.NET Development
Security Solutions

.NET Development Security Solutions™

John Paul Mueller

SYBEX

San Francisco · London

Associate Publisher: Joel Fugazzotto
Acquisitions and Developmental Editor: Tom Cirtin
Production Editor: Leslie E.H. Light
Technical Editor: David M. Clark
Copyeditor: Cheryl Hauser
Compositor: Scott Benoit
Proofreaders: Emily Hsuan, Monique van den Berg, Eric Lach, Nancy Riddiough
Indexer: Lynnzee Elze
Cover Designer: Caryl Gorska/Gorska Design
Cover Illustrator/Photographer: Glen Allison/PhotoDisc

Library of Congress Card Number: 2003107709

ISBN: 0-7821-4266-4

10 9 8 7 6 5 4 3 2 1

With loving thoughts of my wife of 23 years on the occasion of our anniversary.

Acknowledgments

Thanks to my wife, Rebecca, for working with me to get this book completed. I really don't know what I would have done without her help in researching and compiling some of the information that appears in this book. She also did a fine job of proofreading my rough draft and the final result.

David Clark deserves thanks for his technical edit of this book. He greatly added to the accuracy and depth of the material you see here. David also contributed a number of great URLs and interesting ideas. His attention to detail is especially appreciated in a book of this type.

Matt Wagner, my agent, deserves credit for helping me get the contract in the first place and taking care of all the details that most authors don't really consider. I always appreciate his help. It's good to know that someone wants to help.

Finally, I would like to thank Tom Cirtin, Leslie Light, Cheryl Hauser, Scott Benoit, and the rest of the editorial and production staff at Sybex for their assistance in bringing this book to print. It's always nice to work with such a great group of professionals.

About the Author

John Mueller is a freelance author and technical editor. He has writing in his blood, having produced 60 books and over 200 articles to date. The topics range from networking to artificial intelligence and from database management to heads down programming. Some of his current books include several C# developer guides, an accessible programming guide, a book on Web Matrix, and several Windows XP user guides. His technical editing skills have helped over 32 authors refine the content of their manuscripts. John has provided technical editing services to both *Data Based Advisor* and *Coast Compute* magazines. He's also contributed articles to magazines like *SQL Server Professional, Visual C++ Developer,* and *Visual Basic Developer*. He's currently the editor of the .NET electronic newsletter for Pinnacle Publishing (`http://www.freeenewsletters.com/`).

When John isn't working at the computer, you can find him in his workshop. He's an avid woodworker and candle maker. On any given afternoon, you can find him working at a lathe or putting the finishing touches on a bookcase. One of his newest craft projects is glycerin soap making, which comes in pretty handy for gift baskets. You can reach John on the Internet at `JMueller@mwt.net`. John is also setting up a Web site at: `http://www.mwt.net/~jmueller/`. Feel free to take a look and make suggestions on how he can improve it. One of his current projects is creating book FAQ sheets that should help you find the book information you need much faster.

Contents at a Glance

Contents

Part IV	**Other Security Topics**	**335**

Chapter 12	**Active Directory Security**	**337**

Introduction

Carpe Diem—seize the day! Every network administrator, every developer, every user, anyone who even considers touching that bit of technology known as the computer should have this statement implanted in their consciousness. If everyone seized the day to think about security, this book wouldn't be necessary. Security is all too easy to put off until tomorrow, but you have to think about it today—now! The cracker residing on the other end of the line certainly won't wait for you to get around to adding the security you need to your application—crackers count on you putting security off until tomorrow.

Finding the Middle Ground

Now that your adrenaline is pumping, let me bring you back to earth. Thinking about security and implementing security are two different tasks. It's easy to think about security: all you need is a clear day, a warm breeze, and a nice shade tree to enjoy. On the other hand, many developers quickly throw in the towel when they need to implement security because they don't really understand how security should work. Many developers approach the topic in a very draconian way and deprive every user of every right for every reason. Usually, this approach fails. Other developers give every right to everyone for any reason whatsoever. This approach also fails.

Finding the middle ground for security so that you can implement it is tough. The security experts certainly can't make up their minds. During my research for this book, I read several hundred security-specific articles written by accomplished security professionals who are experts in their fields. I have no doubt that what I read was the most correct information the person could provide. Unfortunately, the information provided often contradicted the findings of other security professionals.

My goal in writing this book is to help developers find the practical side of security—the middle ground you need to write a good application. Within these pages, you'll find a wealth of code, ideas, and resources you can use to make your security decisions based on fact. I also tell you when a decision is likely to cause problems no matter what answer you use because there simply isn't a good answer. For example, what do you do about the user who insists on writing their password down? You can use a number of techniques to encourage the user to keep their password secret, but short of depriving them of every possible form of communication, there isn't a good answer for keeping the password secret if the user won't cooperate.

Understanding the Human Side of Security

This book isn't just about coding techniques. Although I do demonstrate many useful techniques (some chapters have seven complete examples), I also help you understand what these techniques mean in human terms. After all, you have to deal with people when it comes to security. The presentation, implementation, and use of security in an application must coincide with the expectations of the user or you won't get their cooperation. The harder you work to force such cooperation, the more often you'll fail to get it. However, you can use coding techniques to point the user in the right direction and make security seem more like a helping hand than a hindrance. This book shows you how to accomplish what seems impossible.

No one knows all the answers. I'm also honest enough to tell you when I don't have a solution to your human problem. In many cases, I'll even tell you what you need to do to resolve the problem on your own or who to contact to get help. The important thing is that I at least give you something to think about—an idea to use or a concept to consider. Even if I can't provide a complete solution, you'll get enough information to make a good choice based on your particular needs.

Overcoming Smoke and Mirrors

A few security experts and some of the people in the media engage in smoke and mirrors security. They would have you believe that every virus is going to gobble up every byte of data on your system and that the outlook is hopeless. According to these sources, the second you attach anything to the Internet your data is going to become hopelessly corrupted. Sometimes it feels like one of those bad dreams where you appear in public unsuitably dressed and everyone laughs at you. However, security isn't hopeless and you're far from helpless. There are solutions to most security problems.

This book helps you find solutions—not just quick solutions, but solutions that actually work because they're based on facts. One of the most important things I wanted to accomplish when I wrote this book is to help developers overcome security issues by using good programming techniques. You don't need to rely on smoke or mirrors when you write an application. What you really need is a list of solutions from which to choose and this book provides more than a few of them.

Knowing It Really Is Broken

You can't develop amazing solutions using broken tools. The problem with security is that someone is always looking for a way to break the lock. Unfortunately, vendors won't tell you that their solution is broken, so many developers literally don't know that their network is an open playground for crackers because they don't have a secure solution. The tool is broken, but no one's willing to admit to the fact. This book tells you about the solutions that are broken as of the time of writing. It also helps you learn where to look for information on tools that get broken in the future. Knowing that a tool is broken is an important step in avoiding a security hole.

The Bottom Line

I'd love to tell you that this book is going to make you a security expert and that somehow you'll become clairvoyant enough to spot every potential cracker exploit weeks before it happens. If you find such a solution, please let me know about it because I'd like to become clairvoyant too. Everyone's applications, data, and network are subject to attack—it's what you do with this knowledge that makes the difference between an adequate programmer and a great programmer. What this book does provide is good solid coding techniques that you can use to create great applications. Yes, someone will figure out a way to break into your code, but you'll have a good chance of knowing the second that they do. In many cases, the techniques in this book will also alert you to data damage, silly user tricks, and a wealth of other problems. In short, you won't become an expert—you'll become proficient. Instead of simply thinking about security, you'll be able to implement it.

Who Should Read This Book?

I've designed this book for Visual Basic .NET and Visual C# .NET developers who need to create secure applications. I'm not just talking about applications that look secure, but applications that really are secure. This book shows how to build the kind of application you aren't afraid to give to the user who writes their name and password on a notepad for the world to see.

You won't find any information on using the language of your choice in this book—this book concentrates on security solutions of all types. In fact, I'll suggest several additional books you might want to try in addition to this book if you don't have the required background. Consequently, you won't want to look at this book until you've already learned to use either Visual Basic or Visual C#. The examples begin working with security in the first chapter and you won't stop until you reach the end of the book. Every chapter has at least one detailed example and most contain several. By the time you finish this book, you'll know how to use all of the security features of the .NET Framework and how to use the Win32 API when the .NET Framework doesn't have the solution you need.

Tools Required

There are some assumptions that I've made while writing the application programming examples in this book. During the writing of this book, I used a Windows 2000 server and Windows XP workstation. There's no guarantee that any of the code in the book will work with Windows 9x—in fact, most of the code won't because Windows 9x doesn't support most of the security features that you need to create a secure application. You must install the latest service packs for all products before the examples will work properly. .NET is a new technology and relies on the latest versions of many DLLs and the .NET Framework. In some cases, I'll list other special requirements that you must observe before the example application will run.

I tested all of the examples in this book with Visual Studio .NET Enterprise Architect Edition and Visual Studio .NET 2003. None of the examples will work with any other programming language products and none of them will work with the educational versions Visual Studio.

All of the desktop application examples will work on a single machine. However, you should test network capable applications using a two-machine setup. The Web examples are set up to work on a two-machine setup—the configuration I encourage you to use to create a true test of the security features of your program. You can easily change them to work on a single machine setup and the book provides instructions on how you can accomplish this task. The mobile device applications are all tested using an actual device, but I also tested them using an emulator. Because the Visual Studio .NET 2003 IDE provides a built-in emulator, you might find this solution the easiest one to use.

PART I

Introduction to .NET Security

CHAPTER 1

Understanding .NET Security

- Understanding the .NET Framework Security Enhancements

- Defining the Security Issues .NET Doesn't Handle

- .NET Framework Architectural Considerations

R ead any trade press magazine and you'll likely run into one or two articles that consider the latest security threat, at least one about the latest security break-in, and several concerning the latest virus. All of these articles make it sound as if every piece of software you own is under attack. In many ways, your software is under attack—even the software you write. Crackers aren't particular; they'll use any hole they find to get into your system and cause damage.

NOTE   For the purposes of this book, the term *cracker* will refer to an individual that's breaking into a system on an unauthorized basis. This includes any form of illegal activity on the system. On the other hand, the term *hacker* will refer to someone who performs authorized (legal) low-level system activities, including testing system security. Hackers also help find undocumented solutions to many computer needs and create workarounds for both hardware and software problems. In some cases, you need to employ the services of a good hacker to test the security measures you have in place, or suffer the consequences of a break-in.

The problem with most software now is that it was written before security threats like the ones today were known. In addition, many developers went to school at a time when security courses were rare or nonexistent. Microsoft is hoping to help with the developer training problem at least. As part of their Trustworthy Computing Initiative, Microsoft recently sponsored a new type of security class at the University of Leeds in England (see http://www.infoworld.com/article/03/03/21/HNmsteachhack_1.html for details on this story). The thing I find interesting about this course is that it employs hacking as part of the curriculum so the students can actually see both the positive and negative parts of applied security.

This chapter provides an overview of what the .NET Framework can do and what it can't do to secure your systems. The book will discuss both the positive and the negative issues of using .NET as a security solution. You may be surprised to learn that .NET isn't a total solution—that there are many areas of your system that it can't protect. A realistic and honest evaluation of any security technology must include both elements. However, you'll also learn that the .NET Framework provides many options not available in previous Windows technologies and that's a step in the right direction.

Along with the practical issues of data and infrastructure protection, this chapter discusses a few necessary theoretical details. For example, you'll learn some new information about the .NET Framework security architecture. I refer you to existing details in the help file and various Web sites to fill in the areas that other sources have already discussed to death.

Finally, you'll see a few simple coding examples that demonstrate specific coding concepts. The examples in this chapter focus on usability or architectural issues. Chapter 2 actually begins showing how to use the .NET Framework namespaces and classes to create secure applications. Consider the examples in this chapter a preview of the information to come. They're also simpler than the examples that follow—this is a starting point.

> **NOTE**   All of the examples for this book are available in both Visual Basic and Visual C#. However, most of the code in the text will appear in Visual C# for consistency reasons. I'll provide you with Visual Basic differences as needed. Otherwise, you can assume the principles I show in Visual C# translate directly to Visual Basic.

An Overview of .NET Framework Enhancements

When Microsoft started designing .NET, the world of computing was moving from the local area network (LAN) and wide area network (WAN) to the Internet. The individual user and group approach Windows used didn't necessarily reflect the best way to pursue security in a distributed environment. In addition, the current environment was too open to potential attacks from outside.

To overcome the security problems inherent in Windows, Microsoft enhanced the role-based security approach originally found in COM+ to work as a general programming methodology. In addition, the managed environment maintains better control over resources that tend to create problems in the unmanaged Windows environment. These two security changes, along with the object-oriented programming strategy of the .NET Framework, summarize what you'll find as security enhancements in the .NET Framework. Here's a list of the critical security enhancements for the .NET Framework.

Evidence-based Security   This feature determines what rights to grant to code based on information gathered about it. The Common Language Runtime (CLR) examines the information it knows about an assembly and determines what rights to grant that code based on the evidence. The evidence is actually matched against a security policy, which is a series of settings that define how the administrator wants to secure a system.

Code Access Security   The CLR uses this feature to determine whether all of the assemblies in a calling chain (stack) have rights to use a particular resource or perform a particular task. All of the code in the calling chain must have the required rights. Otherwise, CLR generates a security error that you can use to detect security breaches. The purpose of this check is to ensure that a cracker's code can't intercept rights that it doesn't deserve.

Defined Verification Process   Before the Just-in-Time (JIT) compiler accepts the Microsoft Intermediate Language (MSIL) assembly, it checks the code the assembly contains for type safety and other errors. This verification process ensures that the code doesn't include any fatal flaws that would keep it from running. The checks also determine whether an external force has modified strongly named code. After these checks are performed, JIT compiles the MSIL into native code. The CLR can run a verified assembly in isolation so that it doesn't affect any other assembly (and more important, other assemblies can't affect it).

Role-based Security   If you know how role-based security works in COM+, you have a good idea of how it works in .NET. Instead of assigning security to individuals or groups, you assign it based on the task that an individual or group will perform. The Windows security identifier (SID) security is limited in that you can control entire files, but not parts of those files. Role-based security still relies on identifying the user through a logon or other means. The main advantage is that you can ask the security system about the user's role and allow access to program features based on that role. An administrator will likely have access to all of the features of a program, but individual users may only have access to a subset of the features.

Cryptography   The advantages of cryptography are many. The concept is simple—you make data unreadable by using an algorithm, coupled with a key, to mix the information up. When the originator supplies the correct key to another algorithm, the original data is returned. Over the years, the power of computers has increased, making old cryptography techniques suspect. The .NET Framework supports the latest cryptographic techniques, which ensures your data remains safe.

Separate Application Domains   You can write .NET code in such a way that some of the pieces run in a separate domain. It's a COM-type concept where the code is isolated from the other code in your program. Many developers use this feature to load special code, run it, and then unload that code without stopping the program. For example, a browser could use this technique to load and unload plug-ins. This feature also works well for security. It helps you run code at different security levels in separate domains to ensure true isolation.

The sections that follow detail the enhancements found in the .NET Framework. There's a lot more to .NET security than you might think. The major shift in strategy may mean that you have to rework your programs, use a new strategy, or rely on alternatives such as using PInvoke (see Chapters 14 and 15 for details).

TIP   Microsoft has made changes to the security implementation for the .NET Framework 1.1. For example, applications assigned to the Internet zone now receive the constrained rights associated with that zone, rather than no rights at all. See the overview at http://msdn.microsoft.com/netframework/productinfo/ for additional security updates.

Using Role-based Security

Role-based security asks the question of whether some entity (a user, the system, a program) is in a particular role. If it's in that role, the entity can likely access a system resource or application feature safely. The concept of a *role* is different from something more absolute like a *group*. When you're a member of a group, you have the same access whether you access the system from a local machine or the Internet. A role does include the idea of group membership, but this is membership based on the environment—the kind of access requested in a given situation from a specific location. An entity's security role changes, rather than being absolute.

Many of the role-based security features you need appear as part of the System.Security.Principal namespace. You'll learn more about this namespace and the class it contains in Chapter 2. However, let's look at a simple example, Listing 1.1, of how role-based security can work for checking a user's information. (You can find this code in the \Chapter 01\ C#\RoleBased or \Chapter 01\VB\RoleBased folder of the source code located on the Sybex Web site.)

Listing 1.1   **Using the *IsInRole()* Method**

```csharp
private void btnTest_Click(object sender, System.EventArgs e)
{
   WindowsPrincipal  MyPrincipal;   // The role we want to check.
   AppDomain         MyDomain;      // The current domain.
   StringBuilder     Output;        // Example output data.
   Array             RoleTypes;     // Standard role types.

   // Set the principal policy for this application.
   MyDomain = Thread.GetDomain();
   MyDomain.SetPrincipalPolicy(PrincipalPolicy.WindowsPrincipal);

   // Get the role and other security information for the current
   // user.
   MyPrincipal = (WindowsPrincipal)Thread.CurrentPrincipal;

   // Get the user name.
   Output = new StringBuilder();
   Output.Append("Name: " + MyPrincipal.Identity.Name);

   // Get the authentication type.
   Output.Append("\r\nAuthentication: " +
      MyPrincipal.Identity.AuthenticationType);

   Output.Append("\r\n\r\nRoles:");

   // Create an array of built in role types.
```

```
RoleTypes = Enum.GetValues(typeof(WindowsBuiltInRole));

// Check the user's role.
foreach(WindowsBuiltInRole Role in RoleTypes)
{

    // Store the role name.
    if (Role.ToString().Length <= 5)
        Output.Append("\r\n" + Role.ToString() + ":\t\t");
    else
        Output.Append("\r\n" + Role.ToString() + ":\t");

    // Store the role value.
    Output.Append(
        MyPrincipal.IsInRole(WindowsBuiltInRole.User).ToString());
}

// Output the result.
MessageBox.Show(Output.ToString(),
                "User Role Values",
                MessageBoxButtons.OK,
                MessageBoxIcon.Information);
}
```

The code begins by obtaining the domain for the current thread. The concept of the application domain appears as the Separate Application Domains bullet. This call is the demonstration of how the feature works. The program is executing in an application domain and you can obtain information about that domain. In this case, the code sets the security policy for this domain equal to the same policy Windows uses. The application is now executing with the same policy that the user has when working with Windows. You could theoretically change that policy depending on conditions such as user location.

Now that the code has set the security policy for the thread, it uses that information to create a WindowsPrincipal object, MyPrincipal. This object knows all kinds of security information about the user. The code shows how you can obtain the username and the method of authentication used.

The most important use for MyPrincipal is to determine which roles the user is in. The book hasn't actually defined any roles yet, so the example uses the WindowsBuiltInRole enumeration to check the standard types. If the user is in the requested role, the IsInRole() method returns true. This value is converted to a string and placed in Output. Figure 1.1 shows typical output from this example. Of course, the results will change when you run the program on your system because the dialog box will reflect your name and rights.

FIGURE 1.1:

A view of the output from an *IsInRole()* method check

The important concept to take away from this example is that role-based security performs a similar task to standard Windows security, but using a different and more flexible technique. Because of the differences between Windows security and role-based security, you may need to rely on the standard Win32 API version, especially when working in an environment that has a mix of managed and unmanaged code. Chapters 14 and 15 discuss the Win32 API approach for the managed environment.

Executing Code in the Managed Environment

Instead of simply monitoring and managing the user and other entities that want access to resources or applications, the .NET Framework also monitors the code. Code access security is an important feature because it places the security burden on the code itself, which makes circumventing security measures much more difficult. Because the focus is on the code, a cracker can't use impersonation techniques. It's still possible to attack the code, but most crackers will look for easier targets.

The .NET Framework uses two techniques to ensure proper code access: *imperative* and *declarative*. Imperative security relies on classes that you use within your code and CLR interprets at runtime, while declarative security relies on attributes you place at the head of an element and CLR interprets at link time. You can find a complete description of the differences and usage techniques in Chapter 4. For now, let's look at the easier of the two: imperative security. Listing 1.2 shows an example of imperative security used for gaining access to a file resource. (You can find this code in the \Chapter 01\C#\Imperative or \Chapter 01\VB\Imperative folder of the source code located on the Sybex Web site—make sure you change the resource file location to match your system.)

Listing 1.2   **Relying on Imperative Security for File Security**

```
private void btnDeny_Click(object sender, System.EventArgs e)
{
   FileIOPermission  FIOP;          // Permission object.
   Stream            FS = null;  // A test file stream.

   // Create the permission object.
   FIOP = new FileIOPermission(FileIOPermissionAccess.Read,
                               "D:\\Temp.txt");

   // Deny access to the resource.
   FIOP.Deny();

   // Try to access the object.
   try
   {
      FS = new FileStream("D:\\Temp.txt",
                          FileMode.Open,
                          FileAccess.Read);
   }
   catch(SecurityException SE)
   {
      MessageBox.Show("Access Denied\r\n" +
                      SE.Message,
                      "File IO Error",
                      MessageBoxButtons.OK,
                      MessageBoxIcon.Error);
      return;
   }

   // Display a success message.
   MessageBox.Show("File is open!",
                   "File IO Success",
                   MessageBoxButtons.OK,
                   MessageBoxIcon.Information);

   // Close the file if opened.
   FS.Close();
}

private void btnAllow_Click(object sender, System.EventArgs e)
{
   FileIOPermission  FIOP;          // Permission object.
   Stream            FS = null;  // A test file stream.

   // Create the permission object.
   FIOP = new FileIOPermission(FileIOPermissionAccess.Read,
                               "D:\\Temp.txt");

   // Allow access to the resource.
```

```
FIOP.Assert();

// Try to access the object.
try
{
    FS = new FileStream("D:\\Temp.txt",
                        FileMode.Open,
                        FileAccess.Read);
}
catch(SecurityException SE)
{
    MessageBox.Show("Access Denied\r\n" +
                    SE.Message,
                    "File IO Error",
                    MessageBoxButtons.OK,
                    MessageBoxIcon.Error);
    return;
}

// Display a success message.
MessageBox.Show("File is open!",
                "File IO Success",
                MessageBoxButtons.OK,
                MessageBoxIcon.Information);

// Close the file if opened.
FS.Close();
}
```

The btnDeny_Click() method will always fail because the imperative security call, FIOP.Deny(), denies access to the file. Notice how the code initializes the FileIOPermission object before using it. The code requires a full path to the file in question. The test actually occurs when the code uses the FileStream() constructor to try to open the file. When the code fails, the catch statement traps the error using a SecurityException object, SE.

The btnAllow_Click() method looks similar to the btnDeny_Click() method. However, this method succeeds because the code calls the FIOP.Assert() method. You can use the Assert() or Demand() methods to allow access to an object. One note on this example: make sure you always use the Close() method to close the file after a successful open. Otherwise, your code could potentially cause problems on the host system.

Security Problems .NET Can't Stop

Security is a problem precisely because it's a system designed by one person to thwart access to resources by another person. What one person can create, another can just as easily destroy.

Consequently, security is an ongoing process. You need to know the threats your system faces so that you can monitor and protect against them. Although the .NET Framework provides a good basis for building applications with robust security, it can't protect you from other sources of security problems. The sections that follow detail these security problems. They provide suggestions on how you can use .NET along with other strategies to at least keep problems to a minimum. Make sure you look at Chapter 3 as well because it discusses how you can avoid many of the common errors and traps associated with using .NET as a security strategy.

Stupid User Tricks

You've likely seen all of the jokes, heard all of the stories, and seen some of user-related problems yourself. The most horrid stories I've read recently appear in an *InfoWorld* article entitled "Stupid User Tricks." One is about a traveler who had taped both the dial-in phone number for his server and his password to the outside of his laptop carrying case. (See http://www.infoworld.com/article/03/01/24/030127Security_1.html for details.) Finding plenty of horror stories is never a problem—solving the security issues users create is another story.

After 17 years of consulting, one of the first security scans I perform at a client site is to check the computer, the desk and surrounding area for pieces of paper with passwords on them. Invariably, I usually find at least one piece of paper with not just one, but several passwords on it. The passwords aren't even hard to figure out. It almost seems that the user is determined to make it easy for the janitor to make off with all of the company passwords.

To an extent, the .NET security features can help overcome problems users create. No, it won't automatically detect Post-it notes placed on the monitor, but it does ensure that the user doesn't gain rights to resources by using code incorrectly. Code access security helps in this regard. For example, when a user requests access to a file, the user's rights are checked and the rights of the code are checked. If either check fails, then access to the file fails. Chapter 4 discusses code access checks in detail.

Training, well-written *policies* (instructions for handling various security situations), and *rules* (requirements that everyone must meet) with some teeth in them can also help with user security problems. However, this is one area where you'll continually have problems because people will normally find a way around rules that are inconvenient. The .NET Framework can help here as well. You can write code in such a way that the network administrator controls security policies, not the user. This technique makes it possible for the network administrator to monitor problems and ensure your program has a reasonable chance of maintaining a secure environment.

It's also important to know how to set the security policies for your application using .NET Framework features. Chapter 5 discusses policies and code groups in detail. While the techniques in this chapter won't fix every user problem, they at least make it harder for someone to destroy the security of your system by accident.

Some External Forces

Most people associate external forces that threaten security with crackers. This group does receive a lot of attention from the media, which is why they're the group that many programmers consider first (and perhaps last). While crackers do cause a great many problems, they aren't the only external force to consider.

Employees on the road or recently let go from the company can cause a great deal of harm to your applications. The problem is twofold:

- Using the old Windows security system, an application might execute at the same privilege level whether the employee accessed it from a desktop or a remote location. The .NET Framework takes this issue into consideration by adjusting the rights of an application based on the zone in which it executes.

- An employee is much more familiar with the security setup and organization of your system than any cracker. Unfortunately, this is a problem that .NET can't help you solve. Someone determined to break into your system is almost certainly going to do it. The only way to overcome this problem is to constantly monitor the system.

Other programs can also affect your application—at least if it's a Web-based application. In a day when distributed applications can rely on services that your program can provide, it's possible that some other programmer you've never met will cause a security problem on your system and not even realize it. The .NET Framework helps you solve this problem by adhering to standards-based security. New standards such as WS-Security and WS-Inspection make it easier to write programs that will work across platforms and provide a secure environment. You can learn more about these standards at Web Services Specifications site (http://msdn.microsoft.com/library/en-us/dnglobspec/html/wsspecsover.asp).

Inept network management can also cause serious problems. A network administrator could restore old policies to a server or overwrite the recently patched files for your application. Newer versions of Windows have some protection for both of these issues. For example, Windows File Protection can help ensure only the latest version of your files remain on disk. The .NET Framework also helps by making version checks before it loads files and executes them. An overwritten file would have the wrong version number and .NET would display an error indicating this fact. This fix may not make the user very happy, but at least you'll know the cause of the problem. Chapter 6 tells you more about validation and verification issues.

Another source of external problems is the connections you create with other businesses. Distributed applications are becoming more common as companies invest more in Web services. The problems with distributed applications are many and you can't expect the .NET Framework to solve them all. However, in Chapter 9 you learn how to protect the .NET-specific areas of a Web server. Chapter 10 shows how to protect .NET application generated data. Finally, Chapter 11 demonstrates methods for protecting the connection between a partner and the organization when using a .NET end-to-end solution. Many of the strategies hinge on standards-based application development such as using the WS-Security standard for your application.

Wireless devices present one of the most prevalent and least understood security problems for developers today. Some wireless networks aren't secured at all. Anyone with the proper equipment can come along and access the network from outside the company. Some people are using this technique to spread illicit e-mail using company Internet connections without anyone knowing. The .NET Framework can't do anything about this kind of security problem. However, once you have some basic security in place, Chapter 13 can show you how to make best use of the features the .NET Framework does provide for security of wireless application communication.

Something's always attacking your data, even nature. Fortunately, keeping your data safe, or at least knowing when someone has tampered with it, is relatively easy because this is an area where security professionals have spent a lot of time. First the bad news—if you have any kind of data transfer at all (even on a LAN), be prepared for situations when that data is compromised. The good news is that the .NET Framework uses the latest technologies to secure your information. Chapter 7 discusses cryptographic techniques.

Poorly Patched Systems

Patches are problematic no matter how you look at them. First, there's the problem that the existence of a patch tells many users that the program wasn't well tested, so it failed in use. This perception is fueled by the media in many cases. In fact, the perception is warranted, in at least a few cases, because the product was rushed to market. However, perceptions aside, even if the program has bugs that will cause security problems, the user of that program has to be encouraged to apply the patch to fix the problem.

Second, there's the issue of compatibility. Some patches actually cause more problems than they fix by creating compatibility problems or introducing new problems onto a system. Consequently, many administrators set up test systems to check the patch for problems before they install it on their production system. Extensive testing means the production system is vulnerable longer—perhaps encountering a security problem while it waits.

Although these issues are probably not going away any time soon, you still need to patch your system to ensure it has the latest security features and that any security holes are fixed. You need to consider the results of not patching your system at all and how it will affect any programs you produce on the system. With this in mind, you'll want to use three tools to check your system for problems before you begin developing a new program.

Windows Update   Always check Windows Update to verify the status of any patches for your system. Windows Update works automatically. All you need to do is select the updates you want to download. The one mistake that some developers make is not reading the information about a patch before they install it. Sometimes this leads to problems on a development machine. You can find Windows Update at `http://windowsupdate.com/`.

Microsoft System Update Services (SUS)   Microsoft SUS can reduce the burden of updating multiple machines for a business. This system helps you download and distribute updates in a safe environment. Learn more about this product at `http://www.microsoft.com/windows2000/windowsupdate/sus`.

Microsoft Baseline Security Analyzer (BSA)   Windows setups can become quite complex. It's easy to miss an update when you have multiple pieces of software to consider. Add to this problem, the issue of individual driver updates, and security can become a considerable problem. The Microsoft BSA won't solve all of your problems, but it can help by providing a comprehensive list of problems within a system. Learn more about this product at `http://www.microsoft.com/technet/treeview/default.asp?url=/technet/security/tools/Tools/MBSAhome.asp`.

All of these update tools should tell you something about your own programs. When I start the Acrobat Reader, it automatically asks if I want to scan for the latest updates. Other programs on my machine are starting to do the same thing. The .NET Framework provides more version checking features than the Win32 API ever thought about providing. The goal of these features is to prevent problems such as DLL hell, an issue that still plagues Windows systems. You can easily use version checking to provide update checking for your application. (Make sure you still give the user the choice of actually installing the update.)

Inept Enterprise Policies

I actually knew of a business that had a policy in place that made every network user an administrator. It was a moderately sized business that lacked a real network administrator. The person who was supposed to administrate the network was simply too lazy to set up the required features and didn't want to hear a lot of user complaints about not being able to access a particular file or feature. That business may still be around, but I found it quite easy to leave before the inevitable security bomb exploded in someone's face. Fortunately, not every business has a policy as absurd as this one.

Setting enterprise policies is one case when the .NET Framework might actually increase the number of security problems your application will have to face. Microsoft assumes that every network administrator is faithful, loyal, hardworking, conscientious, and knowledgeable. The .NET Framework is set up to ensure the network administrator has maximum access to security features. Unfortunately, some network administrators just aren't up to the task and you'll have to find ways to overcome this problem.

Training is one way to help network administrators fulfill their new role with the applications you create. Many will find it quite surprising that they can control who uses a particular function within your components and specific features in an application. Chapter 4 shows you other techniques to work around this problem. The best strategy is to effectively use imperative and declarative security in your applications to ensure they maintain some level of security even if the network administrator doesn't do anything at all.

Enterprise policies are affected by the environment. A well-maintained domain setup is more secure because the policies are set on the server. Even if the user moves to another machine, you have some assurance that your program will have the proper security and work as anticipated. Unfortunately, the alphabet soup of technologies used for LAN-based applications today makes security difficult (perhaps impossible). Chapter 8 shows you how to get around some of the problems with LAN security. This chapter is an open view of what .NET can do for you and more important, what you still need to tackle using other technologies.

Problems begin with local security policies because they're often implemented unevenly and the rights don't move with the user. Code access security ensures that a rogue program can't make use of this scenario to circumvent security. You can also validate the user, computer, and other data using Active Directory. Chapter 12 discusses how you can use Active Directory to reduce some of the local security problems an application will encounter. It also demonstrates techniques for working with Active Directory security information.

Distributed applications are notorious for opening security holes because these applications make resources that are normally hidden visible to users through an Internet connection. It's amazing that some companies don't have security policies in place to protect from these problems. What's even more amazing is that a few companies actually end up opening new holes in their firewall and other security features to enable an application to work. For example, some companies still rely on Distributed Component Object Model (DCOM) applications to create distributed applications. The .NET Framework isn't the only solution at your disposal, but by using modern Web services techniques, you can greatly reduce the risks distributed applications impose.

One of the most interesting security problems is one in which a company follows all other best practices, but then fails to lock the computer up so that no one can access it physically. If someone can gain physical access to a server, they can control the server in a relatively short time. A worst case scenario occurs when the company not only leaves the computer in the open, but thoughtfully provides a monitor and keyboard so that anyone entering the room can modify the server setup. Although the best policy is to lock the computer up, there are alternatives if you must keep the computer in plain view. For example, you can add physical locking to the system. The World of Data Security (`http://www.crocodile.de/`) provides a number of specialized computer-locking mechanisms that make physical access a lot more difficult.

Windows File Protection Vulnerabilities

Windows File Protection is thought to be a safe way to install executable files on a system because those files are supposedly signed. Unfortunately, there's a well-known method to create files that Windows File Protection will trust even if they aren't signed by an appropriate digital certificate. You can read the detailed version of the problem on the Bugtraq site at `http://archives.neohapsis.com/archives/ntbugtraq/2002-q4/0122.html`. A Microsoft security bulletin on the topic appears at `http://www.microsoft.com/technet/security/bulletin/MS00-072.asp`.

The interesting thing about the .NET Framework is that it doesn't rely on this security mechanism. When you sign a control, component, or application, the signature is verified by the CLR. The signature uses a hash mechanism that exists outside the Windows File Protection environment, so the security of the file is ensured. You can always check the token used to secure a file with a strong name that's contained within the Global Assembly Cache by viewing the content of the `\WINDOWS\assembly` folder. Figure 1.2 shows a typical example of the content of this folder.

FIGURE 1.2:

Managed files use a unique signature system that ensures their integrity.

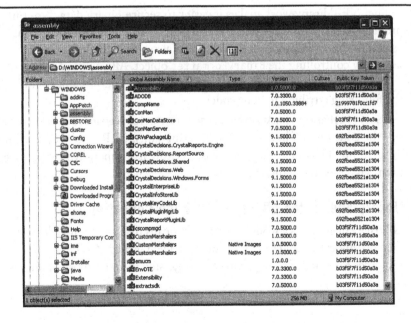

.NET Framework Security Architecture Considerations

It's important to know something about the .NET Framework security architecture and determine how you can use that architecture to fix problems. You also need to know about issues and problems you'll face as a result of the architectural decisions that Microsoft has made. This section of the chapter discusses some architectural issues you need to consider before you begin coding. You'll learn about other architectural considerations (practical versus theoretical) as the book progresses.

NOTE   Microsoft has improved the .NET Framework security features in Version 1.1, the version that I use for this book. Some of the calls in the example programs for this book don't appear in the .NET Framework 1.0. I'll let you know when you'll need Version 1.1 in most cases. However, if you run into a call that obviously isn't in the version of the .NET Framework you're using, make sure you update to the most current version.

Securing the Binary Output

Securing text usually isn't as big a problem for organizations as securing binary information. All you need for text is a good encryption technology and the code to use it. Binary data is entirely different because it usually involves complex protocols and can include code. In fact, security of some older technologies, such as DCOM, makes securing binary data almost impossible. The problem is that these older technologies often use ports indiscriminately and require the data in an unencrypted form to ensure the recipient can read it.

The .NET Framework makes it easier to secure binary data. Not only does it avoid the problem of using multiple ports, it also provides methods for encrypting and decrypting data as part of the serialization stream. You can also rely on code access security to help in this situation by controlling the `BinaryFormatter` object. All you need it a set of permissions to go with the serialization and de-serialization process. A permission could be as simple as adding the following attribute to your code:

```
[SecurityPermissionAttribute(SecurityAction.Demand,SerializationFormatter=true)]
```

If the code doesn't have the proper permissions, CLR won't allow the `BinaryFormatter` to do anything. Of course, you could just as easily use imperative security (the `SecurityPermission` class) to achieve the same goal.

Understanding the Effects of Garbage Collection

Garbage collection is a wonderful idea. It means that you spend a lot less time worrying about memory allocation and freeing resources. The Garbage Collector takes care of freeing these resources for you. Of course, you can always step in and dispose of objects when necessary. In fact, this is a recommended procedure when you have large objects and aren't sure when the Garbage Collector will kick in.

The Garbage Collector also impacts security because it affects memory and resources. What happens if a cracker wants to look around in memory and determine what's going on or look for some interesting data? Your program might think that data's already gone, but there it is, in memory waiting for the Garbage Collector. The issue of waiting for the Garbage Collector is normally not something you need to consider, but it is if the object concerned contains sensitive data.

From an architectural perspective, the Garbage Collector is probably the best thing to happen to developers in a long time. However, from a security perspective, it's a problem because objects have an indeterminate life span. The solution, in this case, is to build your sensitive objects with methods for disposing of the sensitive information. You should then build your code so that it always frees objects immediately. Freeing the objects will get the Garbage Collector busy immediately, rather than waiting for the program to exit.

Considering the Requirements of Object-Oriented Programming

One of the best reasons to use .NET to build secure applications is that it's fully object oriented. You can attach security to every element of your program. The security system will faithfully check every access to every method, property, and event of every object your application creates. In general, you can bind your .NET application to the point where nothing can get in—at least not directly.

The problem with .NET security is that every access requires a stack walk and that takes time. The .NET Framework has some optimization built in to reduce the number of complete stack walks, but the basic idea is that security demands that permissions get checked every time a request is made. This level of checking makes .NET secure, but it also makes .NET slow.

As the book progresses, you'll learn several methods you can use to keep speed problems to a minimum. For example, using *declarative security*, whenever possible, will speed your application because some declarative security requirements are handled at link time, rather than runtime. In addition, declarative security attaches the security to the method, rather than to the object, whereas *imperative security* is handled completely at runtime and focuses on the objects you create in the code.

Understanding Native Code Access Concerns

Just about every developer has a wealth of native Windows code to consider as part of any application development task. Most developers have concluded that they'll need to use PInvoke to continue using the unmanaged code that they've spent so much time and resources developing. However, what happens when you mix managed and unmanaged code in the same project? Obviously, the unmanaged code won't understand role-based security or code access security.

> **TIP** Creating PInvoke code can become difficult if you use complex data structures and require access to some of the less documented Win32 API features. You may also want to move your components and controls from the unmanaged to the managed environment. My book, *.NET Framework Solutions: In Search of the Lost Win32 API* (Sybex, 2002, ISBN: 0-7821-4134-X) can help you overcome any of the problems you'll run into when working with the Win32 API.

One solution to this problem is to use Win32 API security for the entire application. In fact, that's what many developers are doing now because that's what they understand best. Knowing that your application employs the same security techniques across all elements can add a bit of comfort in a world that's increasingly insecure. The benefit of this technique is that it's relatively easy and fast. You also know the problems involved in using this method, so you can easily watch for them as you maintain the security of your system.

Another solution is to place the managed code within a separate domain. This is the solution that affords you the best chance of catching problems early. The .NET Framework security is definitely more robust than the security used by your Win32 API code. The advantage of this method is obvious: greater security is always a good thing when you can get it. However, there are several disadvantages to consider:

- For one thing, there's a performance hit for placing the individual code elements in separate domains.

- You'll also have to consider the problems of maintaining two different security techniques until you make all of your code managed. Complexity always breeds errors, which is anathema for secure systems.

In sum, the .NET Framework architecture gives you two basic choices for handling security when you have a mix of managed and unmanaged code—a condition that will exist for quite some time in the Windows community. What you need to consider are the trade-offs between the two choices. Neither choice is a perfect solution, but one choice might work better than another for your particular application.

You also need to consider some types of native code access in light of the way that .NET handles objects. CLR checks every object for security violations, even those accessed through the interoperability layer. In some cases, you can get a performance boost for your application and reduce interoperability issues by removing these runtime checks using the [SuppressUnmanagedCodeSecurity] attribute.

Summary

This chapter has provided an overview of the features that make .NET Framework security unique. In addition, you've seen that this security has both strengths and weaknesses. Finally, you've learned how the .NET Framework architecture makes using this technology easier, faster, and less error prone than previous Windows security technologies.

Before you go any further, consider again the problems listed in the "Security Problems .NET Can't Stop" section of the chapter. These are real issues that you need to address before most of the techniques in this book will provide you with a reasonable assurance of secure computing. Not all of these issues have a one-time fix—security is an ongoing process. Although you can't absolutely stop users from pasting their passwords on their monitor for future use, you can certainly discourage the practice by putting policies in place and providing training.

Chapter 2 begins a detailed discussion of .NET Framework features. You learn about the namespaces and classes that you can use to create a secure application environment using the .NET Framework. Chapter 2 is also the first chapter that contains code that you can use to create secure applications: consider it a starting point. Subsequent chapters provide detailed examples that help you build robust applications with great security.

CHAPTER 2

.NET Framework Security Overview

- Finding .NET Security Information

- Using the `System.Runtime.Remoting.Contexts` Namespace

- Using the `System.Security` Namespace

- Using the `System.Security.Cryptography` Namespace

- Using the `System.Security.Permissions` Namespace

- Using the `System.Security.Policy` Namespace

- Using the `System.Security.Principal` Namespace

- Using the `System.Web.Security` Namespace

- Using the `System.DirectoryServices` Namespace

The .NET Framework provides a lot of security programming assistance in the form of namespaces and classes. Unlike the Win32 API, Microsoft has actually gathered these features together into a number of areas, making it easy to find what you need. The problem for many developers is learning which namespace to use and determining when to use it. Security is a large topic no matter how much help the underlying programming structure provides.

The first section of this chapter provides some pointers on where to locate security information you need. This section covers a number of topics that you need to know in order to build a strong development platform and assess risks for users of your finished program. Most of the locations are online because these sites generally update the information they provide as Microsoft introduces new features. Of course, some of your best sources of information are the examples in this book.

The remaining sections of the chapter introduce you to important namespaces that you'll use regularly for .NET programming. I chose not to differentiate between distributed and local programming in this case, because most developers need an overall solution that works as well on the desktop as it does on the Web site. Each of the sections will have a short example, in addition to useful programming tips and application usage guidelines. The examples in this chapter are a little on the simple side—each of the namespaces is covered in depth as the book progresses. The important consideration is to gain an understanding of the namespaces and discover what they can do for you.

NOTE   Every one of the namespace sections contains an online source of information for that namespace. You might wonder why this is important given that you have perfectly usable help available on your hard drive. The security information that Microsoft provides is bound to change as the .NET Framework matures. In order to see the most current information about the namespaces, you need to get online and view the information there. The information found on your hard drive might be just enough out-of-date that you miss a *cracker exploit* (security vulnerability) that Microsoft has shown how to remedy through improved examples or documentation. Many other areas of the book will also include online resources so that you can create the most secure programs possible by using current information.

Locating the Security Information You Need

Security information changes almost daily as security threats change. As crackers discover new holes, and vendors come up with new fixes for those holes, your security outlook changes as well. Various updates, new technologies, and revised strategies affect how you handle various security issues and may mean changing application code to meet new security threats. In short, just keeping up with security issues could be a full-time job. Needless to say, paper documentation is a little too permanent for some security requirements, which means looking for what you need online.

Trade press magazines and newsletters are helpful for keeping you up-to-date. It's also important to check the Microsoft Knowledge Base (`http://search.support.microsoft.com/search/default.aspx`) from time to time. You can use the Knowledge Base to search for new articles published within a given timeframe. (Just fill in the dates you're interested in viewing in the form supplied—you can also look for terms, such as *security*.) Between these two sources, you can obtain information about major security threats. The following sections discuss specific security information needs and tell you where to find additional information.

Dealing with Patches

The most important nonprogramming-related security consideration is applying patches to your development machine. Yet, most developers don't install patches because they feel it's a waste of time. After all, they don't use their machine for production work and there's a good chance they'll format the machine's hard drive after the current project. The problem is that if your machine doesn't contain all of the required security patches, a virus could infect it. In addition, testing your program without having the patches in place means you don't actually know how your program will work on the client machine.

Unfortunately, knowing about a security threat isn't always enough. Even if you download and install a patch on your development machine, it's not always safe to assume that the user of your application will do the same. Therefore, you need to know how to check for the patches if the patch will affect your application in some way. Consequently, the second part of a good machine setup is ensuring the user has the same patches you do and keeps their machine updated. Here are some URLs you'll want to check for ideas on locating patches.

Windows Update (*http://windowsupdate.microsoft.com/*)   This is the definitive site to look for patches for your system. It's automatic and has a relatively easy-to-use interface. The problem with this site is that it isn't always current. You may find that it doesn't list all of the patches you need. For example, this site doesn't list any patches needed for your development product—just those needed for the operating system.

Hotfix & Security Bulletin Service (*http://www.microsoft.com/technet/security/current.asp*) The best place to locate patches for your machine is this service. Microsoft keeps it updated with information that may not even appear on the Windows Update site. In addition, the easy-to-use interface means that most users can understand the site and use it to keep their machine updated. The list of updates you receive appears in date order, making it easy to figure out which updates you need to download. You can also look for products besides Windows, such as Visual Studio .NET.

Security Guide for Windows (*http://www.winguides.com/security/*)   The sometimes bizarre language used to write Microsoft security guides is difficult for many people to understand. This site puts the information you need in plain English. It lists the updates by product type and date. You won't find Visual Studio here, but you can find all of the other products you've used to set up your development workstation and server.

One interesting resource that you'll want to read is the SANS Institute article entitled, "Microsoft Windows Security Patches" (`http://www.sans.org/rr/win/patches.php`). This article not only points out where to get the patches, but also why they're important. It's the kind of article that you'll want to keep for reference.

Locating General Security Tips for Everyone

Once you have a safe environment for your application, you still need to use safe coding practices to ensure the program will work as anticipated. Some coding practices are timeless, and you can use them with any programming language, or operating system for that matter. For example, you always want to check user input to ensure it's the right kind of input within the correct range, and doesn't violate any rules. In fact, if you look at many of the latest security issues for common applications, you'll find that problems such as buffer overruns are quite common across all applications and all operating systems. (See Chapter 3 for a list of common problems that you can easily avoid when writing a .NET application.) Here are some Web sites that provide general security information that anyone can use.

Der Keiler (*http://www.der-keiler.de/*)   This site ("Wild Boar" in English) provides a number of English-language mailing lists where you can ask specific security questions. In some cases, you'll also find information on security exploits that includes code and the potential fix. The exploits are things you commonly see in applications such as SQL Server.

IT World (*http://www.itworld.com/AppDev/*)   This site provides links to news stories from a number of trade magazines. The feature that makes this site so interesting is that you can drill down to specific topic areas. The link provided takes you to the general application development area. From there, you can drill down to Security Techniques and from there to topics such as Passwords. The organization of this site helps you locate information on a given topic quickly.

Microsoft Developer Network (*http://msdn.microsoft.com/security/*)   Although it seems like an obvious place to start, many people assume that Microsoft doesn't know anything about security. Actually, the developers at Microsoft have written a number of useful articles about security—more than you'll find elsewhere.

Sometimes a single article can provide the wealth of general information you need to code more effectively. For example, the SANS Institute article entitled, "The Foundation to Secure Computing" provides general security advice that could fit any situation (`http://www.sans.org/rr/code/sec_programming.php`). This particular article comes with a list of interesting links that you can use for further research.

One of the best pieces I've read about security is the MSDN Magazine article entitled, "Defend Your Code with Top Ten Security Tips Every Developer Must Know" (`http://msdn.microsoft.com/msdnmag/issues/02/09/SecurityTips/default.aspx`). This article relies heavily on Visual C++ and Visual C#, but the ideas it conveys are universal.

Finding .NET Framework Specific Security Tips

Finally, you must consider specific .NET Framework threats. This book helps you understand these threats and demonstrates methods for overcoming them. As time progresses, I'll learn new information and post it on my Web site at `http://www.mwt.net/~jmueller/`. Make sure you tell me about any new threats you learn about using my email address `JMueller@mwt.net`. Security is a rather large area, though, and you'll want to know about other general .NET security Web sites. Here are some you should consider adding to your favorites list, if you haven't already.

The Code Project (*http://www.codeproject.com/*)   This site contains a wealth of well-documented programming examples written by other developers. In general, you'll find the examples are somewhat specific, but you can use the principles they teach in your own code. Unfortunately, the owner hasn't organized this site by topic area, so you'll need to search for the security topics. A search for .NET security returned 91 hits as of the time of this writing, so you have a lot from which to choose.

Microsoft .NET Specific Security (*http://msdn.microsoft.com/net/security/*)   In addition to the general security topics you can find on Microsoft's MSDN Web site, you can also find .NET specific topics. They're located in a separate section from the general security topics.

.NET 247 (*http://www.dotnet247.com/*)   One of the more interesting features of this Web site is that it includes a complete list of the .NET Framework namespaces and classes. Click on the links to find articles for that particular element. However, this site also provides articles listed by topic area. Many of the articles are ranked by importance, making it easier to choose the article you want to read.

Most security articles you read contain verifiable information written by conscientious authors. However, it's still important to verify information you receive from the press, a Web site, a friend, or anywhere else for that matter. A report could tell you that a security exploit exists when it doesn't, or provide news of a technique that doesn't actually work. In some cases, Microsoft's Web site will refute a particular charge of vulnerability. One such case is a complaint about the Visual C++ .NET compiler security in a Cigital article entitled, "Microsoft Compiler Flaw Technical Note" at `http://www.cigital.com/news/index.php?pg=art&artid=70`. You'll find Microsoft's refutation at `http://msdn.microsoft.com/visualc/compiler.asp`. You can derive quite a bit of information from both articles, but here's the crux of the matter. The Buffer Security Checking feature of Visual C++ can't protect you from every kind of buffer overflow, so good coding practice is always required. However, anyone who wants to create great applications always uses good coding practices anyway. The fact of the matter is that you might get the wrong idea from Microsoft's original documentation and let down your guard—that's always fatal when it comes to security. Never let anyone tell you that you can get by with less than your best effort.

Understanding the *System.Runtime.Remoting.Contexts* Namespace

This book doesn't discuss all of the intricacies of remoting—you could probably fill several chapters of a general programming book with the required information. However, this section does discuss the security benefits of a context, which is an essential coding consideration for remoting. A context describes the environment in which one or more objects execute. It includes properties that define this environment. The environment includes a number of factors including security. Of course, it also defines synchronization, transactions, and Just-In-Time (JIT) activation. All of these elements combine to define the application environment.

> **TIP**   You can find a complete description of the `System.Runtime.Remoting.Contexts` namespace at `http://msdn.microsoft.com/library/en-us/cpref/html/frlrfsystemruntimeremotingcontexts.asp`. The description includes as list of the classes directly associated with this namespace.

Contexts Namespace Overview

The most important aspect of context for this book is the security that an application domain (`AppDomain`) can provide by isolating an object. The isolation places the object within a different security context than other objects executing with the same process. For example, ASP.NET places each Web page in a separate application domain, but all of the Web pages execute within the same process.

TIP Sometimes you need an alternative view of the .NET Framework. The .NET Framework Class Browser (`http://docs.aspng.com/quickstart/aspplus/samples/classbrowser/vb/classbrowser.aspx`) provides this view. It actually lists all of the classes that Microsoft keeps hidden in the help files. The site doesn't contain any documentation of the sort that you find in the help files, but it does make the interactions between the various .NET Framework elements clearer than the help file does in some situations. For example, look at the class for this section and you'll find a number of related interfaces and classes that aren't associated with the `System.Runtime.Remoting.Contexts` namespace in the help file.

One of the main security benefits of the `System.Runtime.Remoting.Contexts` namespace is the isolation it provides between objects. Whenever your application creates a context-bound object (one based on a context-bound class), the CLR finds a compatible context or places the object in a new context. The object remains in this context for life. Whenever another object wants to access the current object, it does so through a proxy. CLR oversees the entire process, making the environment inherently more secure.

SynchronizationAttribute Attribute Example

The only accessible class in the `System.Runtime.Remoting.Contexts` namespace is SynchronizationAttribute. The main purpose of this class is to enforce the synchronization domain for the current object and all objects that share the same instance. Think of a domain as a method for isolating a set of related objects. Listing 2.1 shows three examples of classes that rely on the `SynchronizationAttribute` attribute. (You can find this code in the `\Chapter 02\C#\Crypto` or `\Chapter 02\VB\Crypto` folder of the source code located on the Sybex Web site.)

Listing 2.1   **Three examples of the *SynchronizationAttribute* attribute**

```
[Synchronization(SynchronizationAttribute.REQUIRES_NEW, false)]
public class Sync1
{
    public String GetName()
    {
        return (AppDomain.CurrentDomain.FriendlyName);
    }
}

[Synchronization(SynchronizationAttribute.SUPPORTED, false)]
public class Sync2 : MarshalByRefObject
{
```

```
    public String GetName()
    {
        return (AppDomain.CurrentDomain.FriendlyName);
    }
}

[Synchronization(SynchronizationAttribute.REQUIRED, false)]
public class Sync3 : ContextBoundObject
{
    public String GetName()
    {
        return (AppDomain.CurrentDomain.FriendlyName);
    }
}
```

The first class uses the SynchronizationAttribute.REQUIRES_NEW argument, which means that the class must appear in a context with a new copy of the synchronization property each time. What this really means is that the resulting object must reside in its own context because the new copy of the synchronization property requires a different context each time.

Notice that this object doesn't derive from anything. The result is a standard system object of the Sync1 type. Figure 2.1 shows the debug view of this object (and the others in this example). When a client attempts to access this object, CLR creates a copy of the object and places the in the client context. The copy contains all of the data and other features of the original. Therefore, if you have a property set to a certain value, the client will see that value. Consequently, a client accesses this class by value. Any changes the client makes to the object won't appear in the original version of the object.

FIGURE 2.1:

The method used to design an object determines the client access type.

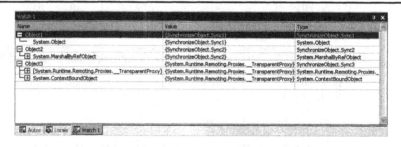

The Sync2 class uses the SynchronizationAttribute.SUPPORTED argument. Using this argument means that CLR can place the object in a context that either does or doesn't have the synchronization property. An alternative to this value is the Synchronization-Attribute.NOT_SUPPORTED argument. This value means that CLR can't place the object within a context that has the synchronization property set. If no context exists, then CLR creates a new one.

This class also demonstrates another access strategy because it derives from the Marshal-ByRefObject class. This addition means that the client will work with the actual object on the server, not a copy. Any changes the client makes will appear to all clients that access the object. When a client exists in a different application domain than the object, CLR creates a proxy for the client. The proxy receives the client requests and passes them to the object. In many respects, this access strategy works the same as COM+. Notice from the debug view in Figure 2.1 that this also adds to the memory footprint of the object by adding an embedded entity.

The Sync3 class uses the SynchronizationAttribute.REQUIRED argument. In this case, CLR can create the object in the same context as other objects, so long as the context has the synchronization property set. Of course, the resource and other requirements of the context must also match.

This class uses the context bound access technique because it derives from the ContextBoundObject class. Using this method means that every client sees the object as if it exists in the same context as the client. However, CLR sends every call through one or more proxies (see the debug view in Figure 2.1) to ensure both the client and the object receive the environment and resources they expect and can access.

The context bound object shown in the debug view in Figure 2.1 provides the isolation and security required for most distributed applications today. Because the proxies are invisible and each party receives what it expects, the program behaves as if it were all on one machine. This is the type of class setup required to ensure maximum benefits from .NET security.

Understanding the *System.Security* Namespace

The System.Security namespace acts as the starting point for the majority of the other security namespaces discussed in the book. This is the first namespace that many people look at when they begin working with security features in the .NET Framework. Actually, this namespace contains a number of utility-type classes. You'll probably use it in every program you create, yet it doesn't contain the underpinnings of the security features. The following sections tell you more about this namespace.

Security Namespace Overview

The System.Security namespace contains a number of interesting classes and attributes, including the AllowPartiallyTrustedCallersAttribute attribute. You use this attribute to allow partially trusted code to call strongly named assemblies. This attribute is one of the double-edged sword decisions you must make when working with security. If you add the attribute to your strongly named assembly, there's a chance that a partially trusted assembly could cause a security breach. On the other hand, not adding the attribute means that some code won't be able to call your strongly named assembly at all.

You always need to add this namespace to your code because it contains the `SecurityException` exception, which allows you to handle security errors, such as authentication failures, gracefully. Normally, you'll want to access secure calls using a `try…catch` structure. When a `SecurityException` exception occurs, your code can catch it and use any logic you have in place for handling the problem. In many cases, the program will exit and send a message to the network administrator. However, you could do something as simple as ask the user to enter a password again.

TIP   You can find a complete description of the System.Security namespace at http://msdn.microsoft.com/library/en-us/cpref/html/frlrfSystemSecurity.asp. You may be surprised at the limited number of classes, interfaces, and enumerations associated with this namespace. To get the bigger picture, make sure you check the name-space hierarchy.

Of all the classes in this namespace, the `SecurityManager` class is one of the most useful because it helps you determine user and code rights to perform certain tasks. In fact, this particular class is so useful, that you may want to commit the routines you write to a separate library so that you can use them in every program. It's important to know what security settings are in place so that you know what the user and the code can do in the current environment. The interesting part about .NET security is that it's flexible enough that you can write a generic routine. You don't have to know the user's name while writing the code because this information is easy to obtain using other means. You'll see this class in action in the next section, "SecurityManager Class Example."

SecurityManager Class Example

This example doesn't show you all of the features of the `SecurityManager` class. However, it gets you started using this important class by demonstrating some basic security features. For example, the class tells you whether the administrator has actually enabled security in the current environment and whether the code has execution rights. Listing 2.2 shows the details of how to use these class features. (You can find this code in the \Chapter 02\C#\SecureManage or \Chapter 02\VB\SecureManage folder of the source code located on the Sybex Web site.)

Listing 2.2   **Obtaining information with the *SecurityManager* class**

```
private void btnTest_Click(object sender, System.EventArgs e)
{
    StringBuilder        Output;      // Output data.
    CodeAccessPermission CAP;         // Permissions object for code.
```

```
PrincipalPermission  PP;          // Permissions object for users.
IEnumerator          Policies;    // Security policies.
PolicyLevel          Policy;      // A single policy.

// Initialize the output string.
Output = new StringBuilder();

// Create the code permissions object.
CAP = new FileIOPermission(FileIOPermissionAccess.AllAccess,
                           @"C:\");

// Create the user permission object.
PP = new PrincipalPermission(SystemInformation.UserName,
                             "Administrator");

// Determine if security is enabled.
if (SecurityManager.SecurityEnabled)
{
   // Security is enabled.
   Output.Append("Security is enabled.");

   // Check the code execution requirements.
   if (SecurityManager.CheckExecutionRights)
      Output.Append("\r\nCode requires execution rights.");
   else
      Output.Append("\r\nCode doesn't require execution rights.");

   // Determine if the caller has administrative rights.
   if (SecurityManager.IsGranted(PP))
      Output.Append("\r\n" + SystemInformation.UserName +
          " has administratrive rights.");

   // Determine if the code can perform all access to drive C.
   if (SecurityManager.IsGranted(CAP))
      Output.Append("\r\nCode can access Drive C.");

   // Get the all of the policies.
   Policies = SecurityManager.PolicyHierarchy();
   Output.Append("\r\n\r\nPolicy Hierarchy:");
   while (Policies.MoveNext())
   {
      // Get the current policy.
      Policy = (PolicyLevel)Policies.Current;

      // Add its label to the output.
      Output.Append("\r\n" + Policy.Label);
   }
}
else
   // Security isn't enabled.
   Output.Append("Security Not Enabled!");

// Output the result.
```

```
MessageBox.Show(Output.ToString(),
                "SecurityManager Results",
                MessageBoxButtons.OK,
                MessageBoxIcon.Information);
}
```

The code begins by creating two types of permissions. A `CodeAccessPermission` determines what the code can do. For example, even though the user has the right (permission) to access the disk drive, the code may not have this right or the administrator may limit the code's access. When you create a new `CodeAccessPermission` object, you can ask about specific code execution rights without worrying about details of other rights the code might have. Note that you don't use the `CodeAccessPermission` constructor directly. You need to create a permission object from one of the resource permissions, such as the `FileIOPermission` shown.

A `PrincipalPermission` object focuses on the user. Notice how the constructor uses the `SystemInformation.UserName` property to determine the current user. Actually, you'll want to view all of the features of the `SystemInformation` class because it's very useful. This class helps you learn more about the system using simple calls. The second argument determines what right you want to check for the given user. In this case, PP will contain the administrator permission for the current user.

After the code creates the two permission objects, it checks the current security state using the `SecurityManager.SecurityEnabled` property. You must make this check before you do anything else because there's a chance that the administrator hasn't enabled security. When this occurs, many of the other `SecurityManager` features won't work properly.

The code checks execution rights next using the `SecurityManager.CheckExecutionRights`. Theoretically, the program should end if it doesn't have proper execution rights. In addition, you'll probably want to create an Event Log entry and raise an error (if one hasn't occurred already). The example simply makes note of the fact and continues with the next check.

The documentation for the `SecurityManager.IsGranted()` method isn't very clear. It tells you that the method requires an object that implements the `IPermission` interface as input, without really telling you what that means. You can theoretically create your own permissions, but the `CodeAccessPermission` and `PrincipalPermission` classes serve most needs. In fact, I can't think of a reason to create another `IPermission` interface class implementation. The example shows how to use both of these classes with the `SecurityManager.IsGranted()` method.

The final element in this example is a quick view of the policy hierarchy. You can actually follow the hierarchy down all the levels, but the example shows just the first level. Because this is a collection, you have several methods of following it at your disposal. The example moves from one entry to the next using the MoveNext() method. You must issue a MoveNext() call to access the first element, which is why the code is set up this way. The PolicyLevel object, Policy, provides complete information about the current level. In this case, the code returns the Label property value, which is the friendly name for that level. If you want to go to the next level, you use the NamedPermissionSets collection. Figure 2.2 shows the output from this program.

FIGURE 2.2:

Rely on the SecurityManager class to learn about code and user rights.

The output shows that the example has security enabled and execution rights. In addition, the user has administrative privileges and the code has all access rights to the C drive. Notice that the policy hierarchy includes Enterprise, Machine, and User—the three standard hierarchy members.

Understanding the *System.Security.Cryptography* Namespace

Security at the most basic level performs two tasks—it protects data and secures resources. Any security feature you build into a program will perform one of these two tasks. Keeping a cracker at bay by denying entrance to your Web site is a method of protecting data and resources. Given this definition of security, the System.Security.Cryptography namespace takes on special importance because it's the only namespace that directly targets data protection. Most of the other namespaces emphasize data and resource protection through other, indirect, methods.

TIP   You can find a complete description of the System.Security.Cryptography namespace at http://msdn.microsoft.com/library/en-us/cpref/html/frlrfSystem-SecurityCryptography.asp. Don't let the large number of classes in this namespace surprise you. Many of the classes perform essentially the same task, such as decryption, using different methodologies. For example, the RSACryptoServiceProvider and SHA1CryptoServiceProvider perform the same task using different encryption methods.

Cryptography Namespace Structure Overview

Some people take one look at all of the classes in this namespace and immediately think that cryptography is difficult. The .NET Framework makes cryptography easy compared to earlier technologies such as the CryptoAPI (see the article entitled, "The Cryptography API, or How to Keep a Secret" at http://msdn.microsoft.com/library/en-us/dncapi/html /msdn_cryptapi.asp for a good overview of this topic). The best way to approach this namespace is to use a divide and conquer approach. You can break the System.Security .Cryptography namespace down into the following distinct areas.

Algorithms   Some classes, such as AsymmetricAlgorithm, define algorithms used to create encryption methodologies. You could theoretically create a class based on one of these algorithms to design your own encryption method. However, it's usually best to leave this task to the experts. Other classes in this category, such as Data Encryption Standard (DES), are used within your application to perform encryption and decryption services based on a particular algorithm. (The example later in this section demonstrates how an algorithm works.) The overall idea is that these classes define an algorithm used to encrypt and decrypt data.

Assistant or Utility   The System.Security.Cryptography namespace includes a number of assistant classes. For example, the CryptographicException class provides help in catching error conditions so you can handle them within your program. The RandomNumberGenerator class generates the random numbers used in all cryptographic calculations.

Data Formatters and Deformatters   The overall goal of these classes is verification. A formatter creates a signature on the sending end that's deformatted (or verified) on the receiving end of a data transmission. For example, the AsymmetricSignatureDeformatter and AsymmetricSignatureFormatter classes act as the base classes for classes that verify signatures. Currently, the Digital Signature Algorithm (DSA) and Rivest, Shamir, and Adleman (RSA) encryption methodologies rely on these classes.

Service Provider   These classes provide a convenient wrapper for using many of the cryptographic algorithm classes. They provide a wrapper that makes using the algorithm easier. For example, the DESCryptoServiceProvider class provides a wrapper around the DES algorithm class.

Transforms   A few of the classes provide data transformation functionality. The two common transforms are FromBase64Transform and ToBase64Transform, which transform data to and from the Base64 format.

Cryptography Namespace Structure Example

Cryptography, the act of making data unreadable to someone else and then converting it back to something readable, is one of the most ancient arts in the world for keeping a secret.

Of course, ancient cryptographic methods can't compete with the modern equivalent, but the idea has been the same since those early times.

One of the ways in which .NET has greatly improved the life of developers is using cryptography to keep data safe. Unlike the CryptoAPI provided with previous versions of Windows, the .NET method is actually easy to understand and use. Listing 2.3 shows an example of the encryption portion of the process. The decryption portion is almost the same with a few minor differences. (You can find this code in the \Chapter 02\C#\Crypto or \Chapter 02\VB\Crypto folder of the source code located on the Sybex Web site.)

Listing 2.3   **Encrypting and Decrypting a File Requires Similar Code**

```
private void btnEncrypt_Click(object sender, System.EventArgs e)
{
    FileStream       FIn;                          // Input file.
    FileStream       FOut;                         // Output file.
    Byte[]           Data = new Byte[100];         // Temporary buffer.
    int              Counter = 0;                  // Total converted.
    int              ReadByte = 0;                 // Currently read counter.
    CryptoStream     CryptStream;                  // Cryptographic stream.
    RijndaelManaged  RM;                           // Encryption Algorithm.
    byte[] Key = {0x01, 0x02, 0x03, 0x04,         // Encryption Key.
                  0x05, 0x06, 0x07, 0x08,
                  0x09, 0x10, 0x11, 0x12,
                  0x13, 0x14, 0x15, 0x16};
    byte[] IV = {0x01, 0x02, 0x03, 0x04,          // Initialization vector.
                 0x05, 0x06, 0x07, 0x08,
                 0x09, 0x10, 0x11, 0x12,
                 0x13, 0x14, 0x15, 0x16};

    // Open the input and output files.
    FIn = new FileStream(txtInput.Text,
                         FileMode.Open,
                         FileAccess.Read);
    FOut = new FileStream(txtEncrypt.Text,
                          FileMode.OpenOrCreate,
                          FileAccess.Write);

    // Create the cryptographic stream.
    RM = new RijndaelManaged();
    CryptStream = new CryptoStream(FOut,
                                   RM.CreateEncryptor(Key, IV),
                                   CryptoStreamMode.Write);

    // Encrypt the file.
    while(Counter < FIn.Length)
    {
        ReadByte = FIn.Read(Data, 0, 100);
        CryptStream.Write(Data, 0, ReadByte);
        Counter = Counter + ReadByte;
```

```
    }

    // Close the open stream and files.
    CryptStream.Close();
    FIn.Close();
    FOut.Close();
  }
```

As you can see from the example code, the idea is to open input and output files. The input file contains the plain text that you want to encrypt. After you open the two files, you need to create an algorithm object to encrypt the data and a stream for handling the encryption. Notice the CreateEncryptor() method call in the CryptoStream() constructor. You would replace this with a CreateDecryptor() call in the decryption portion of the code.

After the code creates the required stream, it simply reads from the input file, encrypts the data, and sends the data to the output file. It's important to track how many bytes the input file actually contained or you'll obtain some odd results from the encryption portion of the program. Once the output is complete, you close the stream first, and then the two files. Make sure you follow this order or you'll receive an error from the application. The output file will also lose data because CLR doesn't flush the CryptoStream object until you close it. Figure 2.3 shows the interface for this program.

FIGURE 2.3:

The sample program can encrypt and decrypt files using the Rijndael algorithm.

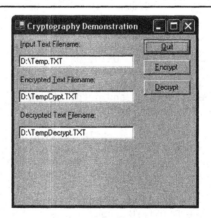

The interface is straightforward, but you need to observe a few rules. First, you must supply three unique filenames or the program will fail. The input and output streams must remain separate. When you click Encrypt, the program encrypts the original input file and places the data in the encrypted file. Figure 2.4 shows typical output from this task. The original text file has a simple statement, "This is some simple text to encrypt." It's unreadable now. Click

Decrypt and the program will decrypt the information into its original state. You can theoretically use this simple program for any encryption needs you have, but other techniques are examined later in the book.

FIGURE 2.4:

Although the encrypted file looks like garbage, it really does contain data.

Understanding the *System.Security.Permissions* Namespace

The System.Security.Permissions namespace provides permission objects used to access resources (see the FileDialogPermission class and the FileDialogPermissionAttribute attribute). These permissions also describe tasks that users and code want to perform (see the RegistryPermission class and the RegistryPermissionAttribute attribute).

Most of the entries come in class and attribute pairs. You use the classes to request access to a resource to perform a task. Use the attributes to define access to the resource or the ability to perform a task. See Listing 2.2 for an example of how to use this namespace. Of course, this namespace is discussed several times throughout the book.

> **TIP**   You can find a complete description of the System.Security.Permissions namespace at
> http://msdn.microsoft.com/library/en-us/cpref/html/frlrfSystemSecurity
> Permissions.asp. The elements in this namespace also have a big effect on the CodeAc-
> cessPermission class discussed in the "SecurityManager Class Example" section. The
> CodeAccessPermission class is part of the System.Security.CodeAccessPermission
> namespace.

Understanding the *System.Security.Policy* Namespace

Most developers are already familiar with some policy concepts. For example, most developers know that a policy defines a set of rules for access to a resource. A user might have read access to a file, but not write access. Consequently, you expect to see classes such as PolicyException, PolicyLevel, and PolicyStatement in the System.Security.Policy namespace.

Network administrators manage policies at the enterprise, machine, and user levels in most cases. Standard additions to these levels include an application and domain level. However, it's possible that a network administrator could require other levels, such as a workgroup.

The concept of a policy extends beyond a set of rules in .NET, however. When an entity requests access to a resource, it must present evidence that the security system allows access. The `System.Security.Policy` namespace supplies a number of classes that present or manage various kinds of evidence. For example, the `StrongName` class presents the strong name of an assembly as evidence. The strong name is important because it uniquely identifies the assembly, provides a hash value for assembly verification, and tells who created the assembly.

> **TIP** You can find a complete description of the `System.Security.Policy` namespace at `http://msdn.microsoft.com/library/en-us/cpref/html/frlrfSystemSecurityPolicy.asp`. Pay particular attention to the classes that affect how a program, administrator, or other entity can make policies, because these classes will likely change most as the .NET Framework security matures. Unlike other namespaces with a lot of classes, these aren't that easy to group by type, so you'll need to look at each class individually to ensure your program makes the best use possible of the features in this namespace.

You need policies to perform a variety of tasks. See Listing 2.2 for an example of how to use this namespace. This example starts at the beginning by showing the policy hierarchy on the local machine.

Understanding the *System.Security.Principal* Namespace

The .NET Framework is a study of contrasts. Some of the classes discussed work specifically with code access security, some with user security, and some with both. The `System.Security.Principal` namespace is the one that you need to remember when working with user-level security. This is actually a very small class for the purpose, but it does the job.

> **TIP** You can find a complete description of the `System.Security.Principle` namespace at `http://msdn.microsoft.com/library/en-us/cpref/html/frlrfSystemSecurityPrincipal.asp`. Even though the number of classes in this namespace is few, you'll find that you use some of them in almost every program. For example, the `WindowsPrincipal` class is exceptionally important when you want to verify the identity and rights of a user.

When working with this class, you're working with implementations of two interfaces. The `IIdentity` interface represents an identity—the essential elements that define the person or other entity. For example, your name is part of your identity. The `IPrincipal` interface is a listing of rights that the person has to some system resource or the ability to perform a task. For example, being a member of the Administrator group gives you complete access to the local machine. See Listing 1.1 for an example of how to use this namespace. Of course, this namespace is discussed several times throughout the book.

Understanding the *System.Web.Security* Namespace

When you think about the System.Web.Security namespace, think about unique Web programming requirements. Don't get the idea that System.Web.Security is an independent namespace that you can use by itself for all of your Web needs—it's in addition to the existing classes. For example, if you want to verify a user identity, you'll still likely need to use the members of the System.Security.Principal namespace.

> **TIP**   You can find a complete description of the System.Web.Security namespace at
> http://msdn.microsoft.com/library/en-us/cpref/html/frlrfSystemWebSecurity
> .asp. Make sure you watch for new security additions for the Internet. It's also important to
> watch for changes as Microsoft updates products such as Passport.

This namespace is the only one where you can find Passport support, which means that you could conceivably use it even with desktop applications. The System.Web.Security namespace includes several Passport-specific classes including PassportAuthentication-EventArgs, PassportAuthenticationModule, and PassportIdentity. You may still need the Passport SDK to meet all of your Passport development needs. See the Microsoft Web site at http://www.passport.net/ for further details. The article entitled, "About the Passport SDK" (http://www.microsoft.com/downloads/details.aspx?FamilyId=89B1BA8B-4AA2-4F1B-B51C-DE4B13581608) provides specifics you need to know. (Also see Chapter 11 for details on what you can do with Passport support in .NET.)

Because security issues in Web development is a complex topic, you'll need additional information before seeing an actual example of this namespace in use. The "Using the System.Web.Security Namespace" section of Chapter 9 contains one of the preliminary examples of this namespace in use.

Understanding the *System.DirectoryServices* Namespace

The System.DirectoryServices namespace provides access to the data stored within Active Directory. This chapter won't discuss the general structure of Active Directory or the utilities you can use to access it. You can find that information in the "Managing Directory Services" section of Chapter 12. However, this chapter does discuss the essentials of the System.DirectoryServices namespace and provides you with an example of how to use it (see Listing 2.4).

TIP   You can find a complete description of the System.DirectoryServices namespace at http://msdn.microsoft.com/library/en-us/cpref/html/frlrfSystemDirectory Services.asp. Checking for changes to this namespace is important because it could change based on Microsoft changes to its server software, as well as the .NET Framework. Of course, you only need to consider this namespace if you're using Active Directory on your network.

DirectoryServices Namespace Overview

The System.DirectoryServices namespace is simply a managed version of the Active Directory Services Interface (ADSI) interface you may have used in the unmanaged environment. It enables you to access Active Directory using managed, rather than unmanaged, techniques in many situations. You'll run into two problems when using this namespace. First, CLR doesn't recognize some Active Directory data types, even though it seems as if it should. Second, the DirectoryServices namespace doesn't provide support for every Active Directory interface, so you'll need to resort to COM to gain access to these interfaces. I'll discuss both problems in the sample applications.

The DirectoryServices namespace includes class counterparts for the ADSI interfaces. The focus of the classes provided in the System.DirectoryServices namespace is implementation of the IADsOpenDSObject interface. (See http://msdn.microsoft.com/library/en-us /netdir/adsi/core_interfaces.asp for a list of core ADSI interfaces and http://msdn .microsoft.com/library/en-us/netdir/adsi/iadsopendsobject.asp for a list of IADsOpenDSObject interface features.) Once you have an open connection to Active Directory, you can begin to manipulate the data it contains.

You can perform most tasks using managed code. In the few cases where you need to perform a task using the COM interfaces, you can obtain a copy of the object using built-in method calls. Of course, several issues besides ease of access remain. One of the most important issues is thread safety—an important consideration in a distributed application. Generally, you'll find that public static class members are thread safe, while instance members aren't. This limitation means you must use class members carefully and take steps to ensure method calls occur in a thread safe manner.

DirectoryServices Namespace Example

The example application performs some essential Active Directory tasks. It accepts a general query for usernames that you use to select an individual user. The application uses this information to create a specific user query, and then displays certain information about that user including their department and job title. Active Directory also provides a note field for each user entry that you can use to make comments. The application enables you to view the current comment and modify it as needed.

Accessing Active Directory

The first task is to gain access to Active Directory generally. Listing 2.4 shows the code you'll need to create a general query. Note that this code works with a WinNT or a LDAP path. (You can find this code in the \Chapter 02\C#\Monitor or \Chapter 02\VB\Monitor folder of the source code located on the Sybex Web site.)

Listing 2.4   **Accessing Active Directory**

```csharp
private void btnQuery_Click(object sender, System.EventArgs e)
{
    // Clear the previous query (if any).
    lvUsers.Items.Clear();

    // Add the path information to the DirectoryEntry object.
    ADSIEntry.Path = txtQuery.Text;

    // The query might fail, so add some error checking.
    try
    {

        // Process each DirectoryEntry child of the root
        // DirectoryEntry object.
        foreach (DirectoryEntry Child in ADSIEntry.Children)
        {
            // Look for user objects, versus group or service objects.
            if (Child.SchemaClassName.ToUpper() == "USER")
            {
                // Fill in the ListView object columns. Note that the
                // username is available as part of the DirectoryEntry
                // Name property, but that we need to obtain the
                // Description using another technique.
                ListViewItem lvItem  = new ListViewItem(Child.Name);
                lvItem.SubItems.Add(
                    Child.Properties["Description"].Value.ToString());
                lvUsers.Items.Add(lvItem);
            }
        }
    }
    catch (System.Runtime.InteropServices.COMException eQuery)
    {
        MessageBox.Show("Invalid Query\r\nMessage: " +
```

```
                              eQuery.Message +
                              "\r\nSource: " + eQuery.Source,
                              "Query Error",
                              MessageBoxButtons.OK,
                              MessageBoxIcon.Error);
        }
    }

    private void lvUsers_DoubleClick(object sender, System.EventArgs e)
    {
        // Create a new copy of the Detail Form.
        DetailForm ViewDetails =
            new DetailForm(lvUsers.SelectedItems[0].Text,
                           lvUsers.SelectedItems[0].SubItems[1].Text,
                           txtQuery.Text);

        // Display it on screen.
        ViewDetails.ShowDialog(this);
    }
```

The application begins with the btnQuery_Click() method. It uses a ListView control to display the output of the query, so the first task is to clear the items in the ListView control. Notice that I specifically clear the items, not the entire control. This prevents corruption of settings such as the list headings.

You can configure all elements of the ADSIEntry (DirectoryEntry) control as part of the design process except the path. The application provides an example path in the txtQuery textbox that you'll need to change to meet your specific server configuration.

The ADSIEntry.Children property is a collection of DirectoryEntry objects. The application won't fail with a bad path until you try to access these DirectoryEntry objects, which is why you want to place the portion of the code in a try…catch block. Notice how the code uses a property string as an index into each DirectoryEntry object. Even if the property is a string, you must use the ToString() method or the compiler will complain. This is because C# views each DirectoryEntry value as an object, regardless of object type.

The output of this portion of the code can vary depending on the path string you supply. Figure 2.5 shows the output for a WinNT path while Figure 2.6 shows the output for a LDAP path. Notice that the actual DirectoryEntry value changes to match the path type. This means you can't depend on specific DirectoryEntry values within your code, even if you're working with the same Active Directory entry. For example, notice that the entry for George changes from WinNT to LDAP. The WinNT entry is simple, while the LDAP entry contains the user's full name and the CN qualifier required for the path.

FIGURE 2.5:

The WinNT path
tends to produce
easy-to-read
DirectoryEntry
values.

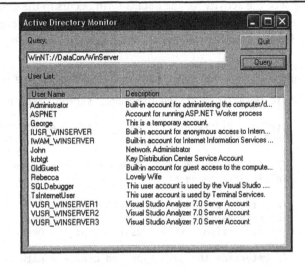

FIGURE 2.6:

LDAP paths tend
to produce complex
DirectoryEntry
values that you'll
need to clean up
for user displays.

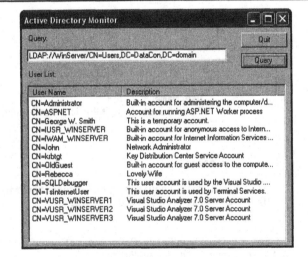

Getting Detailed Active Directory Information

Once you have access to the usernames, it's possible to gain details about a specific user. The
sample application performs this task using a secondary form. When a user double-clicks on
one of the names, the lvUsers_DoubleClick() method creates a new copy of the secondary
form and passes everything it needs to create a detailed query. Notice that the code uses the
ShowDialog() method, rather than the Show() method. This ensures that one query completes
before the user creates another one.

Most of the activity for the details form occurs in the constructor. The constructor accepts the username, description, and path as inputs so it can create a detailed query for specific user information. Listing 2.5 shows the constructor code for this part of the example.

Listing 2.5   The Details Form Displays Individual User Information

```
public DetailForm(string UserName, string Description, string Path)
{
    string    UserPath;    // Path to the user object.
    bool      IsLDAP;      // LDAP provides more information.

    // Required for Windows Form Designer support
    InitializeComponent();

    // Set the username and description.
    lblUserName.Text = "User Name: " + UserName;
    lblDescription.Text = "Description: " + Description;

    // Determine the path type and create a path variable.
    if (Path.Substring(0, 4) == "LDAP")
    {
        IsLDAP = true;

        // LDAP requires some work to manipulate the path
        // string.
        int CNPosit = Path.IndexOf("CN");
        UserPath = Path.Substring(0, CNPosit) +
                    UserName + "," +
                    Path.Substring(CNPosit, Path.Length - CNPosit);
    }
    else
    {
        IsLDAP = false;

        // A WinNT path requires simple concatenation.
        UserPath = Path + "/" + UserName;
    }

    // Set the ADSIUserEntry Path and get user details.
    ADSIUserEntry.Path = UserPath;
    ADSIUserEntry.RefreshCache();

    // This information is only available using LDAP
    if (IsLDAP)
    {
        // Get the user's title.
        if (ADSIUserEntry.Properties["Title"].Value == null)
            lblTitleDept.Text = "Title (Department): No Title";
        else
            lblTitleDept.Text = "Title (Department): " +
```

```
                ADSIUserEntry.Properties["Title"].Value.ToString();

    // Get the user's department.
    if (ADSIUserEntry.Properties["Department"].Value == null)
        lblTitleDept.Text = lblTitleDept.Text + " (No Department)";
    else
        lblTitleDept.Text = lblTitleDept.Text + " (" +
            ADSIUserEntry.Properties["Department"].Value.ToString()
            + ")";
}

// This information is common to both WinNT and LDAP, but uses
// slightly different names.
if (IsLDAP)
{
    if (ADSIUserEntry.Properties["lastLogon"].Value == null)
        lblLogOn.Text = "Last Logon: Never Logged On";
    else
    {
        LargeInteger        Ticks;      // COM Time in Ticks.
        long                ConvTicks;  // Converted Time in Ticks.
        PropertyCollection  LogOnTime;  // Logon Property Collection.

        // Create a property collection.
        LogOnTime = ADSIUserEntry.Properties;

        // Obtain the LastLogon property value.
        Ticks = (LargeInteger)LogOnTime["lastLogon"][0];

        // Convert the System.__ComObject value to a managed
        // value.
        ConvTicks = (((long)(Ticks.HighPart) << 32) +
                     (long) Ticks.LowPart);

        // Release the COM ticks value.
        Marshal.ReleaseComObject(Ticks);

        // Display the value.
        lblLogOn.Text = "Last Logon: " +
            DateTime.FromFileTime(ConvTicks).ToString();
    }
}
else
{
    if (ADSIUserEntry.Properties["LastLogin"].Value == null)
        lblLogOn.Text = "Last Logon: Never Logged On";
    else
        lblLogOn.Text = "Last Logon: " +
            ADSIUserEntry.Properties["LastLogin"].Value.ToString();
}

// In a few cases, WinNT and LDAP use the same property names.
```

```
if (ADSIUserEntry.Properties["HomeDirectory"].Value == null)
   lblHomeDirectory.Text = "Home Directory: None";
else
   lblHomeDirectory.Text = "Home Directory: " +
      ADSIUserEntry.Properties["HomeDirectory"].Value.ToString();

// Get the text for the user notes. Works only for LDAP.
if (IsLDAP)
{
   if (ADSIUserEntry.Properties["Info"].Value != null)
      txtNotes.Text =
         ADSIUserEntry.Properties["Info"].Value.ToString();

   // Enable the Update button.
   btnUpdate.Visible = true;
}
else
{
   txtNotes.Text = "Note Feature Not Available with WinNT";
}
}
```

The application requires two methods for creating the path to the user directory entry. The WinNT path is easy—just add the UserName to the existing Path. The LDAP path requires a little more work in that the username must appear as the first "CN=" value in the path string. Here's an example of an LDAP formatting user directory entry path.

```
LDAP://WinServer/CN=George W. Smith,CN=Users,DC=DataCon,DC=domain
```

Notice that the server name appears first, then the username, followed by the group, and finally the domain. You must include the full directory entry name as presented in the ADSI Viewer utility. This differs from the presentation for a WinNT path, which includes only the user's logon name.

The process for adding the path to the DirectoryEntry control, ADSIUserEntry, is the same as before. In this case, the control is activated using the RefreshCache() method. Calling RefreshCache() ensures the local control contains the property values for the user in question.

LDAP does provide access to a lot more properties than WinNT. The example shows just two of the additional properties in the form of the user's title and department name. While WinNT provides access to a mere 25 properties, you'll find that LDAP provides access to 56 or more. Notice that each property access relies on checks for null values. Active Directory uses null values when a property doesn't have a value, rather than set it to a default value such as 0 or an empty string.

WinNT and LDAP do have some overlap in the property values they provide. In some cases, the properties don't have precisely the same name, so you need to extract the property value depending on the type of path used to access the directory entry. Both WinNT and LDAP provide access to the user's last logon, but WinNT uses LastLogin, while LDAP uses lastLogon.

WinNT normally provides an easy method for accessing data values that CLR can understand. In the case of the lastLogon property, LDAP presents some challenges. This is one case when you need to use the COM access method. Notice that the lastLogon property requires use of a LargeInteger (defined in the ACTIVEDS.TLB file). If you view the property value returned by the lastLogon property, you'll see that it's of the System.__ComObject type. This type always indicates that CLR couldn't understand the value returned by COM. Notice that the code converts the COM value to a managed type, then releases the COM object using Marshal.ReleaseComObject(). If you don't release the object, your application will have a memory leak—so memory allocation problems aren't quite solved in .NET, they just don't occur when using managed types. The final part of the conversion process is to change the number of ticks into a formatted string using the DateTime.FromFileTime() method.

As previously mentioned, the sample application shows how to present and edit one of the user properties. The Info property is only available when working with LDAP, so the code only accesses the property if you're using an LDAP path. The code also enables an Update button when using an LDAP path so you can update the value in Active Directory. Here's the simple code for sending a change to Active Directory.

```
private void btnUpdate_Click(object sender, System.EventArgs e)
{
    // Place the new value in the correct property.
    ADSIUserEntry.Properties["info"][0] = txtNotes.Text;

    // Update the property.
    ADSIUserEntry.CommitChanges();
}
```

The application uses a double index when accessing the property to ensure the updated text from txtNotes appears in the right place. All you need to do to make the change permanent is call CommitChanges(). Note that the change will only take place if the user has sufficient rights to make it. In most cases, COM will ignore any update errors, so you won't know the change took place unless you actually check the entry. Figure 2.7 shows the LDAP output for the sample application.

FIGURE 2.7:

The LDAP output is more complete than the WinNT output, but requires more work as well.

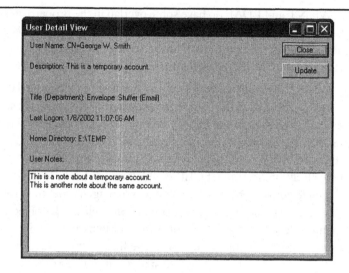

Summary

This chapter has demonstrated techniques for developing applications with the various namespaces provided by the .NET Framework. Although the examples are simple, you now have a better idea of how each namespace fits within the .NET programming arena. You've also gained an understanding of how each of these namespaces can help your programming efforts and when you would use each namespace. Finally, you've gained a list of new and interesting places to look for information online.

The material in this chapter is just the tip of the iceberg. The remainder of the book will show detailed examples of each namespace, but this is the only time you'll get to see all of these namespaces in one place. Consequently, you'll want to spend time familiarizing yourself with each of the namespaces before you move to the next chapter. In addition, make sure you mark this chapter as an overall reference.

Chapter 3 is the last overview chapter. It presents some of the most common security errors gathered from newsgroups, trade magazines, and personal experience. Each of the sections presents a potential trap and tells how you can avoid it. Once you complete Chapter 3, you'll have a better understanding of why some things in the .NET Framework are set up in a certain way. Chapter 3 also discusses a few things that Microsoft could have done better and when these issues can cause problems in your programming efforts.

CHAPTER 3

Avoiding Common Errors and Traps

- Keeping Data Entry Errors Controlled

- Preventing Buffer Overruns

- Understanding Access Control Issues

- Using the Appropriate Privileges

- Deterring Canonical Representation Issues

Many of the worst security problems are due to human error. When a user leaves a password pasted on a monitor for the world to see, that's a significant security problem and it's one that only the user can prevent. (Finding the password later and removing it is hardly a solution to the problem.)

Developers can make security mistakes too. Some of these errors, such as buffer overruns, receive a lot of press. Other errors receive hardly any notice at all. For example, when was the last time you saw a major article on range checking? Yet, this particular error has many serious security implications.

Traps also come in many forms. A developer may need every second allotted to a project to develop the original code. The problem is that there isn't time to check for code that is less utilitarian, but necessary nonetheless. For example, a lack of error-trapping code can present a number of security problems. Many crackers enter systems based on the idea that the system is going to crash and become helpless (unable) to prevent the intrusion.

This chapter discusses many of the traps and errors that cause security problems outside the confines of good coding practice. The purpose of this chapter is to help you discover some of the security issues that you cannot address in your code. The goal is to produce code that not only follows all of the technical requirements for good coding practice, but also reduces the number of human error issues.

Preventing Data Entry Errors

The most common, yet easily preventable, security errors are those that result from data entry and consequent management. For example, if a user inputs a number when you were looking for standard text, then you need to have code that recognizes the error and alerts the user to the problem. Of course, you don't want the application to fail, so it's important to let the user retry after you provide instructions for proper input. However, at some point, you have to consider that multiple attempts fall outside the range of errant input and into the range of a cracker probing for holes in your defenses. Issues such as these cause the majority of security problems and they're all preventable with good programming practices.

The following sections describe various data entry error issues and provide ideas on how to fix them. Not every problem will require the same fix and the text doesn't include every potential problem. For example, you may find that range checking requires a simple check against a numeric limits, in some cases, but requires direct comparison to a list of acceptable entries in others. The important concept is that you must perform some type of range checking to ensure the input data is valid.

Putting the Time back into Access

One of the biggest problems that developers face is time. Often, accountants, managers, and others who don't develop code for a living only understand the ticking of the clock and see how the expenditure of time affects the bottom line. The outside world has tried to quantify developer productivity for years. In a race to deliver code within the time expectations of management, developers often cut corners and leave out the code that we all know should appear in the application.

Would it surprise you to know that most of the errors and security issues in code are there because of time issues? Even the best developers get flustered and fail to provide adequate checks in their code because it's easier to deliver the code now than to hear marketing whine one more time. Time is the enemy of security. Bowing to the demands of time, rather than exercising prudent programming practices, is the biggest mistake any developer can make. Fortunately, the .NET Framework automatically adds code to perform many required security checks. The Common Language Runtime (CLR) uses these automatic code additions to perform security checks during runtime. Unless you trap the error, however, the user sees an ambiguous security error message, rather than a precise message stating how to fix the problem. The .NET Framework does improve the situation, but can't fix it completely.

Explaining the dichotomy of time versus quality to your boss isn't an easy undertaking and will be impossible if you can't quantify the argument in some way. It's important to put the science back into the art of programming by creating an underpinning of quality within your organization. For example, how many developers actually use a checklist to ensure they've met every programming need? (Such as the need to include security exception checking within the code.) A checklist requires validation, but once validated, it can provide the best means of quantifying your progress to those who need to know.

Checking the Data Range

A data range defines the acceptable values for data input. For example, when you define a value in your code as Int32, it means that the user can enter any value from –2,147,483,648 through +2,147,483,647. However, your application might not find this range acceptable. When this happens, you must include special code in your application to check for potential error conditions. You might want to accept numbers from 0 to 40,000 in your code, which is outside the Int16 value range, but well within the Int32 value range. In short, a data range is specific to the need at hand.

Generally, you'll find that value data types are the easiest to range check because they have predefined ranges. The .NET Framework supports more value types than you might think. For example, the .NET Framework considers a color used for drawing (System.Drawing.Color) a value type. You can see the full list of .NET Framework value types at http://msdn .microsoft.com/library/en-us/cpref/html/frlrfsystemvaluetypeclasshierarchy.asp.

TIP   Always use the .NET Framework specific value types, rather than native types, whenever possible. Although the .NET Framework maps native types to their .NET equivalent, using a .NET type at the outset reduces potential confusion. These types are standard across all languages used for .NET development.

Data ranges can encompass a variety of types. For example, it's possible to create a discontinuous numerical set to address specific configuration needs. Strings naturally fall into a discontinuous set because words don't fall into any ordered pattern except as defined for language. In many situations, you can overcome this problem by defining an enumeration and then using that enumeration as input as shown in Listing 3.1. (You can find this code in the \Chapter 03\C#\EnumeratedTypes or \Chapter 03\VB\EnumeratedTypes folder of the source code located on the Sybex Web site.)

Listing 3.1   **Enumerating Discontinuous Data Ranges**

```
// Use the enumeration names directly for strings.
public enum SomeStrings
{
   One,
   Two,
   Three,
   Four
}

// Supply a specific value for numbers.
public enum SomeValues
{
   Value1 = 1,
   Value10 = 10,
   Value100 = 100,
   Value1000 = 1000
}

public class DoMsg
{
   public static void Show(SomeStrings Input1, SomeValues Input2)
   {
      // Convert Input2 to a number.
      Int32 IVal;
      IVal = (Int32)Input2;

      // Display a message box using the inputs.
      MessageBox.Show("The selected string is: " + Input1.ToString() +
                  "\r\nThe selected number is: " + IVal.ToString(),
                  "Selection Results",
```

```
                      MessageBoxButtons.OK,
                      MessageBoxIcon.Information);
    }
}
```

This simple example has two enumerations. The Show() method of the DoMsg class uses these enumerations to define acceptable input values. To any external program, the Show() method will appear to use specific data types. This technique does require more time, but the results are worth it. If an external program were to try to access the Show() method like this:

```
DoMsg.Show("Hello", 2);
```

the program wouldn't even compile. Figure 3.1 shows the error message the developer would see. This technique, in effect, limits the data input to the enumerated values that you provide, making security less of a problem.

FIGURE 3.1:

Use enumerated types to eliminate data range problems whenever possible.

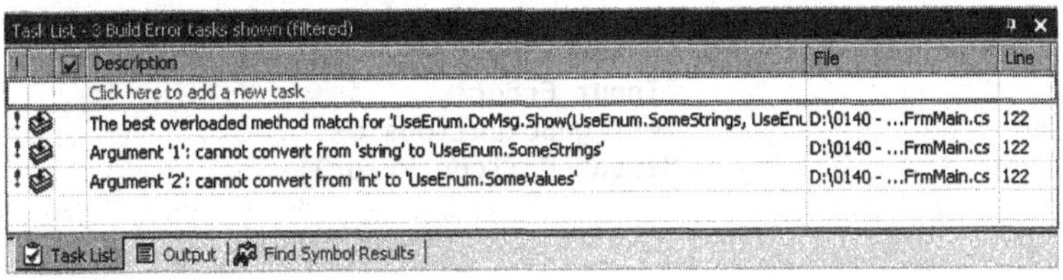

Checking the Data Length

Many of the exploits crackers use depend on the application not checking the length of the incoming data. For example, the buffer overrun technique (discussed in the "Stopping Buffer Overruns" section of the chapter) has become so popular precisely because few developers check the length of incoming data. Fortunately, for the .NET developer, CLR does much of the length checking automatically and raises an exception immediately after it detects data of the wrong length. Even so, CLR only checks for extreme cases—you still have to perform checks for your particular application.

Data that's too short can be just as much a problem as data that's too long. For example, if your program needs a string that it will then parse for appropriate data, it could fail if it suddenly runs out of data before the parsing is complete. Ensuring the data is as long as you need before you begin any processing is the best way to avoid certain kinds of problems. Make sure you tell the user about these requirements (length limits) and present clear messages about the error when it does occur. Listing 3.2 shows a typical example of how you can handle a data length issue. (You can find this code in the \Chapter 03\C#\DataLength or \Chapter 03\VB\DataLength folder of the source code located on the Sybex Web site.)

```
private void btnTest_Click(object sender, System.EventArgs e)
{
   try
   {
      // Process the input text.
      if (ProcessData(txtInput.Text, 8, 4))

         // Display a result message for correct input.
         MessageBox.Show("You typed: " + txtInput.Text,
                     "Input String",
                     MessageBoxButtons.OK,
                     MessageBoxIcon.Information);
   }
   catch (SecurityException SE)
   {
      // Display an error message for incorrect input.
      MessageBox.Show(SE.Message,
                  "Input Error",
                  MessageBoxButtons.OK,
                  MessageBoxIcon.Error);
   }
}

private void btnBadTest_Click(object sender, System.EventArgs e)
{
   try
   {
      // Process the input text.
      if (ProcessData(txtInput.Text, 4, 8))

         // Display a result message for correct input.
         MessageBox.Show("You typed: " + txtInput.Text,
                     "Input String",
                     MessageBoxButtons.OK,
                     MessageBoxIcon.Information);
   }
   catch (ArgumentException AE)
   {
      // Display an error message for incorrect input.
      MessageBox.Show(AE.Message,
                  "Argument Error",
                  MessageBoxButtons.OK,
                  MessageBoxIcon.Error);
   }
}

private Boolean ProcessData(String Input,
                        Int32 UpperLimit,
                        Int32 LowerLimit)
```

```
{
    // Check for an input error.
    if (UpperLimit < LowerLimit)
    {
        System.ArgumentException    AE;
        AE = new ArgumentException("The UpperLimit input must be " +
                                   "greater than the LowerLimit number.",
                                   "UpperLimit");
        throw(AE);
    }

    // Check for a data length error condition.
    if (Input.Length < LowerLimit || Input.Length > UpperLimit)
    {
        SecurityException SE;
        SE = new SecurityException("String is the wrong length. Use a " +
                                   "string between 4 and 8 characters " +
                                   "long.");
        throw(SE);
    }

    // If the data is correct, return true.
    return true;
}
```

This example actually shows two kinds of checking you need to provide—both of which are tested in the ProcessData() method. The first is the user input (demonstrated in the btnTest_Click() method). The input has to be a certain length for this application, and the ProcessData() method checks to ensure it is. The second is the input arguments (demonstrated in the btnBadTest_Click() method). The ProcessData() method uses a separate check for argument errors.

Notice that this example can create one of two exceptions. The ArgumentException object represents cases where the arguments are incorrect, while the SecurityException object represents incorrect user input. It's important to use the right type of exceptions when you track problems such as data that is the wrong length—even if you have to create new exceptions for the job. Tracking potential security problems such as incorrect data length begins when you provide good error documentation by using different exception objects for each error type.

Keeping Unnecessary Characters Controlled

Unnecessary characters are any characters that your application doesn't require as input. For example, if your application doesn't require any slashes, then you shouldn't accept them as input. Likewise, you should avoid any numeric or control character input unless you actually need them to make the application work properly.

TIP   You may think that checking individual characters in a string isn't worth the effort. Until you actually see some of the exploits that crackers use, it might seem that character checking is a solution in search of a problem. The Security Focus site articled entitled, "Abusing poor programming techniques in webserver scripts V 1.0" at `http://www.der-keiler` `.de/Mailing-Lists/securityfocus/secprog/2001-07/0001.html` shows that this is a significant problem. Pay careful attention to this example. Notice that it breaks several of the rules listed in this chapter, including allowing the use of nonstandard characters.

Crackers have devised a number of interesting exploits over the years to make use of extra characters. The problem is especially severe for Web applications where an application could actually end up combining several fields together if the cracker provides specific input. (It's easier to create combined fields in a Web application because form data isn't strongly typed and there is less direct separation of the data through use of individual variables.) However, even desktop applications need to be aware of unwanted characters because some control characters can damage data or cause other problems. Listing 3.3 shows an example of how you can control unwanted characters. (You can find this code in the \Chapter 03\C#\UnwantedInput or \Chapter 03\VB\UnwantedInput folder of the source code located on the Sybex Web site.)

NOTE   The code used to call the CheckChars() method (see Listing 3.3) is similar to the btnTest_Click code show in Listing 3.2. Check the source listing for details.

Listing 3.3   Avoiding Unwanted Characters in Input

```
private Boolean CheckChars(String Input)
{
   // Create a regular expression for match purposes.
   Regex R;
   R = new Regex("[A-Za-z]");

   // Check for a data length error condition.
   if (R.Matches(Input).Count < Input.Length)
   {
      SecurityException SE;
      SE = new SecurityException("String contains incorrect " +
                                "characters. Use only A through Z " +
                                "and a through z.");
      throw(SE);
   }

   // If the data is correct, return true.
   return true;
}
```

The CheckChars() method relies on a Regex (regular expression) object to perform its task. In this case, the Matches() method counts the number of times the letters in the input string match the allowed letters in R. If the number of matches is equal to the length of Input, then the input string doesn't contain any unauthorized letters.

Of course, someone could provide characters that don't match R. This example uses a SecurityException object to raise an exception when the input contains incorrect characters. Your program could react in a number of ways, but displaying the default error message probably works best. The idea is to present the user with the list of acceptable input choices. This is one situation when you might want to track the number of times the user makes incorrect entries to detect crackers looking for weaknesses in your defenses.

TIP   Avoid the problem of free-form text input whenever possible by using any of the controls that provide controlled input such as list boxes, combo boxes, and check boxes. Eliminating the chance of incorrect user input is always better than handling the incorrect input later.

Providing Precise Help

It always pays to provide good help with your application. A good help file can prevent many kinds of user input errors by showing the user precisely what your application expects to receive. Reducing input errors makes it possible to perform thorough analysis of the errors that remain, which reduces security risks from incorrect input in the end.

Some data types present special challenges that your application must handle to ensure data integrity, as well as address security concerns. For example, a date is a common data entry item that could present problems. First, you need to consider the format of the date. A user could type 1 June 2003, 06/01/2003, June 1, 2003, 2003/06/01, or any other acceptable variant. Desktop applications usually don't have many problems with dates, but they can become a problem with Web applications because the application must parse the date into an acceptable format. Allowing just one type of entry and telling the user about the precise data format will reduce the security problems—it's easier to determine when the data is correct.

Note that providing precise help won't eliminate all data entry errors. Some users will insist on attempting to enter data using whatever means they think best. In addition, there are biases to consider. A particular locale may use a specific date form and the user will use that form out of habit. Even so, most users will get the point after a few tries, making good help beneficial. When you begin noticing patterns of constant abuse despite the help, your security screens should go up and you should consider the kind of user making the error.

Stopping Buffer Overruns

The buffer overrun is one of the most common security problems today. In fact, according to a CNET article (http://news.com.com/2100-1001-233483.html?legacy=cnet), it's the most common security problem. You've probably read about buffer overruns in more than one place. A look through recent trade press magazines shows that a week doesn't pass without news of yet another buffer overrun fix from one of the major vendors. It may seem as if buffer overruns are an unstoppable source of security problems for the developer, but they really aren't. In fact, buffer overruns emphasize the need for various types of data checks, especially the length of the data.

The good news for .NET developers is that most causes of buffer overruns don't affect you unless you regularly work with unmanaged code. CLR ensures that most causes of buffer overruns can't occur by managing memory for you. However, any time you interact with any unmanaged code at all, your application is susceptible to this particular problem. Obviously, any problem that affects the .NET Framework due to problems in Microsoft's coding practices will also affect you. Although you might be tempted to think of the .NET Framework as an entirely new world, you should realize that the Win32 Application Programming Interface (API) lurks underneath it all.

Understanding How Buffer Overruns Work

Buffer overruns rely on a somewhat strange idea. A cracker provides input to a program that exceeds the length of a buffer. The extra information ends up overwriting memory other than the memory controlled by the buffer. In some cases, the memory actually holds executable information. In other cases, the cracker overwrites the stack frame for the application and sends a return call to another location where the cracker's code resides. The security community refers to these two types of attacks as:

- Stack buffer overflow

- Heap memory overrun

TIP   You can find an interesting Cyberguard paper on buffer overruns at http://www.utdallas .edu/~aph3x/docs/programming/security/overruns.pdf. The end of this document contains URLs that lead you to cracker code (with explanatory text) for buffer overruns.

A cracker doesn't have to do something too weird to gain control of your machine. For example, the simple act of telling Windows to display a command prompt is enough to gain control of the system in some cases. If the system security is even a little lax, the cracker could gain control of the server. At the very least, a command prompt allows the cracker to probe the system looking for other ways to gain more access. Crackers don't have to gain control of your system on the first try. A little gain here and a little gain there is all they need.

Keeping Exploits Controlled

The best way to control buffer overrun is to check every input your program receives, even from trusted sources. The problem of buffer overruns is so entrenched that you really can't trust any source of information—not even your own code, because some operating system layer could contaminate the data. If you want to write truly secure code, then you need to make constant checks. See the "Checking the Data Length" section for an example of how to check data lengths in your code.

> **TIP**   Microsoft provides a few recommended ways to control buffer overruns at `http://msdn.microsoft.com/library/en-us/security/security/avoiding_buffer_overruns.asp`. While this article isn't very long, it is helpful. This article also lists a third form of buffer overrun called the array indexing error. However, none of the other security sources seems to recognize this exploit as a separate issue.

Developers complained about taking these additional measures in the past. For one thing, writing the addition code takes time. Unfortunately, code writing time is still an issue today, but one that you need to weigh against the cost of fixing problems later. It's no longer convenient to put off writing the code you need today until tomorrow.

Another problem is that the error checking code affects performance. Machine resources were scarce in the past, so developers had a choice of writing fast code or safe code—the fast code usually won out. Today, machine resources are extremely cheap and plentiful. Even though the error checking code still affects performance, the performance hit is inconsequential in most cases. In sum, don't accept the reasoning of the past as a way of avoiding extra coding time today.

Controlling Access

The .NET Framework provides features that control both code and user access to various resources. However, these are new techniques for most developers and poorly explained in many situations. Chapters 4 and 5 discuss the actual mechanics of access control. For now, what you need to know is what issues you'll face when you use these technologies in your application.

Understanding Code Access Control Issues

Any code you created before .NET usually had free reign over any resource the system had to offer (and it could obtain). Unrestrained code has caused a number of problems throughout the history of the PC. For example, I still remember when I had to set multitasking environments to restrict the memory available to applications or they would attempt to grab every byte.

Resource problems aside, unrestrained access can result in other problems. It wasn't too long ago that code would overwrite the memory used by other code. Until processor technology stepped in to ensure that applications had to behave themselves, this problem looked like it would kill any hope of creating a usable environment where multiple applications could reside unmolested. Now, consider for a moment that some of these applications are still around and you understand why code access security is so important.

When you write a program using the .NET Framework, you need to ensure that it doesn't step on any other application's toes. This means checking everything from resource use to the kind of access the code enjoys. If a code doesn't need to access a data stream, don't give it access to that stream. When a cracker comes along and tries to get your code to perform some nefarious task, the code won't be able to comply. Limiting access isn't about restricting performance or creating less capable programs—it's about locking your system down so that crackers can't abduct it.

Understanding User Access Control Issues

Some network administrators and many developers have the wrong idea about user access control. For some people, it's a power issue, but I won't get into that little problem here. The real reason you control user access to system resources is to protect the user. When a user gains unnecessary access to system resources, data, or environmental control, the system can crash, taking the user's data with it.

Most developers don't spend a lot of time with users. However, by defining company-endorsed roles for users and then enforcing the required level of access for each role, your application can keep the user out of trouble.

This control extends to keeping crackers out of the user's account. By limiting user access to specific roles, you limit the appeal of the account to those who would use it for less than honorable reasons. In sum, the issue you face when it comes to user access control is how best to define roles that will meet every need for that particular application.

Setting Privileges Appropriately

One of the most pressing security issues is that of access. Many companies have security problems because they lack proper control of privileges. Any user who thinks they need access to a resource often gains access to that resource without much of an argument. When a cracker creates an exploit, programming problems often grant initial access the network. However, the lack of proper controls makes the problem worse by giving the cracker more access. A programming problem that causes a slight breach becomes worse when the cracker uses a regular user's account to gain access to administrator level resources.

You can avoid at least some of the security problems faced by other developers by incorporating a certain level of security within your application. The use of role-based and code access security won't mean that your application is bulletproof, but these security features do make it less likely that your application will become the source of a major security breach. The idea is to control access to resources programmatically whenever possible. Privilege can become a double-edged sword. On the one hand, granting appropriate privileges make users more productive, but they also leave doors open that crackers are almost certainly going to use.

Avoiding Canonical Representation Issues

Data is in a *canonical representation* when it conforms to the requirements of a particular standard, published or not. The precise representation depends on the standard. For example, the HyperText Markup Language (HTML) is a loose standard with a lot of room for interpretation. (Technologies such as HTML and XML rely on a document type definition, DTD, to define the tags and attributes, and the order in which those elements can appear.) XML defines the format of the data, but not the presentation or content. Adding a schema to XML (which is standard) further defines the data ordering and data types. The Simple Object Access Protocol (SOAP) is a little stricter interpretation of data transfer requirements. In short, the representation varies by standard and the room for error varies by the strictness of the standard.

TIP   You can find many documents and standards that discuss canonical representation issues, but one of the more revealing documents is a W3C document entitled, "Exclusive XML Canonicalization." This document discusses issues such as how a digital signature should affect a subdocument when you remove it from the main XML document. You can learn more about this standard at `http://www.w3.org/TR/2002/REC-xml-exc-c14n-20020718/`.

When you create a data transfer methodology for an application, you create a standard for that data that affects the canonical representation of the information. For example, creating a Web service means defining the information that SOAP presents to the user of the Web service and the expectations your Web service has for data exchange. Just about every kind of application relies on some form of canonical representation. Of course, databases are the most organized of these applications because a database relies on a specific schema. The following list presents ideas on how you can avoid canonical representation issues.

Precise Data Format   The format of the information is important. One of the reasons that browsers have problems with HTML is that the developer defines the data format poorly, in many cases, causing problems when the browser interprets the data. The XML standards, such as the XML/HTML hybrid called eXtensible HyperText Markup Language (XHTML), seek to correct this problem by enforcing specific data formatting rules. For example, every opening tag must have a closing tag. However, this requirement also applies to other application types. It's essential to define a specific data format so that every application requiring the data can understand the form it receives.

Data Type Definition   A standard that doesn't precisely define data types is going to cause problems. For example, it's possible to create a standard where every data element is a string, but this leads to validation and verification problems. Including a numeric data type is a step in the right direction, but even so, a simple numeric type causes problems because one sender could provide an integer (32-bit number), while another provides a long (64-bit number). The standard should also specify how to handle dates, times, Boolean values, and currency. It should also differentiate between integers and real numbers.

Parsing Requirements   One of the more interesting issues that developers have to consider is the problem of data parsing. It's important to answer the question of which party performs this task. In general, developers agree that it's the responsibility of the party receiving the data to parse it and check it for correctness. In other words, you should never rely on the party sending the data to get the information correct.

Data Ordering   Non-ordered data causes security problems because the application must receive data in whatever order the sender chooses. The resulting complexity often leaves holes in the implementation that are hard to find and fix. Using a precise data order doesn't increase the complexity of sending the data, but it does reduce the complexity of receiving the data. If the order of the data is incorrect, the recipient can assume some type of error has occurred.

Error Reporting and Handling   It's essential to provide some type of error reporting and handling mechanism. A .NET application can accomplish this task by raising an error locally. However, when working with a remote data source or *sink* (the recipient of the data), the application must provide some type of error reporting mechanism other than a raising an error. Most technologies today rely on a specially formatted message. For example, SOAP relies on this approach. You can also return an error value, which is the technique used by the Win32 API.

Summary

This chapter has presented some of the human error issues you need to consider for your next coding project. It's shown you how many of these errors creep in because developers lack time or simply don't think about code from a cracker's perspective. Once you see some of the exploits presented in this chapter, it becomes painfully obvious that none of them requires a rocket scientist to figure out—you just need to think outside the box.

Now that you've spent time looking at these human error issues, it's time to create a hit list of your own. One of the best ways to produce more secure applications is to use a checklist to ensure you have all of the bases covered. Of course, this isn't the only step you need to take, but many developers leave this step out of their plans for any of a variety of reasons. Good security begins with a standardized and measured approach to maintaining application quality.

Chapter 4 shows how to use various rule-based security approaches to maintain a secure environment for .NET applications. It pursues a detailed description of some of the relevant .NET Framework namespaces and demonstrates the differences between declarative and imperative security. You'll also see techniques for testing your desktop application. Chapter 4 also covers essentials such as using the .NET Framework Configuration Tool and signing your components and applications to make it harder for people to tamper with their content.

Part II

Desktop and LAN Security

CHAPTER 4

.NET Role-Based Security Techniques

- Defining the Differences in .NET Role-Based Security

- Detecting Permissions with the Permission View Tool

- Working with the .NET Framework Configuration Tool

- Developing Applications that Use Declarative Security

- Developing Applications that Use Imperative Security

- Creating a Secure Registry Environment

- Creating a Secure Desktop Application Installation

- Developing Managed Components and Controls

- Testing Your Desktop Application

The vast majority of the non-code security problems that you'll encounter are user oriented because users are unpredictable and they don't follow rules particularly well. Users cause problems by writing down their passwords, believing crackers performing social engineering exploits, and downloading materials that look interesting, but contain deadly code. However, a program is essentially useless without a user. Why write something that someone can't use to perform useful work? One of the ironies in life is that the applications designed to service user needs are the very applications that require the greatest protection from the user.

> **NOTE** *Social engineering* is an extension of psychology where the cracker exploits a common human attribute such as curiosity to obtain useful information, convince the user to comply with specific requests, simply use the person as a tool for breaking into the system. You can find an excellent paper on the topic of social engineering at `http://www.securityfocus.com/infocus/1527`.

This chapter won't show you how to control users—that's impossible. While it's true that training can help users become more aware of the consequences of their actions, it's very hard to convince a user to apply the training they've received unless the user is willing to do so. (A good whip can also help, but don't let human resources catch you in the act.) However, this chapter does show how you can use role-based security to reduce the risk to applications, resources, and data from users by giving the user access based on the role they must perform. In some cases, the chapter also discusses how you can attempt to mitigate some of the problems that stem from less reliable and dependable users. For example, you can issue some types of access based on the user's ability and willingness to use the access carefully. In many cases, you can base your assessment of the user's behavior on their historical pattern of use.

You'll also learn a few code access techniques in this chapter. These techniques relate to the use of code access to offset some of the problems that role-based security can't address adequately. If you can't keep the user from creating a security breach, perhaps the code can at least make the security breach less severe or even prevent it from occurring in the first place. Code access security is an essential tool in the war on security problems. You really do need to combine both security techniques, along with good coding practice, to achieve a secure system. (Make sure you read about the problems developers have in Chapter 3 before you judge the user too harshly based on this introduction—developers can play a big part in security problems too.)

Understanding How .NET Role-Based Security Differs

Anyone who's spent time working with the security features provided by the Win32 Application Programming Interface (API) knows that these measures concentrate on individuals and groups. (Don't assume that any user is necessarily a person—it could be another application, remote computer, or other device.) If you give an individual user access to a system resource, they always have access to that resource no matter how they access the resource. They have access to the resource from the desktop or from the Internet. This kind of security doesn't consider the environment.

Groups only add to the problem because you can inadvertently give a user access to resources through a group membership that the user shouldn't have. Perhaps a manager hasn't trained the user on how to make entries in the accounting system yet. However, because the user belongs to the accounting department, they have access to the accounting system and can make entries in it.

The Win32 API technique also has other problems. Remember that this system has two kinds of lists. The first grants access to a resource, while the second denies access to a resource. (See the "Considering Access Problems with the Win32 API" section in Chapter 14 for additional details.) It's possible that a single resource could have entries that both grant and deny access. When this situation occurs, a user who should have access to a resource may not be able to access it because the entry granting access to the resource appears earlier in the list than the entry denying access to the resource. The reverse situation can also occur, which means there's a hidden security hole in your system.

The following sections further refine the differences between role-based, code access, and user identity security. The coding examples show how to overcome some of the limitations of Win32 API security using the new features in the .NET environment. The big thing to remember, however, is that the Common Language Runtime (CLR) still depends on the Win32 API, so you need to exercise care in saying that these measures are perfect. Until the underlying operating system is secure, you'll always have to look at these security features as useful, but not complete.

> **TIP**   For many developers, the main issue in shifting gears from Win32 to .NET is how each system manages security. Under .NET an object doesn't have any rights until it provides evidence that CLR feeds through a policy to produce a permission. The idea is that CLR grants all rights. An object seeks permission to perform a task. If you can keep this basic concept in mind, then all the complexities discussed in this book become easier to understand.

Defining Code Access Security versus Role-based Security

Previous chapters have mentioned code access and user identity security in passing. The example in the "Executing Code in the Managed Environment" section of Chapter 1 demonstrated principles of using code access security, while the "Using Role-based Security" section demonstrated role-based security. The "Controlling Access" section of Chapter 3 introduced the idea that both techniques provide some level of control over the computing environment. The concepts in these two chapters discuss some of the hows of .NET security, but not the why, where, or when. Unfortunately, these three questions are the ones that developers ask most often. The following sections answer all three questions.

Why Use Code Access or Role-based Security

Before you proceed any further, it's important to realize that the .NET programs you write always use both code access and role-based security. Even if you don't include a single line of security code in your program, .NET provides default levels of security for your application. Therefore, the advantage of including custom security code in your application isn't one of adding security—it's already there. The real advantage is controlling security, which is what everyone should be worrying about now.

The fact that a security breach is going to occur is well established. However, knowing that the breach has happened, and then controlling the breach, is the basis for many security schemes today. The .NET approach to security helps you control not only the user, but also the code that the user relies on to perform work.

You probably have a good understanding of user issues, but code access security can present a problem because developers haven't had to work with it in the past. At one time, every piece of code you ran on a computer came from one source. There was no need to worry about online connections, email, and crackers knocking on your firewall door (or looking for cracks to sneak in). Today, users face a deluge of code from myriad sources. Sometimes the code enters a system without anyone knowing. In short, code could be trusted at one point, but you don't have that luxury anymore.

Systems are also more complex today. The advances in computer speed and resources have fueled unheard levels of development. This speed and complexity places a burden on you as a developer to protect users of your code. The second reason you want to use code access security is to ensure that no one uses your code incorrectly. Code access security lets you define how someone can use the code and more important, what types of tasks they can't use the code to perform. For example, if you decide that your code should never access the hard drive, you can tell .NET that you don't want it to perform that task using declarative security. (See the "Defining Effective Declarative Security" section for details on this kind of security.) In short, you can ensure that even if a cracker somehow gains access to your code, that the cracker can't force your code to perform tasks that you never envisioned it doing.

One of the special features that you probably won't see mentioned a lot is that your code can insist that a user have a digital signature. In addition, a vendor can provide a digital signature as evidence for gaining access to specific resources. Your code can actually check for a particular strong name using the StrongNameIdentityPermission class. (See the "Developing a Secure Desktop Application Installation" section to see how you can implement strong name identity security.) Although digital signature technology probably has flaws (see the "Beware of the Cracked Symmetric Algorithm" section of Chapter 7 for details), it's considered very reliable.

Using a digital signature is only an option if you add the correct code to your application, which means you have to become proactive.

Another good reason to declare security requirements is error handling. If you don't define the security requirements for your code, CLR will assume the current environment meets all the code requirements when it runs the program. Unfortunately, the environment varies by user, mode of access, and a number of other characteristics that you can't determine when you write the program. Failure to declare security requirements for your program means you must be ready to handle every potential security problem that could crop up. Of course, developers of unmanaged code have to handle every security problem because they don't have a means for declaring the requirements—at least .NET gives you the choice.

When to Use Code Access or Role-based Security

It's important to consider when you should use a particular mode of security. One tendency of developers today is to create a secure user environment. The draconian security measures imposed by a recent version of Outlook and Outlook Express regarding attachments are just one example. After applying this patch, users found it nearly impossible to do anything with attachments sent to their email. You can find a particularly interesting InfoWorld take on this patch at `http://archive.infoworld.com/articles/hn/xml/01/05/04/010504hnairf.xml`. Another good view of the topic appears on Woody's Office Watch at `http://www.woodyswatch .com/winxp/archtemplate.asp?2-n45`. The point is that the user security is often the wrong approach to take—sometimes you need to control the code.

TIP   You can avoid the whole issue of securing some types of code for Internet use by employing zone security using the `ZoneIdentityPermission` class. This class simply states that if the caller comes from anything other than the requested zone, the code won't execute. Zones are explained in the section "Understanding Zones," and you can see an example of this type of security in the "Using Principal and Identity Objects" section of the chapter.

Look at the issue from this perspective. If you know that you signed all of the code on your system, then any unsigned code probably came from a nonsecure source and you shouldn't execute it. This is an oversimplification of the problem, but it often helps to look at issues from this perspective. Because any code you execute can check for the security of other .NET code, it becomes possible to maintain good security even when the user downloads a virus from the Internet. The .NET Framework provides a number of ways to check the caller's identity and the source of the code. For example, you can use the `SiteIdentityPermission` or `URLIdentityPermission` classes to verify the source of an Internet call.

Here's the reality check on when to use a particular coding technique. I'd love to say that code access security works completely today, but there's a lot of unmanaged code out there and it's not going to go away anytime soon. Consequently, you have to make a judgment call somewhere along the way. Do you restrict unmanaged code? That's not practical because even Windows is unmanaged code. (Even Microsoft's latest Windows 2003 Server is composed entirely of unmanaged code.) Consequently, role-based security that not only defines the level of trust you have in the user, but also defines the user's training and expertise levels is important. Role-based security can fulfill this need, but only if you stretch the Microsoft definition to the breaking point.

Where to Use Code Access or Role-based Security

One of the most important features of the .NET security scenario is that network administrators have better control over permissions. A network administrator can use the .NET Framework Configuration Tool (see the "Using the .NET Framework Configuration Tool" section of the chapter) to configure any code you create. The network administrator changes are manual, however, and .NET defaults to any security you define as the automatic option. Therefore, the quick answer to the question of where to use code access and role-based security is everywhere within reason. You need to assume that no one is ever going to look at the security provided by your code and create reasonable defaults based on that decision.

Given that most developers have severe restrictions on the time they can spend writing an application, however, adding complete security everywhere can become problematic. The reality is that you have to choose the areas where you add code access or role-based security carefully. In addition, you need to decide whether to demand a certain level of security and decide whether imperative or declarative security is the best approach. This chapter helps you make those decisions and you'll see a number of coding examples that demonstrate these techniques as the book progresses.

Understanding Zones

The zone from which code loads determines a basic level of security. For example, code contained on your local machine is generally safer than code downloaded from the Internet. Knowing the original location of code can help you determine its trustworthiness. By default, CLR defines five different zones (most of which look familiar to anyone who uses Internet Explorer).

- MyComputer
- Intranet
- Trusted
- Internet
- Untrusted
- NoZone

Anything that resides on the local machine is in the MyComputer zone. The Intranet zone includes any code downloaded using a Universal Naming Convention (UNC) location such as \\ServerName\Drive\Folder\Filename.TXT. CLR also uses the Intranet zone for code downloaded from a Windows Internet Name Service (WINS) site, rather than a standard IP site, such as a local Web server. Anything outside of these two zones is in the Internet zone. Initially, the Trusted and Untrusted zones are empty. However, the network administrator can place sites that are normally in the Internet zone into either the Trusted zone (to raise its confidence level) or the Untrusted zone (to lower its confidence level). The NoZone zone is a temporary indicator for items that CLR has yet to test. You should never see this zone in use.

Defining Membership and Evidence

The word *evidence* brings up the vision of a court with judge and jury for many people. The image is quite appropriate for the .NET Framework because any code that wants to execute must present its case before CLR and deliver evidence to validate any requests. CLR makes a decision about the code based on the evidence and decides how the evidence fits within the current policies (laws) of the runtime as set by the network administrator. Theoretically, controlling security with evidence as CLR does allows applications built on the .NET Framework to transcend limitations of the underlying operating system. Largely, this view is true. However, remember that CLR is running on top of the underlying operating system and is therefore subject to its limitations. Here's the typical evidence-based sequence of events.

1. The assembly demands access to data, resources, or other protected elements.

2. CLR requests evidence of the assembly's origins and security documents (such as a digital signature).

3. After receiving the evidence from the assembly, CLR runs the evidences through a security policy

4. The security policy outputs a permission based on the evidence and the network administrator settings.

5. The code gains some level of access to the protected element if the evidence supports such access; otherwise, CLR denies the request.

Note that the assembly must demand access before any part of the security process occurs. The Win32 API normally verifies and assigns security at the front end of the process—when the program first runs. (A program can request additional rights later or perform other security tasks.) CLR performs verifications as needed to enhance system performance.

Evidence includes a number of code features. CLR divides code into verifiable and nonverifiable types. Verifiable code is type safe and adheres to all of the policies defined by the .NET Framework. Consequently, code output by Visual Basic is always verifiable. Visual C#

can output non-verifiable code because it includes direct pointer manipulation features. However, in general, CLR considers C# code verifiable. Visual C++ is a little less verifiable because it not only includes pointer support, but also functions such as `reinterpret_cast`. Older code, such as that found in most Windows DLLs and COM objects, is always non-verifiable. Interestingly enough, loading non-verifiable code is a right that CLR grants to local applications only as a default. Remote programs have to request this right.

CLR defines two kinds of evidence: assembly and host. You can create any number of custom evidence types by deriving from the `Evidence` class. Custom evidence resides within the assembly as assembly evidence. CLR also ships with seven common evidence classes that cover most needs. These seven classes provide host evidence because Microsoft implemented them as part of the host (CLR).

- `ApplicationDirectory`
- `Hash`
- `Publisher`
- `Site`
- `StrongName`
- `URL`
- `Zone`

The `ApplicationDirectory`, `Site`, `URL`, and `Zone` classes show where the code came from. The `Publisher` and `StrongName` classes tell who wrote the code. Finally, the `Hash` class defines a special number that identifies the assembly as a unique entity—it shows whether someone has tampered with the content of the assembly. See the "Developing a Secure Desktop Application Installation" for an example of how to use these classes to implement security for an application.

Each of the host evidence classes has an associated membership condition class. For example, the `ApplicationDirectory` class, which is the evidence presented to the policy, uses the associated `ApplicationDirectoryMembershipCondition` class to determine its membership status. When CLR passes evidence to one of the membership classes, the object determines whether the assembly in question belongs to a particular code group. If the assembly is a member of the code group, then CLR authorizes the assembly to perform code group tasks. Listing 4.1 shows a typical example of membership testing. (You can find this code in the `\Chapter 04\C#\CheckMembership` or `\Chapter 04\VB\CheckMembership` folder of the source code located on the Sybex Web site.)

⊃ **Listing 4.1**   **Discovering Code Group Membership**

```
private void btnTest_Click(object sender, System.EventArgs e)
{
    // Get the current assembly.
    Assembly Asm;
    Asm = Assembly.GetExecutingAssembly();

    // Get the evidence from the assembly.
    Evidence EV;
    EV = Asm.Evidence;

    // Create a membership condition check.
    ZoneMembershipCondition ZoneMember;
    ZoneMember = new ZoneMembershipCondition(SecurityZone.MyComputer);

    // Check for application directory membership.
    if (ZoneMember.Check(EV))
        MessageBox.Show("Assembly is a member.");
    else
        MessageBox.Show("Assembly doesn't belong.");
}
```

This code is relatively straightforward. You need access to the assembly to get the evidence needed for this check. The example gains access to the current assembly using the GetExecutingAssembly() method. However, you could also use calls such as LoadAssembly() to load an external assembly.

Once the code has access to the assembly, it uses the Evidence property to get all of the evidence for the assembly. As shown in the example in the "Using the System.Reflection .Assembly.Evidence Property" section, most assemblies support four kinds of evidence as a minimum: Zone, URL, StrongName, and Hash.

This code checks for Zone class membership using the ZoneMembershipCondition class. The Check() method returns a simple Boolean value indicating whether the assembly is part of the specified class, which is SecurityZone.MyComputer in this case. Because you're executing this program from your desktop, the check likely passes in this case. However, if you were to check for some other zone, the check would fail. Note that checking membership doesn't generate a permission object—all this check does is tell you whether an assembly has a particular membership.

Using Permission Objects

So far, the chapter has covered the kinds of security you can use, how the system uses evidence, and how to determine membership in a particular code group. All of these facts help you understand how security works, but your code still doesn't have permission to perform any tasks. When CLR loads an assembly, the assembly lacks any rights—it can't even execute code. Consequently, the first task CLR must perform with the assembly is to use the evidence and the code group memberships to determine what permissions the assembly has. To perform this task, CLR must run the evidence through the policies set up by the network administrator. Listing 4.2 shows an example of how you determine rights based on policies. (Note that this listing isn't complete. You can find the complete listing in the \Chapter 04\C#\GetPermission or \Chapter 04\VB\GetPermission folder of the source code located on the Sybex Web site.)

Listing 4.2   **Getting a Permission List Using a Policy**

```
private void btnTest_Click(object sender, System.EventArgs e)
{
    IEnumerator       Policies;   // Security policies.
    PolicyLevel       Policy;     // A single policy.
    PolicyStatement   Statement;  // A list of permissions.
    Assembly          Asm;        // Current assembly.
    Evidence          EV;         // Security evidence.
    StringBuilder     Output;     // Output data.

    // Initialize the output.
    Output = new StringBuilder();

    // Get the current assembly.
    Asm = Assembly.GetExecutingAssembly();

    // Get the evidence from the assembly.
    EV = Asm.Evidence;

    // Get the all of the policies.
    Policies = SecurityManager.PolicyHierarchy();
    while (Policies.MoveNext())
    {
        // Get the current policy.
        Policy = (PolicyLevel)Policies.Current;

        // Get the policy name.
        Output.Append("Policy: " + Policy.Label);

        // Determine the permissions for this policy.
        Statement = Policy.Resolve(EV);
        Output.Append("\r\n" + Statement.PermissionSet.Count +
            " Permissions:\r\n" + Statement.PermissionSet);

        // Get the attributes.
        Output.Append("Attributes: " +
            Statement.Attributes + "\r\n\r\n");
```

```
        }

        // Display the results.
        txtOutput.Text = Output.ToString();
    }
```

The code begins by getting the executing assembly and the evident it contains. It uses this information to create a list of polices using the `PolicyHierarchy()` method. This method actually returns a list of policy objects you can enumerate using an `IEnumerator` object.

The `PolicyLevel` object, `Policy`, contains the individual policies associated with the assembly. Notice the `Policy.Resolve()` method call. This call sends the assembly evidence to the policy for evaluation. The output is a `PolicyStatement` object, which includes the permissions generated by the policy. Each `PolicyStatement` includes a `PermissionSet` property that defines the permissions for the assembly based on that policy.

You can use other techniques to build a set of permissions. For example, you can determine the permissions for a Web site. However, you must build the evidence because it doesn't already exist in a neat package. In addition, you need to consider which evidence to present to the policy. Listing 4.3 shows an example of building evidence to access a Web site (you can supply any URL you wish).

Listing 4.3   **Building Evidence to Obtain Permissions**

```
private void btnUrlTest_Click(object sender, System.EventArgs e)
{
    PermissionSet    Perms;    // A single policy.
    Evidence         EV;       // Security evidence.

    // Create evidence based on the URL.
    EV = new Evidence();

    // Fill the evidence with information.
    EV.AddHost(new Url(txtUrl.Text));
    EV.AddHost(Zone.CreateFromUrl(txtUrl.Text));

    // Determine the current permissions.
    Perms = SecurityManager.ResolvePolicy(EV);

    // Create the output.
    txtOutput.Text = Perms.ToString();
}
```

This example still relies on evidence. However, you must build the evidence using the `AddHost()` method. The evidence consists of an URL and a Zone in this situation, but you can any acceptable form of evidence. Notice that this example uses the `SecurityManager` object to resolve the policy. Figure 4.1 shows the output from this example.

FIGURE 4.1:

Code access
permissions
generally appear
in XML format.

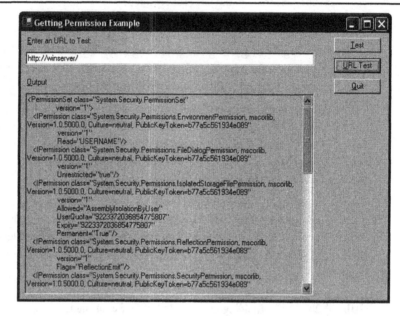

Notice that the information uses an XML format. You'll see in the "Using the .NET Framework Configuration Tool" section that this information can come in quite handy for defining policies.

Each of the permissions listed includes the full class information, which makes it easier to determine precisely what the permission means. For example, the first permission is `System.Security.Permissions.EnvironmentPermission`. This permission controls access to environmental data. The Web site in question can't access all of the environmental information, but it can access the username. One of the last items in the list (at least for this URL) is the `System.Security.Permissions.ZoneIdentityPermission`. This permission shows that the URL is within the Intranet zone for my machine. Testing URLs on the Web correctly shows zone change.

TIP   You can find a complete list of standard permissions for the .NET Framework at `http://msdn.microsoft.com/library/en-us/cpref/html/frlrfSystemSecurity Permissions.asp`. It's also easy to find additional class resources on the .NET 247 site at `http://www.dotnet247.com/247reference/System/Security/Permissions/ System.Security.Permissions.aspx`.

Once you have access to permission objects, you can modify the permissions for the object by using the `PermissionSet` members. For example, you can add a permission using either the `AddPermission()` or the `Assert()` methods. Be aware, however, that the `Assert()` method can cause security vulnerabilities by giving an object rights that other objects in the hierarchy don't have. In addition, the `Assert()` method requires that the code have the `Security PermissionFlag.Assertion` permission, which CLR doesn't grant in some cases (making an `Assert()` method call harder to make than `AddPermission()`). Neither of these methods will allow you to add permissions that the current policy doesn't allow—you can't use these calls to circumvent security measures. You can also use the `FromXml()` method to load an XML formatted file that contains rights the object should have.

Using Principal and Identity Objects

Much of the conversation so far in this chapter has dealt with the code calling a method. Code access security is the main component you'll use to ensure the safety of your applications in a distributed environment. In addition, you'll use role-based security to ensure the caller has the proper credentials. Principal and identity objects generally relate to users or at least a caller of some type. You'll find the essentials for these two categories of objects in the `System.Security.Principal` namespace.

An *identity* object represents the user. It includes the user's name, credentials, and other personal information that belongs to the user. On the other hand, a *principal* object is the security context in which the user is operating. The security context varies by location, application, and other criteria. The combination of identity and principal objects determines the user's rights to use resources and request services. The example in the "Using Role-based Security" section of Chapter 1 demonstrates the use of identity and principal objects for role-based security.

Fortunately, you can use the principal and identity objects for more than checking the user's identity and verifying they're in a specific role. For example, using a simple login mechanism is great when a system setup confines the user to their local machine. It begins to break down as the user moves on to the LAN. When you get to a fully distributed environment where the user could be anyone with the right password, the whole idea of validating a user with a password alone seems absurd.

Principal and identity objects help you maintain a secure environment in a distributed application. The `LinkDemand` and `InheritanceDemand SecurityAction` enumeration members help in this environment because they place the burden of proof on the caller. For example, you can create a `LinkDemand` that includes a `StrongNameIdentityPermission` requirement for a caller with a specific public key. Even when a method is marked public, the caller can't use it unless they supply the required security key. The same holds true for abstract classes. You can mark methods is an `InheritanceDemand` that forces anyone deriving from that class to implement security based on the permissions provided with your base class.

Here's an example of a class marked for use in a specific zone. (Note that this listing isn't complete. You can find the complete listing in the `\Chapter 04\C#\IdentityPermission` or `\Chapter 04\VB\IdentityPermission` folder of the source code located on the Sybex Web site.)

```
public class Secured
{
    [ZoneIdentityPermission(SecurityAction.LinkDemand,
        Zone=SecurityZone.MyComputer)]
    public static void SaySomething(String Input)
    {
        // Display the input messsage.
        MessageBox.Show(Input);
    }
}
```

The implementation is simple. The biggest problem is that IntelliSense breaks down, in this case, and doesn't really show you how to create the declarative statement shown in the example. (This pop-up help doesn't tell you which arguments you can use after the `SecurityAction` entry.) Once you have the protected class method in place, all you need to do is write code to access it. Executing the example on the local machine always works because the local hard drive is in the `SecurityZone.MyComputer` zone. However, the simple act of moving the program to a network hard drive makes the code fail. Figure 4.2 shows the error information.

FIGURE 4.2:

Even small security additions can greatly affect the execution of a program.

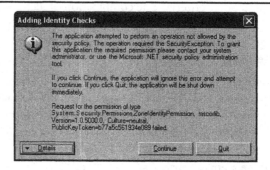

The interesting feature of this program is that you can run the program locally, but not from a remote location. The local user is unaffected by the change. This example has the effect of making remote access impossible (or at least highly unlikely), which make certain types of cracker exploits impossible. The identity of the user remains unchanged, but the context (principal) in which the user operates changes when you move the example program from a local drive to a remote drive. This example wouldn't be possible using the Win32 API because that environment only checks the user's identity. This example demonstrates one way in which the .NET Framework can help you perform additional checks on how a user accesses a program.

Using the Permission View Tool

Configuring the environment to support an assembly properly is just fine if you know what the assembly needs. However, you may never meet the network administrator who adds your application to a network environment. This lack of communication can cause problems because the network administrator might not have any clue as to what your program needs. (This is another good reason to declare security requirements in your code.) Fortunately, the Permission View Tool (PermView.EXE) can help.

The Permission View Tool meets two different needs. First, you can use it to detect PermissionSetAttribute declarations such as the ones shown here:

```
// Security declarations.
[assembly:PermissionSetAttribute(SecurityAction.RequestOptional,
                                 Name="FullTrust")]
[assembly:PermissionSetAttribute(SecurityAction.RequestMinimum,
                                 Name="Execution")]
[assembly:PermissionSetAttribute(SecurityAction.RequestRefuse,
                                 Name="SkipVerification")]
```

Second, you can use the Permission View Tool to check the declarative security within a program. Listing 4.4 shows a simple program containing declarative security. (You can find this code in the \Chapter 04\C#\Declarative or \Chapter 04\VB\Declarative folder of the source code located on the Sybex Web site.)

Listing 4.4   **Using Declarative Security Definitions**

```
[System.Security.Permissions.FileIOPermission(SecurityAction.Deny,
                                              All="C:\\Temp.txt")]
private void btnDeny_Click(object sender, System.EventArgs e)
{
    Stream   FS = null;  // A test file stream.

    // Try to access the file.
    try
    {
        FS = new FileStream("C:\\Temp.txt",
                            FileMode.Open,
                            FileAccess.Read);
    }
    catch(SecurityException SE)
```

```
        {
            MessageBox.Show("Access Denied\r\n" +
                            SE.Message,
                            "File IO Error",
                            MessageBoxButtons.OK,
                            MessageBoxIcon.Error);
            return;
        }

        // Display a success message.
        MessageBox.Show("File is open!",
                        "File IO Success",
                        MessageBoxButtons.OK,
                        MessageBoxIcon.Information);

        // Close the file if opened.
        FS.Close();
    }

[System.Security.Permissions.FileIOPermission(SecurityAction.Assert,
                                              All="C:\\Temp.txt")]
private void btnAllow_Click(object sender, System.EventArgs e)
{
    Stream   FS = null;  // A test file stream.

    // Try to access the file.
    try
    {
        FS = new FileStream("C:\\Temp.txt",
                            FileMode.Open,
                            FileAccess.Read);
    }
    catch(SecurityException SE)
    {
        MessageBox.Show("Access Denied\r\n" +
                        SE.Message,
                        "File IO Error",
                        MessageBoxButtons.OK,
                        MessageBoxIcon.Error);
        return;
    }

    // Display a success message.
    MessageBox.Show("File is open!",
                    "File IO Success",
                    MessageBoxButtons.OK,
                    MessageBoxIcon.Information);

    // Close the file if opened.
    FS.Close();
}
```

Declarative syntax relies on attributes. The attributes can appear at the assembly, class, or member levels, and they can request, demand, or override the security options currently in place. Applications use requests to change their current security settings. A request can ask for more or less access to objects. Demand and overrides appear within library code. A demand protects the object from caller access, while an override changes the default security settings.

Even if you include declarative security in your program, it can never request more rights than the network administrator is willing to allow. In short, if the network administrator decides to deny access to the C drive, then your program can't access it even if it makes the request. Using declarative security does make it easier for the network administrator to know your application needs and means that the application will fail immediately, rather than later when the system can meet specific security needs.

The `btnDeny_Click()` method in Listing 4.3 will always fail because the `FileIOPermission` attribute it set to deny all access to the file. The `Assert()` or `Demand()` methods would allow access to the same file (the example uses the `Assert()` method). As you can see, the result of this code is that CLR protects the `TEMP.TXT` file, even if the user would normally have access to it. This is an example of how CLR can transcend the limitations of the operating system when conditions are right.

The Permission View Tool won't locate imperative security entries. For example, you can't use it to locate a security demand such as the one shown here:

```
public FrmMain()
{
    // Required for Windows Form Designer support
    InitializeComponent();

    // Demand that users have the FileIOPermission.
    FileIOPermission  RequiredIO;
    RequiredIO = new FileIOPermission(FileIOPermissionAccess.AllAccess,
                                      @"C:\");
    RequiredIO.Demand();
}
```

This imperative security entry demands access to the C drive. The application will fail if the environment doesn't meet the need. However, the Permission View Tool won't display this entry for the network administrator because imperative security doesn't appear within the assembly manifest in a manner that allows access.

You can use the Permission View Tool in several ways. In general, you'll want to output the results to a text file for easy viewing in a program such as Notepad, so you'll always want to include the /Output argument. Type `PermView /Output OutputFileName ExecutableName` at the command prompt to detect just the assembly level security information (where *OutputFileName* is the name of the text file you want to create and *ExecutableName* is the name of the executable file, such as `Declarative.EXE`). Figure 4.3 shows the assembly level output for the example in this section.

FIGURE 4.3:

Add assembly level information to your application for general security needs.

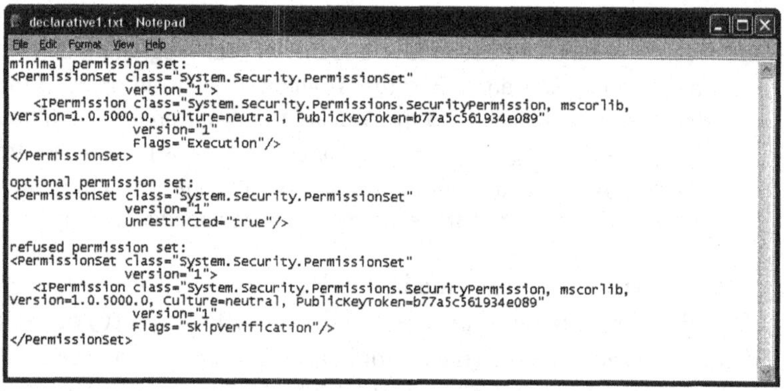

```
declarative1.txt - Notepad
File  Edit  Format  View  Help
minimal permission set:
<PermissionSet class="System.Security.PermissionSet"
               version="1">
      <IPermission class="System.Security.Permissions.SecurityPermission, mscorlib,
Version=1.0.5000.0, Culture=neutral, PublicKeyToken=b77a5c561934e089"
               version="1"
               Flags="Execution"/>
</PermissionSet>

optional permission set:
<PermissionSet class="System.Security.PermissionSet"
               version="1"
               Unrestricted="true"/>

refused permission set:
<PermissionSet class="System.Security.PermissionSet"
               version="1">
      <IPermission class="System.Security.Permissions.SecurityPermission, mscorlib,
Version=1.0.5000.0, Culture=neutral, PublicKeyToken=b77a5c561934e089"
               version="1"
               Flags="SkipVerification"/>
</PermissionSet>
```

The output file contains a plain text header, followed by XML entries for each security requirement. Notice that the Permission View Tool outputs three sections of information:

Minimum Permission Set   Contains the minimum rights the program can accept for normal execution. The program must have these to do anything at all, even if it's at a reduced operating level.

Optional Permission Set   Defines the rights the program would like to have, but doesn't necessarily need. Your program may need these rights to perform ancillary or enhanced functionality tasks.

Refused Permission Set   Includes all of the permissions that the operating system could bestow on the program, but you don't want the program to have. For example, you might not want the program to have the right to skip verification or allow the user to access the program from the Internet.

When you want the output file to also include all of the declarative security information, you need to include the /Decl argument. In this case, you'd type `PermView /Decl /Output`

OutputFileName ExecutableName at the command prompt. Figure 4.4 shows the output from the example in this section.

FIGURE 4.4:

Include declarative elements in your code when you want to control access to individual elements.

This file contains all of the same information as the file in Figure 4.3, but it also contains the additional declarative security shown in Figure 4.4. Every method or other element that includes some kind of declarative security appears in this list. Using declarative security lets you define how users can access individual methods within a class or use properties. The Permission View Tool helps the network administrator understand how you've set security so that any new security conditions can work with, instead of against, the program.

Using the .NET Framework Configuration Tool

The .NET Framework Configuration Tool has a lot to offer the developer. It's a tool that you should spend time learning, even if you aren't using it for security needs. For example, this tool lets you view registered assemblies and add new ones using a graphical interface, as shown in Figure 4.5. Using this tool is easier than using utilities such as GACUtil (Global Assembly Cache Utility), which you use to register assemblies with strong names for global use.

FIGURE 4.5:

Add the .NET
Framework
Configuration
Tool to your list
of security aids.

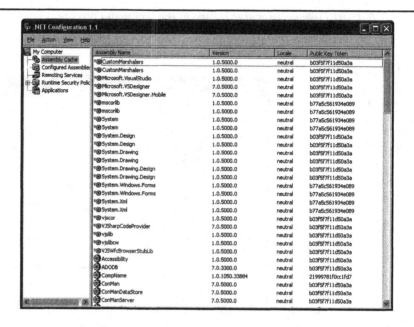

> **NOTE**   This chapter assumes that you're using the .NET Framework version 1.1 and associated .NET Framework Configuration Tool. The older 1.0 version is very similar, but you may see a few differences in screenshots, wording, and changes in some options or features. Even if you own the older version, you'll find this discussion helpful.

The following sections describe the security uses of the .NET Framework Configuration Tool. I'll also include some usage notes as the book progresses and show how the tool affects the output of programs. For now, however, concentrate on how you can use the tool to reduce your workload.

Working with Code Groups

The "Defining Membership and Evidence" section discussed the idea of code groups and I demonstrated how you could determine code membership characteristics. The .NET Framework only comes with one code group by default, the A11_Code group. The Enterprise, Machine, and User policies all support this code group and you'll generally use it for all local programs. However, you can modify how the code groups work and even add new code groups as the need arises. Any new code group you add will appear below the A11_Code group in the hierarchy.

When you first select the Runtime Security Policy\<Level>\Code Groups\A11_Code entry in the left pane of the .NET Framework Configuration Tool, you'll see a help screen.

This screen contains options for adding new code groups or configuring the existing code group, as shown in Figure 4.6. (This figure also shows the location of the All_Code entry in the hierarchy.)

FIGURE 4.6:

Add or edit code groups using this help screen.

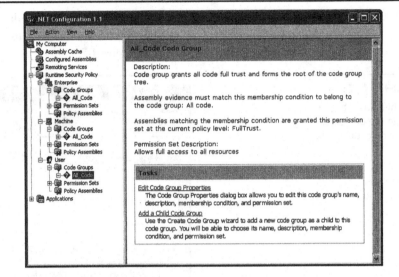

You can use one of three ways to create a new code group. Click the Add a Child Code Group link and you'll see a Create Code Group dialog box. This dialog box contains an option to create the code group manually (the first method), or you can import an XML file that contains the code you want to use (the second method). The third method is to right-click an existing code group and choose the Duplicate entry from the context menu. This technique creates a code group with the same characteristics as the parent.

TIP You don't have to use the .NET Framework Configuration Tool to edit policies for a system. The configuration files are actually XML based, so you can edit them with any good XML editor. In fact, the Visual Studio .NET IDE reads these files without any problem. If you prefer a command line approach, you can use the CASPol utility to make any required changes. The enterprise, application domain, and machine level configuration files appear in the \WINDOWS\Microsoft.NET\Framework\<Version Number>\CONFIG folder, while the user information appears in the \Documents and Settings\<User Name>\Application Data\Microsoft\CLR Security Config\<Version Number> folder. The example in the "SecurityManager Class Example" section of Chapter 2 shows how to obtain the precise locations of these files using the SecurityManager.PolicyHierarchy() method. The PolicyLevel.StoreLocation property contains the directory information.

When you choose to create a code group manually, you pass through several dialog boxes. Each dialog box asks a question about the new code group including the condition type (such as `ApplicationDirectory`, `Zone`, or `Hash`) and the permission set (such as Full Trust, Execution, or Internet).

Editing a code group means changing features such as the condition type and the permission set. When you click Edit Code Group Properties on the help screen, you see a Properties dialog box similar to the one shown in Figure 4.7.

FIGURE 4.7:

Use this dialog box to change the characteristics of a code group.

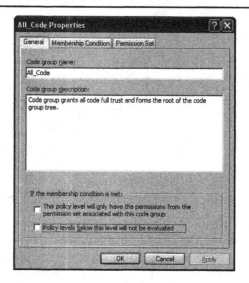

Notice that you can use this dialog box to determine how the code group will work with the policy levels. The first check box lets you set the code group to use permissions associated with the permission set for the code group exclusively. The second tells CLR not to evaluate policy levels below the existing policy level. In other words, this check box creates an exclusive code group.

Creating and Defining Permission Sets

The .NET Framework comes with a standard set of permissions. You can create additional permission sets as required to meet specific programming needs. In addition, you can modify the definitions for existing permissions. However, modifying a current permission isn't a good idea because that action will change the default meaning of the permission and could cause applications written by other developers to fail. (CLR prevents you from changing .NET Framework specific permission sets.)

You have the same options for creating a new permission set as described in the "Working with Code Groups" section. When you create a new permission manually, you'll see the Create Permission Set dialog box. The first screen asks for a name and description for the permission set. The second screen asks you to define the permission for the permission set, as shown in Figure 4.8.

FIGURE 4.8:

Define the permissions for your new permission set carefully to avoid security breaches.

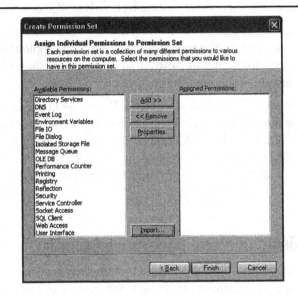

Whenever you add a new permission, the .NET Framework Configuration Tool displays a Permission Settings dialog box that helps you configure that particular permission. The dialog boxes vary by permission. For example, the File IO permission includes a setting that lets you define individual permissions for each drive you want the permission set to access, or you can grant unlimited drive access. You can click Import to import an XML file containing the permissions you want to use. Custom permission sets include a help screen that lets you view, change, and rename the permission set.

Defining Policy Assemblies

Policy assemblies contain the code used by CLR to evaluate the evidence presented by an object to obtain a permission. The default .NET Framework configuration is all you need unless you design a special policy that requires additional code. If you decide to create a unique policy, then you must add the assembly to the appropriate list or the evaluation will always fail. Unfortunately, you may find that .NET is less than helpful in telling you about the problem. It always appears as a security error.

Adding Configured Applications

The Applications folder isn't strictly a security setting, but entries in this folder can affect individual applications. When you look at the help screen for the Applications folder, you see two entries. The first helps you add a new configured application to the list. The second helps you fix the configuration of an application. For example, the developer of an application may design it to use an assembly that isn't available or is outdated.

You need to consider two configured application features. First, this utility lets you change the code bases for the application. Several of the applications in this chapter rely on the code base provided by the application, so it's easy to see how changing the code base could affect the security of the application as well.

The second feature appears on the Properties dialog box for the application. To display this dialog box, right-click the application entry and select Properties from the context menu. The .NET Framework Configuration Tool normally checks the Enable Publisher Policy check box by default. However, it's possible that someone could clear this check box, which will affect the security of the application. You could find that the application fails because someone has turned the publisher policies off.

Defining Effective Declarative Security

Declarative security defines application security requirements as part of the declaration of main application elements such as a namespace, class, or method. It relies on attributes defined as part of an application element declaration, such as a method. The compiler normally processes these attributes during compile time, which means the declaration appears as part of the application manifest.

You've already seen several examples of declarative security throughout the book (and will see several more before the completion of the book). For example, the "Using the Permission View Tool" section of the chapter relies on declarative security. This example points out one of the reasons you should use declarative security in some cases. Declarative security creates entries in the assembly metadata that are easy to retrieve and use as a basis for setting assembly security. Someone who knows what an assembly requires in the way of security is less likely to make setup mistakes.

Declarative security is also good from a documentation standpoint. All of the security requirements for a particular element appear as part of the declaration. You don't have to wade through the code to find the security statement that could cause coding problems down the road.

You can use declarative and imperative security interchangeably for many needs, but declarative security is more effective in some situations. Whenever you need to consider the documentation aspects of an application as a higher priority than ease of use or dynamic data manipulation, declarative security is the tool of choice.

Defining Effective Imperative Security

Imperative security appears as statements within the application code. You define a security object, and then use methods provided by that object to grant or deny access to various resources. CLR processes these statements at runtime. Consequently, imperative security doesn't appear as part of the application manifest. The example in the "Executing Code in the Managed Environment" section of Chapter 1 shows just one way to use imperative security in an application.

Declarative security is important because it provides so many good features, such as instant documentation and good metadata access. In fact, declarative security may provide so many good features that you might be tempted to use it exclusively. However, you do need to use imperative security in some situations.

Whenever a security need requires a dynamic data path or other resource information, you must use imperative security. Because the compiler processes declarative security attributes during the compilation stage, you can't change it at runtime. Using imperative security is the only way around this problem.

Many developers also find that imperative security is inherently easier to use because it appears as statements. Using declarative security means placing all security requirements at the very beginning of a module, which breaks up the code flow and means moving back and forth to really understand what the code means. In addition, attribute coding is relatively new. Most developers who learned to code before .NET arrived on the scene will find using statements more intuitive because they've always used statements in the past.

Securing the Registry

The registry is the central storage area for all kinds of information for the local machine, the user, and applications. Consequently, keeping the registry secure is an important issue. Fortunately, the .NET Framework makes working with the registry a lot easier. These new ease of use features include added functionality for setting registry permissions. The following sections describe how you can keep the settings for your application secure.

Using the *RegistryPermission* Class

The RegistryPermission class provides code access security for the registry as long as you implement it correctly. The operative words are *code access* and *correctly*. The "A Word about Registry Security" section points out serious flaws in the implementation of the RegistryPermission class. The most serious issue is that it doesn't actually affect the registry. You can still use any unmanaged application such as the Registry Editor to access the keys and their values. The second problem is that you must implement the security correctly, which leaves a lot of room for error. Listing 4.5 shows the code for this example. (The listing for this example contains only the essential information. You can find the full listing for this code in the \Chapter 04\C#\RegSecure or \Chapter 04\VB\RegSecure folder of the source code located on the Sybex Web site.)

Listing 4.5   **Implementing Code Access Security for the Registry**

```
class AccessReg
{
    // Some global variables used to make registry access easier.
    private RegistryKey       HKey;    // HKEY_CURRENT_USER reference.
    private RegistryKey       CKey;    // Company key reference.
    private RegistryKey       AppKey;  // Application key reference.
    private RegistryPermission RegPerm; // Registry permission object.
    private Boolean           RegStat; // Registry lock status.

    public AccessReg()
    {
        // Permission for the company registry setting.
        RegPerm =
            new RegistryPermission(RegistryPermissionAccess.AllAccess,
                @"HKEY_CURRENT_USER\Software\" + Application.CompanyName);

        // Permission for the application registry setting.
        RegPerm.AddPathList(RegistryPermissionAccess.AllAccess,
            @"HKEY_CURRENT_USER\Software\" + Application.CompanyName +
            @"\" + Application.ProductName + @"\0");

        // Ensure access initially.
        RegPerm.Demand();

        // Get the HKEY_CURRENT_USER key.
        HKey = Registry.CurrentUser.OpenSubKey("Software", true);

        // Verify the company key exists.
        CKey = HKey.OpenSubKey(Application.CompanyName, true);
        if (CKey == null)
            CKey = HKey.CreateSubKey(Application.CompanyName);

        // Verify the application key exists.
```

```
      AppKey = CKey.OpenSubKey(Application.ProductName, true);
      if (AppKey == null)
         AppKey = CKey.CreateSubKey(Application.ProductName);
}

public void Finalize()
{
   // Close the keys.
   AppKey.Close();
   CKey.Close();
   HKey.Close();

   // Clear the references.
   AppKey = null;
   CKey = null;
   HKey = null;
}

public void WriteData(String Value, String Data)
{
   // Check the registry lock status.
   if (RegStat)
      RegPerm.Deny();
   else
      RegPerm.Assert();

   try
   {
      // Write data to the registry.
      AppKey.SetValue(Value, Data);
   }
   catch (SecurityException SE)
   {
      // Display an error message.
      MessageBox.Show("Write Access Denied", "Security Error",
         MessageBoxButtons.OK, MessageBoxIcon.Error);
   }
}

public String ReadData(String Value)
{
   // Check the registry lock status.
   if (RegStat)
      RegPerm.Deny();
   else
      RegPerm.Assert();

   try
   {
      // Read data from the registry.
      return (String)AppKey.GetValue(Value);
   }
```

```
        catch (SecurityException SE)
        {
            // Display an error message.
            MessageBox.Show("Read Access Denied", "Security Error",
                MessageBoxButtons.OK, MessageBoxIcon.Error);

            // Return an error string.
            return "Key Access Error!";
        }
    }

    public void LockRegKey()
    {
        // Lock the registry key.
        RegStat = true;
    }

    public void UnlockRegKey()
    {
        // Release any registry key lock.
        RegStat = false;
    }
}
```

The `AccessReg` class shows a number of tasks you can perform using the `Microsoft.Win32` `.RegistryKey` and `System.Security.Permissions.RegistryPermission` classes. Yes, for whatever odd reason, Microsoft decided to place the two registry classes you need to use together in completely separate locations.

The code begins by creating `RegPerm`, the registry permission for the key used to store registry data for this program. The `RegistryPermission` constructor call creates a path to the company registry key. The code uses the `AddPathList()` method to add the application key to the list. You must include both paths to provide an adequate level of security. Otherwise, a caller could access the company key first, and then use that key to access the application key. The `AccessReg()` constructor uses the `RegPerm.Demand()` call to ensure the caller has the proper registry rights.

This portion of the code ends by opening three registry keys using the `OpenSubKey()` method. The first key accesses `HKEY_CURRENT_USER\Software\`, which is always available. The second key accesses the company key. If the company key is unavailable, then the code uses the `CreateSubKey()` method to create it. The third key is the application sub-key. Like the company key, the code creates this key if it isn't available.

The code includes a `Finalize()` method. All that this method does is ensure that the registry keys are closed and the global variables cleared. Otherwise, strange things can happen when you try to access the registry. One common error is that the key becomes unavailable, even though you know it's in the registry.

The `WriteData()` and `ReadData()` methods are essentially the same. Both methods begin by inspecting a local variable, `RegStat`. This value determines when the registry is locked or opened to the current application. If the registry is locked, the code executes `RegPerm.Deny()`, which blocks access to both the company and application keys. Otherwise, the code uses `RegPerm.Assert()` to ensure the code can access the registry values. The code then uses the `SetValue()` method to write information to the registry or `GetValue()` to read information from the registry.

A Word about Registry Security

Securing the registry is important because it contains entries crucial to your machine's functionality. Registry security in the Win32 API world depends on the `RegSetKeySecurity()` and `RegGetKeySecurity()` functions. The Win32 API also requires use of functions such as `RegOpenKeyEx()` and `RegSetValueEx()` to interact with the registry. You can find a list of these functions at `http://msdn.microsoft.com/library/en-us/sysinfo/base/registry _functions.asp`.

The `Microsoft.Win32.RegistryKey` class provides access to the registry without relying on Win32 API or Platform Invoke (PInvoke) calls. You can learn more about this class at `http://msdn.microsoft.com/library/en-us/cpref/html/frlrfMicrosoftWin32 RegistryKeyMembersTopic.asp`. The `System.Security.Permissions.RegistryPermission` class provides code access security for your .NET application. However, the security measures leave the registry wide open to attack from any unmanaged application that happens along because this class doesn't actually lock the registry.

To actually lock a registry key from prying eyes, you'd need an equivalent for the `RegSetKeySecurity()` and `RegGetKeySecurity()` functions. Consequently, if you really want to protect the registry, you need to use PInvoke calls. The "Using the `RegGetKeySecurity()` and `RegSetKeySecurity()` Functions" section of Chapter 15 demonstrates use of these two calls in securing the registry.

The massive holes in registry security aren't limited to problems with physical locking and code access only security. If you don't lock every path for a particular registry entry, it's possible to use the `RegistryKey` class to access the value even though your code supposedly locked it. Read the "Canonicalization Problems Using Deny" write-up on the `Deny()` method at `ms-help://MS.MSDNQTR.2003FEB.1033/cpguide/html/cpcondeny.htm` for a fuller explanation of the problem. (This topic doesn't appear online, so you need a local copy of MSDN to see it.) In short, you have to be very careful when relying on the .NET Framework to secure the registry. Microsoft may fix this problem sometime in the future.

Developing a Secure Desktop Application Installation

This chapter has already demonstrated a number of ways to make your application more secure. For example, you can use zone security to ensure that no one can execute the code outside its intended environment. The following sections contain two additional ways to make your desktop applications more secure. The first section describes the `StrongNameIdentityPermission` class, which requires the caller to provide a specific public key to access an external module. This technique is extremely useful if you want to ensure that only those with proper identification can access your classes from a remote location. The second section describes the `System.Reflection.Assembly.Evidence` property in detail. This property will appear several times throughout the book, so you need to know more about it.

Using the *StrongNameIdentityPermission* Class

The `StrongNameIdentityPermission` class is one of the better innovations for the .NET Framework. You generate a public/private key set that you use to sign all of your components and controls (or at least those that you want to access using this technique). Someone who wants to use the component or control, presents the public key as evidence that they're granted access. Once CLR determines the public key is valid, the caller accesses the code as usual. This technique works exceptionally well when you know the parties you want to access your code. Given that many distributed applications fall into this category, this technique will work for a broad range of needs. Of course, you have to exercise care in handing out the keys to your code. Even this technique won't work if a malicious third party gains access to your key and knows how to use it to access the code. Read the "Strong-Name versus Publisher Evidence" sidebar for additional information on this topic. The following sections take you through the process of using this technique.

StrongName versus Publisher Evidence

A strong name consists of a public/private key pair that a developer can generate on the local machine using the SN (Strong Name) utility. The developer applies the certificate using the [assembly: AssemblyKeyFile("")] entry in the AssemblyInfo file. This kind of security relies on your ability to determine the public key in advance. A trusted source would need to send the public key to you or you could use a key pair generated for your own use. A strong name doesn't provide verification, nor can you determine who owns a key based on the information in the assembly alone. The StrongName evidence type is useful for personal or shared projects, but it isn't something you could trust for projects with someone you don't know.

Continued on next page

On the other hand, Publisher evidence relies on an X.509 certificate (digital signature) created by a third party or Certificate Authority (CA) such as VeriSign (http://www.verisign.com), Entrust (http://www.entrust.com), or Thawte (http://www.thawte.com). A CA verifies the identity of an application independently of the Internet. This technique ensures that you can trust the identify information because you trust the CA. You'd normally use this technique to validate code received from a third party that you don't know. Microsoft also provides the Make-Cert (Make X.509 Certificate) and Cert2SPC (X.509 Certificate to Software Publisher Certificate) utilities to create temporary, test certificates. The certificate generated by these utilities is only good for testing purposes because it doesn't contain the CA information. No matter what certificate source you use, you apply the certificate to an assembly using the SignCode utility.

You may read some texts that appear to say that one or the other form of evidence is better (usually with a strong emphasis on the Publisher evidence). Both forms of evidence have specific uses and you should use the form of evidence that best meets your needs. The important consideration is keeping the certificate or key file in a secure location to ensure that no one can sign code that you create. Neither form of evidence is worth anything once a third party has access to your key file.

Writing the *StrongNameIdentityPermission* Class Code

The signing takes place in the client code—that's what makes this method of code access so perfect. If the client doesn't present the correct signature when it accesses your component code, the call fails. You can also reverse this process to improve mutual trust, but the example concentrates on the client. Listing 4.6 shows the simple client for this example. (The listing for this example contains only the essential information. You can find the full listing for this code in the \Chapter 04\C#\SignedClient or \Chapter 04\VB\SignedClient folder of the source code located on the Sybex Web site.)

Listing 4.6   **Signed Client Example Code**

```
private void btnTest_Click(object sender, System.EventArgs e)
{
    MathFuncs   MyComp;  // The test component.

    // Examine the evidence for this client.
    IEnumerator Enum =
        Assembly.GetExecutingAssembly().Evidence.GetHostEnumerator();

    // Get the strong name for this client.
    StrongName SN = null;
```

```
while (Enum.MoveNext())
   if (Enum.Current.GetType() == typeof(StrongName))
      SN = (StrongName)Enum.Current;

// Create the required permission.
StrongNameIdentityPermission  ClientPer;
ClientPer =
   new StrongNameIdentityPermission(
   SN.PublicKey, SN.Name, SN.Version);
ClientPer.Assert();

// Try to access the secure component.
try
{
   // Create the test component.
   MyComp = new MathFuncs(SN.Name);

   // Perform a math operation.
   Int32 MyValue;
   MyValue = MyComp.MyAdd(1, 2);

   // Display the result.
   MessageBox.Show(
      "The calculated value is: " + MyValue.ToString(),
      "Calculation Result",
      MessageBoxButtons.OK,
      MessageBoxIcon.Information);
}
catch (SecurityException SE)
{
   // The client didn't have permission.
   MessageBox.Show(SE.Message,
                   "Error Creating Component",
                   MessageBoxButtons.OK,
                   MessageBoxIcon.Error);
}
}
```

The code begins by gathering evidence about the executing assembly. You must present evidence to the component before it will grant permission for use. The code creates the `StrongName` object for this assembly and grants itself the `StrongNameIdentityPermission` permission. If you don't take this step, the component will never grant the program access, even if you sign it with the correct key. The error message you receive will never indicate that this is the problem, so this particular error is nearly impossible to find and fix. The code looks like it should work, but always remember that you must have permission. The remainder of the code is a simple object creation and test.

Of course, you haven't signed the client yet. To do that, you need to generate a key pair using the Strong Name (SN) utility. Simply type **SN -k MyKey** at the command line and press Enter. Once you generate the key pair, open the AssemblyInfo file and locate the AssemblyKeyFile attribute. Your entry should look like this:

```
[assembly: AssemblyKeyFile("..\\..\\MyKey")]
```

Make sure you compile the program with the new key. Once you do, you can use the procedure in the "Using SecUtil to Extract the Public Key from an Assembly" section to extract the public key.

NOTE   The example includes a second key for testing purposes, MyKey2. This key won't match the key expected by the component, so the example will fail. Make sure you use the MyKey key for your initial test so you can see the code succeed!

Using SecUtil to Extract the Public Key from an Assembly

The SecUtil tool helps you extract the public key from a signed assembly. The public key helps you validate the signed assembly. To use this utility, you type **SecUtil -s SignedClient.exe >> Out.txt** at the command line. The resulting file contains a public key similar to the one shown in Figure 4.9.

FIGURE 4.9:

Define the permissions for your new permission set carefully to avoid security breaches.

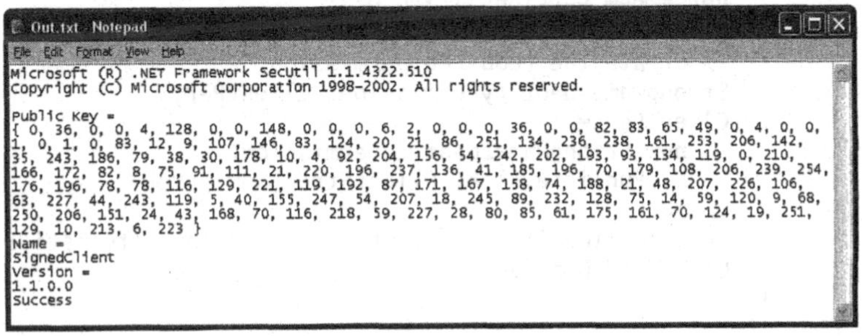

Notice that this file contains the public key and the version number. You must include both elements as part of the security check. This means that the version number of your client application must remain stable or the security check will fail. Always set the AssemblyVersion attribute to a stable number, as shown here:

```
[assembly: AssemblyVersion("1.1.0.0")]
```

Creating the Component

The job of the component is to check the credentials of anyone making a request. The best place to perform this task is in the constructor. Listing 4.7 shows a typical example of a component constructor that checks for specific credentials.

Listing 4.7   **Using a Component Constructor to Check Credentials**

```
public MathFuncs(String ClientStrongName)
{
    // Create an array for the public key.
    Byte[]   PublicKey = {
        0, 36, 0, 0, 4, 128, 0, 0, 148, 0, 0, 0, 6, 2, 0, 0, 0, 36,
        0, 0, 82, 83, 65, 49, 0, 4, 0, 0, 1, 0, 1, 0, 83, 12, 9,
        107, 146, 83, 124, 20, 21, 86, 251, 134, 236, 238, 161,
        253, 206, 142, 35, 243, 186, 79, 38, 30, 178, 10, 4, 92,
        204, 156, 54, 242, 202, 193, 93, 134, 119, 0, 210, 166,
        172, 82, 8, 75, 91, 111, 21, 220, 196, 237, 136, 41, 185,
        196, 70, 179, 108, 206, 239, 254, 176, 196, 78, 78, 116,
        129, 221, 119, 192, 87, 171, 167, 158, 74, 188, 21, 48, 207,
        226, 106, 63, 227, 44, 243, 119, 5, 40, 155, 247, 54, 207,
        18, 245, 89, 232, 128, 75, 14, 59, 120, 9, 68, 250, 206,
        151, 24, 43, 168, 70, 116, 218, 59, 227, 28, 80, 85, 61,
        175, 161, 70, 124, 19, 251, 129, 10, 213, 6, 223 };

    // Create a public key blob using the public key.
    StrongNamePublicKeyBlob PublicKeyBlob;
    PublicKeyBlob = new StrongNamePublicKeyBlob(PublicKey);

    // Create a version number.
    System.Version Ver;
    Ver = new Version("1.1.0.0");

    // Create the required permission.
    StrongNameIdentityPermission  ClientPer;
    ClientPer =
        new StrongNameIdentityPermission(
            PublicKeyBlob, ClientStrongName, Ver);

    // Determine if the client has these characteristics.
    ClientPer.Demand();
}
```

If you compare the public key in this constructor with the public key in Figure 4.9, you'll notice they match. You know the public key of the client because you added that key when you built the application. Consequently, this key should match the public key you used.

The constructor builds a StrongNamePublicKeyBlob and a Version object. You could also designate your own client name, making it possible for the constructor to check three elements of the caller. These three elements appear as input to the StrongNameIdentityPermission constructor. The code then uses the Demand() method to check security. If the caller's credentials don't match, the code generates a security exception.

Testing the Program

This example requires two tests. After you make each change, be sure to recompile the example so the changes take effect. Both tests require changes to the AssemblyInfo file. For the first test, change the AssemblyVersion attribute. Changing this attribute means the version number will no longer match the one anticipated by the component and the security access will fail.

After you test the AssemblyVersion attribute, change the value back to 1.1.0.0 and change the AssemblyKeyFile attribute to MyKey2. Changing this attribute means the signature will no longer match and the security access will fail.

These two tests show that you can provide very explicit access to components on your server. Writing the code using this technique makes it very tough for a cracker to break in using falsified information. However, nothing is foolproof, so you need to change keys as needed and maintain vigilance on your system.

Using the *System.Reflection.Assembly.Evidence* Property

Working directly with the various permissions and evidence can provide a lot of information. However, you'll probably find that you don't need this detailed level of interaction very often, which is why I only include a few of the vast number of security classes in this chapter. In many cases, the only thing you need to check for security needs is the System .Reflection.Assembly.Evidence property. Listing 4.8 shows how you can use this property to get four of the most important types of information from any object. (Note that this listing isn't complete—it only shows the vital code. You can find the complete listing in the \Chapter 04\C#\EvidenceCheck or \Chapter 04\VB\EvidenceCheck folder of the source code located on the Sybex Web site.)

Listing 4.8   **Using Reflection to Obtain Evidence**

```
private void btnTest_Click(object sender, System.EventArgs e)
{
   // Create a text object.
   StringBuilder SB;
   SB = new StringBuilder();

   // Get the evidence for this object.
   Evidence EV;
   EV = SB.GetType().Module.Assembly.Evidence;

   // Define an enumerator for the evidence.
   IEnumerator Enum;
   Enum = EV.GetHostEnumerator();

   // Create an output string containing security information.
```

```csharp
while (Enum.MoveNext())
{
    // Check for the Zone.
    if (Enum.Current.GetType() == typeof(Zone))
    {
        // Define a Zone variable.
        Zone  TheZone;
        TheZone = (Zone)Enum.Current;

        // Create an output string for it.
        SB.Append("Zone: ");
        SB.Append(TheZone.SecurityZone);
        SB.Append("\r\n");
        SB.Append(TheZone.ToString());
        SB.Append("\r\n");
    }

    // Check for the URL.
    if (Enum.Current.GetType() == typeof(Url))
    {
        // Define a Zone variable.
        Url  TheURL;
        TheURL = (Url)Enum.Current;

        // Create an output string for it.
        SB.Append("URL: ");
        SB.Append(TheURL.Value);
        SB.Append("\r\n");
        SB.Append(TheURL.ToString());
        SB.Append("\r\n");
    }

    // Check for the StrongName.
    if (Enum.Current.GetType() == typeof(StrongName))
    {
        // Define a Zone variable.
        StrongName  TheSN;
        TheSN = (StrongName)Enum.Current;

        // Create an output string for it.
        SB.Append("Name: ");
        SB.Append(TheSN.Name);
        SB.Append("\r\n");
        SB.Append("Version: ");
        SB.Append(TheSN.Version);
        SB.Append("\r\n");
        SB.Append("Public Key: ");
        SB.Append(TheSN.PublicKey);
        SB.Append("\r\n");
```

```
            SB.Append(TheSN.ToString());
            SB.Append("\r\n");
        }

        // Check for the Hash.
        if (Enum.Current.GetType() == typeof(Hash))
        {
            // Define a Zone variable.
            Hash  TheHash;
            TheHash = (Hash)Enum.Current;

            // Create an output string for it.
            SB.Append("MD5 Hash: ");
            SB.Append(ReadArray(TheHash.MD5));
            SB.Append("\r\n");
            SB.Append("SHA1 Hash: ");
            SB.Append(ReadArray(TheHash.SHA1));
            SB.Append("\r\n");
        }
    }

    // Display the results.
    MessageBox.Show(SB.ToString(),
                    "Object Evidence",
                    MessageBoxButtons.OK,
                    MessageBoxIcon.Information);
}
```

The code begins by creating a `StringBuilder` object to store the textual evidence. You literally can use this technique on any object, so the example uses `SB` as the source of evidence as well. Notice the use of the `Evidence` class for this example. The code places the evidence for `SB` into `EV` using the `GetType().Module.Assembly.Evidence` property.

Most objects have four kinds of evidence: `Zone`, `URL`, `StrongName`, and `Hash`. The code creates an `IEnumerator` object to hold the content—the pieces of evidence, obtained using the `GetHostEnumerator` method.

All four evidence types have different information to offer, so you must check for their type within the enumeration (there isn't any guarantee of order) and create a variable based on the `Enum.Current` property. Once the code coerces the property into the correct type, it can look at the evidence. The code presents the various types of information you can obtain. Each evidence object also contains methods to perform various tasks such as creating a permission, so this technique normally provides everything you need to validate the evidence an object presents. Figure 4.10 shows the output from this program.

FIGURE 4.10:

Use the information
gathered from the
Evidence property to
validate objects
loaded by your
program.

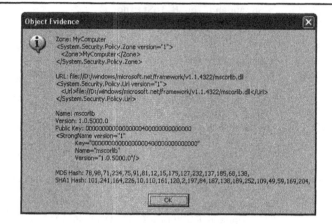

Summary

This chapter has shown you how to use role-based security to keep your system secure—at least to a point. I hope you also noticed all of the tips, caveats, and warnings telling you that role-based security isn't perfect. I don't imagine any system can provide perfect security so long as you need to address the peculiar behavior of some users. In addition to all of the new programming techniques you've learned, you should also realize that constant monitoring and vigilance are the only tools that actually keep your system safe. Once a security breach occurs, you must act quickly to seal it or suffer the consequences.

The number one problem that this chapter doesn't solve is the issue of setting up roles and implementing the security. Sure, you can write a program right now that will contain role-based security and provide your application with everything it needs to keep crackers at bay. However, that's the coding side of the issue and it's not enough to keep your system safe. If you really want to make your application safe, you also need to spend time setting up roles that make sense for your application and add human safeguards into the equation. Consequently, before you write one line of code, you need to create a security plan. The plan has to include everything you want to add to your application or the security system simply won't work.

Chapter 5 discusses two important topics: code groups and security policies. You'll learn that code groups are code access security specific, but that security policies affect both role-based and code access security. The important issue in this chapter is the idea of security documentation. A code group and a security policy define security. It's like writing the goals of a security measure down so that the implementation is consistent throughout a particular range of resources, machines, users, and groups.

CHAPTER 5

Policies and Code Groups in Detail

- Using the Code Access Security Policy Tool

- Working with Code Groups

- Creating Custom Permissions

- Using Policy Objects

Policies are the mechanism that the Common Language Runtime (CLR) uses to examine evidence presented by an object and create a permission that the object uses to access the requested resource. Code groups are the mechanism that grants code a level of trust based on a number of criteria, such as location. All_Code must have membership in at least one code group to execute. Chapter 4 started the discussion of policies and code groups. However, that discussion only covered the basics.

This chapter presents detailed information about both policies and code groups. You'll discover additional methods for creating, editing, and deleting policies and code groups from any system. In addition, the chapter covers more techniques for working with code groups and policies in code—including programmatic techniques for managing these elements. Finally, you'll learn how to create a default security policy for your system (an individual workstation or server). This is an important step because the .NET Framework only installs a default policy that may not meet your specific needs.

Using the Code Access Security Policy Tool

The Code Access Security Policy (CASPol) tool is a command line utility you can use to add and remove policies from a system, as well as make other adjustments. Normally, you want to use the .NET Framework Configuration tool demonstrated in the "Using the .NET Framework Configuration Tool" section of Chapter 4 to make changes, but this tool can come in quite handy for a number of tasks. Generally, you won't use it directly at the command prompt, but will call on the CASPol tool from a batch file or a program to perform specific types of tasks automatically.

CASPol provides an extensive number of command line switches. There are so many, in fact, that you'll quickly find yourself getting lost in switches if you try to use them all in your first program. You can find a complete list of these switches at `http://msdn.microsoft.com/library/en-us/cptools/html/cpgrfcodeaccesssecuritypolicyutilitycaspolexe.asp`. This section demonstrates some of the more common switches. Here's the command line syntax for CASPol:

```
CASPol [Option] [Arguments]
```

When you type `CASPol` by itself or with the ? switch, you receive a list of options. The list is relatively long, so knowing what you want to do is always best. An option tells CASPol what type of information you want to see or defines how you want CASPol to perform. For example, the `-machine` option tells CASPol to make all commands act at just the machine level, while the –addgroup adds a new group. Only use one of each option type in any command. Typing **CASPol –machine –addgroup** would add a group to the machine level. You use the arguments to provide additional information. In general, use only the arguments that you actually need to perform a task.

CASPol is a task-oriented tool. You use it in different ways depending on the task you need to perform. Microsoft provides an overview of a large number of CASPol tasks at http://msdn.microsoft.com/library/en-us/cpguide/html/cpconusingcodeaccesssecurity-policytoolcaspolexe.asp. You can also find a list of CASPol command line options at http://msdn.microsoft.com/library/en-us/cptools/html/cpgrfcodeaccesssecuritypolicy-utilitycaspolexe.asp. This chapter only reviews a limited number of common tasks, but covers those tasks in a relatively detailed manner. CASPol is a powerful tool that you can use to automate a variety of tasks.

Listing the Permissions and Code Groups

Even a default .NET Framework setup includes a number of policies and code groups, so listing them at the command prompt is often useful. For that reason, it's usually better to list them to a file using the CASPol –list >> Filename command, where Filename is the name of the file you want to use. (You can find a sample listing in the \Chapter 05\FullListing.TXT file of the source code located on the Sybex Web site.) The default setup includes all policies and code groups for all levels. CASPol formats the file so that you can potentially parse it using an external program.

You can reduce the amount of information by specifying a particular level. For example, typing **CASPol –user –list** displays just the policies and code groups at the user level. Of course, now you can't compare differences between levels, but you do gain access to all of the information at one level.

Another way to list policies and code groups is by type. For example, you can type **CASPol –enterprise –listgroups** to list just the enterprise groups. Typing **CASPol –machine –list-description** displays a description of the various groups, as shown in Figure 5.1. You also have options for listing all of the permissions (the –listpset switch) and all of the assemblies that have full trust (the –listfulltrust switch). The combination of all these switches provides relatively full access to all of the security information for the .NET Framework. Unfortunately, you have to issue the commands one at a time—you can't combine them to create custom listings in a single pass.

Employ various
lists as needed to
see a snapshot of
the information on
your system.

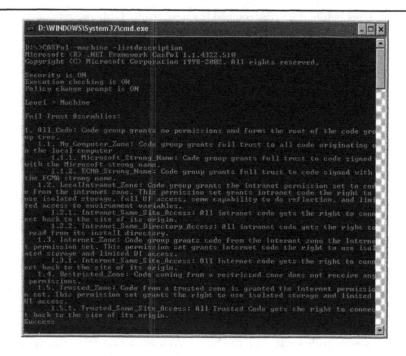

NOTE   Many of these switches also come in a shortened version that you can use to reduce your typing. For example, you could type the command in this example as **CASPol -m -ld**. The chapter uses the longer form to make the meaning of the command line entries clearer.

The **CASPol -listgroups** command is particularly handy when you want to see the hierarchical structure of the zones. Notice that there are actually subzones in some cases. For example, the My_Computer_Zone entry includes Microsoft_Strong_Name and ECMA_Strong_Name entries.

Of course, the question remains as to why you'd want to use this approach to list the various security elements when you can use the .NET Framework Configuration Tool. As you work with the various outputs, you'll notice that they're structured, which means you can process the output information in a variety of ways. The simple text makes it easy to manipulate the entries for storage in a permanent form in either a database or a written report.

Using this utility is also the only way to obtain information when you use a remote connection that doesn't have the bandwidth required to use the .NET Framework Configuration Tool. A text interface is faster and uses fewer resources. These reasons keep many developers using text-based utilities, even when GUI alternatives exist.

Making Group Modifications

The .NET Framework security features work like a hierarchical database in some respects. Consequently, you can add and delete entries as needed to create new policies and setups. You can also modify existing policies. For example, you can add a new permission set to an existing group. This is one area where CASPol really shines. Imagine having to set up a new server using the .NET Framework Configuration Tool. Yes, you can eventually do it, but it's going to take considerable time (assuming you can keep the network administrator awake). A simple batch file lets CASPol perform the required configuration for you using a single command.

The reason that I mentioned the hierarchical database approach is that you can visualize how a change will affect the system better when you use this perspective. Look again at the hierarchy in Figure 5.1. You can add a new code group at any point along that hierarchy. For example, if you wanted to add a super secret strong naming convention to the `Microsoft_Strong_Name` entry, you could type the following command: `CASPol -addgroup 1.1.1. -zone MyComputer Full-Trust -name MyStrongGroup -description "This is a special group."`, CASPol will display the security policy message shown in Figure 5.2. Type **yes** (lowercase and the full word) and CASPol will display the success message shown in Figure 5.2.

FIGURE 5.2:

When adding a new group, CASPol asks whether you want to change the security policy.

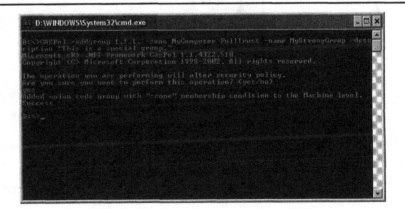

> **TIP** You can turn the policy change message shown in Figure 5.2 off using the `CASPol -polchgprompt off` command. This feature works well for batch processing because you don't want the processing to stop to wait for input. However, it's dangerous to turn policy change messages off when working at the command line because you won't receive any warnings. It's always better to receive the policy change message so that you can validate any changes before you make them. The best method is to turn the policy change messages off at the beginning of a batch file and turn them back on using the `CASPol -polchgprompt on` command at the end of the batch file.

When you execute the -addgroup command, CASPol adds a new group to the Microsoft_Strong_Name entry, as shown in Figure 5.3. (Figure 5.3 uses the .NET Framework Configuration Tool to make the addition clear, but you could also use the listing commands in the "Listing the Permissions and Code Groups" section.) The -addgroup command has several components. First, notice that the -addgroup entry specifies the location in the hierarchy as 1.1.1. You could also use a group name. Second, this new entry belongs to the MyComputer zone and it has the FullTrust permission. Figure 5.3 shows both of these elements. Third, the new group has a name of MyStrongName and a description of "This is a special group". The examples in the Microsoft help file make it look like you can create a name with spaces, but this feature doesn't appear to work without error. However, you can create a description with spaces by enclosing the description in double quotes.

FIGURE 5.3:

Defining a new group adds the entry to the specified location in the group hierarchy.

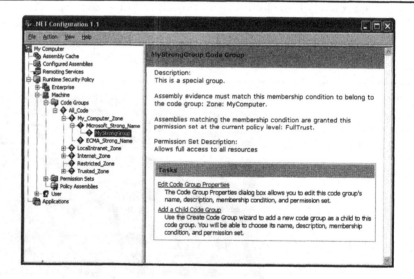

Removing a group is actually easier than adding one. All you need is either the hierarchical level or the code group name. Type **CASPol -remgroup MyStrongGroup** to remove the MyStrongGroup added earlier. CASPol will ask you whether you're sure about making the change as it did before. After you type **yes**, CASPol will remove the group and display the success message shown in Figure 5.4.

FIGURE 5.4:

Removing a group is relatively easy using CASPol, which makes the policy change notice more important.

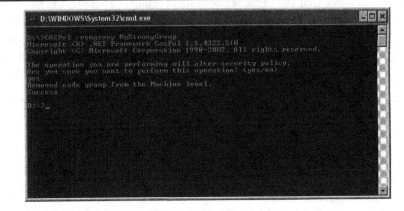

WARNING The –remgroup command is a one-way process. Removing a group is permanent and there's no undo command. Make sure you actually want to remove a group before you execute this command.

Making Permission Modifications

Working with permissions is similar to working with groups. To add a permission, you use the –addpset command. For example, you might want to add a new permission set to the machine level by typing: **CASPol -machine -addpset MyPermission.XML**. Figure 5.5 shows the results of this example command using the .NET Framework Configuration Tool.

FIGURE 5.5:

Adding a permission lets you create custom setups for a code group.

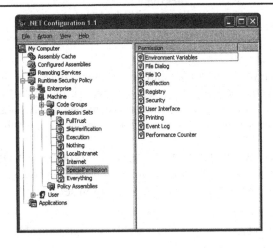

Notice that the -addpset command requires an XML file that includes the permission information. You can create a custom permission or you can use a combination of named permissions. The example uses a combination of named permissions, as shown in Listing 5.1. (This listing isn't complete. You can find the complete XML file in the \Chapter 05\ MyPermission.XML file of the source code located on the Sybex Web site.)

Listing 5.1   Permission XML File Example

```
SpecialPermission (Allows access to some resources.) =
<PermissionSet class="System.Security.NamedPermissionSet"
              version="1"
              Name="SpecialPermission"
              Description="Allows access to some resources.">
    <IPermission
       class="System.Security.Permissions.EnvironmentPermission,
              mscorlib,
              Version=1.0.5000.0,
              Culture=neutral,
              PublicKeyToken=b77a5c561934e089"
              version="1"
              Unrestricted="true"/>

... Other IPermission Entries ...

    <IPermission class="System.Diagnostics.PerformanceCounterPermission,
              System,
              Version=1.0.5000.0,
              Culture=neutral,
              PublicKeyToken=b77a5c561934e089"
              version="1"
              Unrestricted="true"/>
</PermissionSet>
```

TIP   When you want to work with named permissions, start with one of the existing permission sets such as Everything. Modify the permissions in the XML file to meet your specific needs. You can obtain a file with the existing named permissions using the CASPol -listpset >> Filename command, where Filename is the name of the file you want to use.

Creating a permission set always entails the same features. You define the permission set itself using the <PermissionSet> tag, and then add any number of <IPermission> tags to define the permissions in the permission set.

The <PermissionSet> tag always includes a reference to the System.Security.NamedPermissionSet class as shown. The current version of the .NET Framework and all previous versions use a version number of 1 for this class, so you set the Version argument to 1. You must also provide a Name argument that includes the name of the permission set. The Description argument is optional, but you should consider including it.

You can undo most current policy change by using the CASPol -recover command. Make sure you specify a level when you want to undo just the change at a specific level. Otherwise, CASPol will undo all of your changes and you'll need to start again. Note that CASPol doesn't have an undo cache, so you can only undo the last change that you made.

Each of the <IPermission> tags includes the name of the class, the name of the file that contains the class, a version number, the culture, and the public token key for that permission class. All of these entries identify the class. You must also provide a version number for the <IPermission> tag and the level of access the permission provides. When you include Unrestricted="true", the permission grants all of the access the class provides. All of the permission classes provide at least one property that accepts access levels. Look at the SecurityPermission entry and you'll notice that it uses the Flags property to control the number of permissions this entry provides. Figure 5.6 shows the effect of using these flag values. Likewise, the FileDialogPermission entry uses the Access property. In this case, the permissions are the same as providing unrestricted access, so CASPol actually sets this entry to Unrestricted="true".

FIGURE 5.6:

Setting access permissions using a property changes the way CASPol makes the policy change.

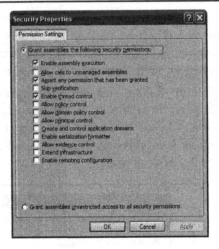

Defining the <IPermission> tags means creating pointers to code that contains the permission handling functionality. The Everything permission contains all of the permissions that the .NET Framework supports, so you can use it as a template for your own permission set. Giving access to everything is usually too much; however, some of the supplied permissions are too restrictive. The reason you want to create custom named permissions is to ensure that the code group has enough permission to perform a given task, but not so much permission that it becomes a security risk. For example, the code in Listing 5.1 lacks the IsolatedStorageFilePermission because there's little reason for most code to access isolated file storage. The example also lacks the DirectoryServicesPermission and other permissions that you would want to grant only as needed.

Removing a permission set requires use of the -rempset command. For example, to remove the previous example, you'd type **CASPol -rempset SpecialPermission**. As with most policy changes you make, the system will ask if you really want to remove the permission.

Adding an Assembly

Adding an assembly to the security setup lets you use it for permissions, which in turn affects code groups. Microsoft assumes that you want to place this custom permission in a class. Consequently, you need to add the resulting assembly to the Global Assembly Cache (GAC), which means giving it a strong name.

Experimentation shows that you can place any assembly with a strong name in the policy assembly list even if it doesn't appear in the GAC. This means you could create a very specific permission for an application that would reside in the application assembly. The security is self-contained within the application it supports.

As an experiment, you can use the application found in the Signed Client example for Chapter 4. (You can find the full listing for this example in the \Chapter 04\C#\SignedClient or \Chapter 04\VB\SignedClient folder of the source code located on the Sybex Web site.) Type **CASPol -machine -addfulltrust SignedClient.EXE** to add the assembly to the list. Figure 5.7 shows the results of this command.

FIGURE 5.7:

Adding any assembly with a strong name to the Policy Assemblies list lets you reference that assembly.

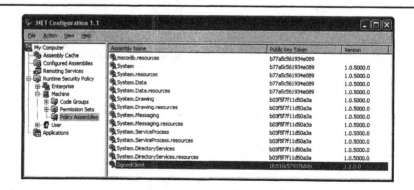

Obviously, this assembly doesn't really do anything to demonstrate permissions, but it does show how to use the command. The "Creating a Permission Assembly" section of the chapter shows how to create a permission class, design a permission around that class, and then use the custom permission as the basis for a code group. The resulting applications won't work without the custom permission object in place on the machine, which means that the application is useless without the proper support.

Interestingly enough, the help file doesn't say how to remove an assembly from the Policy Assemblies list. Type **CASPol −machine −remfulltrust SignedClient.EXE** to remove the assembly from the list. This command will fail if the assembly is currently in use, but will succeed otherwise. The command must be able to find the assembly for removal, just as it does when you add it.

Resolving Security Errors in Assemblies

You can use CASPol to locate security problems in an assembly. An assembly may not run if it lacks permissions to execute or to perform specific tasks. For example, let's say you want to check the Declarative example in Chapter 4 for errors. (You can find the full listing for this example in the \Chapter 04\C#\Declarative or \Chapter 04\VB\Declarative folder of the source code located on the Sybex Web site.) Type **CASPol −machine −resolvegroup Declarative.EXE** to determine the groups that this assembly belongs to at the machine level. Figure 5.8 shows typical output.

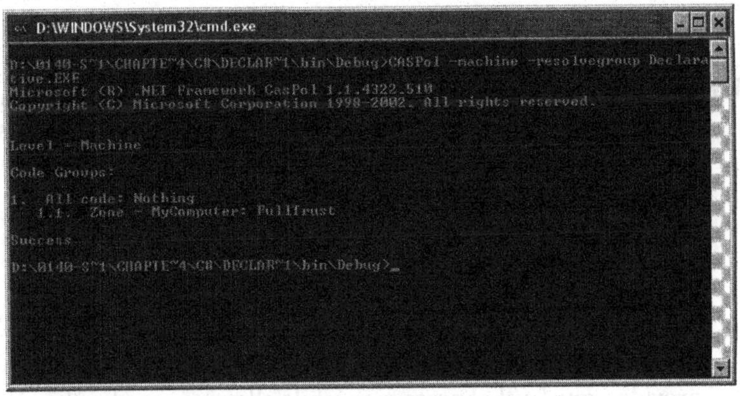

FIGURE 5.8:

Check for security errors in an assembly by using one of the resolve commands.

The example belongs to the All_Code group, but that group doesn't provide any access. However, the MyComputer zone that appears below the All_Code group does grant full access to system resources.

Working with permissions is similar to checking groups. For this example, you'd type **CASPol -machine -resolveperm Declarative.EXE** to determine the permissions of the Declarative example. In this case, the example has full access through the System.Security.PermissionSet class. The example also has permissions from both the System.Security.Permissions.Url-IdentityPermission and System.Security.Permissions.ZoneIdentityPermission classes.

Using the .NET Wizards

You have another choice in addition to using CASPol or the .NET Framework Configuration Tool for modifying security. Using the .NET Wizards is an alternative when the security changes you need to make are extremely simple and straightforward. Figure 5.9 shows these three tools.

FIGURE 5.9:

Depend on the .NET Wizards to help you make simple configuration changes.

As you can see, the three wizards help you perform simple security adjustments, trust an assembly, or fix an application setup. All you need to do to use these three wizards is double-click the appropriate icon and follow the prompts. It's important to remember that these wizards can help in some situations, so you shouldn't forget that they exist. However, most security needs are more complex than these wizards can handle.

WARNING   Unfortunately, it's not a good idea to use the wizards as a starting point and then make modifications using some other tool. Using the same tool from start to finish for a given task is less error prone because you don't have to remember where you stopped making security changes when switching from one tool to another.

Using Code Groups

An essential part of maintaining a secure environment is defining code groups that actually provide some level of protection while allowing membership of code that does require specific resources. The permissions that you give the code group define how much security the code group provides as contrasted to the access it grants. These two concepts contrast with each other. Granting a code group greater access means reducing the amount of security that it provides.

The following sections describe code groups in detail. First, the benefits and limitations of the default code group are discussed. Once you understand the default code groups better, this section will demonstrate how to create custom groups of your own.

Understanding the Default Groups

The default .NET Framework setup doesn't assume anything about the individual user or the enterprise—it focuses on the requirements of an individual machine. Consequently, the Code Groups folder for the User and Enterprise levels only contain the All_Code group. The Machine level contains all of the default groups that the .NET Framework supplies, as shown in Figure 5.10.

FIGURE 5.10:

Look for the default .NET Framework groups at the machine level.

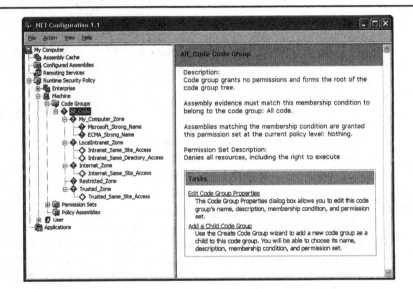

As shown in Figure 5.10, the default groups start with zone level security. You can see that each group defines a different zone, such as the Internet zone. Below each of these code groups are groups that define levels of access. At the My_Computer_Zone level, the code gains full access using either the Microsoft or European Computer Manufacturer's Association (ECMA) strong naming conventions.

Notice that some of the entries in this list (Figure 5.10) have white diamonds in place of the more common purple diamonds. You can't edit these custom code groups directly. In most cases, these custom code groups provide specific features that the originator doesn't want changed in any way. Viewing the custom code group properties does show the XML used to create it, however, which is an important way to learn more about how to construct custom code groups yourself. Figure 5.11 shows a typical custom code group representation. (Display this dialog box by clicking the View Custom Code Group Properties link and selecting the Custom Code Group tab.)

FIGURE 5.11:

Define a custom code group for specific situations where you don't want any changes.

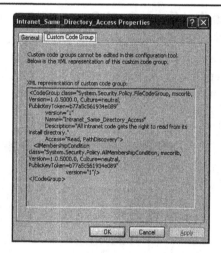

Custom code groups are one situation where it becomes important to import the information from an XML file, rather than to define the group directly. Figure 5.11 shows that defining a custom code group is similar to defining a custom permission set as we did in Listing 5.1.

TIP   You can add custom code groups using the `-custom` option of the CASPol utility. For example, you could type **CASPol -addgroup 1.1.1. -custom MyMembershipCond.XML FullTrust -name MyStrongGroup -description** "**This is a special group.**" to add a new group based on the MyMembershipCond.XML file content. Note that no matter how you add an XML-based membership condition, it's always going to appear as a custom code group.

Working with Code Groups

Code groups can help you perform real work with applications by ensuring that a particular application actually has the required access. However, it's not just about ensuring correct security. A code group can reduce your coding burden and add consistency to the verification process.

You've already seen pieces of this concept. The "Making Group Modifications" section of this chapter emphasizes the hierarchical structure of the security setup. The "Writing the `StrongNameIdentityPermission` Class Code" section of Chapter 4 discusses how to use strong names in your code. Finally, the "Defining Membership and Evidence" section of Chapter 4 shows how to verify membership in a particular code group. The example in this section combines all of these features and shows how to access them using a code group that you've defined.

> **WARNING** If you suddenly notice that all code access security requests succeed, even from locations such as the Internet, someone may have turned code access security off. To turn code access security back on, type **CASPol -security on**. Obviously, if this solution fixes the problem, you need to investigate further. A cracker may have gained valuable access to your system.

Defining the Special Code Group

A special code group lets you check for a particular membership. However, before you can create a special code group, you need a component that will check for this membership as part of allowing access to the features it provides. Listing 5.2 shows one way to approach the problem. This is the technique that many developers will use because it's easy and fast. (You can find the full listing for this example in the \Chapter 05\C#\CodeGroupComponent or \Chapter 05\VB\CodeGroupComponent folder of the source code located on the Sybex Web site.)

Listing 5.2   **Specialized Code Group Component**

```
// Use attributes to define the security requirements.
[ZoneIdentityPermission(SecurityAction.LinkDemand,
   Zone=SecurityZone.MyComputer),
 StrongNameIdentityPermissionAttribute(SecurityAction.LinkDemand,
   PublicKey=
     "0024000004800000940000000602000000240000525341310004000001" +
     "000100530C096B92537C141556FB86ECEEA1FDCE8E23F3BA4F261EB20A" +
     "045CCC9C36F2CAC15D867700D2A6AC52084B5B6F15DCC4ED8829B9C446" +
     "B36CCEEFFEB0C44E4E7481DD77C057ABA79E4ABC1530CFE26A3FE32CF3" +
     "7705289BF736CF12F559E8804B0E3B780944FACE97182BA84674DA3BE3" +
     "1C50553DAFA1467C13FB810AD506DF")]
public class SayHello2
{
    public String DoSayHello2()
    {
        return "Hello from DoSayHello2!";
    }
}
```

Each of these attributes checks a specific security attribute. To use this component, the caller must appear on the local computer and be signed with the correct key. You can place these two attributes in various locations. Placing them at the class level secures all of the methods, events, and properties in the class as well. Securing individual elements means placing the two attributes immediately before those elements.

Considering a Code Group Component Alternative

The .NET Framework normally provides multiple ways to perform any given task, but you have to consider the tradeoffs of each option. This example could also use membership checks to achieve essentially the same effect. The advantages of using membership checks are that you can perform custom processing and you don't have to provide a specific public key. The disadvantages of this approach are that you can't place the check at multiple levels (at least not easily) and you have to write a lot more code. Listing 5.3 shows the code for the alternate version of the CodeGroupComponent. (You can find the full listing for this example in the \Chapter 05\C#\CodeGroupComponent or \Chapter 05\VB\CodeGroupComponent folder of the source code located on the Sybex Web site.)

Listing 5.3   Alternative Code Group Component

```
public SayHello()
{
   // Get the calling assembly.
   Assembly Asm;
   Asm = Assembly.GetCallingAssembly();

   // Get the evidence from the assembly.
   Evidence EV;
   EV = Asm.Evidence;

   // Create a zone membership condition check.
   ZoneMembershipCondition ZoneMember;
   ZoneMember = new ZoneMembershipCondition(SecurityZone.MyComputer);

   // Check for application directory membership.
   if (!ZoneMember.Check(EV))
   {
      DialogResult   Result;  // Return value.

      // Ask whether the user wants to continue.
      Result = MessageBox.Show("Using this component from an " +
                              "intranet connection can cause " +
                              "a security " breach.\r\nContinue?",
                              "Potential Security Error",
                              MessageBoxButtons.YesNo,
                              MessageBoxIcon.Warning);

      if (Result == DialogResult.No)
         // Throw an exception.
         throw(new
```

```
                    PolicyException("Calling assembly zone incorrect."));
    }

    // Examine the evidence for this component.
    IEnumerator Enum =
        Assembly.GetExecutingAssembly().Evidence.GetHostEnumerator();

    // Get the strong name for this component.
    StrongName SN = null;
    while (Enum.MoveNext())
        if (Enum.Current.GetType() == typeof(StrongName))
            SN = (StrongName)Enum.Current;

    // Create the strong name membership condition.
    StrongNameMembershipCondition StrongMember;
    StrongMember =
        new StrongNameMembershipCondition(SN.PublicKey, null, null);

    // Check the strong name membership.
    if (!StrongMember.Check(EV))
    {
        // Throw an exception.
        throw(new PolicyException("Calling assembly isn't a " +
                                  "Demonstration_Strong_Name member."));
    }
}
```

The code begins by getting the calling assembly—the client that's calling on the component for service. It uses the Asm object to obtain evidence. The first check determines whether the caller is in the correct zone. It does this by creating the ZoneMember object and using the Check() method against the caller's evidence.

When the caller is in the wrong zone, the code asks about the potential for a security breach. If the user answers no, the code throws an exception. This is an example of how the second technique is superior to the first because you've added flexibility in handling the situation. The example uses a PolicyException with a custom message. You can also use a SecurityException. However, the PolicyException is more precise and specific.

The second check determines whether the caller has the correct strong name. Of course, this means constructing a StrongName object. The code obtains the strong name using an enumeration that checks the executing assembly, rather than the calling assembly. The executing assembly is the component and you want to verify that both the caller and the component have the same strong name. The code uses an enumeration to find the executing assembly strong name. The strong name handling demonstrates another way in which the second method is superior to the first. You don't have to hard code the public key, so changing keys is a simple change and recompile.

WARNING It's easy to confuse the calling and executing assemblies, especially when you need to work with multiple client levels. Always verify the use of the GetExecutingAssembly() method for the host application and the GetCallingAssembly() method for the calling application. Otherwise, you could perform comparisons that end up checking the caller against itself.

After the code locates the strong name information for the executing assembly, it creates a StrongNameMembershipCondition object using just the SN.PublicKey value. Notice that the code uses a null value for both the name and version arguments. The StrongMember object will match any caller signed with the same public key as the component. If you also added the name and version number, the call would fail unless the caller is the same as the current component. As with the zone check, the code throws a policy exception if the public keys don't match.

Installing the *CodeGroupComponent*

You must sign this component. Add the example component to the GAC by typing **GAC-Util /i CodeGroupComponent.DLL** at the command prompt. (You can remove the component later by typing **GACUtil /u CodeGroupComponent.DLL**.) However, there's no requirement that you always add your component to the GAC. This step does make working with the component easier. The following steps tell you how to create the specialized strong name code group based on this component using the .NET Framework Configuration Tool:

1. Highlight the My_Computer_Zone entry within the Machine\Code Groups folder.

2. Click the Add a Child Code Group link. The .NET Framework Configuration Tool displays an Identify the New Code Group dialog box.

3. Type **Demonstration_Strong_Name** in the Name field and **A code group used for demonstration purposes.** in the Description field. Click Next. The .NET Framework Configuration Tool displays a Choose a Condition Type dialog box.

4. Select Strong Name from the condition list. The Choose a Condition Type dialog box changes to accept strong name information.

5. Check the Name and Version entries to enable these security entries.

6. Click Import. You'll see an Import Strong Name from Assembly dialog box.

7. Locate the `CodeGroupComponent.DLL` file and highlight it. Click Open. The Choose a Condition Type dialog box should look similar to the one shown in Figure 5.12.

FIGURE 5.12:

Use the strong name information from the component to create a strong name membership.

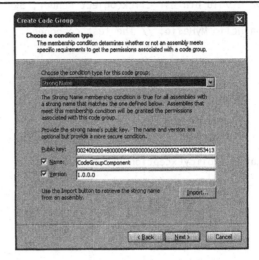

8. Click Next. The .NET Framework Configuration Tool displays an Assign a Permission Set to the Code Group dialog box.

9. Select FullTrust from the permission set list, and then click Next.

10. Click Finish to complete the process.

The current setup lets anyone using the current machine also access the component. If the user isn't part of the current machine or tries to access the machine from another location, then the call will fail. You could easily change this to a user specific check by moving the code group to the User list.

Writing the Code Group Access Code

The example component file actually contains two components. The first uses the attribute technique, while the second uses the membership technique. The code in Listing 5.4 shows how to test both components. Notice that this code isn't anything special—it could easily represent nonsecure code. (You can find the full listing for this example in the \Chapter 05\C#\CodeGroup or \Chapter 05\VB\CodeGroup folder of the source code located on the Sybex Web site.)

Listing 5.4   **Code Group Component Testing Example**

```
private void btnTest_Click(object sender, System.EventArgs e)
{
   SayHello MyHello; // The test component.

   try
   {
      // Create the component.
      MyHello = new SayHello();

      // Test the component.
      MessageBox.Show(MyHello.DoSayHello());
   }
   catch (PolicyException PE)
   {
      // Display an error message.
      MessageBox.Show(PE.Message);
   }

}

private void btnTest2_Click(object sender, System.EventArgs e)
{
   SayHello2   MyHello; // The test component.

   try
   {
      // Create the component.
      MyHello = new SayHello2();

      // Test the component.
      MessageBox.Show(MyHello.DoSayHello2());
   }
   catch (SecurityException SE)
   {
      // Display an error message.
      MessageBox.Show(SE.Message);
   }
}
```

In both cases, the code creates the component and then calls on the one method it contains to display a string on screen. The only difference between this application and any application you might have created in the past is that this application requires a key—the same key you used for the component. Once you sign the test program, it becomes part of the Demonstration_Strong_Name code group created earlier. Run the **CASPol -machine -resolvegroup CodeGroup.EXE** command. You'll see output similar to that shown in Figure 15.13. This output demonstrates that the application is part of the code group.

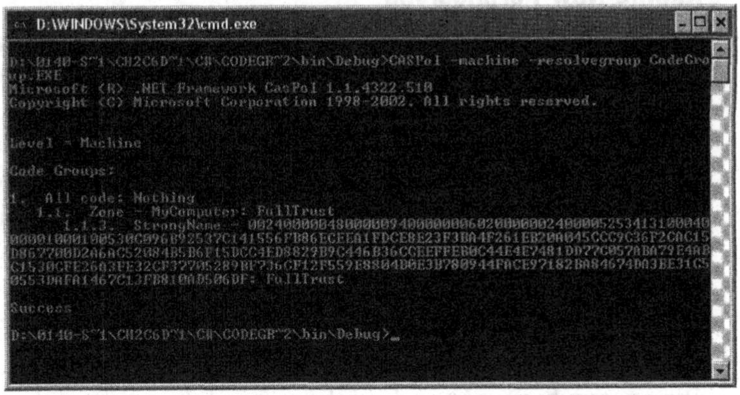

FIGURE 5.13:

Signing the test
program automatically
adds it to the strongly
named group.

Testing the Code Group

Both versions of the test program always run on the local machine as long as you sign the calling
application and the component with the same key. Try compiling the test application without a
key and you'll notice that it fails. One interesting test is to compile both the test application and
the component using MyKey2 supplied with the Signed Client example in Chapter 4. The more
flexible membership testing technique shown in Listing 5.3 still works, but the simpler technique fails because the attribute hard codes the key.

The real test occurs when you place the test application on a network drive. Because of the
way that we installed the Demonstration_Strong_Name code group, the test applications will fail.
However, you can easily change that outcome. Right-click the Demonstration_Strong_Name
code group entry in the .NET Framework Configuration Tool and choose Cut from the context menu. Right-click the LocalIntranet_Zone entry and choose Paste from the context menu.
These two steps move the Demonstration_Strong_Name code group entry.

WARNING Make sure you cut the entry and don't copy it—if you copy the entry the test won't work
as anticipated.

Try the test application again. Notice that the attribute method still fails because the
attribute hard codes the zone error reaction. The membership testing technique displays
an error message. When you click Yes, this application succeeds because the custom coding
enables the user to decide the severity of the security risk. Of course, you can choose any of
a number of mechanisms to make the decision. The important point is that you can make a
decision.

Adding New Permissions

The permissions that Microsoft provides as part of the .NET Framework will address many (if not most) common situations. However, one consistent element of programming is that the unexpected is the normal condition that developers face. A company usually has some kind of special need for their data that Microsoft can't consider as part of the common scenario. The need could be something as simple as ensuring that no one outside the selected group can use the program. You may need to limit the functionality of a program based on the needs of the requestor. Perhaps managers have access to features that other employees don't need.

In the Win32 environment, handling special situations is difficult because security is a hard-wired element of the operating system. You can only go so far in protecting an operating system because the role of the user and the nature of the environment aren't considered. In fact, you can't even garner enough information to develop a kludge to handle this situation in many cases.

The .NET Framework makes it possible to create a new permission. This permission can describe any set of security requirements you can imagine. When you want to limit application access based on some criteria, you can build a permission to handle that requirement. The permission acts as input to a code group that defines access to the permission based on a membership criteria. Finally, your application can demand the requisite permission and perform analysis of which features the requestor can access. It's an extremely flexible way to define security.

The following sections take you through the process of creating a new permission and testing it within an application. In short, when you finish this section, you should know the basic process for creating any security requirement needed to ensure the integrity of your data, the safety of your resources, and the use of resources.

Creating a Permission Assembly

In general, you must create a new permission to implement a new security requirement that's part of a code group. You can take several routes to achieve this goal. For example, you can create a new permission out of the available named permissions. We discussed that possibility in the "Making Permission Modifications" section of the chapter. In that example, we created an XML file to hold the existing definitions in a new combination. You can assign that definition to a code group and use it as part of an application setup.

This section takes a different approach. It assumes that the existing permissions are inadequate for your particular needs. Listing 5.5 shows the code used to create a custom permission. Of course, this is just the permission assembly. You still have more work to do to implement the permission, but this is the starting point. (Note that this listing isn't complete. You can find the full listing for this example in the \Chapter 05\C#\CustomPermission or \Chapter 05\VB\CustomPermission folder of the source code located on the Sybex Web site.)

Listing 5.5   A Typical Custom Permission Assembly

```
// This enumeration contains the acceptable permission values.
public enum SpecialSet
{
   All = 0,
   Some,
   None
}

[Serializable()]
public class Special : CodeAccessPermission, IUnrestrictedPermission
{
   // A required variable for unrestricted access.
   private Boolean _unrestricted;

   // A special variable for tracking access to this class.
   private SpecialSet _setValue;

   // At least one constructor should set the restricted state.
   public Special(PermissionState State)
   {
      if (State == PermissionState.Unrestricted)
         _unrestricted = true;
      else
         _unrestricted = false;

      // Make sure you also set any special property values.
      if (_unrestricted == true)
         _setValue = SpecialSet.All;
      else
         _setValue = SpecialSet.None;
   }

   // At least one constructor should set your special properties.
   public Special(SpecialSet SetValue)
   {
      // Set the property value.
      _setValue = SetValue;

      // You can assume an unrestricted state in some cases.
      if (SetValue == SpecialSet.All)
         _unrestricted = true;
      else
         _unrestricted = false;
```

```
      }

      // This implementation also requires a special property.
      public SpecialSet SetValue
      {
         get { return _setValue; }
         set
         {
            // Set the new value.
            _setValue = value;

            // Determine whether unrestricted has changed.
            if (_setValue == SpecialSet.All)
               _unrestricted = true;
            else
               _unrestricted = false;
         }
      }

      public override IPermission Copy()
      {
         // Create a new copy of the permission.
         Special Copy = new Special(PermissionState.None);

         // Define the properties.
         Copy._setValue = this.SetValue;

         // Set the restriction level.
         if (this.IsUnrestricted())
            Copy._unrestricted = true;
         else
            Copy._unrestricted = false;

         // Return the copy.
         return Copy;
      }

      public override void FromXml(SecurityElement elem)
      {
         // Get the SetValue value.
         String Element;
         Element = elem.Attribute("SetValue");

         // Set the property values according to the
         // SetValue entry.
         if(Element != null)
         {
            switch (Element)
            {
               case "All":
                  this._setValue = SpecialSet.All;
                  this._unrestricted = true;
```

```
                    break;
                case "Some":
                    this._setValue = SpecialSet.Some;
                    this._unrestricted = false;
                    break;
                case "None":
                    this._setValue = SpecialSet.None;
                    this._unrestricted = false;
                    break;
            }

            // Don't perform any more processing.
            return;
        }

        // The XML file didn't contain a SetValue entry. Try
        // the Unrestricted entry.
        Element = elem.Attribute("Unrestricted");

        if (Element != null)
        {
            // Process using the Unrestricted value.
            this._unrestricted = Convert.ToBoolean(Element);

            // Set the SetValue value.
            if (_unrestricted)
                this._setValue = SpecialSet.All;
            else
                this._setValue = SpecialSet.None;
        }
        else
        {
            // No one saved anything, so use defaults.
            this._setValue = SpecialSet.None;
            this._unrestricted = false;
        }
    }

public override IPermission Intersect(IPermission target)
{
    // Use a try...catch statement in case the caller sends
    // the wrong kind of permission.
    try
    {

        // If the permission is null, return null.
        if(target == null)
        {
            return null;
        }

        // Create a new copy of the permission. This is where the
```

```
            // code will fail if the supplied permission is the wrong
            // type.
            Special Perm = (Special)target;

            // Start checking permissions. Begin with the case where
            // the incoming permission allows everything.
            switch (Perm.SetValue)
            {
                case SpecialSet.All:
                    return this.Copy();
                case SpecialSet.Some:
                    if (this.SetValue == SpecialSet.None)
                        return this.Copy();
                    else
                        return Perm;
                case SpecialSet.None:
                    return Perm;
            }

            // If all else fails, return a copy of this object.
            return this.Copy();
        }
        catch (InvalidCastException)
        {
            // Tell the caller there is an argument error.
            throw new ArgumentException("Wrong Argument Type ",
                this.GetType().FullName);
        }
    }

    public override bool IsSubsetOf(IPermission target)
    {
        // Use a try...catch statement in case the caller sends
        // the wrong kind of permission.
        try
        {

            // If the permission is null, return false.
            if(target == null)
            {
                return false;
            }

            // Create a new copy of the permission. This is where the
            // code will fail if the supplied permission is the wrong
            // type.
            Special Perm = (Special)target;

            // Start checking permissions. Begin with the case where
            // the incoming permission allows everything.
            switch (this.SetValue)
            {
```

```
            case SpecialSet.All:
                return true;
            case SpecialSet.Some:
                if (Perm.SetValue == SpecialSet.All)
                    return false;
                else
                    return true;
            case SpecialSet.None:
                if (Perm.SetValue == SpecialSet.None)
                    return true;
                else
                    return false;
        }

        // If all else fails, return false.
        return false;
    }
    catch (InvalidCastException)
    {
        // Tell the caller there is an argument error.
        throw new ArgumentException("Wrong Argument Type ",
            this.GetType().FullName);
    }
}

public override SecurityElement ToXml()
{
    // Create a security XML encoding element.
    SecurityElement SE = new SecurityElement("IPermission");

    // Determine the permission type.
    Type Inst = this.GetType();

    // Determine the assembly name.
    StringBuilder AssemblyName;
    AssemblyName = new StringBuilder(Inst.Assembly.ToString());

    // Replace double quotes with single quotes for the XML file.
    AssemblyName.Replace('\"', '\'');

    // Create the required attributes.
    SE.AddAttribute("class", Inst.FullName + ", " + AssemblyName);
    SE.AddAttribute("version", "1");
    SE.AddAttribute("Unrestricted", _unrestricted.ToString());
    SE.AddAttribute("SetValue", _setValue.ToString());

    // Return the resulting security element.
    return SE;
}

public bool IsUnrestricted()
{
```

```
        // Return the current restricted state.
        return _unrestricted;
    }
}
```

Notice that the Special class derives from the CodeAccessPermission class and implements the IUnrestrictedPermission interface. When you create a permission class, you must implement the IPermission interface in some way. Microsoft recommends that you use the CodeAccessPermission class to meet this requirement because otherwise you have to write code for all of the common IPermission interface members.

> **TIP** It may be tempting to say that the CodeAccessPermission class is the only class you can use to derive a new permission class. This statement isn't true. You can derive from any permission class and it may be better if you do derive from other classes in some situations. The CodeAccessPermission class is code access specific. When you need to create a new identity permission, you may want to derive your new permission from one of the identity permissions such as the ZoneIdentityPermission class. The point is that you don't want to limit your choices based on the methods used in this section or online—choose the best class to meet your specific need and then modify that implementation as needed.

The Special class also has the [Serializable()] attribute attached. You don't have to include this attribute if you only intend to use imperative security with the new permission. However, it's usually a good idea to include the [Serializable()] attribute in case you decide to implement declarative security later. Otherwise, you see a strange error message (it seems to vary by phase of the moon) that has nothing to do with the actual problem when you attempt to use the permission in declarative mode.

The code begins by creating two private variables. Part of the custom permission specification states that you must keep track of the unrestricted state. However, you'll also want to track custom values.

The example provides two constructors. Look at most of the .NET Framework permission classes and you'll notice that they also have a minimum of two constructors. The reason is that you must create one constructor that accepts a PermissionState enumeration value as input. This value sets the unrestricted value. Notice that the example code also sets the custom _setValue variable based on this input. Although this isn't a requirement, you'll find that your custom permission works better if you make some assumptions based on the unrestricted value when a caller uses the PermissionState enumeration as input. Likewise, the second constructor handles the unrestricted state based on the SetValue input.

It may not seem like a very important addition, but you should provide a property for every custom status value your permission supports. The example provides this feature to make it easier to implement declarative security. It's also a good addition when the caller wants to learn the current permission state. A component may rely on specific caller states to grant or deny permissions.

Another rule for creating permissions based on the CodeAccessPermission class is that you must override the Copy(), Intersect(), IsSubsetOf(), ToXml(), and FromXml() methods. It's also helpful to override the Union() method, but not absolutely required. The example code shows typical implementations that include functionality for a special security state property. Notice, for example, that the Copy() method sets the values of the new copy of the Special object before returning it.

The FromXml() and ToXml() methods are paired. Microsoft doesn't place any restrictions on the format of the XML file except that the FromXml() must be able to read anything produced by the ToXml() method. The XML tags must also conform to the format produced by the SecurityElement object. This XML data isn't strictly correct or even readable by a typical XML utility. Figure 5.14 shows typical SecurityElement object XML output. As you can see from the figure and the associated code, the general idea is to use an existing object to generate XML settings that the code can read in and use to create a replica object.

FIGURE 5.14:

Create the specialized XML used for security needs in the FromXml() and ToXml() methods.

The Union(), Intersect(), and IsSubset() methods all perform manipulations of security settings based on the comparison of the existing permission with an input permission. The Union() method creates a result that's the complete set of settings of the two permissions. The Intersect() method returns a result that's the least of the two permissions. The IsSubset() method returns a Boolean value that states whether the input permission is a true subset (or an equal) of the existing permission. In all three cases, the code must check for a null input and act accordingly. After checking for a null input, the code coerces the input permission to an object of the same type as the current permission. If the coercion succeeds, the code performs the required comparison. As shown in the examples, you must provide handling for the InvalidCastException exception.

The IUnrestricted interface is relatively easy to implement. All you need to provide is an IsUnrestricted() method that returns the unrestricted value of your permission.

Listing 5.5 showed the imperative portion of the permission. However, you'll likely want to implement declarative security too. Listing 5.6 shows a typical declarative security implementation. The attribute class appears as part of the Special class module, which makes it easy for the two to work together (and lessens the work you must perform to create the declarative version).

Listing 5.6   Declarative Security Addition

```
// Add an attribute class so the permission includes both imperative
// and declarative security support.
[AttributeUsageAttribute(AttributeTargets.All, AllowMultiple = true)]
public class SpecialAttribute: CodeAccessSecurityAttribute
{
   // A required variable for unrestricted access.
   private Boolean _unrestricted;

   // A special variable for tracking access to this class.
   private SpecialSet _setValue;

   // You must include a property for changing the unrestricted value.
   public new Boolean Unrestricted
   {
      get { return _unrestricted; }
      set { _unrestricted = value; }
   }

   // This implementation also requires a special property.
   public SpecialSet SetValue
   {
      get { return _setValue; }
      set { _setValue = value; }
   }

   // Create the constructor.
   public SpecialAttribute(SecurityAction Action) : base (Action)
   {
   }

   // Override this method so the attribute returns the correct
   // object type.
   public override IPermission CreatePermission()
   {
      // Handle the case where the SetValue argument is supplied.
      switch (SetValue)
      {
         case SpecialSet.All:
```

```
            return new Special(SpecialSet.All);
        case SpecialSet.Some:
            return new Special(SpecialSet.Some);
        case SpecialSet.None:
            return new Special(SpecialSet.None);
    }

    // Handle the case where the Unrestricted argument is supplied.
    if(Unrestricted)
    {
        return new Special(PermissionState.Unrestricted);
    }
    else
    {
        return new Special(PermissionState.None);
    }
    }
}
```

The `SpecialAttribute` class derives from `CodeAccessSecurityAttribute`. However, as with the imperative version of this example, you can implement a completely custom declarative version.

You must provide properties for every value that the user can change as part of the attribute. These properties contain the values when the system calls your code. For example, when the caller uses the

```
[SpecialAttribute(SecurityAction.Demand, SetValue=SpecialSet.All)]
```

Attribute, the `SetValue` property receives the `SpecialSet.All` value. If you don't provide the requisite property, then your code won't receive the value.

The only method you must implement is `CreatePermission()`. The example shows one method of handling the input. If the `SetValue` property isn't set, the code looks at the `Unrestricted` property. You must handle the unrestricted setting at a minimum because many types of XML file handling rely on it. Note that in all cases, the `SpecialAttribute` class merely returns a new copy of the `Special` class.

Designing a Component to Use the Custom Permission

It's time to use the new `Special` permission class to protect a component. Listing 5.7 shows typical component code. It depends on the imperative method, but you could easily use the declarative method as well. (You can find this example in the \Chapter 05\C#\ `CustomPermissionComponent` or \Chapter 05\VB\CustomPermissionComponent folder of the source code located on the Sybex Web site.)

Listing 5.7   **A Custom Permission Test Component**

```
public class TestClass
{
   public TestClass()
   {
      // Demand the required permission.
      Special  ClientCheck;
      ClientCheck = new Special(SpecialSet.All);
      ClientCheck.Demand();
   }

   public String Random()
   {
      // Create a random number and place it in a string.
      Random MyRand;
      MyRand = new Random(DateTime.Now.Second);
      return "Next random number: " + MyRand.Next().ToString();
   }
}
```

When a caller tries to instantiate a copy of the component, the code checks for the correct security level using the Demand() method. Incorrect credentials produce a SecurityException exception. The Random() method is only used to test component access—it generates a string that includes a random number.

Designing an Application to Test the Custom Permission

The test program checks grant and deny security conditions when using the Special permission. Listing 5.8 shows the code used to instantiate a copy of the test component and display a string using the Random() method. (You can find this example in the \Chapter 05\C#\ CustomPermissionTest or \Chapter 05\VB\CustomPermissionTest folder of the source code located on the Sybex Web site.)

Listing 5.8   **Custom Permission Test Application**

```
private void btnGrant_Click(object sender, System.EventArgs e)
{
   // Create a new permission.
   Special Perm;
   Perm = new Special(SpecialSet.All);
   Perm.Demand();

   // Try to create the custom component.
   try
   {
      TestClass TC;
```

```
        TC = new TestClass();

        // Display a result.
        MessageBox.Show(TC.Random());
    }
    catch (SecurityException SE)
    {
        // Display the error.
        MessageBox.Show(SE.Message);
    }
}

private void btnDeny_Click(object sender, System.EventArgs e)
{
    // Create a new permission.
    Special Perm;
    Perm = new Special(SpecialSet.All);
    Perm.Deny();

    // Try to create the custom component.
    try
    {
        TestClass TC;
        TC = new TestClass();

        // Display a result.
        MessageBox.Show(TC.Random());
    }
    catch (SecurityException SE)
    {
        // Display the error.
        MessageBox.Show(SE.Message);
    }
}
```

As you can see, both methods are essentially the same. The only difference is that one uses the Demand() method to gain access to the required permission and the other uses the Deny() method to refuse the permission. Clicking Deny produces a message box that contains a security error message. The message box correctly identifies the CustomPermission.Special class as the source of the error.

Using Policy Objects

Creating a permission lets you create custom policy objects using the CASPol command line tool or the .NET Framework Configuration Tool. As your organization depends more on .NET to ensure the safety of your data, creating custom policies becomes more important.

You may run into a situation where you want to return a system to the default security policy before you make any other changes. For example, this technique works well if you use a batch file for setup and want to ensure the system is in a baseline configuration before you begin the batch file. To return the system to a default security configuration, type **CASPol -reset**.

This section of the chapter relies on the custom permission created in the "Adding New Permissions" section of the chapter. In this case, we'll use the Special permission class as the basis for defining a new policy.

Installing a New Permission

When you create a code group, you begin by looking at the membership condition and the permission granted by fulfillment of that condition. However, before you can grant a permission, it must appear as part of the standard security policy used by the .NET Framework. You must make the system aware of the permission in order to use it as a basis for any policy. The first task is to add the permission class to the Policy Assemblies folder at one or more levels. Repeated attempts show that this part of the .NET Framework Configuration Tool doesn't work as expected, so you must type **CASPol -machine -addfulltrust CustomPermission.DLL** and press Enter at the command prompt.

At this point, you need to create the permissions used with the code groups. Unfortunately, you can't just use the existing CustomPermission.DLL file as you might for other purposes. Neither of the utilities discussed so far will accept anything other than an XML file as input, which means you need to build the requisite program. Listing 5.9 shows that this program isn't difficult to write—just annoying. (This listing isn't complete. However, you can find the complete listing for this example in the \Chapter 05\C#\CustomPermissionXMLGen or \Chapter 05\VB\CustomPermissionXMLGen folder of the source code located on the Sybex Web site.)

Listing 5.9   XML Generator for a Custom Permission

```
private void btnTest_Click(object sender, System.EventArgs e)
{
    Special              Perm;    // Special permission object.
    NamedPermissionSet   NPS;     // Permission set container.
    StreamWriter         Output;  // Data storage to disk.

    // Create the All special permission.
    Perm = new Special(SpecialSet.All);

    // Define a named permission set.
    NPS = new NamedPermissionSet("SpecialPermissionAll",
                                 PermissionState.None);
```

```
    NPS.Description = "Grants all permissions for special permission.";
    NPS.AddPermission(Perm);

    // Generate the All permission output file.
    Output = new StreamWriter("SpecialPermissionAll.XML");
    Output.Write(NPS.ToXml());
    Output.Close();

    ... Some and None Permission Generation ...

    // Operation complete.
    MessageBox.Show("Output Complete!");
}
```

As you can see, the code begins by building a named permission set and a permission to place in it. It's important to create one permission for each permission state that you want a code group to support. Because the code is relatively easy, the example creates permission files for all three of the example permission states. The program uses a StreamWriter to output the information to an XML file. The result of running this program is three XML files that you can use to create permissions. The following steps show how to perform this part of the process using the .NET Framework Configuration Tool.

1. Select the Runtime Security Policy/Machine/Permission Sets folder.

2. Click Create New Permission Set. You'll see a Create Permission Set dialog box.

3. Select the Import a permission set from an XML file option.

4. Click Browse to locate the XML file or type the location of the file. Your dialog box should look similar to the one shown in Figure 5.15.

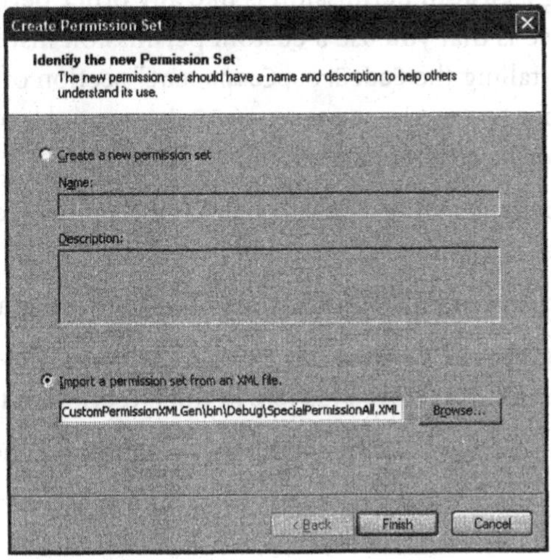

FIGURE 5.15:

Define the location of the XML file containing the new permission you want to create.

5. Click Finish. The .NET Framework Configuration Tool will add the new permission to the list.

6. Repeat Steps 2 through 5 for each of the permissions you want to add (three for this example).

Figure 5.16 shows the Permission Sets folder with all three permissions added.

FIGURE 5.16:

A view of the Permission Sets folder with custom permissions added.

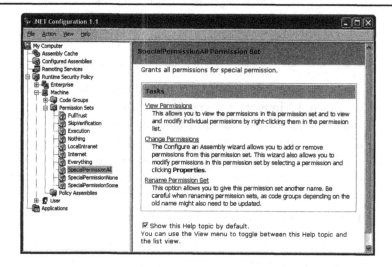

Creating a Code Group Based on the Permission

Now that you have a new permission to use, you'll likely want to create a code group to use it. Using a custom permission is like any other permission you might have used. The only difference is that you use a custom permission instead of one of the supplied permissions. The "Installing the CodeGroupComponent" section of the chapter provides an example of the techniques you use to create a new code group. Here are the quick steps for creating a code group for the custom permission.

1. Select the Runtime Security Policy/Machine/Code Groups/All_Code/My_Computer_Zone folder.

2. Click Add a Child Code Group. You'll see a Create Code Group dialog box.

3. Type **Special_Permission_Test** in the Name field and **Tests the CustomPermission .Special class permission.** in the Description field, and then click Next.

4. Select All_Code as the membership condition and click Next.

5. Select SpecialPermissionAll as the permission and click Next.

6. Click Finish. The .NET Framework Configuration Tool creates the new code group.

Designing a Named Permission Test Program

It's the decisive moment. The example in this section shows how to check for the existence of a named permission on your system. In this case, the program only provides output for the custom permissions you just installed. Listing 5.10 shows the code that you'll need. (The listing in this chapter is incomplete. You can find the complete listing for this example in the \Chapter 05\C#\NamedPermission or \Chapter 05\VB\NamedPermission folder of the source code located on the Sybex Web site.)

Listing 5.10   Obtaining a Named Permission

```
private void btnTest_Click(object sender, System.EventArgs e)
{
    IEnumerator          Policies;    // Security policies.
    PolicyLevel          Policy;      // A single policy.
    NamedPermissionSet   NPS;         // The special permission set.
    Special              Perm;        // The special permission.
    StringBuilder        Output;      // The output value.

    // Initialize the output.
    Output = new StringBuilder();

    // Get the all of the policies.
    Policies = SecurityManager.PolicyHierarchy();
    while (Policies.MoveNext())
    {
        // Get the current policy.
        Policy = (PolicyLevel)Policies.Current;

        // Check for the SpecialPermissionAll named permission set.
        NPS = Policy.GetNamedPermissionSet("SpecialPermissionAll");

        // Process the named permission set when available.
        if (NPS != null)
        {
            // Get the named permission and check its values.
            Perm = (Special)NPS.GetPermission(typeof(Special));
            Output.Append("SpecialPermissionAll\r\nUnrestricted: ");
            Output.Append(Perm.IsUnrestricted().ToString());
            Output.Append("\r\nSetValue: ");
            Output.Append(Perm.SetValue.ToString());
        }

        ... Other Permission Checks ...
```

```
        }
    // Output the results.
    MessageBox.Show(Output.ToString(),
                    "Named Permission Sets",
                    MessageBoxButtons.OK,
                    MessageBoxIcon.Information);
}
```

The code begins by accessing the `SecurityManager` and gaining access to the policy hierarchy. The code moves from one policy to the next in search of the named permission sets you created. You use the `GetNamedPermissionSet()` method to access a named permission set. If the permission set is missing, the return value is `null`.

Once the code locates the named permission set, it uses the `GetPermission()` method to obtain access to the actual permissions. The code coerces the `IPermission` output to the `Special` type. The permission has all the same features as the custom permission you created. Figure 5.17 shows the output from this example. Note that all of the values reflect the custom permission code.

FIGURE 5.17:

Viewing the output
of the named
permission program
shows custom
permissions
really work.

TIP   You'll likely find that the `GetPermission()` method doesn't work as advertised in Visual Basic .NET. The technique to get around this problem is to use an enumeration. While using this method isn't as fast or memory efficient as the C# alternative, it is reliable. In addition, you'll run into casting problems with Visual Basic when using the `Special` permission. The alternative in this case is to use an `Object` instead of the actual type. See the Visual Basic .NET version of this example for details.

Summary

This chapter has demonstrated several new features of code groups and policies. Now that you've completed this chapter, you should have a better idea of how both .NET security features work at a low level. More important, you know how to manage these security features so that you can prevent most security problems and detect those that do get past your defenses. The goal of this chapter is to help you understand how policies and code groups work together to create a cohesive .NET security strategy.

Now that you have a better idea of how policies work, you should define a default security policy for your system at all three levels: enterprise, machine, and user. Make sure you use the tips found in the chapter to refine your security strategy. Remember that it's important to have a written policy that works with the software policies you create.

Chapter 6 discusses the process of validation and verification. Validation is the process of checking that code, data, and resources are intact. You use validation to detect any changes that a cracker makes to your system. It's also useful for ensuring your code doesn't contain any changes before you run it. Verification is the process of determining identity. In this case, identity includes both the caller and recipient. It's important to verify the identity of both servers and workstations in a world where crackers use both ends of the communication channel to overcome and overwhelm security measures.

CHAPTER 6

Validation and Verification Issues

- Creating Trust Relationships in the Managed Environment

- Defining Features to Validate Your Code

- Defining and Overcoming .NET Verification Issues

- Using the `AppDomain` for Managed Code Security

- Developing the `AppDomain` to Secure Unmanaged Code

Validation and *verification* are two essential security issues that many developers confuse and some developers feel are the same issue worded in a different way. However, validation and verification are separate issues and you must manage both if you want to create a reasonably secure application:

- Validation is the process of checking credentials to ensure they're correct in every way.

- Verification is the process of ensuring that any requestor with validated (authenticated) credentials actually has permission to access a resource or system service.

The overall purpose of this chapter is to discuss the concept of earned trust (at the code, user, and machine levels). At some point, you need to trust the code running on the machine or the client accessing resources in order to accomplish anything. You don't necessarily trust the code or the client completely, but they do require some level of trust. The concept of earned trust isn't new. Any secure system has to have this concept to work. However, the .NET method of managing earned trust is new. Consequently, this chapter helps you understand how the .NET Framework manages earned trust.

The .NET Framework does have some special problems to overcome. The greatest problem is unmanaged code. Unlike the managed code an application uses, unmanaged code lacks the level of security discussed in previous chapters. You still have to provide some kind of trust mechanism for unmanaged code or do without the functionality it provides. At this point, you can't run many complex applications without unmanaged code, so let's say this need is a given. In short, this chapter not only discusses earned trust, but also the problems with earned trust in the .NET environment.

Don't assume that unmanaged code is the only validation or verification problem you have to overcome. This chapter also demonstrates how to perform techniques such as validating the Intermediate Language (IL) code for an application. This check is important when security is the highest priority. A cracker can make subtle code changes that turn your application from a benign manipulator of data to a shark chewing up the data it's supposed to protect. As part of this validation and verification process, the chapter also helps you to understand how the .NET Framework deals with verification issues and what you can do improve this process within your code.

Ensuring Trust in the Managed Environment

Trust is an essential part of any relationship or interaction between client and server. The job of the server is to protect and manage the resources and services that the network administrator has configured. This task runs counter to providing access to those same services and resources. Absolute security means denying all access to anyone requesting it. The definition of a secret is something that you keep to yourself—if anyone else knows the information, it's no longer truly secret. The trust relationship indicates that the server has some level of confidence that the requestor will maintain the integrity of the secret. The server can't guarantee the requestor will absolutely maintain the secret, but there's some level of confidence in this fact.

The reason I keep stressing layers of security and quantities of security is that many developers have gotten the idea from security vendors that they can whisper some kind of magic enchantment that provides absolute security. Absolute security is a fallacy unless you maintain absolute control over the data, which makes the data useless. Sharing is a requirement for information exchange.

Fortunately, the .NET Framework does make it easier to assess the level of risk that you take in making information accessible to a requestor, even one from the same machine. For one thing, the .NET Framework ensures flexible security. If you must grant access to data, resources, or services to a requestor, then ensuring that the requestor actually has the proper rights is important. Chapter 5 covered one application of this principle in the "Adding New Permissions" section. This section demonstrates that you can create a flexible security solution using the .NET Framework—one that Microsoft couldn't consider when it designed the system. Expecting the unexpected is an essential part of trustworthy security—any good security plan is flexible enough to change with the conditions.

Validating Your Code

At one time, the code you wrote stayed on a local machine or a network, so there was little chance that someone could get a copy of it—much less change it. The probability that you would suffer a major security problem due to the code alone was relatively small. Any code you wrote that also included reasonable protection from user mistakes and malicious tampering was safe.

However, now your code is accessible through Web services or through sharing with partners. In addition, .NET has certain weaknesses that are less inherent in native code. For example, it's very easy to disassemble .NET code into a text file that anyone with reasonable programming skills can modify. For these and many other reasons, it's no longer safe to assume that the code you write and distribute today is going to be safe tomorrow.

Chapter 4 covered the issue of code validation to an extent. The Signed Client example in Chapter 4 (see the "Writing the `StrongNameIdentityPermission` Class Code" section) shows one way to verify the identity of the caller. This verification process entails checking the validity of the code. A change in the code would cause issues when Common Language Runtime (CLR) tried to run it. In general, the check in this chapter alone is enough to provide satisfactory security for many needs. However, some applications need better security than the example in Chapter 4 provides.

The following sections discuss issues you should consider for code validation when security is at least as important as performance. For example, if you're developing any kind of application that handles money, you need to validate the code to ensure that even small or odd bits of tampering haven't occurred.

Checking the Intermediate Language (IL) Code

The first question you need answered is whether you can assume that your signed code is safe—the answer is no. Although you can sign your code and make it very tough for someone to misrepresent you or your organization, the fact remains that anyone with the .NET Framework installed on their system has the tools required to view and modify your code (not that it's an easy task).

Let's look at a simple example. (You can find this example in the \Chapter 06\C#\ SimpleSigned or \Chapter 06\VB\SimpleSigned folder of the source code located on the Sybex Web site.) The code of interest is the btnTest_Click event handler shown here.

```
private void btnTest_Click(object sender, System.EventArgs e)
{
   // Display a message box.
   MessageBox.Show("Hello",
                   "Message",
                   MessageBoxButtons.OK,
                   MessageBoxIcon.Information);
}
```

This simple example is signed with the MyKey key used for many of the other examples in the book. To open this file, create a command prompt, type **ILDASM SimpleSigned.EXE**, and press Enter. Figure 6.1 shows the disassembly of this signed file. Notice that signing this assembly doesn't prevent you from reading it. You can learn anything you want about this assembly and .NET does nothing to stop you.

FIGURE 6.1:

Security information in a .NET IL file is easily readable.

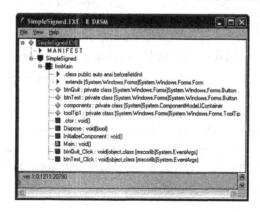

There are many pieces of interesting information in this file, but the piece to focus on now is the MANIFEST entry displayed near the top of Figure 6.1. Double-click this entry. Look near the bottom of the file that opens and you'll see information similar to the information shown in Figure 6.2.

FIGURE 6.2:

Reading what should be protected information is excessively easy in .NET.

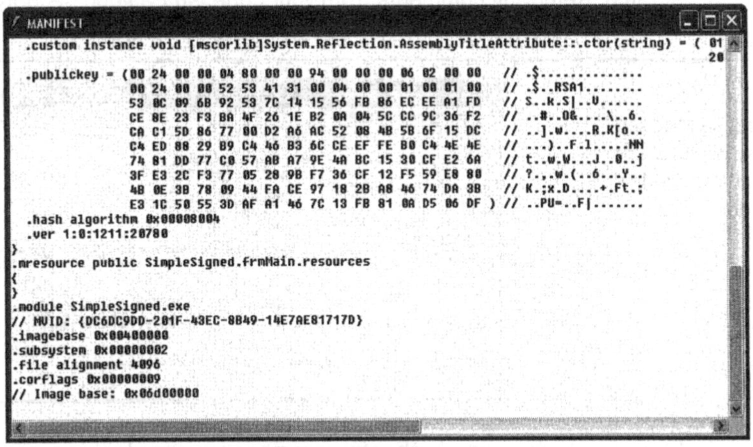

From previous chapters you know that Microsoft provides tools for extracting at least some of this information from the manifest. However, few developers realize that all this information is so easy to access using a single utility. It would appear that your code is completely open to abuse and misuse. Even if you include public key checks and perform other types of validation, the fact that your code is so easy to read makes it unlikely that any security methodology will ensure complete code security. Native code compilation has a definite advantage here because the compiler can obfuscate the code sequence and the use of machine instructions makes the information nearly unreadable. (As a connoisseur of disassemblers, I can tell you that nothing is certain even with native code.)

Validating the Standard Check

CLR doesn't leave your code completely helpless if you sign it. The checks it performs will detect a moderate level of tampering from an inexperienced .NET developer. It's easy to check out this part of your protection package. Begin by creating a source code file. Type **ILDASM /Source /Out=SimpleSigned.IL SimpleSigned.EXE** at the command prompt, press Enter, and you receive text and resource files that define the example.

Make a simple change to the SimpleSigned.IL file. For example, you could change the word Hello to Goodbye, as shown in Figure 6.3. Notice that this is the IL version of the btnTest_Click event handler. You may find it interesting to look through this file. Many developers are unaware that their comments appear in the IL file, which can make for interesting reading.

> **NOTE**   Some developers might consider the problem of comments in an IL file as an argument for removing comments from production level code, but the cure would be worse than the disease. Uncommented code causes more than a few problems and some companies even hire consultants to determine whether to salvage uncommented code or start from scratch. Removing comments from your code isn't a good security policy.

FIGURE 6.3:

Creating a disassembly of a .NET application lets you modify the code.

```
private void btnTest_Click(object sender, System.EventArgs e)
//000115:
//000116:        {
//000117:            // Display a message box.
//000118:            MessageBox.show("Goodbye", "Message", MessageBoxButtons.OK,
MessageBoxIcon.Information);
    IL_0000:    ldstr       "Goodbye"
    IL_0005:    ldstr       "Message"
    IL_000a:    ldc.i4.0
    IL_000b:    ldc.i4.s    64
    IL_000d:    call        valuetype [System.Windows.Forms]System.Windows.Forms.DialogResult
[System.Windows.Forms]System.Windows.Forms.MessageBox::Show(string,

                                                             string,

                                                             valuetype
[System.Windows.Forms]System.Windows.Forms.MessageBoxButtons,

                                                             valuetype
[System.Windows.Forms]System.Windows.Forms.MessageBoxIcon)
    IL_0012:    pop
//000119:        }
```

Once you make a simple change, you need to compile the program back into an executable. At the command prompt, type **ILASM /EXE /Resource=SimpleSigned.RES /Output=Simple-SignedMod.EXE SimpleSigned.IL** and press Enter. The new file, SimpleSignedMod.EXE, still uses the original key as a signature. When you run it, you receive the error message shown in Figure 6.4.

FIGURE 6.4:

Casual crackers are unlikely to remain undetected during the standard CLR checks.

This part of the example demonstrates that CLR does, in fact, detect modifications to your signed executable (your unsigned executable is completely helpless). Note that you can dismiss the debugging dialog that appears after you click OK at the security message in Figure 6.4.

Circumventing and Fixing the Standard Check

What happens, though, if someone signs the new version of the file with their key using the ILASM command? At the command prompt, type **ILASM /EXE /Resource=SimpleSigned.RES /Output=SimpleSignedMod2.EXE /Key=MyKey2 SimpleSigned.IL** and press Enter. The ILASM command creates a new version of the program, just as it did before.

The exploit demonstrated in this section becomes much harder if you use a digital signature issued by a third party Certificate Authority (CA) because a cracker can't simply substitute one key for another without notice. However, even using this method means that you need to alert users who are going to notice that the signature is no longer the same. Experience shows that most users simply aren't that observant.

Run the resulting program. Suddenly, there's no error message. Again, your code is completely helpless because CLR sees that the code is signed using a legitimate key—one supplied by the cracker. Unless you incorporate an internal check, there's no hope of catching this problem. Now you see the benefit of the example in Chapter 4—at least no one can access your components unless they change them as well.

You can perform several checks to ensure that no one has changed your code. These checks won't stop everyone, but they do add another security layer. Listing 6.1 shows the constructor for an improved version of the SimpleSigned program. (You can find this example in the \Chapter 06\C#\SimpleSigned2 or \Chapter 06\VB\SimpleSigned2 folder of the source code located on the Sybex Web site.)

Listing 6.1   Adding Security Checks to a Client

```
public frmMain()
{
    StrongNamePublicKeyBlob        PublicKeyBlob;  // Public Key Check
    Assembly                       Asm;            // Current assembly.
    Evidence                       EV;             // Assembly evidence.
    StrongNameMembershipCondition  StrongMember;   // Strong Member Check.
    IEnumerator                    MyEnum;         // Security enumerator.
    HashMembershipCondition        HashMember;     // Hash Member Check.
    Hash                           ClientHash;     // Current client hash.
    RegistryKey                    AppKey;         // Registry entries.

    // Required for Windows Form Designer support
    InitializeComponent();

    // Create an array for the public key.
    Byte[]   PublicKey = {
        0, 36, 0, 0, 4, 128, 0, 0, 148, 0, 0, 0, 6, 2, 0, 0, 0, 36,
        0, 0, 82, 83, 65, 49, 0, 4, 0, 0, 1, 0, 1, 0, 83, 12, 9,
        107, 146, 83, 124, 20, 21, 86, 251, 134, 236, 238, 161,
        253, 206, 142, 35, 243, 186, 79, 38, 30, 178, 10, 4, 92,
        204, 156, 54, 242, 202, 193, 93, 134, 119, 0, 210, 166,
        172, 82, 8, 75, 91, 111, 21, 220, 196, 237, 136, 41, 185,
        196, 70, 179, 108, 206, 239, 254, 176, 196, 78, 78, 116,
        129, 221, 119, 192, 87, 171, 167, 158, 74, 188, 21, 48, 207,
        226, 106, 63, 227, 44, 243, 119, 5, 40, 155, 247, 54, 207,
```

```
           18, 245, 89, 232, 128, 75, 14, 59, 120, 9, 68, 250, 206,
           151, 24, 43, 168, 70, 116, 218, 59, 227, 28, 80, 85, 61,
           175, 161, 70, 124, 19, 251, 129, 10, 213, 6, 223 };

// Create a public key blob using the public key.
PublicKeyBlob = new StrongNamePublicKeyBlob(PublicKey);

// Create the strong name membership condition.
StrongMember =
   new StrongNameMembershipCondition(PublicKeyBlob, null, null);

// Get the calling assembly.
Asm = Assembly.GetExecutingAssembly();

// Get the evidence from the assembly.
EV = Asm.Evidence;

// Check the strong name membership.
if (!StrongMember.Check(EV))
{
   // Throw an exception.
   throw(new SecurityException("Failed Internal Security Check"));
}

// Get the hash value for this client.
MyEnum = EV.GetHostEnumerator();
ClientHash = null;
while (MyEnum.MoveNext())
   if (MyEnum.Current.GetType() == typeof(Hash))
      ClientHash = (Hash)MyEnum.Current;

// Check for the Hash value.
AppKey = Registry.LocalMachine.OpenSubKey(@"Software\SimpleSigned");

// The registry key does exist.
if (AppKey == null)
{
   // Create the registry key.
   AppKey =
      Registry.LocalMachine.CreateSubKey(@"Software\SimpleSigned");

   // Set the registry value.
   AppKey.SetValue("HashValue", ClientHash.MD5);
}
else
{

   // Create the Hash membership condition.
   Byte[] HashValue = (Byte[])AppKey.GetValue("HashValue");
   HashMember =
      new HashMembershipCondition(new MD5CryptoServiceProvider(),
```

```
                              HashValue);

        // Verify the hash value hasn't changed.
        if (!HashMember.Check(EV))
            throw(new SecurityException("Failed Internal Hash Check"));
    }
}
```

This code may look a little bizarre, but it's quite effective in securing your application. The code performs two checks. First, it looks for the public key assigned to the application. This check overcomes the problem of someone using another key to sign your application. Second, it looks at the hash value of the program. Even if someone should decide to replace your public key value with the new ones for their key, replicating the hash value is extremely hard. In addition, this value isn't stored in plain view in the disassembled code.

The strong name check has appeared in several other examples in various forms. This is yet another form of that very useful check. The code creates a StrongNameMembershipCondition object and then uses the Check() of that object to verify a standard strong name value against the strong name value in the current client.

The hash check begins with the code obtaining the hash value of the application, as it currently exists. If a cracker has changed the code in any way, the current hash value won't match a stored hash value. However, there's a problem. You can't extract the hash value easily and it doesn't appear in the disassembled code. Finding the hash value so you have something to use for comparison purposes could be a bit problematic.

The example solves this problem by using the registry. The registry solution actually works very well if you also set policies that restrict access to that key and its values. Even if you don't secure the key, the probability that someone will know where to look in the registry for your application's key is small. For the purpose of this example, the registry check can take one of two courses. If the registry key doesn't exist, the code creates it and adds a value. On the other hand, if the key does exist, the code extracts the known good hash value from it. If this were a production application, you would add the key to the registry during installation and raise an error if the application couldn't find it. The code creates a HashMembershipCondition object and uses the Check() method to validate the hash key.

I would love to say that this technique is foolproof, but only a fool would believe that statement. This two-phase check greatly increases the security of your program at a very modest cost in startup time. It doesn't cost any performance once the program is running, nor does it cause the program to use any more resources (at least not once the Garbage Collector does its work). However, it's possible that a determined cracker could still overcome both checks. All the cracker would need to do is add a new public key and create a new hash value for the registry. It's possible, but more difficult than just making a change and recompiling the code.

As previously mentioned, multiple layers of security will slow a determined cracker down, but you can never stop a cracker completely.

Protecting Your Code with Dotfuscator

All of the problems mentioned so far have hinged on one factor, the ability of the cracker to read your code. This is a very big security problem because a cracker can analyze any security measures you take. There's a strong third party market in programs that make your code unreadable using ILDASM. In fact, Microsoft has recognized that code readability is a problem, so they included Dotfuscator Community Edition with Visual Studio .NET 2003. If you're using an older version of Visual Studio .NET, you can download this product from http://www.preemptive.com/dotfuscator/.

You can use Dotfuscator directly from the command line, which means you can simply add it to the compile process for your program. However, it pays to use the GUI the first few times, so you better understand how the product works and discover which features you want to use for your application security needs. Figure 6.5 shows the initial Dotfuscator display.

FIGURE 6.5:

The initial Dotfuscator display shows that this product can perform a number of tasks.

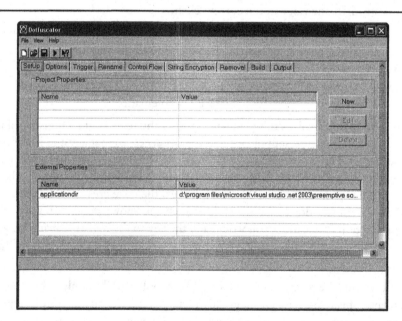

As you can see, the product can do quite a bit—each task area is on a separate tab. The following steps show how to perform the essential task of making your code unreadable. (You can find this example in the \Chapter 06\Dotfuscator folder of the source code located on the Sybex Web site.)

1. Select the Options tab and check the Verbose option. This option is important because it lets you see what Dotfuscator is doing and provides a better sense of the product's utility. Notice that you can also set the product to keep output to a minimum using the Quiet option. Use the Investigate option if you want to see the product work without producing any output and the Library option if the modules you specify as input are part of a library of modules.

2. Select the Trigger tab. The Professional Edition performs application optimization by only including methods in the output that the code calls in the application. The Community Edition only uses this tab as a means of selecting the assemblies that you want to work with. In both cases, type the name of the assemblies you want to work with or use the Browse button to find them.

3. Select the Rename tab. You'll see the display shown in Figure 6.6. (It's interesting to compare the list shown in Figure 6.6 with the one shown in Figure 6.1—Dotfuscator does a great job of analyzing your code.) In general, Dotfuscator renames everything in a module. This could be a problem if you call a specific method from an unrelated program. Use this tab to select elements that you don't want to rename. It's important to remember that anything that you don't rename provides crackers with valuable clues. The default setup of renaming everything works for most applications.

FIGURE 6.6:

Renaming all of the elements in your program makes it harder for crackers to locate specifics.

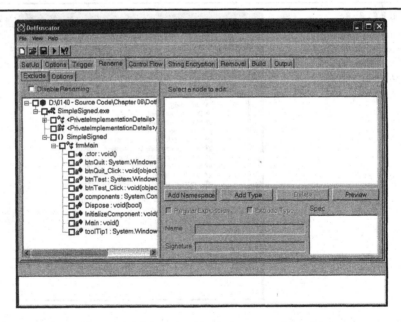

4. Select the Build tab. Type entries in the Temporary Directory and Destination Directory fields. These fields define the temporary and permanent location of data for the selected program.

5. Save the project using the File ➤ Save command. Dotfuscator saves its configuration files as eXtensible Markup Language (XML), making them relatively easy to read. Figure 6.7 shows the configuration file for this example. You can use this information to define your own custom project files.

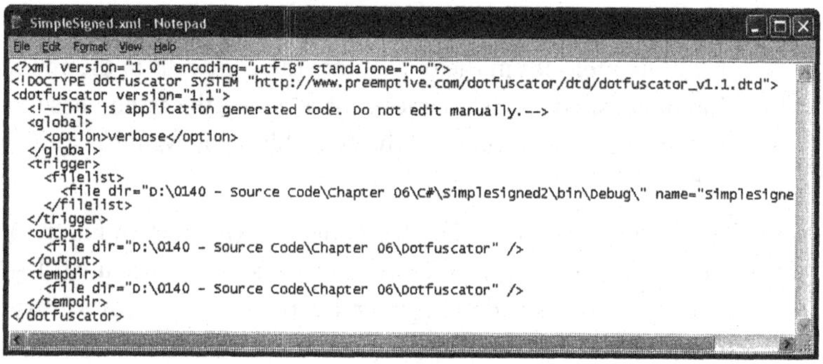

FIGURE 6.7:

Reading the GUI generated XML files can help you build your own custom versions.

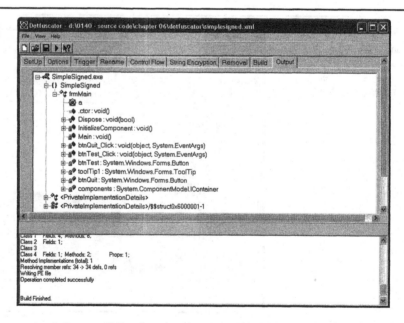

6. Click Build. Dotfuscator builds the program for you. The lower window shows the build progress. You can see the results of the build process on the Output tab shown in Figure 6.8.

FIGURE 6.8:

Building the application generates information on the Output tab and in the lower window.

Of course, the question is how well Dotfuscator does in making your code unreadable. The initial output that appears in Figure 6.9 looks good. ILDASM displays a program organization that doesn't look much like the original in Figure 6.1. However, if someone is determined, they can still learn the details of your program. Dotfuscator does confuse things, but it's nothing like trying to disassemble native code.

FIGURE 6.9:
Using Dotfuscator will
make your code harder
to read and interpret.

Unfortunately, some aspects of the program are still all too readable. For example, the MANIFEST entry hasn't changed at all. You can still read the public key without any problem at all. The constructor is also easy to find. Dotfuscator makes subtle changes to the code that makes it more difficult to figure out what's going on, but again, a determined cracker can learn what your code is doing.

In the end, Dotfuscator is another piece of the security you should use to protect your application, but you can't count on it as the only piece. Although the product sounds promising and does some of what it promises, it's not a complete solution. You still need to sign your code and use techniques such as the hashing method shown in the "Circumventing and Fixing the Standard Check" section. Even so, you must realize that someone who is determined to modify your code can probably do so, which means you must remain vigilant if you plan to make your system secure.

Creating a Security Deployment Package

The .NET Framework Configuration Tool helps you create a security deployment package that contains the settings needed to support your application. The advantage to using this method is that you can create a security policy on a test machine, verify that it works, and then deploy it to your entire organization using the resulting Microsoft Installer (MSI) file. Whenever the user logs in after deployment, Windows automatically installs the new policy, which means you have fewer security problems due to security setup issues.

The disadvantage to this method is that it's level oriented. You have to install the entire level to the MSI file. This means you couldn't develop the policy on a standard machine—one that could have policies you don't want the user to have. The only way to use this method effectively is to create the policy on a machine that has no other policies installed—preferably one with a fresh installation of Windows. The following steps tell how to use this technique from within the .NET Framework Configuration Tool. (You can find an example file in the \Chapter 06\MyPolicy.MSI file of the source code located on the Sybex Web site.)

1. Highlight the Runtime Security Policy folder.

2. Click Create Deployment Package. You'll see a Deployment Package Wizard dialog box.

3. Select the level you want to deploy (Enterprise, Machine, or User).

4. Type the location you want to use for the MSI file.

5. Click Next. You'll see a completion dialog box.

6. Click Finish. The wizard creates the deployment package for you.

Relying on the *AppDomain* for Managed Code

The application domain in which your program executes determines its access to resources and services. The application domain is a kind of container that determines the security settings for an application and isolates it (from a security perspective) from other applications. A single application can have more than one application domain—you can create a different application domain for each assembly that you load. In short, every assembly for an application can have different security settings, which means your control over the assemblies is robust. At the center of all this control is the AppDomain class.

We initially discussed the AppDomain class in Chapter 1 as part of the "Using Role-based Security" section discussion. The example in Chapter 1 assumed that the application has a single application domain and used that fact to determine information about the principal of that domain. The context in which the program executes determines how role-based security works. (See the "Understanding the System.Runtime.Remoting.Contexts Namespace" section of Chapter 2 for a discussion of the effects of context on your application.) By controlling the application domain, you not only control the application, but also the code access and role-based security for that application.

Accessing Another Application

The example in this section goes further than simply telling you that every application has at least one AppDomain object you can use to discover information about the user's role or the ability of code to access specific features. The example demonstrates how you can create multiple application domains in which you can load assemblies to control their access to specific functionality. Listing 6.2 shows the code you need for this example. (You can find this example in the \Chapter 06\C#\ManagedAppDomain or \Chapter 06\VB\ManagedAppDomain folder of the source code located on the Sybex Web site.)

Listing 6.2   **Using Multiple *AppDomain* Objects to Control Access**

```
private void btnTest2_Click(object sender, System.EventArgs e)
{
    AppDomainSetup APS;        // Setup information for the domain.
    Evidence       EV;         // New evidence for the domain.
    AppDomain      LoadApp;    // The application domain.
    DoSomething    MyComp;     // An intance of the component.

    // Create the domain setup information.
    APS = new AppDomainSetup();
    APS.ApplicationName = "MyLoadedApplication";

    // Get evidence for the domain.
    EV = AppDomain.CurrentDomain.Evidence;

    // Create the application domain.
    LoadApp = AppDomain.CreateDomain("MyLoadedApplication", EV, APS);

    // Execute the program.
    LoadApp.ExecuteAssembly(Application.StartupPath +
                            "\\LoadedApplication.EXE");

    // Create a local copy of the test component.
    MyComp = new DoSomething();

    // Execute the SayHello() method.
    MessageBox.Show(MyComp.GetDomain());
}
```

The code begins by creating a new application domain setup. CLR passes this object to the new application domain and can contain any of a number of values. The example is defined only the ApplicationName property because that's all you really need to verify the actual domain the other application uses. In general, you want to define the AppDomainSetup object to ensure that the new domain uses the features you want and for testing purposes—to ensure that the security measures work the way you think they will.

You also need to create evidence for the new AppDomain object. This evidence can include anything we've discussed in other areas of the book. For example, you can provide specific permissions as part of the evidence. The point is that you can define the security environment to meet specific needs.

The next step is to create the application domain and execute the application. The code uses the CreateDomain() method to create the new application domain. You can use other sets of arguments. For that matter, you can create a domain by providing the friendly name, which is `MyLoadedApplication` for the example. Executing the code is relatively easy—just use the `ExecuteAssembly()` method as shown. Some versions of this call even accept command line parameters.

This portion of the example ends by creating a copy of the text component used by the sample application. It uses the `MyComp.GetDomain()` method to display the `AppDomain` value of the current assembly. You'll find that the sample application has an `AppDomain` value of `MyLoadedApplication`, while the current assembly uses `ManagedAppDomain.EXE`. Listing 6.3 shows the code used for the sample application.

Listing 6.3   A Simple Test Application

```
namespace LoadedApplication
{
    public class LoadTest
    {
        [STAThread]
        static void Main()
        {
            DoSomething MyComp;    // Create the test component.

            // Instantiate the component.
            MyComp = new DoSomething();

            // Display the friendly name.
            MessageBox.Show(MyComp.GetDomain());
        }
    }
}
```

All this application does is load a test component and use the text component's `GetDomain()` method to detect the current domain `FriendlyName` value. The example doesn't even use a full Windows application—this is a modified console application used to display a `MessageBox` object. Listing 6.4 shows the test component used for this example.

Listing 6.4   Domain *FriendlyName* Detection Component

```
namespace LoadedAssembly
{
    public class DoSomething
    {
        public String GetDomain()
        {
            AppDomain   MyDomain;   // The current domain.

            // Get the current domain.
```

```
        MyDomain = Thread.GetDomain();

        // Return the friendly name to the caller.
        return MyDomain.FriendlyName;
    }
  }
}
```

This component obtains a copy of the current domain using the Thread.GetDomain() method. It uses this object to return the FriendlyName value to the caller. Using this simple component lets you see that the sample application is actually executing in its own AppDomain because the name differs from the AppDomain value of the main application.

Understanding Component Access Problems

Executing code in a separate AppDomain is relatively easy. The code in Listing 6.2 shows that you only need to add a few lines of code to create the AppDomain, place an application in it, and execute that application. Some people may confuse the idea of an AppDomain and a thread. However, if you spend some time in the debugger, you'll find that the example in Listing 6.2 executes in the current thread. Threads can have multiple AppDomain objects (they can only use one at a time) and AppDomain objects can use multiple threads.

Components present a problem that you might not consider because of the ease with which you can create an application. Listing 6.5 shows how you would use an AppDomain to create an instance of a component. (You can find this example in the \Chapter 06\C#\ManagedAppDomain or \Chapter 06\VB\ManagedAppDomain folder of the source code located on the Sybex Web site.)

Listing 6.5 **Creating a Component from an *AppDomain* Object**

```
private void btnTest_Click(object sender, System.EventArgs e)
{
    AppDomainSetup APS;       // Setup information for the domain.
    Evidence       EV;        // New evidence for the domain.
    AppDomain      LoadComp;   // The application domain.
    Assembly       ExtComp;    // External assembly.
    DoSomething    CompInst;   // An instance of the component.

    // Create the domain setup information.
    APS = new AppDomainSetup();
    APS.ApplicationName = "LoadedComponent";

    // Get evidence for the domain.
    EV = AppDomain.CurrentDomain.Evidence;

    // Create the application domain.
    LoadComp = AppDomain.CreateDomain("LoadedComponent", EV, APS);

    // Load the assembly.
```

```
ExtComp = LoadComp.Load("LoadedAssembly");

// Create an instance of the component.
CompInst =
  (DoSomething)ExtComp.CreateInstance("LoadedAssembly.DoSomething");

// Execute the SayHello() method.
MessageBox.Show(CompInst.GetDomain());
}
```

Notice that this example (Listing 6.5) uses the same three step process to create the application domain as Listing 6.2: create the AppDomainSetup object, create an Evidence object, and then create the AppDomain using the CreateDomain() method. You know from the previous example that the AppDomain is most definitely different from the AppDomain used by the current application. It would seem that anything you do with that AppDomain would remain separate.

The example code uses the Load() method to load an assembly that contains a component. Note that you can't use the ExecuteAssembly() method because you have to instantiate the component. The loaded assembly is, in fact, in a separate domain. However, the moment you use the CreateInstance() method to create an instance of the component located in the loaded assembly, something happens. CLR moves the component from the AppDomain of the loaded assembly into the AppDomain of the current application. The MessageBox.Show(CompInst.GetDomain()) call proves that the component is executing in the ManagedAppDomain.EXE AppDomain and not the LoadedComponent AppDomain.

The important thing to remember is that you must test the security setup you create to determine how CLR actually uses the objects you create. An incorrect assumption can give you the illusion of executing in a separate AppDomain even when the separation doesn't exist. This code executes without error—you would never know there's a potential security hole without checking the FriendlyName value. (See Listing 6.4 for an example of the FriendlyName property in use.)

Extending the *AppDomain* to Unmanaged Code

Unmanaged code requires special handling if you want to make access secure. The problem is that you can't guarantee the actions of the unmanaged code because you can't control it using the same security system as the rest of your .NET application. In fact, giving your code permission to access unmanaged code of any type can prove detrimental to any security plan you have in place.

TIP   Microsoft recommends sorting your unmanaged code into three classes to make classification easier. You can use the unsafe moniker for code that shouldn't run except under strict supervision. The native moniker denotes code that runs when the caller has the `SecurityPermissionFlag.UnmanagedCode` permission. Use the safe moniker only when the code is so safe there's no chance that anyone could use it for nefarious reasons. Learn more about this naming scheme at `http://msdn.microsoft.com/library/en-us/cpguide/html/cpconnamingconventionforunmanagedcodemethods.asp`.

The following sections show two techniques for working with unmanaged code. The first shows a technique for working with functions within a DLL. The second shows how to call external applications.

Working with External Functions

The Win32 API provides a wealth of functionality not found in the .NET Framework. Microsoft will eventually incorporate some of the function, but they've already said that some functionality will never appear in the .NET Framework. Consequently, your need to access the Win32 API will decrease as the .NET Framework becomes more mature, but won't ever go completely away. With this in mind, Listing 6.6 shows one technique for calling external functions. (This listing shows only the essential elements of the code. You can find the complete listing in the \Chapter 06\C#\TestNativeMethods or \Chapter 06\VB\TestNativeMethods folder of the source code located on the Sybex Web site.)

Listing 6.6   Calling External Functions

```
private void btnTest_Click(object sender, System.EventArgs e)
{
    // Create a new permission and deny access to it.
    SecurityPermission Perm;
    Perm = new SecurityPermission(SecurityPermissionFlag.UnmanagedCode);
    Perm.Deny();

    // A call to native methods, even those marked safe, should fail.
    try
    {
        Safe.Beep(2000,1000);
    }
    catch (SecurityException SE)
    {
        MessageBox.Show(SE.Message);
    }

    // This call sends the native code access outside the current method
```

```
        // and could succeed.
        try
        {
            DoMakeSound();
        }
        catch (SecurityException SE)
        {
            MessageBox.Show(SE.Message);
        }
    }

    private void DoMakeSound()
    {
        // Grant permission to make calls to unmanaged code.
        SecurityPermission Perm;
        Perm = new SecurityPermission(SecurityPermissionFlag.UnmanagedCode);
        Perm.Assert();

        // This call will succeed.
        try
        {
            Safe.Beep(1000, 1000);
        }
        catch (SecurityException SE)
        {
            MessageBox.Show(SE.Message);
        }
    }
```

In this case, the ability to call unmanaged code resides within a single secure function. The btnTest_Click() method begins by creating a SecurityPermission object that contains the SecurityPermissionFlag.UnmanagedCode flag and denying itself this permission. When the btnTest_Click() method calls the Win32 API Beep() function, the call fails. The code then calls on the DoMakeSound() method.

The DoMakeSound() method also creates a SecurityPermission object that contains the SecurityPermissionFlag.UnmanagedCode flag. In this case, it asserts the permission. A call to the Win32 API Beep() function succeeds, even though the caller, btnTest_Click(), lacks the required permission. As you can see, this example also demonstrates the power and potential problems of the Assert() method. However, the Assert() call would still fail if security conditions warranted the action—CLR can't grant rights that don't exist. For example, the application user could have a security restriction that would prevent this program from working.

Working with External Programs

The example in Listing 6.7 shows how to work with external programs. In this case, the code creates a copy of Notepad and tells it to open a file named Temp.TXT on the C: drive. You could use a technique similar to the one shown in Listing 6.6 for this task, but the example shows how to keep the program in a separate AppDomain to increase security. (The two listings in this section form one program and only show essential elements of each module. You can find a complete listing in the \Chapter 06\C#\UnmanagedAppDomain or \Chapter 06\VB\UnmanagedAppDomain folder of the source code located on the Sybex Web site.)

Listing 6.7   Accessing External Programs

```
private void btnTest_Click(object sender, System.EventArgs e)
{
    AppDomainSetup      APS;        // Domain setup information.
    Evidence            EV;         // New evidence for the domain.
    AppDomain           LoadApp;    // The application domain.
    String              WinDir;     // Windows directory.
    String[]            Args;       // Application arguments.

    // Get the Windows directory.
    WinDir =
        Environment.GetFolderPath(Environment.SpecialFolder.System);
    WinDir = WinDir.Substring(0, WinDir.LastIndexOf("\\") + 1);

    // Define the arguments.
    Args = new String[2];
    Args.SetValue(WinDir + "Notepad.EXE", 0);
    Args.SetValue(@"C:\Temp.TXT", 1);

    // Create the domain setup information.
    APS = new AppDomainSetup();
    APS.ApplicationName = "UnmanagedApp";

    // Get evidence for the domain.
    EV = AppDomain.CurrentDomain.Evidence;
    EV.AddHost(new
        SecurityPermission(SecurityPermissionFlag.UnmanagedCode));

    // Create the application domain.
    LoadApp = AppDomain.CreateDomain("RunApp", EV, APS);

    // Run the program.
    LoadApp.ExecuteAssembly(
        Application.StartupPath + @"\RunApp.EXE", EV, Args);
}
```

The code begins by creating a pointer to the Notepad.EXE file location. It places this information and the name of the file you want to open in a string array named Args. The code will pass these two arguments to the safety class.

As with any AppDomain coding task, you should define the AppDomainSetup and Evidence objects for the new AppDomain. Notice that the permissions for the new AppDomain include the ability to run unmanaged code. Once the code creates the new AppDomain, it uses the ExecuteAssembly() method to call the RunApp application. Listing 6.8 shows the contents of this program.

Listing 6.8   Using the *Process.Start()* Method

```
namespace RunApp
{
    [SecurityPermissionAttribute(SecurityAction.Assert,
        Flags=SecurityPermissionFlag.UnmanagedCode)]
    class RunWinApp
    {
        [STAThread]
        [SuppressUnmanagedCodeSecurity()]
        static void Main(String[] Args)
        {
            // Determine the number of arguments. If the number of
            // arguments is one or two, then use the Process.Start()
            // method to run the application.  Otherwise, throw an error.
            switch (Args.Length)
            {
                case 0:
                    throw new
                        ArgumentException("Provide 1 or 2 array arguments.");
                case 1:
                    Process.Start(Args.GetValue(0).ToString());
                    break;
                case 2:
                    Process.Start(Args.GetValue(0).ToString(),
                                  Args.GetValue(1).ToString());
                    break;
                default:
                    throw new
                        ArgumentException("Provide 1 or 2 array arguments.");
            }
        }
    }
}
```

The `Main()` method uses the `[SuppressUnmanagedCodeSecurity()]` attribute to ensure it can run unmanaged code, even if the caller lacks this ability. The code begins by testing the number of arguments. This is an important check for the `Process.Start()` method because you could end up with problems such as an uncontrolled program crash otherwise, which is always an invitation to a crash. To make this program completely secure, you'd also validate the arguments supplied by the caller. The "Checking the Data Range" section of Chapter 3 provides some ideas of what to check in this area. Once the program determines that the number of arguments is correct, it calls `Process.Start()` and starts Notepad with the requested file loaded.

Summary

This chapter has discussed the differences between validation and verification. You now know how each of these factors contributes toward the concept of earned trust. In addition, this chapter has demonstrated methods for working with both managed and unmanaged code in a single application. The techniques in this chapter will help you decide the level of trustworthiness each kind of code deserves given a particular set of circumstances.

Knowing about a potential security problem and actually dealing with it are two different things. The issues in this chapter are important because you need some verifiable and consistent method for handling security issues. Crackers rely on uneven security implementations and inadequate policies to gain access in situations where everything else is secure. Now is the time to put what you've learned in this chapter into practice by verifying and validating your applications.

Chapter 7 discusses an issue of particular importance given the number of distributed applications that developers are building. The data transmitted from one point of a company to another is the most important asset the company owns. Nothing is more important than the data. Consequently, using cryptographic methods to protect that data is equally important. Chapter 7 shows you how cryptography works in .NET and helps you build applications to demonstrate these techniques. You'll find that the .NET Framework is wonderfully easy to use in this regard, which makes it even more important that you secure data using cryptography whenever possible.

.NET Cryptographic Techniques

- Updating Your Machine's Cryptographic Settings

- Considering the Cryptographic Methods That .NET Supports

- Developing Applications That Encrypt and Decrypt Files

- Understanding the `System.Security.Cryptography.X509Certificates` Namespace

- Creating Applications That Use Hash Functions

Cryptography is a math-based technique for changing data from a readable to an unreadable format for transport to another location and back to a readable format when it arrives at the destination. This application feature causes a lot of consternation and you read about it all the time. In fact, you hear about this technology so often that you might be tempted to think that it's relatively new. However, cryptography has appeared in one form or another for many centuries. It's probably the oldest technology that you'll ever use with a computer and definitely the most fragile.

NOTE   This book won't provide you with a history of cryptography or all of the cryptographic technologies used throughout history. However, you can find interesting articles about cryptography during World War II at `http://www.cs.miami.edu/~harald/enigma/enigma.html` and `http://www.pbs.org/wgbh/nova/decoding/`. If you would like to read about some of the ways in which modern computer cryptography came into being, check out `http://www.turing.org.uk/turing/`. The true beginnings of cryptography are unknown, but you can read the suspected beginnings at `http://www.sans.org/rr/encryption/history.php`. If you're really interested in the historical aspects of cryptography, try the book *The Codebreakers: The Comprehensive History of Secret Communication from Ancient Times to the Internet* by David Kahn (Scribner, 1996).

Every form of cryptography relies on math to perform its task. An algorithm accepts input values and calculates an output based on those inputs. The goal is to find an algorithm and associated inputs that are so complicated that calculating the output becomes impossible. The problem is that computers constantly become faster, making a cipher (the name of the algorithm) that was perfectly safe yesterday unsafe today.

Using cryptography can create strong security, but you must still maintain a constant vigilance. As crackers devise new ways to break old encryption methods, you must upgrade to newer methods. Consequently, cryptography is a brittle technology at best—something you should suspect every time you use it. Fortunately, the .NET Framework is quite capable of accepting new cryptographic standards. As crackers break old standards, you can add new standards to your repertoire.

This chapter explores cryptographic techniques. I won't espouse a particular cryptographic standard because it's impossible to know when new standards will arrive on the scene. However, the techniques for using these ciphers will remain the same. Your code will change to use the new ciphers, but the process for using the cryptographic technique is unlikely to change.

Administering the Cryptographic Settings

One of the biggest problems you'll ever experience with cryptographic techniques is that someone will forget their password. (An employee's sudden death or departure from the company are also things to consider and just as problematic as forgetting the password.) Forgetting the password makes the data inaccessible unless you know how to crack the cipher, in which case, the cryptographic technique is useless anyway. Unfortunately, this problem isn't small or isolated to a few individuals. There's a booming market of vendors who can recover your Office documents after you lose the password used to encrypt them. Office is just one of many examples. Consequently, your first administrative task is to ensure that any cryptographic method you use is not only safe but also reversible. Usually this means retaining some type of database of account statistics in a safe (locked) location that you use only in emergencies. Many organizations call this an escrow account.

In addition to user-related administrative tasks, you may need to perform a number of other cryptographic-related tasks, such as managing the authorization store or creating certificates for your organization. The following sections look at a number of configuration tasks you should know about. At the very least, you'll want to know how to manage cryptographic classes to obtain maximum effect.

Using the Certification Authority Utility

A *digital certificate* is a series of numbers forming an identity that acts as a key to lock and unlock files, identify a particular individual or company, and perform other cryptographic tasks. It's more secure than the public/private key combination generated by the Strong Name utility (SN.EXE). The "StrongName versus Publisher Evidence" sidebar in Chapter 4 provides an overview of digital certificate issues. The "Circumventing and Fixing the Standard Check" section of Chapter 6 describes some of the problems in using a public/private key pair for code verification. In general, the public/private key pair is more secure than using nothing at all, but you can't verify the source of the key easily, nor can you validate that the code has permission to run on the host machine without a lot of extra work, such as using a hash as was shown in Chapter 6.

Many organizations do make use of third-party Certificate Authorities (CAs) to obtain digital certificates for signing their code. This is always the best approach if you intend to make your code available to third parties that don't know you or your organization. For example, this is the approach you should use when developing shrink-wrap software. However, this approach isn't necessarily cost effective for an organization that plans to send its software to a few trusted partners who know the developer well. In this case, using the CA built into server operating systems such as Windows 2000 Server or the newer Windows 2003 Server is a less expensive alternative.

The following sections provide some configuration tips developers can use to ensure that a stand-alone or enterprise CA works efficiently for in-house applications. In addition, this section describes techniques for generating your own certificates for use in code signing. This task is especially important in cryptographic applications where trust is everything.

(While it might be tempting to say that trust is only one piece of a greater whole, the greater whole doesn't matter much if you don't trust the individual or organization in the first place.)

NOTE   The CA setup for the following sections is a Windows 2000 server with all the latest patches and an enterprise CA installed. Your browser views will vary from the ones shown if you use a non-patched version of Windows 2000 or a stand-alone CA. Some of the options mentioned in the following sections aren't available to systems that lack Active Directory support or if you perform the setup using a server that isn't a domain controller. However, even with these differences, the basic concepts are the same. You still need to obtain a code-signing certificate using the server options that you do have available.

Viewing the CA Configuration

The Certification Authority Microsoft Management Console (MMC) shown in Figure 7.1 provides the means to monitor your CA setup. You won't generally use this utility to perform configuration tasks.

FIGURE 7.1:

Use the Certificate Authority console to view your certificates.

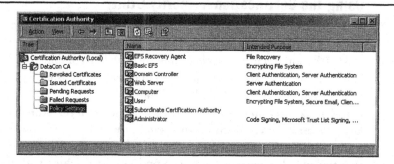

The first four folders contain certification information. Revoked certificates include those that someone has compromised or have expired because you didn't renew them. The Issued Certificates folder contains a list of certificates the system has issued and who has them. The Pending Requests folder contains a list of certificates that require approval. If you set up your system to use the default settings, this folder should be empty (except for momentary entries during an initial request). The presence of entries in the Failed Requests folder requires further investigation. When you set your CA up correctly, a certificate request from an authorized user should pass, which means that these entries normally show requests from those who lack authorization.

Of the four folders, the Issued Certificates folder is the most important. When you want to revoke an existing certificate, locate the certificate in this folder, right-click the certificate, and choose Revoke from the context menu. This folder also lets you look at the certificate by double-clicking its entry. The Certificate dialog box lets you verify the status of the certificate and the period the certificate is valid. You can also view details such as the type of public key and the issuing authority.

A quick look at the Policy Settings folder holds the promise of actually making some kind of CA change. The truth is that these entries tell you which settings are in place. However, the information is useful for making quick checks and lets you track information without exposing the information to potential change. You can use the information you see to make quick decisions. For example, double-click the Administrator entry and you'll learn that this certificate is useful for signing code.

You must perform an important developer task before going any further. Notice that most of the default certificates lack any kind of code-signing capability, with the exception of the Administrator certificate. Unfortunately, you want a code-signing certificate and it may not be such a good idea to give every programmer in your organization an Administrator certificate. Use the following steps to create a Code Signing certificate type.

1. Right-click Policy Settings and choose the New ➤ Certificate to Issue option on the context menu. You'll see a Select Certificate Template dialog box.

2. Highlight the Code Signing option and Click OK. The Certificate Authority console adds the new policy to the list.

Making CA Configuration Changes

When you want to make a change in the CA setup, you need to use the Active Directory Users and Computers console shown in Figure 7.2. Most CA changes involve policies used to manage the certificate. In addition, you can control the distribution of certificates.

FIGURE 7.2:

Use the Active Directory Users and Computers console to configure the CA.

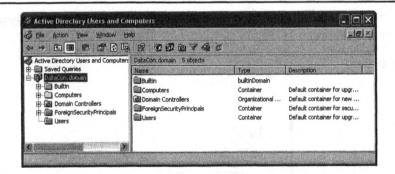

The second configuration process is the most important to a developer because any code you distribute using a certificate must be trusted on the client machine—this requirement means getting the certificate to all client machines. The following steps show how to get your CA set up to distribute the root certificate (the basis for all trust) automatically.

1. Right-click the domain entry (DataCon.domain in Figure 7.2) and choose Properties from the context menu. You'll see a domain Properties dialog box.

2. Select the Group Policy tab (see Figure 7.3). Highlight the Default Domain Policy entry and click Edit. You'll see the Group Policy dialog box.

FIGURE 7.3:

Select the Default Domain Policy entry.

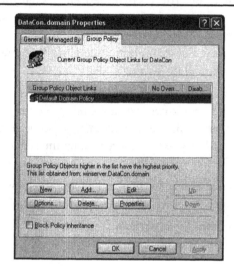

3. Select the Automatic Certificate Request Settings entry shown in Figure 7.4. This entry lets you set the certificates that the server sends to the clients in a domain automatically. Verify that there aren't any entries for the certificate that you want to automatically place on the client.

FIGURE 7.4:

Choose the Automatic Certificate Request Settings entry.

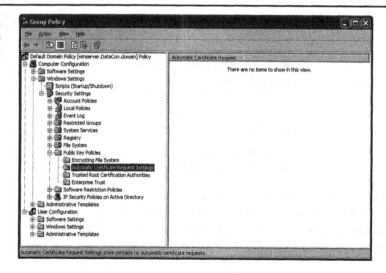

4. Right-click Automatic Certificate Request Settings and choose New ➤ Automatic Certificate Request. You'll see the Automatic Certificate Request Settings Wizard.

5. Click Next. You'll see the Certificate Template dialog box shown in Figure 7.5. The list in Figure 7.5 is generic. You can import additional entries into this list using the Import option of the Trusted Root Certification Authorities or Enterprise Trust entry of the Group Policies dialog box.

FIGURE 7.5:

Highlight the certificate you want to install automatically.

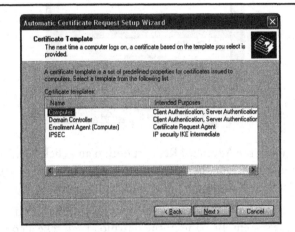

6. Select the certificate that you want to install, and then click Next.

7. Click Finish. The Wizard adds the certificate to the list shown in Figure 7.4.

Getting Your Own Certificate

At some point, you'll want your own certificate to use for programming needs. A certificate store identifies the issuing authority, making it a lot more difficult for someone to forge a key using the technique shown in the "Circumventing and Fixing the Standard Check" section of Chapter 6. The easiest way to obtain a certificate is to use your browser. The following steps show how.

1. Open your browser and access the certificate server using an URL similar to `http://YourServerName/CertSrv/Default.asp`. (The URL you type very likely points to your company's intranet site, rather than a location on the Internet.) Make sure your browser has scripting and cookies enabled (it probably will). You'll see the initial Microsoft Certificate Services Web site.

2. Select the Request a Certificate option, and click Next. You'll see a Choose Request Type screen. This is where knowledge of the various policies in the Policy Settings folder of the Certificate Authority console is helpful. Notice that the only entry is a User certificate. Double-click the User entry in the Policy Settings folder and you'll see a User Properties dialog box similar to the one shown in Figure 7.6. Notice that the User certificate doesn't include code signing. Consequently, this certificate would be useless for a developer.

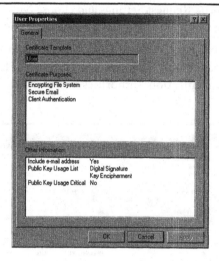

3. Choose the Advanced Request option and click Next. You'll see an Advanced Certificate Requests screen. Because you probably don't have a smart card or an existing certificate, you'll need to choose the first (default) option of filling out a form.

4. Click Next. The Web server will tell you that it's downloading an ActiveX Control to your system. Be patient; the download can take a considerable amount of time even on a high-speed network. After some time, you'll see the form shown in Figure 7.7. This is where you fill in the requirements for your certificate.

FIGURE 7.7:

Wait for the ActiveX
Control to download so
you can see this form.

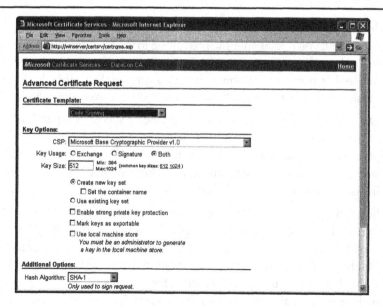

5. Select the Code Signing option in the Certificate Template field.

6. Select a Cryptographic Service Provider (CSP) from the list in the CSP field. One of the best choices is the Microsoft Strong Cryptographic Provider, but even the Microsoft Base Cryptographic Provider 1.0 works well. The various CSPs feature different options such as key length. A longer key makes the key harder to break but can also increase some factors such as code size.

7. Set the Key Usage option to Both so that you can use the Code Signing key for both needs.

8. Set the Key Size. A larger key is more secure, while a smaller key is more efficient. The minimum key size you should consider for code is 1,024, but some CSPs offer keys up to 16,384 bits in length. If your security needs are exceptional, you should also check the Enable Strong Private Key Protection option.

9. Check the Mark Keys as Exportable option. This check enables the Export Keys to File option. Check this option as well and type the name of a file in the File Name field. This step is essential because it gives you a physical key you can use as input to Visual Studio.

10. Select a Hash Algorithm option. Pay careful attention to this step. You must select one of the options that Visual Studio supports such as Secure Hashing Algorithm 1 (SHA-1) or Message Digest 5 (MD5). Don't select options such as MD2 or MD4 because you'll run into problems getting them to work right.

11. Click Submit. Internet Explorer will display a Generating Request message for a moment, and then you'll see a Create Private Key Password dialog box.

12. Type a password in the Password field, and again in the Confirm Password field. Click OK. Internet Explorer will display a success message.

Managing the Cryptographic Classes

You might not think that you have to do anything with the existing cryptographic classes. In most cases, you don't. However, you can manage the classes to produce better (or at least different) results. The following sections describe some techniques you can use to manage the cryptographic classes so that you can obtain the results you need using the least amount of code.

Deciding Which Cryptographic Object Creation Method to Use

The .NET Framework actually provides four distinct methods for creating cryptographic objects. All four methods result in the same cryptographic object, so there's no reason to use one method over another for purely result motives. However, personal taste, availability of resources, self-documentation, and efficiency of coding do play a part in the selection. Here are the four choices:

Use the New Operator   This is the easiest method of creating a cryptographic object and the one that most developers know. Using the New operator will guarantee that anyone reading your code will understand your code. The disadvantage is that this method isn't flexible. You must create a specific object that relies on a specific cryptographic technology. For example, you couldn't substitute the MD5 technique for the SHA-1 technique because this method won't handle that kind of change.

Use the Abstract Class `Create()` Method   This method requires slightly more work than using a specific provider. For example, instead of using the `DESCryptoServiceProvider` class, you'd use the Data Encryption Standard (DES) class. The advantage of using this method is that you can specify a particular DES encryption methodology, rather than use the default Cryptographic Service Provider (CSP). So, even though the code is slightly harder to read, you can use this method to extend the functionality that the .NET Framework provides.

Use the `CryptoConfig.CreateFromName()` Method   The `System.Security.Cryptography` namespace contains the `CryptoConfig` class. Because the .NET Framework doesn't attach this class to any particular cryptographic method such as MD5, SHA-1, or DES, you can use it to create any of these objects. This means the same code could work with any of the standard cryptographic methods as long as you code carefully. This particular method also supports algorithm mapping (described in the "Using Configuration Files to Map Algorithm Names" section). Algorithm mapping lets you change the result of a method call based on the content of a configuration file.

Use the `Create()` Method of an Abstract Class that Implements a Class of Cryptographic Algorithms   Use this method when you need maximum flexibility and coding efficiency isn't necessarily a concern. To use this technique, you create an object using the `Create()` method of a high-level cryptographic class such as the `System.Security` `.Cryptography.SymmetricAlgorithm` class. The resulting object provides access to all of the cryptographic methods supported by the master class. For example, the `SymmetricAlgorithm` class supports the DES, Ron's Code 2 (RC2), Rijndael, and Triple DES methods. This technique also supports algorithm mapping (described in the "Using Configuration Files to Map Algorithm Names" section).

Using Configuration Files to Map Algorithm Names

Algorithm mapping is the process you use to change the result of a call to specific cryptography classes. Normally the `DES.Create()` and `CryptoConfig.CreateFromName("DES")` method calls produce a `DESCryptoServiceProvider` object as output. However, you can change the system to output another cryptographic object by modifying the settings in the `Machine.Config` file. For example, you may want to use a third party CSP in place of the CSP provided by Microsoft. You can create this mapping so that your existing code also uses the new CSP without any changes. In short, the change modifies your code to use an updated CSP.

NOTE You can find the Machine.Config file in the \WINDOWS\Microsoft.NET\Framework\ <Version>\CONFIG folder. The examples in this section rely on the contents of the \WINDOWS\Microsoft.NET\Framework\v1.1.4322\CONFIG folder.

The Machine.Config file is XML-based. This format means that you use tags to identify major sections, elements to hold data, and attributes to modify the meanings of the tags. Here's an example of an entry that modifies the DES.Create() and CryptoConfig.CreateFromName("DES") methods. Listing 7.1 shows a typical mapping entry.

Listing 7.1:   **Mapping an Algorithm to a Class**

```
<configuration>
<!-- Bunches of other entries -->
   <mscorlib>
      <cryptographySettings>
         <cryptoNameMapping>
            <cryptoClasses>
               <cryptoClass ThirdPartyDES="ThirdPartyDESClass,
                           ThirdPartyDESAssembly,
                           Culture='en',
                           PublicKeyToken=1234567890123456,
                           Version=1.0.0.0"/>
            </cryptoClasses>
            <nameEntry name="DES"
                       class="ThirdPartyDES"/>
            <nameEntry name="System.Security.Cryptography.DES"
                       class="ThirdPartyDES"/>
         </cryptoNameMapping>
      </cryptographySettings>
   </mscorlib>
</configuration>
```

The Machine.Config file is relatively large and you shouldn't change any of the entries without knowing what they do. I prefer to place this entry at the end of the file so that I can find it easily. Placing the entry at the beginning of the file may not work because there are other definitions you need.

The first entry is the <cryptoClasses> tag. You can add more than one entry to the list. However, the example only uses one entry. The <cryptoClass> tag contains the information for the class you want to map to a particular algorithm. You can use any legitimate .NET class, even existing classes. For example, you might want to ensure that everyone uses triple DES encryption at all times, so mapping the `TripleDES` class to the `DES` class makes sense. The `<cryptoClass>` tag must include the following information:

- A string that describes the class

- The name of the assembly that contains the class

- The culture (the language and elements associated with a particular country) associated with the assembly

- A public key token associated with the assembly

- The assembly version number

The assembly must appear in the GAC. You can add the assembly to the GAC using the GACUtil utility. All of the information you need to create a class entry appears in the \WINDOWS\assembly folder as shown in Figure 7.8.

FIGURE 7.8:

Validate the information for a class entry using the assembly folder information.

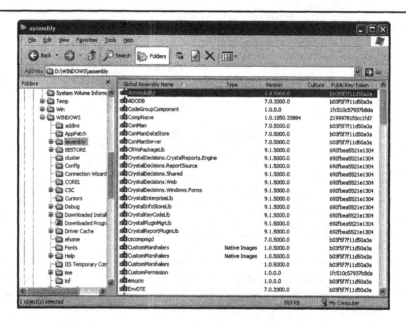

After you create and verify the `<cryptoClasses>`, you must create one or more `<nameEntry>` tags. Each `<nameEntry>` tag contains the name of an existing algorithm-associated class such as the two shown in Listing 7.1. You then use the `class` attribute to define the name of the class you want associated with the class defined by the `name` attribute.

Using Configuration Files to Map Object Identifiers (OIDs)

Some forms of data encryption rely on Abstract Syntax Notation One (ASN.1) OID entries. These entries appear as additions to the hash value and identify the maker or type of the encryption algorithm. The CSP signs both the hash value and the OID, so this added information becomes part of the signed package—making it nearly impossible for someone to change the encryption source information.

> **TIP** You'll find that companies use ASN.1 entries for more than just cryptographic work. The best place to learn about these entries is the ASN.1 Consortium at http://www.asn1.org/.

Normally, you don't need to worry about ASN.1 OIDs because Microsoft provides them for any encryption technology provided as part of .NET. In addition, most third party vendors don't use this technology. However, you might want to use an encryption technology that relies on an ASN.1 OID, making a map to that OID required.

As with the algorithm name map described in the "Using Configuration Files to Map Algorithm Names" section, you must make the map entry in the Machine.Config file. See that section for details on this file. The vendor should provide you with everything needed to create the entry. Listing 7.2 shows a typical Machine.Config OID entry.

Listing 7.2   Mapping an OID to a Class

```
<configuration>
<!-- Bunches of other entries -->
   <mscorlib>
      <cryptographySettings>
         <cryptoNameMapping>
            <cryptoClasses>
               <cryptoClass ThirdPartyDES="ThirdPartyDESClass,
                            ThirdPartyDESAssembly,
                            Culture='en',
                            PublicKeyToken=1234567890123456,
                            Version=1.0.0.0"/>
            </cryptoClasses>
            <nameEntry name="NewDES" class="ThirdPartyDES"/>
         </cryptoNameMapping>
         <oidMap>
            <oidEntry OID="1.2.3.4.5.6"
                      name="NewDES"/>
         </oidMap>
      </cryptographySettings>
   </mscorlib>
</configuration>
```

The `<cryptoClasses>` and `<cryptoClass>` tags work just like those used for an algorithm map. You can obtain the information you need from the `\WINDOWS\assembly` folder as shown in Figure 7.8. It's important to include all of the entries to ensure that CLR can identify your particular class.

The `<nameEntry>` tag doesn't reference one of the .NET Framework classes in this case. Instead, you must provide the name of the new class as it appears to the application developer. The `class` attribute associates the new class with the class definition provided by the `<cryptoClass>` tag.

The `<oidMap>` tag and its associated children associate the new class with the OID for the hashing method. The problem with this entry is that you can't readily access the information on your machine. The vendor must provide this information to you or you must find it from a third party source when using a generally accessible algorithm.

Understanding the Supported Cryptographic Methods

It's important to understand how the .NET Framework arranges the various cryptographic methods and how CLR uses them. Not every cryptographic algorithm is equal and you need to use the right algorithm for your specific need. The cryptographic hierarchy begins with the two types of cryptography in use on computers today: symmetric (`SymmetricAlgorithm` class) and asymmetric (`AsymmetricAlgorithm` class). You can't use either class directly, but these classes do form the basis for cryptographic analysis for .NET applications. In fact, these classes are basic dividers in the functionality that the .NET Framework provides.

> **NOTE**   The `System.Security.Cryptography` namespace also contains a `HashAlgorithm` class that you won't use for cryptographic purposes. See the "Circumventing and Fixing the Standard Check" section of Chapter 6 for details on using this algorithm for verifying code. You can also use this algorithm for verifying data integrity and for detecting changes to essential security elements such as digital signatures. See the "Using Hash Functions" section of this chapter for further details on other hash uses.

A symmetric algorithm relies on a single private key. Anyone who wishes to decrypt data encrypted with a certain key must have access to that key. The advantages of symmetric algorithms include relative simplicity and fast data translation speed. In addition, a symmetric algorithm tends to produce a smaller encrypted file. For example, given a 209-byte input file, the `RijndaelManaged` class produces a 224-byte encrypted result, while the Rivest, Shamir, and Adleman (RSA) class produces a 768-byte result. (See the `TempCryptA.TXT` and `TempCryptA.TXT` files in the \Chapter 07 folder located on the Sybex Web site as examples.) This is the kind of algorithm to use when encrypting personal data or transferring a large quantity of data between trusted associates. The symmetric algorithms supported by the .NET Framework include:

- DES
- RC2
- Rijndael
- TripleDES

An asymmetric algorithm relies on a public and private key pair. The cryptographic cipher relates the keys through a very large prime number, which means you can't realistically expect to guess the private key by knowing the public key. You encrypt data using the private key and use the public key to decrypt the information (or vice versa—encrypt using the public key and decrypt using the private key). The advantage of the asymmetric system is that you can give the public key out to anyone who needs to decrypt the data without making it possible for them to also encrypt data using your private key. You can also receive information from multiple sources that the senders encrypted using the public key that only you can decrypt using your private key. Consequently, an asymmetric algorithm is also more secure than a symmetric algorithm when two parties are involved (such as an email sender and a recipient). The asymmetric algorithm classes include:

- Digital Signature Algorithm (DSA)
- RSA

> **NOTE** In some cases, a cryptographic technique will combine symmetric and asymmetric methods. The cryptographic technique will exchange symmetric keys using asymmetric encrypting. Because the technique encrypts the symmetric key before transmitting it, there's little chance of someone eavesdropping and discovering this key. The two parties might use the symmetric key only during the current session, so the two parties exchange new symmetric keys for each session—increasing security. The two parties use the symmetric key to encrypt the data, making the data encryption, transferral, and decryption process faster.

Beware of the Cracked Symmetric Algorithm

It's important that you use a trustworthy algorithm to encrypt your code. This means researching the algorithm before you use it in your current project to see what the current threats to that algorithm are. Don't assume that the encryption technique you used yesterday is still fine today. For example, many people are still under the assumption that DES is safe—it isn't. This particular algorithm was cracked five years (or even more) ago.

A number of online sources chronicle the fall of the venerable DES algorithm. For example, the five-year-old Wired article at `http://www.wired.com/news/technology/0,1282,13800,00.html` states that computers of that time could break the DES encryption in about 3 days. A 1999 article from Network World Fusion (`http://www.nwfusion.com/news/1999/0120cracked.html`) shows the time has gone down to around 22 hours. The reason that Triple DES exists is that the government is trying to extend the life of this aging algorithm. You can use DES as long as you create a large key, but some people steadfastly refuse to move beyond the 56-bit key that a five-year-old computer can crack in 3 days and a modern computer can crack in a few hours. It's best to consider the DES class as the backward compatibility addition to the .NET Framework and move on from there.

Before you latch on to the TripleDES class as the solution for your problems, consider the complaints of some developers that this algorithm is extremely slow. The Network World Fusion article at `http://www.nwfusion.com/links/Encyclopedia/D/596.html` explains why. This algorithm actually encrypts the data three times—no wonder it's slow. The article also states that the National Institutes of Standards and Technology (NIST) has moved to the Advanced Encryption Standard (AES). It so happens that AES appears as the Rijndael class in the .NET Framework. Although you can use any symmetric algorithm that the .NET Framework supports natively or you add using techniques such as those shown in the "Using Configuration Files to Map Algorithm Names" section, the Rijndael class provides good value for today and is still a safe method to use. You can read more about the origins of this algorithm at `http://www.esat.kuleuven.ac.be/~rijmen/rijndael/`.

Learning about the Asymmetric Algorithm

Now that we've covered the symmetric algorithm, what do you need to know about the asymmetric algorithm? The good news is that there's little evidence to suggest that either of the asymmetric algorithms supported by the .NET Framework are even close to getting cracked. However, you're going to run into news stories that say a hacker in the Philippines recently cracked the RSA algorithm. According to articles on many sites including Slashdot (`http://slashdot.org/articles/01/02/05/1911258.shtml`), the hacker was less than successful. Unfortunately, the article is still circulating on the Internet. If you have any doubts about RSA, you can use the newer DSA algorithm instead.

The problem with the DSA algorithm is that it's less flexible than RSA and you can only use it for digital signatures. Many developers also claim that the algorithm is slower than using RSA for similar tasks. You can read a professional evaluation of DSA at `http://www.rsasecurity.com/rsalabs/faq/3-4-1.html`.

Encrypting and Decrypting Files

One of the most common tasks you can perform with cryptography is data encryption. In fact, you'll perform this task far more often than any other cryptography task (such as encrypting code or digital signatures). The .NET Framework provides access to a number of data storage methodologies. For example, you can store information in files or memory structures. The form that data takes can also vary from straight text to a variety of XML-based formats. The fact remains that you're working with data that requires protection.

The sections that follow consider a specific case of data encryption and decryption—the data file. The target is a simple text file that you'll find in the \Chapter 07 folder of the source code located on the Sybex Web site. Although the data is simple by design to make the encryption and decryption techniques clearer, the techniques shown will work with any kind of data.

Using Symmetric Cryptography

This section of the chapter shows how to encrypt and decrypt simple text using the symmetric methodology. The example uses the RijndaelManaged algorithm class based on the discussion in the "Beware of the Cracked Symmetric Algorithm" section of the chapter. Listing 7.3 shows an example of the encryption portion of the process. The decryption portion is almost the same with a few minor differences. You'll find this example in the \Chapter 07\C#\Crypto and \Chapter 07\VB\Crypto folders of the source code located on the Sybex Web site.

Listing 7.3   **Encrypting Data Using Symmetric Cryptography**

```
private void btnEncrypt_Click(object sender, System.EventArgs e)
{
    FileStream        FIn;                          // Input file.
    FileStream        FOut;                         // Output file.
    Byte[]            Data = new Byte[100];         // Temporary buffer.
    int               Counter = 0;                  // Total converted.
    int               ReadByte = 0;                 // Currently read counter.
    CryptoStream      CryptStream;                  // Cryptographic stream.
    RijndaelManaged   RM;                           // Encryption Algorithm.
    byte[] Key = {0x01, 0x02, 0x03, 0x04,           // Encryption Key.
                  0x05, 0x06, 0x07, 0x08,
                  0x09, 0x10, 0x11, 0x12,
                  0x13, 0x14, 0x15, 0x16};
    byte[] IV = {0x01, 0x02, 0x03, 0x04,            // Initialization vector.
                 0x05, 0x06, 0x07, 0x08,
                 0x09, 0x10, 0x11, 0x12,
                 0x13, 0x14, 0x15, 0x16};

    // Open the input and output files.
```

```
    FIn = new FileStream(txtInput.Text,
                         FileMode.Open,
                         FileAccess.Read);
    FOut = new FileStream(txtEncrypt.Text,
                          FileMode.OpenOrCreate,
                          FileAccess.Write);

    // Create the cryptographic stream.
    RM = new RijndaelManaged();
    CryptStream = new CryptoStream(FOut,
                             RM.CreateEncryptor(Key, IV),
                             CryptoStreamMode.Write);

    // Encrypt the file.
    while(Counter < FIn.Length)
    {
       ReadByte = FIn.Read(Data, 0, 100);
       CryptStream.Write(Data, 0, ReadByte);
       Counter = Counter + ReadByte;
    }

    // Close the open stream and files.
    CryptStream.Close();
    FIn.Close();
    FOut.Close();
}
```

No matter which symmetric encryption technology you choose, they all rely on the cipher chaining method of encryption. The encryption algorithm uses the previous cipher block in a chain of blocks to determine the encryption seed for the current block. Of course, there's no previous block for the first block of code, so you must supply a seed value for the encryption algorithm called the initialization vector (IV). Consequently, all of these encryption techniques require that you provide both a Key and an IV Byte array as basic input values. Notice how these two values work with the RM.CreateEncryptor() method. As the example shows, the CSP is part of this constructor call, so you don't use the Key and IV with the CSP, but you do use it to create the data transfer object.

WARNING   The Key and IV values shown in Listing 7.3 are for demonstration purposes only. Don't use values such as these for your own code (I chose them specifically because you shouldn't use these values). Make sure you choose unique Byte arrays for both values. Anything you can do to make it harder for a cracker to discover the input for your encrypted files is worth the effort.

As you can see from the example code, the idea is to open an input and an output file. The input file contains the plain text that you want to encrypt. After you open the two files, you need to create an algorithm object to encrypt the data and a stream for handling the encryption.

Notice the `CreateEncryptor()` method call in the `CryptoStream()` constructor. You would replace this with a `CreateDecryptor()` call in the decryption portion of the code.

After the code creates the required stream, it simply reads from the input file, encrypts the data, and sends the data to the output file. It's important to track how many bytes the input file actually contained or you'll obtain some odd results from the encryption portion of the program. Once the output is complete, you close the stream first, and then the two files. Make sure you follow this order or you'll receive an error from the application. The output file will also lose data because CLR doesn't flush the `CryptoStream` object until you close it.

Figure 7.9 shows the results of using the encryption portion of the program. Notice that the text is completely garbled (see the `TempCrypt.TXT` file). However, the decryption portion of the program proves that the original text is easy to recover (see the `TempDecrypt.TXT` file).

FIGURE 7.9:

Viewing the output of the cryptographic program shows that the text is completely garbled.

Using Asymmetric Cryptography

The asymmetric method is different from the symmetric method shown in Listing 7.3. You perform a two-step process to encrypt a file using this technique as shown in Listing 7.4. The first step is to create a key, which is actually harder than you might think. The .NET Framework provides a number of ways to perform this task, but the best way is to create a key every time you want to encrypt a file, and then find secure storage for that key for the decryption process. You'll find this example in the `\Chapter 07\C#\Asymmetric` and `\Chapter 07\VB\Asymmetric` folders of the source code located on the Sybex Web site.

Listing 7.4 **Creating a Key Pair**

```
public frmMain()
{
    String          KeyPath;        // The location of the key.
    CspParameters   Params;         // Cryptographic parameters.
    FileStream      KeyFile;        // Key disk storage.
    Char[]          KeyData;        // Key data as a Char array.
    Byte[]          KeyConv;        // Converted key data.
    StringBuilder   KeyString;      // Key data as a String.
    Int32           Counter;        // Loop counter.

    // Required for Windows Form Designer support
```

```
InitializeComponent();

// Create the key path string.
KeyPath = Application.ExecutablePath;
KeyPath = KeyPath.Substring(0, KeyPath.LastIndexOf(@"\") + 1)
        + "SpecialKey";

// Define the cryptographic parameters.
Params = new CspParameters();
Params.KeyContainerName = "TemporarySpecialKey";
Params.KeyNumber = 1;
Params.ProviderName =
    "Microsoft RSA SChannel Cryptographic Provider";
Params.ProviderType = 12;
Params.Flags = CspProviderFlags.UseMachineKeyStore;

// Detect the presence of a key pair file.
if (!File.Exists(KeyPath))
{
    // Generate a key pair.
    RSACrypto = new RSACryptoServiceProvider(2048, Params);

    // Convert the key data for storage.
    KeyData = RSACrypto.ToXmlString(true).ToCharArray();
    KeyConv = new Byte[KeyData.Length];
    for (Counter = 0; Counter < KeyData.Length; Counter++)
        KeyConv[Counter] = Convert.ToByte(KeyData[Counter]);

    // Save the key to a file.
    KeyFile = File.Open(KeyPath, FileMode.CreateNew);
    KeyFile.Write(KeyConv, 0, RSACrypto.ToXmlString(true).Length);
    KeyFile.Close();
}
else
{
    // Open the key file for reading.
    KeyFile = File.Open(KeyPath, FileMode.Open);
    KeyConv = new Byte[KeyFile.Length];
    KeyFile.Read(KeyConv, 0, (Int32)KeyFile.Length);
    KeyFile.Close();

    // Convert the key file.
    KeyString = new StringBuilder(KeyConv.Length);
    for (Counter = 0; Counter < KeyConv.Length; Counter++)
        KeyString.Append(Convert.ToChar(KeyConv[Counter]));

    // Create the key.
    RSACrypto = new RSACryptoServiceProvider(2048, Params);
    RSACrypto.FromXmlString(KeyString.ToString());
}
}
```

The code begins by creating a key path. You can store the key anywhere safe, but the example uses a file so that you can see how certain elements of the key generation work. In general, you'll need to produce a file that contains the public key to send to others, but you might want to keep the private/public key pair on your machine. It's relatively easy to use the machine's key storage for this purpose. Unfortunately, if you have to reformat the hard drive or lose contact with the machine for other reasons, the key is also lost. Although the machine's key storage is safer than using a file, it's also beneficial to create a file for the private/public key pair to store in an offsite location so you can recover your data should an emergency occur.

Next, the code creates a CspParameters object. Although this object is optional, you should create it so that you can better control the encryption process. Otherwise, the system will make all of the critical decisions for you. This object has four fields and one property that you should fill with data. Microsoft's documentation says you should look at the Windows CryptoAPI documentation for details on everything. In short, this object is almost undocumented.

The KeyContainerName property contains a simple string that identifies the key container. A single container can contain multiple keys. You would use this name if you wanted to access the key using the machine's store. If you plan to create just a disk version of the key or if you want to use the default key container, you don't need to include this value.

The KeyNumber property is the number of the key within the container. Unless you create multiple keys for a given container, set this value to 1.

The ProviderName property is where things get interesting. You must supply a specific text value—one that the system supports, but these values don't appear in the .NET documentation. The fastest way to locate these values is to look in the WinCrypt.H file found in the \Program Files\Microsoft Visual Studio .NET 2003\Vc7\PlatformSDK\Include folder. The supported names include:

- Microsoft Base Cryptographic Provider v1.0
- Microsoft Enhanced Cryptographic Provider v1.0
- Microsoft Strong Cryptographic Provider
- Microsoft RSA Signature Cryptographic Provider
- Microsoft RSA SChannel Cryptographic Provider
- Microsoft Base DSS Cryptographic Provider
- Microsoft Base DSS and Diffie-Hellman
- Microsoft Enhanced DSS and Diffie-Hellman
- Microsoft DH SChannel Cryptographic Provider
- Microsoft Base Smart Card Crypto Provider
- Microsoft Enhanced RSA and AES Cryptographic Provider

Unfortunately, not every server supports every potential CSP. Look again at Figure 7.7. The CSP field of this figure contains a list of the CSPs supported by your server and tells you which of these values you can use for your program.

The `ProviderType` field value must match the `ProviderName` field value because this is the numeric equivalent of that field. Again, you'll find the values you need in the `WinCrypt.H` file. Table 7.1 shows a list of typical values, the Visual C++ define value, and their associated strings.

TABLE 7.1: *ProviderType* Value to *ProviderName* Value Correlation

Constant	Visual C++ Define	Associated String
1	PROV_RSA_FULL	Any string so long as you use the RSA provider
2	PROV_RSA_SIG	Microsoft RSA Signature Cryptographic Provider
3	PROV_DSS	Microsoft Base DSS Cryptographic Provider
4	PROV_FORTEZZA	Used with Skipjack encryption and the Key Exchange Algorithm (KEA)—not supported by the .NET Framework
5	PROV_MS_EXCHANGE	Used with C. Adams and S. Tavares (CAST) encryption and the RSA algorithm—not supported by the .NET Framework
6	PROV_SSL	Supported by the .NET Framework for Internet applications, but not used for desktop applications
12	PROV_RSA_SCHANNEL	Microsoft RSA SChannel Cryptographic Provider
13	PROV_DSS_DH	Microsoft Base DSS and Diffie-Hellman
14	PROV_EC_ECDSA_SIG	Used for Windows CE development
15	PROV_EC_ECNRA_SIG	Used for Windows CE development
16	PROV_EC_ECDSA_FULL	Used for Windows CE development
17	PROV_EC_ECNRA_FULL	Used for Windows CE development
18	PROV_DH_SCHANNEL	Microsoft DH SChannel Cryptographic Provider
20	PROV_SPYRUS_LYNKS	Used for Windows CE development
21	PROV_RNG	Used for Windows CE development
22	PROV_INTEL_SEC	Used for Windows CE development
23	PROV_REPLACE_OWF	This entry isn't documented anywhere
24	PROV_RSA_AES	Microsoft Enhanced RSA and AES Cryptographic Provider

The `Flags` property can have one of two values from the `CspProviderFlags` enumeration. When you define a `KeyContainerName` field value, use the `UseMachineKeyStore` value as shown in the example. If you keep the `KeyContainerName` field value blank, use the `UseDefaultKeyContainer` value.

Now that you have everything needed to create a key, it's time to see if the key file exists using the `File.Exists()` method. If the file doesn't exist, the code creates a new `RSACryptoServiceProvider` object that includes the key length and the `Params` defined earlier. Windows ties the size of the key to the CSP that you use. When you're unsure as to which values you can use, look at the display in Figure 7.7, select the CSP you want to use, and view the pertinent key sizes in the Key Size field entries.

The code performs a two-step conversion of the key. First, it converts the key into an XML string. The ToXmlString() method argument determines if the CLR outputs just a public key (false) or both a public and private key (true). Second, the code converts the XML string into a Byte array. After the code changes the key data into a Byte array, it outputs it to a file for later retrieval. Figure 7.10 shows the results of the conversion. Notice that you can read the various values, which is why you want to keep this key locked in a safe place.

FIGURE 7.10:

Viewing the output of the cryptographic program shows that the text is completely garbled.

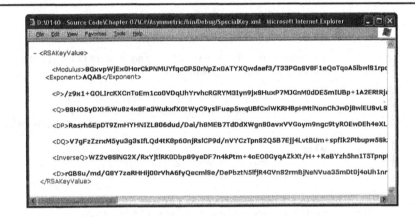

The process for reading the saved key into memory is the reverse of saving it. First, the code reads the data into a Byte array. Second, it uses the FromXmlString() method to read the information into the key.

Once you have a key, you use it to encrypt or decrypt a file. Listing 7.5 shows an example of the encryption portion of the process. The decryption portion is almost the same with a few minor differences.

Listing 7.5   **Encrypting and Decrypting Data Using Asymmetric Cryptography**

```
private RSACryptoServiceProvider RSACrypto;  // The key pair.

private void btnEncrypt_Click(object sender, System.EventArgs e)
{
    FileStream       FIn;           // Input file.
    FileStream       FOut;          // Output file.
    Byte[]           InData;        // Input buffer.
    Byte[]           OutData;       // Output buffer.
    int              Counter = 0;   // Total converted counter.
```

```
int                  ReadByte = 0;  // Currently read counter.

// Open the input and output files.
FIn = new FileStream(txtInput.Text,
                     FileMode.Open,
                     FileAccess.Read);
FOut = new FileStream(txtEncrypt.Text,
                      FileMode.OpenOrCreate,
                      FileAccess.Write);

// Initialize the buffers.
InData = new Byte[100];
OutData = new Byte[256];

// Encrypt the file.
while(Counter < FIn.Length)
{
    // Determine if we're encrypting a partial packet.
    if ((FIn.Length - Counter) < 100)
    {
        // If so, create a small encryption value.
        InData = new Byte[FIn.Length - Counter];
        ReadByte = FIn.Read(InData, 0, (Int32)(FIn.Length - Counter));
    }
    else
        // Otherwise, create a full encryption value.
        ReadByte = FIn.Read(InData, 0, 100);

    // Output the encrypted data.
    OutData = RSACrypto.Encrypt(InData, false);
    FOut.Write(OutData, 0, OutData.Length);
    Counter = Counter + ReadByte;
}

// Close the open stream and files.
FIn.Close();
FOut.Close();
}
```

Unlike the symmetric processing method, you have to be very careful about block sizes when using the asymmetric method. The code shows that the OutData array contains 256 bytes. This value depends on the size of key you use. For example, when you use a 1,024-byte key, the block size is 128 bytes. If you don't use the proper sized blocks, decryption can become impossible. The error message will simply read, "bad data." When you see this error message, check your block size to make sure you're using the correct size for the key and CSP.

The encryption process is only a little more complex than the symmetric method. You must ensure that the InData array contains only enough entries for the remaining data on the last pass.

Otherwise, the decrypted file will contain the wrong number of bytes and include corrupted data at the end of the file.

Deriving a Key from a Password

Just about every program that performs cryptography asks the user for a password. The password acts as part of the input for generating the cryptographic key. The example in this section demonstrates a method for accepting a password as input from the user and generating an encryption key from it. You won't actually use the key to encrypt data—you can see these techniques in Listings 7.3 through 7.5. Listing 7.6 shows how to use the CryptDeriveKey() method. You'll find this example in the \Chapter 07\C#\PasswordKey and \Chapter 07\VB\PasswordKey folders of the source code located on the Sybex Web site.

Listing 7.6   Generating a Key from a Password

```
private void btnTest_Click(object sender, System.EventArgs e)
{
    PasswordDeriveBytes          PDB;        // Creates the key.
    RC2CryptoServiceProvider     RC2CSP;     // Contains the key.
    Int32                        IVSize;     // Required IV size.
    Byte[]                       IV;         // Initialization vector.
    Int32                        Counter;    // Loop counter.
    StringBuilder                Output;     // An output string.
    Byte[] Seed = {0x01, 0x02, 0x03, 0x04,  // PDB seed value.
                   0x05, 0x06, 0x07, 0x08,
                   0x09, 0x10, 0x11, 0x12,
                   0x13, 0x14, 0x15, 0x16};

    // Create the PasswordDeriveBytes object.
    PDB = new PasswordDeriveBytes(txtPassword.Text, Seed, "MD5", 5);

    // Initialize the key.
    RC2CSP = new RC2CryptoServiceProvider();

    // Initialize the IV.
    IVSize = RC2CSP.BlockSize / 8;
    IV = new Byte[IVSize];
    for (Counter = 0; Counter < IV.Length; Counter++)
        IV[Counter] = Convert.ToByte(Counter);

    // Create a key.
    RC2CSP.Key = PDB.CryptDeriveKey("RC2", "MD5", RC2CSP.KeySize, IV);

    // Display a result.
    Output = new StringBuilder();
    Output.Append("The Generated Key:\r\n");
    for (Counter = 0; Counter < RC2CSP.Key.Length; Counter++)
    {
```

```
            Output.Append(RC2CSP.Key.GetValue(Counter));
            Output.Append(" ");
        }
    MessageBox.Show(Output.ToString(),
                    "Key Output",
                    MessageBoxButtons.OK,
                    MessageBoxIcon.Information);
    }
```

The example begins by creating a `PasswordDeriveBytes` object. This object is the key to working with user passwords. Notice that the constructor for this object accepts the password, a seed value (range of `Byte` values), the hash method you want to use, and the number of hash iterations used to generate the `PasswordDeriveBytes` object. The main use for the resulting object is to generate a cryptographic key based on the user's password.

The next step is to create the IV value for the cryptographic key. This value is a specific length, and you compute it by dividing the number of bits in the `RC2CSP.BlockSize` property by 8 to obtain the number of bytes for the IV Byte array. Because you don't know the size of the IV array at the outset, you need to create a method of generating byte values that you can reproduce later. The example uses a simple progression of numbers, but this isn't sufficient to keep crackers at bay.

At this point, the code generates the cryptographic key using the `CryptDeriveKey()` method. You must supply a cryptographic algorithm name, the hashing algorithm name, the size of the key you want, and the IV. For maximum compatibility, use the `RC2CSP.KeySize` property to obtain the key size. The application ends by displaying the resulting key.

Using the *System.Security.Cryptography.X509Certificates* Namespace

The `System.Security.Cryptography.X509Certificates` namespace is especially important because it provides the classes you use to work with these digital signatures. Many developers know the X.509 certificate by another name, the Public Key Infrastructure (PKI). You can learn more about the relationship between these two terms and obtain a list of associated standards at the Internet Engineering Task Form (IETF) site at `http://www.ietf.org/html.charters/pkix-charter.html`.

NOTE   The standard lists this certificate type as X.509 (with the period between the X and the 5). The .NET Framework leaves the period out, so it shows up as X509. Make sure you keep the two representations separate.

Whenever you get a certificate from a third party or generate one using a local server (see the "Getting Your Own Certificate" section for details), the resulting certificate is an X.509 certificate. However, not all X.509 certificates are created alike. The certificate still isn't quite standardized, so a certificate that works fine in some places may not work everywhere.

Double-click on a CRT (certificate) file and you'll see a General tab that contains information about the issuer and recipient of the certificate, along with dates the certificate is valid. This tab also contains an Install Certificate button you can use to install the certificate on your machine. The Details tab shown in Figure 7.11 is the one that you're interested in as a developer. Notice that this tab lists the specifics of the certificate including the all-important Version field (highlighted in the figure). To use a certificate with .NET, it must be version 3 or above.

FIGURE 7.11:

The Details tab of the Certificate dialog box provides interesting facts about the certificate and its origin.

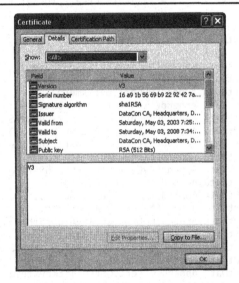

Click the Copy to File button shown in Figure 7.11 and you'll see a Certificate Export Wizard dialog box. If you want to use an exported certificate in a Visual Studio .NET program, you must export it using the DER Encoded Binary X.509 (.CER) option or the certificate will fail to load. The example shown in Listing 7.7 assumes that you've created a certificate and exported it as a Distinguished Encoding Rules (DER) encoded binary. I've included a sample certificate with the source code for this chapter. You'll find this example in the \Chapter 07\C#\X509Cert and \Chapter 07\VB\X509Cert folders of the source code located on the Sybex Web site.

Listing 7.7   Reading an X.509 Certificate

```
private void btnTest_Click(object sender, System.EventArgs e)
{
    String          CertPath;    // Certificate path.
    X509Certificate MyCert;      // The certificate.
    StringBuilder   CertData;    // Certificate information to display.

    // Create the certificate path string.
    CertPath = Application.ExecutablePath;
    CertPath = CertPath.Substring(0, CertPath.LastIndexOf(@"\") + 1)
               + "MyCertificate.CER";

    // Load the certificate.
    MyCert = X509Certificate.CreateFromCertFile(CertPath);

    // Get the certificate information.
    CertData = new StringBuilder();
    CertData.Append("Issuer Name: ");
    CertData.Append(MyCert.GetIssuerName());
    CertData.Append("\r\nName: ");
    CertData.Append(MyCert.GetName());
    CertData.Append("\r\nEffective Date: ");
    CertData.Append(MyCert.GetEffectiveDateString());
    CertData.Append("\r\nExpiration Date: ");
    CertData.Append(MyCert.GetExpirationDateString());
    CertData.Append("\r\nHash: ");
    CertData.Append(MyCert.GetCertHashString());
    CertData.Append("\r\nFormat: ");
    CertData.Append(MyCert.GetFormat());
    CertData.Append("\r\nKey Algorithm: ");
    CertData.Append(MyCert.GetKeyAlgorithm());
    CertData.Append("\r\nKey Algorithm Parameters: ");
    CertData.Append(MyCert.GetKeyAlgorithmParametersString());
    CertData.Append("\r\nPublic Key String: ");
    CertData.Append(MyCert.GetPublicKeyString());
    CertData.Append("\r\nSerial Number: ");
    CertData.Append(MyCert.GetSerialNumberString());

    // Display the information on screen.
    MessageBox.Show(CertData.ToString(), "Sample Certificate Data",
                MessageBoxButtons.OK, MessageBoxIcon.Information);
}
```

As you can see, the .NET Framework provides a wealth of information about the X.509 certificates. You can load either a DER encoded file using the CreateFromCertFile() method or a signed file using the `CreateFromSignedFile()` method. Once you load a certificate, you can use any of the methods shown to determine facts about the certificate, such as its expiration date.

The .NET Framework also makes an `X509CertificateCollection` class available. This class lets you work with cerificates in the local machine store. You can list the existing certificates, delete old certificates, or add new certificates. None of the existing classes lets you work with other machines. For example, you couldn't easily build a program to add certificates to a remote machine.

Using Hash Functions

Hash functions are an essential part of any security setup. However, hash functions are also used for nonsecurity needs too. A hash is simply a mathematical result of some type of data comparison. For example, you could use the Unicode number assigned to each character in a data file as the basis for a numeric comparison. Add all of the character number representations up and you have a unique number that identifies that file. Other files could have the same number, but that chance is infinitely small compared to the number of text files as a whole. In short, hash functions provide means of identifying the content of a file. By using the same algorithm to compare the file each time, you know whether something inside the file has changed (because the hash will change) without performing a character-by-character comparison. The output of a hash is often called a message digest because it's a representation of the data.

Most hash functions are far more complex than the one I've just described, but the idea is always the same. A hash is a numeric representation of the content of the file derived by some mathematical means. The .NET Framework lumps all hashes under the `HashAlgorithm` class. Like the `SymmetricAlgorithm` and `AsymmetricAlgorithm` classes, you can't use the `HashAlgorithm` class directly, but every class you can use derives from this one. The .NET Framework supports the following hash algorithms:

- MD5
- SHA-1
- SHA-256
- SHA-384
- SHA-512

All of these options are called cryptographic hashes because they are commonly used for cryptographic purposes. Hashes don't impart any significant security feature by themselves—they're always used in combination with something else. For example, the Digital Signature Standard (DSS) relies on the160-bit number produced by the SHA-1 hash. The SHA-256 hash is similar to the SHA-1 hash but outputs a 256-bit number instead of a 160-bit number. The larger the number, the less likely that the message digest for two documents will be the same. The SHA-384 and SHA-512 hashes require 64-bit processing and can become quite slow on a 32-bit processor. However, if you're looking for maximum cryptographic potential, the SHA-512 hash is the best to use because it outputs a 512-bit number. You can read about the merits of these various standards at `http://islab.oregonstate.edu/koc/ece575/03Project /Watson/watson-project.doc`.

The MD5 hash is a little less capable than any of the SHA variants, but it's very fast. Many people use the MD5 because it's fast and more than adequate for many needs. This hash outputs a 128-bit number, which means the message digest is also more efficient than the others discussed in this section. You can read about the merits of the MD5 hash and its predecessors at `http://www.rsasecurity.com/rsalabs/faq/3-6-6.html`.

The .NET Framework also supports keyed hashes that derive from the `KeyedHashAlgorithm` class. When using a standard cryptographic hash, anyone can verify the file because the hash function always works. A keyed hash requires a key in addition to the file. Only someone who knows the key can verify the authenticity of the file because both inputs are required. This makes keyed hashes both more secure and slower than standard cryptographic hashes. The .NET Framework supports the following keyed hashes.

- Hash-based Message Authentication Code Secure Hashing Algorithm 1 (HMACSHA1)

- Message Authentication Code Triple Data Encryption Standard (MACTripleDES)

Hashes have been used in a number of examples in the book. For example, the password example in Listing 7.6 requires use of a hash. Hashes figure so prominently in security that you'll see other examples as the book progresses.

Summary

This chapter has explored cryptography and shown you how to use the various cryptographic methods that the .NET Framework provides. It's important to remember that the ciphers you use to encrypt and decrypt data will change over time because crackers will discover ways around the old ciphers. However, some of the techniques used for cryptography today—the actual processes used to perform the work—have remained unchanged for centuries. The code you write today will require change for the cipher, but it's not likely you'll change the process used to perform the work any time soon.

Writing the code to encrypt and decrypt data is only a small part of the actual work you need to perform. Cryptography requires a concerted effort by everyone involved. Humans are often the weakest link in any cryptographic process. Consequently, you need to help create a cryptographic policy for your company and ensure that policy remains up-to-date.

Chapter 8 discusses LAN security requirements. The trade press would have you believe that the LAN is stale and that not many organizations even rely on it anymore because Web services and other new technologies are so important. The problem with this view is that most companies do rely heavily on LANs and these networks aren't secure. Chapter 8 helps you understand how you can write code with .NET that will make your network more secure. A secure network translates into an application environment that's less susceptible to the problems created by online communication.

CHAPTER 8

LAN Security Requirements

- Programming with Sockets

- Creating a Secure RPC Environment

- Developing DCOM Applications

- Creating a Secure Server Application Installation

- Creating COM+ Applications

All eyes are focused on the Internet, and therein lies a problem that will cause you more grief than any other security problem. Because the trade press hammers you day and night with news of the truly bizarre attacks that occur on the Internet, it's easy to forget that the biggest security problem lies on the network that you depend on to accomplish anything at all (including accessing the Internet in many cases). Securing the desktop is a good first step, but if you want a truly secure system, then the network has to be your next priority.

Most of the techniques discussed in the book so far work equally well in a desktop or network situation. For example, a server requires good default security (see Chapter 4) and policies (see Chapter 5). No matter if your code comes from a local or remote source, you still need to validate it to ensure that no one has tampered with it (see Chapter 6). Likewise, you need to check signatures and hashes to ensure that no tampering has occurred (see Chapter 7). If anything, a network environment merely intensifies the requirements for checking every bit of code and data for potential problems. For example, while you might leave code on your local machine unencrypted, many developers make it common practice to encrypt sensitive information for transfer over the network.

Networks also have special requirements and that's the topic of this chapter. For example, when you transfer data over the wire, you normally rely on sockets to do it. The Remote Procedure Call (RPC) protocol is old, but still used for most data transfers over a network. The fact that you've moved to .NET doesn't mean that you've also moved all your code, so you'll definitely need to work with the Distributed Component Object Model (DCOM) in some way. All of these wire concerns are important because the wire is the first place crackers try to extract data.

A secure network also requires a secure server. Again, by verifying code, users, and data, you can prevent a wide range of problems from occurring. This chapter won't discuss verification or validation issues that affect the server in general because they were already covered in Chapter 6. However, we haven't discussed some server specific technologies such as Message Queuing or COM+ yet. In addition, you should employ extra measures for server installations. The second half of the chapter discusses these server-specific issues.

NOTE   This chapter focuses on what many developers view as the Local Area Network (LAN) environment: a well-defined group of known users connected together to share resources and data. However, this term refers to computers networked within the same physical location. The techniques shown in this chapter also work well with Metropolitan Area Networks (MANs) and Wide Area Networks (WANs). A MAN is a specialized term that refers to computers that reside in the same metropolitan area. It's larger than a LAN, but smaller than a WAN, and often relies on fiber optic or other high-speed connections. A WAN is a set of remote locations networked together using anything from telephone connections, to satellites, to the Internet. The use of *LAN* throughout the chapter is generic and can refer to these other configurations. I'll use a specific reference when you need to know about exceptions.

Working with Sockets

The .NET Framework provides access to an impressive array of socket-oriented communication methodologies—everything from the typical Transmission Control Protocol/Internet Protocol (TCP/IP) communication to the Infrared Data Association (IrDA) connection used for laptops and other equipment. You can use the various classes to create both clients and listeners. In short, the System.Net.Sockets namespace contains a class for most needs. If you don't see what you need, third party vendors such as Dart (http://www.dart.com/dotnet/sslsockets_faq.asp) supply socket-based add-on products you can use.

> **NOTE**   A complete discussion of sockets and a description of how they work under Windows are outside the scope of this book. You can find a number of good Windows Sockets (WinSock) tutorials, including the documentation with MSDN. A number of online sites such as Windows Sockets: A Quick and Dirty Primer (http://world.std.com/~jimf/papers/sockets /winsock.html) and Windows Sockets Programming (http://www.snible.org /winsock/) provide good general information. The .NET Framework removes a lot of the complexity from working with sockets, so it also pays to know the .NET side of things. You'll find a good selection of TCP/IP articles on the .NET 247 site at http://www.dotnet247 .com/247reference/System/Net/Sockets/TcpClient.aspx. Another good article that shows how to use sockets is "Using .NET Sockets" at http://www.ondotnet .com/pub/a/dotnet/2002/10/21/sockets.htm.

A good understanding of the WinSock interface is important if you want to create a secure .NET application with the .Net.Sockets.Sockets class. In most cases, the sockets implementation provided by .NET merely marshals the requests to the underlying WinSock implementation (normally found in WinSock.DLL). Any flaws in the standard WinSock implementation provided by Microsoft also affect your .NET application. In addition, you have the added burden of the .NET layer to consider, so the number of potential security issues is higher for a .NET application than they are for an equivalent native application. Fortunately, the .NET Framework also provides classes that can help you maintain better control over the application environment.

The following sections describe several security measures you can use when working with sockets. Don't assume that you only use sockets with Internet applications—the LAN relies on them as well and you might find that you actually use sockets more often in a LAN environment.

Using the *SocketPermission* Class

One of the advantages of using the .NET Framework to develop applications from a security standpoint is that it contains a permission for most activities. The application can't do much if it lacks the required permissions—it can't even execute. With this in mind, the .NET Framework includes a special permission for working with sockets. The SocketPermission class doesn't grant other rights, just the right to work with sockets.

Before we get into the permission, however, let's look at some typical code. Listing 8.1 shows how to define code that makes a basic connection to the LocalHost connection (available on every computer) using the Telnet service. The `SocketPermission` entry in Listing 8.1 grants permission to use the socket. The source code also includes an example of how to deny this permission. Although the second example doesn't appear in the listing, I'll tell you about the differences in the code discussion. You'll find this example in the `\Chapter 08\C#\SocketPerm` and `\Chapter 08\VB\SocketPerm` folders of the source code located on the Sybex Web site.

Listing 8.1   **Using the *SocketPermission* Class**

```
private void btnAllow_Click(object sender, System.EventArgs e)
{
    SocketPermission  SP;             // Containt the permission object.
    Socket            LocalConnect;   // A local connection.
    IPHostEntry       HostList;       // A list of addresses.
    IPAddress         LocalHost;      // The address of the localhost.
    IPEndPoint        LocalHostEnd;   // The localhost endpoint.
    Byte[]            DataBuffer;     // Holds received data.
    Char[]            ConvertBuffer;  // Data converstion buffer.
    String            DataString;     // Human readable string.
    Int32             Counter;        // Loop counter.

    // Define the permission.
    SP = new SocketPermission(NetworkAccess.Connect,
                              TransportType.All,
                              "LocalHost",
                              23);

    // Allow the access.
    SP.Assert();

    // Define the socket.
    LocalConnect = new Socket(AddressFamily.InterNetwork,
                              SocketType.Stream,
                              ProtocolType.Tcp);

    // Get the host addresses.
    HostList = Dns.Resolve("LocalHost");

    // Create the connection.
    LocalHost = new IPAddress(HostList.AddressList[0].Address);
    LocalHostEnd = new IPEndPoint(LocalHost, 23);

    // Open the connection.
    try
    {
        LocalConnect.Connect(LocalHostEnd);
    }
    catch (SocketException SockExc)
    {
```

```
        // Display a socket error and exit.
        MessageBox.Show("Socket Error\r\n" + SockExc.Message,
                        "Socket Exception",
                        MessageBoxButtons.OK,
                        MessageBoxIcon.Error);
    return;
}
catch (SecurityException SE)
{
    // Display a security error and exit.
    MessageBox.Show("Secuirty Error\r\n" + SE.Message,
                    "Secuirty Exception",
                    MessageBoxButtons.OK,
                    MessageBoxIcon.Error);
    return;
}

// Display the connected status.
if (LocalConnect.Connected)
    MessageBox.Show("Connected", "Connection Status",
                    MessageBoxButtons.OK,
                    MessageBoxIcon.Information);
else
{
    MessageBox.Show("Connection Failed", "Connection Status",
                    MessageBoxButtons.OK,
                    MessageBoxIcon.Information);
    return;
}

// Telnet will send some initial options. Clear these options.
DataBuffer = new Byte[LocalConnect.Available];
LocalConnect.Receive(DataBuffer);

// Load the Are You There? command and send it.
DataBuffer = new Byte[2];
DataBuffer[0] = 255;
DataBuffer[1] = 246;
LocalConnect.Send(DataBuffer);
LocalConnect.Poll(1000, SelectMode.SelectRead);

// Read the answer to the question.
DataBuffer = new Byte[LocalConnect.Available];
LocalConnect.Receive(DataBuffer);

// Convert it to a string.
ConvertBuffer = new Char[DataBuffer.Length];
for (Counter = 0; Counter < DataBuffer.Length; Counter++)
    ConvertBuffer[Counter] = Convert.ToChar(DataBuffer[Counter]);
DataString = new String(ConvertBuffer);

// Display the result.
MessageBox.Show("Are you there?" + DataString, "Query Result",
                MessageBoxButtons.OK, MessageBoxIcon.Information);
```

```
    // Close the connection.
    LocalConnect.Close();
}
```

The code begins by declaring and defining a `SocketPermission` object. Unlike many of the other permissions discussed in the book, this permission is very specific. You must provide input that determines how the program uses sockets. The first argument determines whether the program will act as a client or server. Selecting the `NetworkAccess.Connect` value means the permission acts on behalf of the client. On the other hand, selecting the `NetworkAccess.Access` value lets the code listen for incoming requests and act as a server. The second argument defines the method of communication. The example uses `TransportType.All`, but you could also select a specific transport methodology such as TCP or User Datagram Protocol (UDP). The permission is also specific to a particular host. In this case, the code makes a connection to LocalHost (third argument) on port 23 (fourth argument). The specific nature of this input means you'll likely define multiple permissions and combine them to provide a permission list.

Once the code creates the `SocketPermission` object, it uses the `Assert()` or `Deny()` method to allow or deny access. However, you'll notice that nothing happens right away. Follow the code with the debugger and you'll notice the code can create the `Socket` object, resolve the `LocalHost` address using the `Dns.Resolve()` method, and even create the connection by defining an `IPAddress` and `IPEndPoint` object. None of these actions actually involves using the sockets, so there's no security breach. However, the security breach does occur when the code executes the `LocalConnect.Connect()` method. Notice that the example code catches both `SocketException` and `SecurityException` errors. Proper security and good coding practice require that you handle both. If the `LocalConnect.Connect()` method fails for either reason, there's a possibility of unauthorized access.

The example program relies on the Telnet service. If the program fails with a socket error, it's usually an indicator that the Telnet service is stopped—you need to verify that Windows has started the Telnet service. The Services snap-in appears in Figure 8.1. Right-click the Telnet service shown in the figure and choose Start from the context menu. Many machines have this service set to Manual so it doesn't start automatically for security reasons. Telnet does offer a security opening that many crackers have used to gain entrance in the past, so setting this service to Manual if you don't need it is always a good idea.

FIGURE 8.1:

Make sure you start the Telnet service before you run the program.

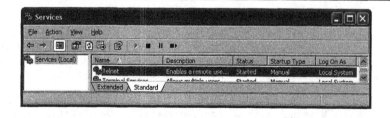

The program code continues by testing the connected state of the code and then sending and receiving some information. It's important to consider the effect of flag options when you work with the `Send()` or `Receive()` methods. For example, sending a message with the `SocketFlags` `.DontRoute` flag means that you can determine precisely where a message goes without worrying that the server will route it elsewhere. Some exploits depend on the router's sending a message to another location, such as the cracker's client or server. Likewise, including the `SocketFlags` `.OutOfBand` flag can open your client up to unexpected data. A number of exploits make use of out-of-band (OOB) data. The server sends and the client receives OOB data independently of normal data (the data sent by your application). The cracker can use this extra channel to send damaging code. To see the effects of one of these exploits, read the Wired article at `http://www` `.wired.com/news/technology/0,1282,3809,00.html`. Of course, OOB does have a legitimate use—it enables your application to handle error (or emergency) messages.

The `"Are you there?"` command is an easy way to test a Telnet connection. In this case, the program displays an answer of `[Yes]` when successful. It's not within the scope of this book to tell you about all of the Telnet commands and options. You can learn more about these features in Microsoft Knowledge Base article Q231866. This source is unfortunately incomplete. Look at the Rexx Sockets to Telnet Session site (`http://w3.hethmon` `.com/os2isp/1998/Aug/Msgs/12w03532.html`) for a list of some commands and options that Microsoft doesn't document. You should also view the original standard, RFC854, at `http://www.faqs.org/rfcs/rfc854.html`.

WARNING Some developers make the mistake of thinking that a secure desktop, a secure wire, and a secure server equate to a secure computing environment. Unfortunately, even the large companies are still making this assumption. For example, consider the recent InfoWorld article where the Windows Media Player required a patch so it inspects incoming data more carefully (`http://www.infoworld.com/article/03/05/07/HNmediapatch_1.html`). You must verify and validate every part of the communication, including the data. A cracker has no rules about how a virus gets onto your system—any hole will do.

Using the Secure Socket Layer (SSL) Protocol

Many developers associate SSL with the Internet. Web servers use this protocol when you type HTTPS in the URL rather than HyperText Transfer Protocol (HTTP). Depending on how the network administrator sets up the Web server, using this special protocol designation automatically creates a secure connection. However, don't assume that this protocol is only for use on an Internet connection. Although the use of HyperText Transfer Protocol Secure (HTTPS) sockets will cost you some application performance, using it on a local intranet is also helpful. Local connections should be just as secure as those you use on the Internet.

In addition to the obvious Web connections, SSL is also an option for more traditional communication. For example, SSL is one of the options that you can choose when setting security up for a message queue. The `Message.AuthenticationProviderType` property relies on the `CryptographicProviderType` enumeration, which includes SSL as one of the options you can choose.

Unfortunately, SSL support is far from universal in the .NET Framework. For example, you can't use SSL with the `NetworkCredential` class explained in the "Using the `System.Net .NetworkCredential` and `System.Net.CredentialCache` Class" section of the chapter. For the most part, SSL is limited to Internet communication or communication that could occur over the Internet. The point to remember is that an intranet, which is an internal network, can use SSL too, making this particular protocol quite versatile. (An intranet uses most of the same technologies and processes as the Internet; however, the functionality differs in that an intranet is private to a company and not exposed to the public.)

Using the *System.Net.NetworkCredential* and *System.Net.CredentialCache* Classes

The `System.Net.NetworkCredential` class let's you store security information about a user in a compact form and use the resulting object to access resources locally and on a network. You can use the resulting object for basic, digest, Windows NT LAN Manager (NTLM), and Kerberos authentication. This object contains a single credential, which means that you need one object for each unique network object that you want to access. Of course, if the user has a single password for all network resources, then you only need one credential. In addition to the username and password, a credential can also include the user's domain.

The `System.Net.CredentialCache` class works with the `NetworkCredential` class to store multiple credentials in one object. Each credential is associated with a particular resource using a Uniform Resource Identifier (URI). The Microsoft examples tend to associate this class with Internet resources. However, a URI can also include local drives, network drives, or any other resource that you can identify with a URI. Listing 8.2 shows an example of how to use the `CredentialCache` and `NetworkCredential` classes together. You'll find this example in the `\Chapter 08\C#\Credential` and `\Chapter 08\VB\Credential` folders of the source code located on the Sybex Web site.

Listing 8.2   **Using the *CredentialCache* and *NetworkCredential* Classes**

```
private void btnTest_Click(object sender, System.EventArgs e)
{
    NetworkCredential OneCred;    // A single credential.
    CredentialCache   CredCache;  // A group of credentials.
    WebRequest        WebReq;     // The access request.
    WebResponse       RespData;   // Response data.
```

```
Stream          DataStream; // The file data.
StreamReader    SR;         // The I/O stream.

// Clear the output.
txtOutput.Text = "";

// Create the network credential.
OneCred = new NetworkCredential(txtUsername.Text, txtPassword.Text);

// Create the credential cache.
CredCache = new CredentialCache();

// Add the credential.
CredCache.Add(new Uri(txtURI.Text), "Basic", OneCred);
CredCache.Add(new Uri(txtURI.Text), "Digest", OneCred);
CredCache.Add(new Uri(txtURI.Text), "NTLM", OneCred);
CredCache.Add(new Uri(txtURI.Text), "Kerberos", OneCred);

// Make the request.
WebReq = WebRequest.Create(txtURI.Text);
WebReq.Credentials = CredCache;

// Get the response.
RespData = WebReq.GetResponse();

// Get the data.
DataStream = RespData.GetResponseStream();
SR = new StreamReader(DataStream);
txtOutput.Text = SR.ReadToEnd();
}
```

This example program is interesting because it lets you retrieve the text content of any URI. It works equally well with the text file on your local drive as it will with a Web site. Of course, the program can't access resources that the WebRequest class can't access. In addition, it doesn't work particularly well with binary files. The program doesn't crash, but the output is understandably less than readable.

One of the secrets of this program is that it lets you enter a username and password for the resource. This information doesn't have to be the same as your normal name and password—it can be specific to that resource. The example creates the NetworkCredential object using the username and password as input. The constructor for this class also accepts input such as a domain name. The example doesn't provide this functionality.

After the code constructs a CredentialCache object named CredCache, it uses the CredCache .Add() method to add the credential to the cache. The cache makes the credential URI specific and requires a specific authentication method. The example shows how to add multiple authentication methods to the cache for the same URI and credential. The WebRequest object will evaluate the credentials in order, so you should place them in order of preference. The order in the example is basic, digest, NTLM, and finally Kerberos.

When you access a secured site, the code will fail at the `WebReq.GetResponse()` method. This call is the first time that the code actually accesses the resource. Consequently, you'll want to surround this call and the remaining data handling statements in a `try...catch` statement for error handling purposes. The example doesn't include this code for the sake of clarity.

Understanding RPC Security

The Remote Procedure Call (RPC)—a protocol that defines the set of rules used to initiate, perform, and end a data communication—is the basis of all networked application communication. Whenever a local application requires access to the services provided by code on another machine, it must use some type of RPC to obtain those services. The term *RPC* is somewhat generic because both DCOM and Common Object Request Broker Architecture (CORBA) rely on an RPC. Of course, DCOM relies on the Distributed Computing Environment (DCE) RPC supported by the Open Software Foundation (OSF). DCOM and CORBA can't communicate because they rely on a different RPC—more precisely, they rely on a different set of rules (or protocol) when communicating.

You might wonder how this discussion affects the security of your application. The protocol you choose for communication between applications—the RPC—defines the security issues you must consider. The .NET Framework supports both DCOM and the Simple Object Access Protocol (SOAP)—the differences between the two from a security perspective are nothing less than astounding.

> **NOTE** Earlier versions of the SOAP specification defined this term as Simple Object Access Protocol. Starting with the 1.2 version of SOAP, the implementers changed the definition to Service Oriented Application Protocol (SOAP). Because the 1.2 version of the protocol hasn't been accepted and the older definition is commonly in use, this book uses Simple Object Access Protocol as the definition for SOAP.

DCOM is the selection of choice for non-Internet communications because it includes security as part of the protocol. You can set a number of DCOM security measures using the DCOM Configuration Tool (DCOMCnfg). The security measures include encryption and various levels of authentication. Unfortunately, this utility only works for unmanaged out-of-process servers. Your managed component is still accessible through DCOM, but you'll need to include security features for it as part of the program code (as usual). Even with the lack of managed component configuration, DCOM is relatively secure compared to other RPCs. The DCOM Configuration Tool appears in the DCOM Config folder of the Component Services console located in the Administrative Tools folder of the Control Panel when using Windows XP. See the "Using the DCOMCnfg Utility" section of Chapter 15 for details.

SOAP is the selection of choice for Internet communications for many companies because older technologies such as DCOM are binary and use multiple ports. SOAP is XML-based and relies on the same ports as standard HTTP or Simple Mail Transfer Protocol (SMTP) for communication (it's possible to use other transport protocols, but these are the two most common protocols in use now). Obviously, there are no restrictions of the ports that SOAP can use, but the use of a single standard port makes firewall setup considerably easier. Text data transfer makes it easier for the recipient to scan the data for potential viruses. However, SOAP has no built-in security and it doesn't appear that it will have good security any time soon. The only way around this problem is to encrypt your data and send it using Base64 encoding (this encoding technique helps you send binary data using a standard text message). (See the article entitled "How Does Base64 Encoding Work?" at `http://email.about`
`.com/library/weekly/aa070201a.htm` for details.)

It's important to understand the two types of RPC support supplied by the .NET Framework because you can secure DCOM easily, but SOAP requires a lot of work. (See some of the reasons for the difficulty in the article entitled "Schneier worried about SOAP security" at `http://www.xmlhack.com/read.php?item=1541`.) This chapter discusses the DCOM RPC and the security measures you can use with it. To learn more about SOAP security, read the "Working with WS-Security" section of Chapter 11. It discusses both the Microsoft solution to the problem and the World Wide Web Consortium (W3C) solution, which is the SOAP Security Extensions standard.

Working with DCOM

DCOM is one of the oldest methods for performing object communication across machine boundaries. When a client application attempts to instantiate a component, Windows looks the entry up in the registry. This entry can point to another machine, in which case, Windows calls on DCOM to make the connection. DCOM is a wire protocol (an RPC)—it affects communication between two machines over the network wire (no matter how long that wire might be). In fact, DCOM is the basis for COM+ communication. You can read more about DCOM at `http://msdn.microsoft.com/library/en-us/dndcom/html/msdn_dcomtec.asp`. Learn more about how COM+ uses DCOM as a wire protocol at `http://www.microsoft`
`.com/msj/0398/dcom.aspx`.

The sections that follow won't teach you DCOM basics. You need to know about DCOM and understand how it works before these sections will prove very helpful. However, these sections will help you understand how DCOM and the .NET Framework interact to a certain extent, especially in the area of security. The sections also provide a little general information because you need it to know how the security features work.

Maintaining Control with COM Attributes

One of the best security guidelines you can follow is to maintain control over the environment. The .NET environment is completely different from the COM environment, which means you have to exercise extreme care if you want to maintain a secure server. COM uses an entirely different set of rules from the ones you've used with the .NET Framework. Consequently, you need to address some compatibility and maintainability issues when working with COM in a managed environment.

> **NOTE**   The use of COM in this section is generic. The attributes described also affect DCOM and COM+ applications.

One of the first problems that you'll need to consider is how to create a managed version of a COM interface. The best way to do this is to add one or more of four COM interface attributes to the interface description. These attributes tell the compiler to add information to the assembly that it wouldn't normally provide. The following list tells you about each of the attributes.

[ComImport]   This attribute tells the compiler that the interface is based on a COM interface with the same name. The .NET environment will actually import the COM definition for you. To use this attribute, the class in question must derive from Object, which means that many COM interfaces won't work with this attribute. Make sure you read the documentation for the interface completely. Always use the [ComImport] attribute with the [Guid] attribute—you must specify the GUID of the COM class that the interface will use. Finally, the class must not have any members—the .NET environment creates the required public constructor (without any parameters) automatically. In sum, this is a fast way to create an interface definition, but it's limited.

[InterfaceType]   This attribute describes the type of exposure to provide for the interface when exposed to COM. The acceptable values include dual, IUnknown, and IDispatch. Generally, implementing a dual interface is best because older versions of Visual Basic rely on IDispatch, while older versions of Visual C++ rely on IUnknown. However, you can make the component slightly smaller by implementing one interface or the other if the component has a specific target environment.

[ClassInterface]   This attribute tells the compiler that it should expose a particular class as an interface definition to COM callers. You use this attribute as part of a class/interface pair, as shown in Listing 8.3 (see the "Developing a Component with Attributes" section). In general, you expose the interface, but keep the class implementation hidden. This attribute helps keep the class hidden. Of course, you can also use it expose the class directly (as in the [InterfaceType] attribute description).

[Guid]   This attribute assigns a globally unique identifier (GUID) to the interface. This must be the same GUID used by the COM unmanaged counterpart. If you aren't implementing an existing interface, then use the GUIDGen utility to create a new GUID. Using the [Guid] attribute isn't mandatory, but it should be to ensure that the GUID for your component remains consistent.

Component Management Considerations for GUIDs

Here's an important housekeeping issue for COM+ components. Using .NET components that lack the [Guid] attribute with COM+ could create a mess that you never dreamed possible in the registry. A globally unique identifier (GUID) provides a method for unmanaged applications to identify your component. The GUID must remain the same if you want to use any of the calls that rely on the GUID to instantiate the component. Therefore, the first reason to use the [Guid] attribute is to ensure that you can document the GUID for unmanaged application calls that require it.

However, the importance of using the [Guid] attribute doesn't end with simple identification. Another reason to use the [Guid] attribute is to keep your development machine reasonably clean. Every time you register a component, the registration application makes entries in the registry. If you don't assign a GUID to the component, the Common Language Runtime (CLR) will select a new GUID each time automatically for you. CLR assigns this GUID at random and the GUID won't be the same from registration to registration.

Theoretically, unregistering the component removes the registry entry, but experience shows otherwise. In some cases, developers have ended up with dozens of entries for the same component in the registry, all of which required manual removal. Trying to find all of the entries for a complex component is time consuming and error prone. These leftover entries can act as breadcrumbs for someone trying to discover information about your system, so cleaning them up isn't optional.

COM+ also requires the [Guid] attribute for another reason. Imagine that you're using servers in a cluster and that each server has a copy of your component installed on it. If the component doesn't use the [Guid] attribute, each server could have a registry entry for the component under a different GUID, which effectively means that each server has a unique version of your component. This little problem makes it impossible for load balancing to work properly because COM will view each component as being different. In sum, even though every server has a copy of the same component, load balancing will see only one copy of the component on one server and won't work as intended.

Developing a Component with Attributes

Developing a secure component means controlling every aspect of that component, including the GUID and the method of interface exposure. In many ways, the entire issue of security rests on control. You control exposure to ensure that only those with the proper access can use your code. Listing 8.3 shows a typical example of a managed version of the COM interface. When you compile and register this component, it will appear to any client as a COM component. The important thing is that you've maintained control over the environment so that the component works as intended without side effects. You'll find this example in the \Chapter 08\C#\DCOMComp and \Chapter 08\VB\DCOMComp folders of the source code located on the Sybex Web site.

Listing 8.3   **Using Attributes in a Managed Component**

```
namespace DCOMComp
{
    [Guid("EA82646C-2531-42ff-AABF-55028FE0B0B5"),
     InterfaceType(ComInterfaceType.InterfaceIsDual)]
    public interface IMathFunctions
    {
        Int32 DoAdd(Int32 Value1, Int32 Value2);
        Int32 DoSubtract(Int32 Value1, Int32 Value2);
        Int32 DoMultiply(Int32 Value1, Int32 Value2);
        Int32 DoDivide(Int32 Value1, Int32 Value2);
    }

    [Guid("0C4340A2-C362-4287-9A03-8CDD3D1F80F6"),
     ClassInterface(ClassInterfaceType.None)]
    public class MathFunctions : IMathFunctions
    {
        public Int32 DoAdd(Int32 Value1, Int32 Value2)
        {
            return Value1 + Value2;
        }

        public Int32 DoSubtract(Int32 Value1, Int32 Value2)
        {
            return Value1 - Value2;
        }

        public Int32 DoMultiply(Int32 Value1, Int32 Value2)
        {
            return Value1 * Value2;
        }

        public Int32 DoDivide(Int32 Value1, Int32 Value2)
        {
```

```
            return Value1 / Value2;
        }
    }
}
```

To build this component (or any component that will interact with COM), you need to construct the interface first. As you can see from Listing 8.3, the `IMathFunctions` interface simply lists the public members of the `MathFunctions` class. After you type the `MathFunction` declaration, press Tab (Visual Studio will prompt you to do this) and Visual Studio will automatically populate the class with the required public methods.

Notice that the example code uses both the `[InterfaceType]` and `[ClassInterface]` attributes. The `ComInterfaceType.InterfaceIsDual` argument tells the compiler to make the `IMathFunctions` interface available to both `IDispatch` and `IUnknown` users. The `Class-InterfaceType.None` value tells the compiler to keep the class interface hidden. Not only is this a good practice for making your component easier to use, but it also makes the component more secure because unmanaged code will have a harder time seeing the implementation details of your component.

Some developers discount the benefit of giving the component a strong name, but that's a mistake. Even if you don't intend to provide global access to the component by registering it in the Global Assembly Cache (GAC), the strong name tends to ensure that no one modifies your code. See the "Circumventing and Fixing the Standard Check" section of Chapter 6 for a discussion of potential problems with the security that the .NET Framework provides for code. The solutions in Chapter 6, such as using a hash stored in a secret location, work even better with components than they do with applications because components tend to change less often (therefore, the secret hash remains valid longer).

You must register this component with the registry if you intend to use it with unmanaged code. Use the **RegAsm DCOMComp.DLL /tlb:DCOMComp.TLB** command at the command prompt to perform the registration. To unregister the component, use the **RegAsm DCOMComp.DLL /unregister** command. The **GACUtil -i DCOMComp.DLL** command lets you add the assembly to the GAC so that it's available for global use. Likewise, the **GACUtil -u DCOMComp** removes the component from the GAC (notice there's no file extension used with the removal command. Always unregister an old version of a component and remove it from the GAC before you install a new version of the component on a machine.

Creating a Test Application

It's important to consider the client that the component in Listing 8.3 targets. If you simply wanted to create a component for a .NET application, you'd use the standard procedures to do it and then rely on the remoting services that .NET provides to provide access. However, this section of the book is about using DCOM and allowing unmanaged applications to interact with your managed component in the safest manner possible. Listing 8.4 shows a typical unmanaged code implementation with full security using Visual C++. You'll find this example in the \Chapter 08\C#\DCOMCompTest folder of the source code located on the Sybex Web site.

Listing 8.4   **Safely Calling .NET Components from Unmanaged Code**

```cpp
void CDCOMCompTestDlg::OnBnClickedTest()
{
    IMathFunctions*    MF;            // Object pointer.
    COAUTHIDENTITY     UserInfo;      // User identity information.
    COAUTHINFO         Authorize;     // Component authorization.
    COSERVERINFO       ServInfo;      // Server information structure.
    MULTI_QI           Comps;         // Return container for interface.
    long               Result;        // Calculation result.
    CString            Output;        // Output from call.

    // Initialize the object and COM.
    MF = NULL;
    CoInitialize(NULL);

    // Set the user information.
    ZeroMemory (&UserInfo, sizeof (UserInfo));
    UserInfo.Domain = (USHORT*)OLESTR("YourDomain");
    UserInfo.DomainLength = strlen("YourDomain");
    UserInfo.Password = (USHORT*)OLESTR("YourPassword");
    UserInfo.PasswordLength = strlen("YourPassword");
    UserInfo.User = (USHORT*)OLESTR("YourName");
    UserInfo.UserLength = strlen("YourName");
    UserInfo.Flags = SEC_WINNT_AUTH_IDENTITY_UNICODE;

    // Set the authorization information.
    ZeroMemory (&Authorize, sizeof (Authorize));
    Authorize.dwAuthnLevel = RPC_C_AUTHN_LEVEL_CONNECT;
    Authorize.dwAuthnSvc = RPC_C_AUTHN_WINNT;
    Authorize.dwAuthzSvc = RPC_C_AUTHZ_NONE;
    Authorize.dwCapabilities = EOAC_NONE;
    Authorize.dwImpersonationLevel = RPC_C_IMP_LEVEL_IMPERSONATE;
    Authorize.pAuthIdentityData = &UserInfo;
    Authorize.pwszServerPrincName = NULL;

    // Create the server information structure.
    ZeroMemory (&ServInfo, sizeof (ServInfo));
    ServInfo.pwszName = L"Winserver";
    ServInfo.pAuthInfo = &Authorize;

    // Create the interface container.
    Comps.pIID = &IID_IMathFunctions;
```

```
        Comps.pItf = NULL;
        Comps.hr = 0;

        // Instantiate the object.
        CoCreateInstanceEx(CLSID_MathFunctions,
                           NULL,
                           CLSCTX_REMOTE_SERVER,
                           &ServInfo,
                           1,
                           &Comps);

        // Cast the returned interface to a local object.
        MF = (IMathFunctions*)Comps.pItf;

        // Perform the addition.
        Result = MF->DoAdd(1, 2);

        // Display the result.
        itoa(Result, Output.GetBuffer(10), 10);
        Output.ReleaseBuffer(-1);
        Output = "1 + 2 = " + Output;
        AfxMessageBox(Output);

        // Uninitialize COM.
        CoUninitialize();
    }
```

Overall, this is a standard call to a component using Visual C++. The important piece of information for this book is the security setup at the beginning of the listing. Many developers don't set any security on components—they make them available to the Everyone group because they feel that secure access is too much trouble. Even with Visual C++, which is notoriously difficult to use for writing code, you can set up secure access with relatively few steps.

Authorization centers on the three data structures shown in the code. The COAUTHIDENTITY data structure contains the user's name, password, and domain name. I haven't used real values in the listing for the obvious reason—my name and password would never work on your system. The COAUTHINFO data structure contains information on how to authorize the user. The example provides standard values that you can use for most situations when working with a managed component. Finally, the COSERVERINFO structure provides the name of the server and packs the rest of the authorization information. In short, security is only mildly difficult and you should use it with every component you create.

If you decide to use this example on a single machine, you'll need to make two changes to the CoCreateInstanceEx() function call. Change the CLSCTX_REMOTE_SERVER entry to CLSCTX_ALL. This change allows local access. In addition, change the &ServInfo entry to NULL. You don't need to provide server information for local component access.

Developing a Secure Server Application Installation

Many developers fail to realize that their development server is a server. If the server has any contact at all with other machines, it can become a source of possible contamination. A recent DevX article (http://www.devx.com/SummitDays/Article/6699) points out the substantial problems of having any server with security problems attached to the network. Microsoft Best Practices (http://www.microsoft.com/technet/security/bestprac/mcswebbp.asp) also underscore the issues of development and other rogue servers that aren't secure. For this reason, your development server must have all of the required security updates and patches installed (see the "Poorly Patched Systems" section of Chapter 1 and the "Dealing with Patches" section of Chapter 2 for details). Any other course of action almost ensures that you'll have security problems.

You should be concerned about patching your development server for other reasons. When you test an application that other people in the company will use, you need to test it in the same environment that they'll use. Otherwise, your testing won't reflect the user environment. Flawed environment testing can lead to all kinds of interesting and difficult to find problems. For example, you might write the program to work around a known problem with the server. If Microsoft issues a patch that fixes that problem and the network administrator installed the patch on the production machines, your program might not work as anticipated. The patch fixes the problem that you anticipated and corrected in your program. Because Microsoft support assumes that you have all patches installed, you won't find much help from them either.

Working with COM+

The .NET Framework provides full support for COM+. In fact, if you want to create a distributed component that works equally well for managed and unmanaged clients, this is the way to do it. When using COM+ 1.5 (supported on Windows XP and the Windows 2003 Server), you can even make your COM+ application into a Web service by making extremely small changes to the COM+ application setup. In short, you can create a local and remote access setup using relatively little code and few setups. Unlike other technologies, you don't need separate component setups for each need—one setup does everything. (I'm not saying that COM+ is easy; it's just better than anything Microsoft produced in the past.) Of course, all of this functionality comes at the price of increased security needs.

NOTE   This section doesn't provide a description of COM+, but does describe security concerns for COM+ in a .NET environment completely. I'm assuming that you already have some knowledge of how COM+ works with the .NET Framework. If you need a good .NET COM+ reference, my book, *COM Programming with .NET* (Microsoft Press, 2003) contains everything you need. This book also includes message queuing examples, so you can see how disconnected applications work with .NET.

The following sections look only at COM+ security. Reading them won't make you a COM+ wizard. However, you'll find that even security can become interesting when you don't do a little advance planning. These sections help you get your component started in the right direction.

Creating a COM+ Component

From a functional perspective, the component in this example isn't much different from the one shown in Listing 8.3. In fact, I purposely made them similar for comparison purposes. Listing 8.5 shows a version of the MathFunctions class designed to work in a COM+ environment. Notice that I changed the [Guid] attributes to ensure this component doesn't clash with the one in the previous example. You'll find this example in the \Chapter 08\C#\COMPlusComp and \Chapter 08\VB\COMPlusComp folders of the source code located on the Sybex Web site.

Listing 8.5   Creating Math Function Methods for the COM+ Environment

```
// Control the COM+ access requirements.
[assembly: ApplicationAccessControl(
    true,
    Authentication = AuthenticationOption.Call,
    AccessChecksLevel = AccessChecksLevelOption.ApplicationComponent,
    ImpersonationLevel = ImpersonationLevelOption.Default)]

namespace COMPlusComp
{
    [Guid("19D3ED98-1F80-4983-89CA-CA84FD054110"),
     InterfaceType(ComInterfaceType.InterfaceIsDual)]
    public interface IMathFunctions
    {
        Int32 DoAdd(Int32 Value1, Int32 Value2);
        Int32 DoSubtract(Int32 Value1, Int32 Value2);
        Int32 DoMultiply(Int32 Value1, Int32 Value2);
        Int32 DoDivide(Int32 Value1, Int32 Value2);
    }

    [Guid("A4A59B2B-08FC-48d7-9D56-F9EA915242EE"),
     ClassInterface(ClassInterfaceType.None)]
    public class MathFunctions : ServicedComponent, IMathFunctions
    {
        public Int32 DoAdd(Int32 Value1, Int32 Value2)
        {
            return Value1 + Value2;
        }

        public Int32 DoSubtract(Int32 Value1, Int32 Value2)
        {
            return Value1 - Value2;
        }

        public Int32 DoMultiply(Int32 Value1, Int32 Value2)
```

```
        {
            return Value1 * Value2;
        }

        public Int32 DoDivide(Int32 Value1, Int32 Value2)
        {
            return Value1 / Value2;
        }
    }
}
```

The first piece of code to consider is the assembly level [ApplicationAccessControl] attribute. Always set this attribute to true because otherwise, your component won't use COM+ security (unless the administrator sets it up manually). The remaining properties define various security elements. The administrator can change these elements, but at least the code provides a starting point and sets the security to a reasonable default level if the administrator doesn't configure it. Here's a description of each property:

Authentication   This property defines how the server authenticates the caller. The default level only checks the caller's credentials at the beginning of a session. This option ensures that the application functions at the maximum speed that still allows some level of authentication check. However, checking the credentials during each call is far more secure, especially if you plan to use this component as part of a Web services solution.

AccessChecksLevel   This property determines how far COM+ applies security checks to a component. You can choose to check security at just the process level. However, it's a lot more secure to perform checks at the component, interface, and method levels as well. The AccessChecksLevelOption.ApplicationComponent option does incur a small performance penalty, but the benefit is that you can perform security checks at a granular level. For example, you can grant individual users access to one method, but not another, depending on the role they perform in the organization.

ImpersonationLevel   This property determines how the component can impersonate the caller when it requires services from another component or service. Impersonation is important because it allows the component to request resources on behalf of the caller. If you set this property to ImpersonationLevelOption.Anonymous, at least some calls will fail due to a lack of resources or services. The ImpersonationLevelOption.Delegate option can become dangerous because it gives the component the ability to impersonate the caller at any level. The ImpersonationLevelOption.Default option shown in the code is the safest setting because it changes the impersonation level to meet enterprise policies.

The other major change in this component code is that it derives from the ServicedComponent class. Even though the Microsoft documentation just assumes that everyone will derive from this class, the fact is that you can use the code from Listing 8.3 just fine from COM+. You can also derive from the Component class, should you wish to. However, deriving from the ServicedComponent class is safest from a security perspective because it provides full access to all of the required COM+ interfaces, including those used to perform full security checks. For example, you'll want to check the caller's role in some cases and that means creating the required COM+ interface. The disadvantages of this particular class are that it adds a little to the size of your component and can incur a small performance penalty.

Working with the *SecurityCallContext* Class

Now that you have a component to use, let's discuss how you use those interfaces in a little more detail. The main security interface that you need to know about when creating a COM+ component is ISecurityCallContext. You'll find the functionality of this unmanaged interface in the SecurityCallContext class of the EnterpriseServices namespace. Don't add a reference to the COM+ Services Type Library to your application to gain access to the ISecurityCallContext support. The IDE will allow the addition, but it's important that you use the SecurityCallContext class members instead because they provide full marshaling of any data.

The SecurityCallContext class provides access to the security data for a particular component in a particular context. What this means to you as a developer is that you determine what role the current user is in and what their rights are. The fact that this interface is for a particular context means that you can only work with the request associated with this particular instance of the component. In addition, you won't be able to gain information about the component as a whole.

This interface is normally accessible to your COM+ component if the administrator enables role-based security, but you won't always need to use it. The only time you'll need to use the methods of this class is when you decide to handle security within the component, rather than allow the administrator to handle security as part of the component's configuration.

You'll normally use the SecurityCallContext class methods to learn specific kinds of information about the current component context. All of this information is contained in the security call context collection—essentially an array of information about the currently executing instance of your component. Here's a list of the information that you can obtain from the security call context collection.

- Number of callers
- Minimum authentication level
- Callers
- Direct caller
- Original caller

In addition to the security call context collection information, the SecurityCallContext class helps you to determine if a caller or user is in a specific role. You'd use this kind of information to either grant or reject a request for access to specific methods within the component. You can also determine if the administrator has enabled role-based security for this component (versus being available on the server).

Now that you have a little better idea of what the SecurityCallContext class can do for you, let's look at the available methods. Here's a list of the methods that you'll use most often.

IsCallerInRole   This method determines whether the direct caller is in a specified role. Although the method doesn't list all of the roles that the caller is in, it does allow you to determine whether the caller is a member of the role you specify. You can use this method to determine whether a caller should have access to a specific method or resource within the component.

IsUserInRole   This method performs essentially the same task as IsCallerInRole, but for a specific user. The difference between the caller and a user is that the caller is the one currently using the component. The user call can refer to any user who has access to the server—not necessarily the user making the current call.

The SecurityCallContext class also supports a number of interesting properties. In most cases, these properties replace method calls used by the ISecurityCallContext interface, which means you need to consider which technique will work best. Here's a list of common properties.

Callers   This property returns one or more SecurityCallers objects. Each object describes a specific caller in the list of callers to the component method. Consider this a paper trail type of property. This property accesses the Callers item in the ISecurityCallContext collection in COM+.

CurrentCall   This static property obtains a SecurityCallContext object for the current call. Essentially, this is your gateway for gaining access to the information provided by the ISecurityCallContext interface.

DirectCaller   This property returns the SecurityIdentity object for the direct caller of this method. The direct caller is the last caller in the caller hierarchy list. Use this property to determine whether the last caller in the list has the proper rights to request access to the component. Otherwise, there's little point in continuing to process the request.

IsSecurityEnabled   This property determines whether the administrator has enabled role-based security for this instance of the component. The method won't determine whether the administrator has enabled role-based security for other instances of the component.

MinAuthenticationLevel   This property returns the security information for the least secure caller in the caller hierarchy. By examining this property, you can determine if any of the callers in the caller chain lack the proper credentials for component access.

NumCallers   This property returns the number of callers in the caller list. This property accesses the NumCallers item in the ISecurityCallContext collection in COM+.

OriginalCaller   This property returns the SecurityIdentity object for the original caller of this method. The original caller is the first caller in the caller hierarchy list. Use this property to determine whether the first caller in the list has the proper rights to request access to the component. Sometimes the original caller tries to overcome security issues by hiding behind the rights of another caller.

Adding Security to a COM+ Application

At some point, you'll create a COM+ application using Component Services and add the example component to it. I'm assuming you know how to perform those tasks and won't cover them here. (The example COM+ application has a name of TestCOMPlus, as you'll see in the figures in this section.) Figure 8.2 shows the general setup I've used for this example, including all of the interfaces added by the SecurityCallContext class and the IMathFunctions interface added by the component.

FIGURE 8.2:

The COM+ application setup for this example

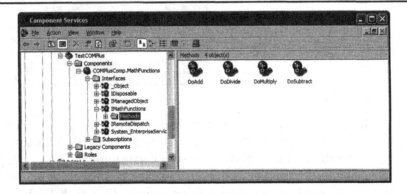

Unfortunately, many developers stop immediately after setting up security and never get any further. Theoretically, you could get by without adding security since Windows already protects the application. However, role-based security is one of the features of COM+ that makes life a lot easier for network administrator and developer alike because you can refine the security measures used to protect a component, the interfaces it contains, and the methods required to perform the application's work. Unlike Windows security where you have to use a one-size fits all approach to security, role-based security allows you to base security on the work a user will perform.

Adding COM+ Component Roles

To add role-based security to the component, you'll need to create at least one, preferably two, roles. We'll call the first role Administrator so that someone logged in as this role will be able to access all of the methods within the COMPlusComp component shown in Listing 8.5. The second role can be any other value, but for this example, we'll use User. The User role will be able to access just the four math functions.

1. Highlight the Roles folder, then use the Action ➤ New ➤ Role command to display the Role dialog box.

2. Type a name for the role, and then click OK. For the example, use Administrator for one role and User for the second.

3. Open the Administrator (or User) folder, and then highlight the Users folder. Use the Action ➤ New ➤ User command to display the Select Users or Groups dialog box shown in Figure 8.3. You'll choose the users that can access components using the Administrator role at this point.

FIGURE 8.3:

Choose which users or groups will perform the task specified by the role.

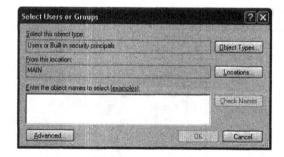

4. Type the users or groups that you want to include for each role in the field provided. The example uses the Administrators group for the Administrator role and a test user for the User role. Make sure you separate multiple entries using a semicolon and that you use the proper form for the entries. If you want Windows to do the work, click Advanced and you'll see a Select Users or Groups dialog box that will help you find individual users or groups.

5. Click OK. Component Services will add the selected users or groups to the Users folder for the appropriate role in the Component Services window.

6. Repeat Steps 1 through 5 for the User role. However, in this case, use your own name, a test username, or the Users group instead of the Administrators group for the Users folder. Figure 8.4 shows a typical example of the security setup for this example. Obviously, any

production components you create will have a more complex security setup that allows users to access the components you create in specific roles.

Creating a typical role-based security setup

Changing COM+ Component Security

COM+ doesn't include security at just one level—you need to monitor it at the application, component, interface, and method levels. To check application level security, right-click the TestCOMPlus entry, and then choose Properties from the context menu. You'll see TestCOMPlus Properties dialog box. Choose the Security tab of this dialog box and you'll see the security options shown in Figure 8.5. This dialog determines the kind of security an application will use.

Set security at the application level before you can use role-based security.

WARNING   You can't use role-based security with library applications. This feature only works with server applications, which means that library applications are inherently less secure than server applications. The Component Services console will let you set role-based security for a library application, but generally, this change results in a malfunctioning application, rather than a secure application. Library applications are also less secure because they execute in the client memory space, rather than on the server. A cracker could use a variety of methods to gain access to the component image in memory and save it to a local disk drive.

You need to consider two of the settings in this dialog box. First, make sure you check the Enforce access checks for this application option. This setting enforces security at the component, interface, and method levels. Second, make sure you allow access checks at both the process and component levels. That's the second option in the Security level group shown in Figure 8.5 (the figure shows the Security level properly configured). You need to select this option if you plan to use role-based security within your components as well. Otherwise, your components will be limited to whatever security Windows provides at the application level.

The next security level is the component. To check component security, right-click the COMPlusComp.MathFunctions component and choose Properties from the context menu. You'll see a COMPlusComp.MathFunctions Properties dialog box. Click the Security tab and you'll see a dialog box similar to the one shown in Figure 8.6. Notice that both of the roles you've created are available for use with this component.

FIGURE 8.6:

You can use any roles that you've created for a COM+ application at all application levels.

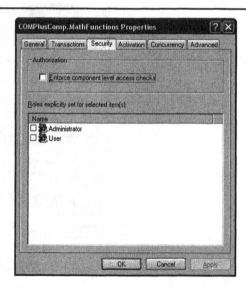

As you can see in Figure 8.6, none of the role-based security options are checked. The way that the Security tab of the COMPlusComp.MathFunctions Properties dialog box is set, no one can access the component right now. What you'll need to do is check the roles that you want to access the component. Let's assume that the Administrator role will have full access to this component, so check the Administrator entry, then click OK to make the change permanent.

Now, let's look at the effect of your decision at a lower level of the application. Right-click the IMathFunctions interface (located in the Interfaces folder for the application), and then choose Properties from the context menu. Click the Security tab. Notice that you still have two options to choose from with regard to role-based security, but that Administrator appears in the Roles Inherited by Selected Item(s) list box. This means that you don't have a choice about the Administrator role—anyone in this role already has access to this interface. You'll find that the same rule holds true for methods. In other words, everyone in the Administrators group can access everything that this component has to offer. On the other hand, the Users role still hasn't been defined.

Right-click the DoAdd entry in the Methods folder and choose Properties. Select the Security tab. You'll see the same list of inherited roles and defined roles as before. This time, select the User role and click OK. The User role now has access to the DoAdd() method. Perform the same task for the other three simple math entries: DoSubtract, DoMultiply, and DoDivide.

Summary

This chapter has demonstrated many of the techniques you need to ensure the security of your network and servers. It's essential to remember that good security begins with the same basics that you use on the desktop, such as code and user verification and validation, but that network environments need even stricter management. Once you consider these requirements, you can move on to other issues such as network data transmission and the use of special features such as COM+.

The problem in trying to create a definitive network solution is that one doesn't exist. You need all of the parts of a good security strategy in place to develop applications that are reasonably secure. It's important to remember that a single check usually isn't enough and even constant vigilance may prove inadequate in some situations. Checking a client's identification at one end of the wire usually isn't enough—you must check the other end as well and then you have to be suspicious of the findings you do verify. If I sound suspicious of everything, it's because that's the only way to create secure solutions on a network.

Chapter 9 moves from desktop and LAN development to development on the Internet. It begins by looking at the requirements for a Web server. As with your LAN server, a Web server requires careful setup and the same good coding strategies discussed for the LAN server. However, the Internet opens a wide range of other possible problems. For example, you must now deal with unknown entities accessing your server. Viruses that exploit problems in code beyond your control are also an issue. Chapter 9 helps you write programs that deal with situations that are beyond your control. While you can't prevent some things from happening, you can at least protect your own code.

PART III

Web-based Security

CHAPTER 9

Web Server Security

- Developing Ways to Keep the Server Safe

- Understanding Good Server Administration Methods

- Overcoming Distributed Denial of Service (DDOS) Attacks

- Detecting Apparent Communication Errors

- Developing Web-based Application Testing Techniques

- Creating a Secure Web-based Application Installation

W hile desktop and LAN security has become passe, and you don't hear much about it anymore, the media hasn't let us forget about Web servers. Some of the articles in the trade press verge on paranoia as industry pundits scream tirades of imminent Internet destruction from forces unknown. The screams have long drowned out any sense that anyone could make of the situation. Certainly, the potential for danger is real—reports of every sort tell of the damage done by the current viruses—but just how vulnerable are your application, server, data, and users? Sitting quietly and reading some of the reports presented by reputable security agencies and consultants will tell you that the danger isn't as extreme as everyone else seems to think it is. The real danger is a lack of preparation, maintenance, and vigilance on the part of those who are supposed to maintain the Web server in some semblance of readiness against attack, which includes the developer in many cases. Of course, the silliness of the user plays a significant role in the demise of your server as well (see the "Stupid User Tricks" section of Chapter 1 for details).

This chapter mixes administration and programming techniques designed to keep your server safe. There are no fixes. No patch in the world will keep your server safe—only constant vigilance can attain that goal. The programming and administration techniques in this chapter reduce the amount of work you need to maintain your network and make detection of potential threats easier.

> **NOTE**   Most of the security articles you'll read still say that internal threats are much greater than those from outside. Disgruntled employees can become your worst security nightmare. However, growing evidence shows that outside forces might be gaining as a threat. For example, the vnunet.com article at `http://www.vnunet.com/News/1140907` says as much as 90% of attacks could come from outside sources. Of course, the biggest reason for this change is increased server exposure due to Web-based applications.

Once you get past simple administration and good programming methods, it's time to discuss some specific threats. For example, this chapter covers methods you can use to keep someone from turning your server into a *zombie* (think of the movie caricature—a computer with no will of its own that goes out of its way to destroy other computers). Crackers use a number of interesting techniques to gain a foothold on your system and many of them don't involve patches to existing DLLs. For example, the simple act of processing an out-of-band (OOB) message (essentially an exception) can ruin your whole day. Threats to your server also include apparent (not real) communication errors, poor testing techniques, and installation problems.

Keeping the Server Safe

It's easier to keep a problem at bay than it is to resolve the problem once it occurs. For example, it's much easier to scan incoming email for a virus than it is to clean the virus off the system once it executes. Virus makers are producing new versions of their product every day, so vigilance is an essential element of keeping the virus out of the system. The virus scanner requires constant updates to keep the system safe. However, the media tells network administrators that they don't have time to keep the virus scanner up-to-date, so the network administrator doesn't perform the work and the virus arrives—costing the network administrator more time. If the network administrator truly lacks the time required to maintain the virus scanner, where did the time come from to clean up the virus? This simple paragraph illustrates a problem in believing everything you read. Often, if the media tells people something long enough, they tend to believe it. However, the bottom line with security is that if you don't have time to perform a preventative task, make the time. It's always going to cost you more time to clean up a problem created by virus than to simply prevent it in the first place.

TIP   The developers that are most successful at creating secure applications often think outside the usual range of security threats. Sometimes security is a study of the absurd. A cracker isn't going to wait for you to discover the next method of exploiting your system. In fact, the cracker hopes that you never discover the method used to enter your system illegally. To demonstrate just how absurd some cracking methods can become, consider the CNET article at `http://news.com.com/2100-1009_3-1001406.html?tag=fd_top`. In this case, the cracker uses a simple lamp to introduce an error into a computer system, which allows the cracker to run his code. This technique is very similar to the buffer overrun technique described in the "Understanding How Buffer Overruns Work" section of Chapter 3.

The following sections contain essential coding techniques you need to employ to ensure that the Web server remains safe. These techniques are the ones that you must make time to use, even if you don't have time to spare. Obviously, they won't fix every problem, but they'll help you add essential functionality to your applications. As part of the content in these sections, you'll also discover a few new development tricks you need to know, such as setting up a Web server to allow remote debugging of an application. Internet Information Server (IIS) doesn't come set up to provide support for remote debugging, in most cases, and the Microsoft supplied instructions often leave you without a functional setup.

A Case for Using Multiple Machines

I'm a strong proponent of using multiple physical machines for testing and debugging any application with a network task, but especially those designed to work on the Internet. Although testing the application on the local machine using the LocalHost server (or using multiple virtual machines) is very convenient, it's also not very realistic. When you test an application, especially when security is involved, you need to create the same kind of environment that user will have. A LocalHost setup just doesn't mimic the Internet very well, so there are going to be holes in your testing if you use it.

When you use two machines, a client and a server, you create an environment that's different from a single machine setup. For one thing, the information has to travel across a wire to the other machine. You aren't using the local machine anymore—the information travels to another machine that you haven't logged on to and even if you do log on, you can set the system up so that you have the same limited rights as any other Internet user. All too often, an application tested on a LocalHost setup fails during deployment because the tester didn't actually check access conditions on the server using the same setup as the user.

The multiple machine configuration can offer other functionality that you can't duplicate effectively on a single machine. For example, you can't duplicate the requirements of passing data through a firewall on a local machine. The data performs an internal loop from the application into the Web server on a local machine, so the application effectively bypasses any firewall. This problem occurred with one developer who wrote an application to use secure communication over a specific port. The application worked fine locally, but failed during deployment because the network administrator didn't leave that port open on the firewall. Testing on a two-machine setup would have made this problem apparent long before the deployment stage—saving hundreds of hours of debugging time during a critical phase.

Although it might not seem relevant at first, a two-machine setup also lets you test application performance. This question is important because any security you add to the application will affect performance. The internal loop of a LocalHost connection is almost instantaneous, so any performance problems induced by security additions remain hidden. Only when you deploy the application does it become apparent that your application is now so secure that no one can use it because it's too slow. With a two-machine setup, it's possible to create the slowest common connection—a dial-up. It's often a good idea to check your application with this kind of setup to ensure that anyone who needs it can use it.

Authentication Techniques

Remember from previous chapters that *authentication* is the act of validating the identity of a caller. You authenticate the caller to ensure that they have the right to access the system. Authentication doesn't give the caller any rights, but it does provide them with a key for accessing resources and services. Consequently, authentication is your first line of defense for a Web server. If someone can't prove that they have the right to access the system by providing a verifiable identity, the communication with them should stop immediately. Unfortunately, this first line of defense is usually breached without too much trouble because crackers have access to an interesting array of software that helps them discover passwords used for authentication on most Web sites all too easily.

Intelligent Password Guidelines

You can reduce the attacks on your system by ensuring that users employ hard to guess, but easy to remember passwords. If the password a user selects is too hard to remember, they'll write it down, which means reduced, not enhanced, security. I usually recommend a random word, followed by a special character, followed by another random word such as lizZard#fiLe. Notice the use of mixed case lettering to make the password harder to guess—the use of capitalization doesn't always work well, but it can help. Also, notice that this password is relatively long—use a minimum of a ten-character password. A random list of letters, numbers, and special symbols such as rApu9u##s8E6 won't work because the password is too hard to remember. For this reason, most automatic password generators won't work. One exception is Random Password Generator-Pro at `http://www.hirtlesoftware.com/p_passpr.htm` because you can use it to generate the random word technique I described and it uses a very large dictionary (making the random words harder to guess).

Use hard to guess usernames as well. Some companies use the first initial of the user's first and middle name, along with their last name. In this situation, my username is JPMueller. That's too easy for the cracker to guess—you're giving the cracker half the entry immediately. Try a username followed by some numbers such as John_1234 or Gerry(1212. Again, make sure you keep things hard to guess, but easy for the user. You don't want the user to write their username down.

Make sure you have strict limits on the number of retries your application will accept. Log a security event in the Event Log when the number of retries exceeds this limit. In addition, disable the account until the network administrator determines the cause of the password entry over the limit. Don't use automatic resets because crackers will rely on the password resetting itself after a specific time interval (usually 24 hours). Configurable limits are best, but typically three to five password retries work well.

Yes, this advice flies in the face of what many security experts tell you. In fact, crackers can easily access your system if you don't combine all three techniques. Believe it or not, crackers have special programs that will try various word and special character combinations one at a time until they find the password for your system. Crackers are patient—they'll keep trying as long as you make it easy for them to do so. That's why the non-automatic reset password entry limit is important. The administrator must be aware of any attempt to crack the system. When the administrator detects a cracker attempt by monitoring usage patterns and an unusual number of bad password attempts, they can change both the username and the password for the account.

The following sections describe special authentication techniques for Web servers. However, before we discuss any coding techniques, we'll discuss some of the problems you can run into when setting Visual Studio .NET up for remote debugging. This helpful advice came from a combination of newsgroup discussions, Microsoft sources, and personal research.

Enabling Authentication for Debugging

Microsoft used to ship Windows and IIS with a modicum of security in place and depended on the network administrator to perform the secure configuration such a system requires. Today, both Windows and IIS come with a wealth of security features already in place, which makes the network administrator's job a lot easier. Unfortunately, these additional security features often prevent your Visual Studio .NET installation from working correctly, especially when you attempt to perform remote debugging.

One of the major problems that developers run into on the server is that they install Visual Studio .NET in the wrong order. Always install IIS on the server first, and then install Visual Studio .NET. The Visual Studio .NET installation makes some changes to the IIS configuration that you need to ensure the two products will work together properly.

Unfortunately, a simple installation order won't fix completely the problems that many developers have. A number of developers have also reported an IIS configuration issue that you need to resolve. Given a default installation of a single default Web site, the following procedure helps you make this change. If you have multiple Web sites installed, simply change the procedure to use your test Web site, rather than the default Web site.

1. Start the Internet Information Services console found in the Administrative Tools folder of the Control Panel.

2. Right-click the Internet Information Services entry and select Connect from the context menu. You'll see a Connect to Computer dialog box.

3. Type the name of the remote server and click OK. The Internet Information Services console will create the connection.

4. Open the Web Sites folder so you can see the Web sites on the server. Right-click the Default Web Site entry and choose Properties from the context menu. You'll see a Default Web Site Properties dialog box.

5. Select the Directory Security tab. You'll see three groups of entries, as shown in Figure 9.1.

FIGURE 9.1:

The Directory Security tab contains three groups of security entries.

6. Click Edit in the Anonymous Access and Authentication Control group. You'll see an Authentication Methods dialog box like the one shown in Figure 9.2. This figure shows a typical default setup.

FIGURE 9.2:

Check the authentication methods allowed by the Web server.

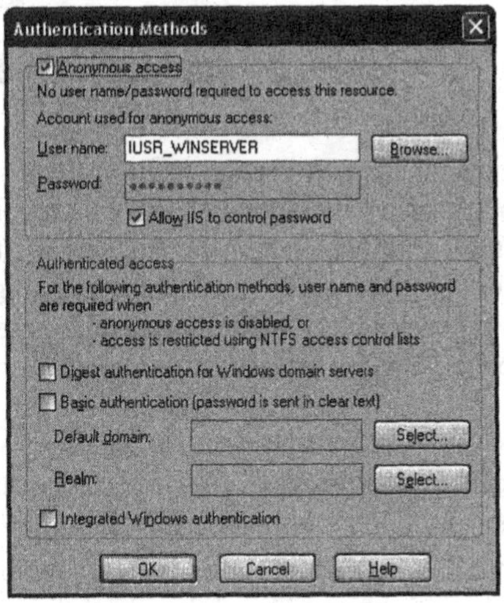

7. Check the Integrated Windows Authentication option at the bottom of the dialog box.

Most people set their browser up to reject certain server activities today. The problem is that these settings can interfere with your ability to debug a Web application properly. Make sure you add your test server to the list of trusted sites for the browser on both your server and your development machine. Use the Tools ➤ Internet Options command to display the Internet Options dialog box. Select the Security tab and you'll see a list of zones. Highlight Trusted, as shown in Figure 9.3, and click Sites. Add the URL of your test site to the list in the Trusted Sites dialog box and click OK twice to close the various dialog boxes.

FIGURE 9.3:

Verify that your test Web site is part of the Trusted zone for your browser.

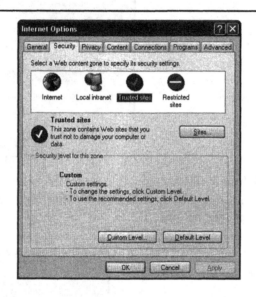

NOTE   Keep your production and development systems separate. Even though the development system configuration should match the production system as closely as possible, using the same system for both purposes usually leads to security problems. Installing the special components you need for remote debugging makes it easier for crackers to gain access to the system. In addition, the test code tends to make the system unstable, which helps the cracker achieve certain exploits, such as buffer overflows.

Some developers forget that their rights are different when working with a Web application than a desktop application. In some cases, this difference means the application you could access using a LAN connection is no longer available using an Internet connection. Make sure you have sufficient rights to debug your Web application. One of the most commonly missed requirements is ensuring that you're part of the Debugger Users group (added by Visual Studio .NET to the Users folder of the Active Directory Users and Computers console when using Active Directory).

Make sure you start all of the services required for complete IIS access. For example, if you don't start the World Wide Web Publishing Service, the debugger won't start either. In addition, check the Visual Studio Debugger Proxy Service to ensure that it starts when you start the debugger. If you don't see this service start, try starting it manually. Verify that the ASP.NET State Service starts when using the debugger for remote debugging (you may find it stopped at other times). You can find all of these services in the Services console located in the Administrative Tools folder of the Control Panel.

You'll also run across a number of project-specific problems. For example, creating a project in a folder that has one or more spaces in the name can cause problems because Visual Studio .NET might continue using the space, rather than insert a %20 to represent the space. Consequently, IIS looks for the part of the URL before the space and fails because it can't find the resource. In short, don't use folder names with spaces in them. However, this problem points to the larger issue of project-specific problems. If the debugger suddenly stops working with a specific project, look for errors in that project's setup, rather than with IIS or the Visual Studio .NET setup.

Using the *AuthenticationManager* Class

The AuthenticationManager class serves a similar purpose to the SecurityManager class used for several examples in the book such as the one found in the "SecurityManager Class Example" section of Chapter 2. You can use the AuthenticationManager class in a number of ways. Two common ways are to obtain information about the current authentication setup and to manage the authentication modules. For example, you can use this class to install a custom authentication module. You also use the AuthenticationManager class to pre-authenticate and to authenticate client requests.

Most developers understand authentication. The client makes a request, the server challenges the client to provide proof that the client has permission to access the resource, and the client provides the proof. At a minimum, the standard authentication technique requires three trips across the wire. When you're working on a LAN, three trips isn't such a big deal. However, if you're using a dial-up connection, three trips can seem like an eternity.

TIP   Don't assume that pre-authentication is another in a long line of special Microsoft behaviors for IIS. Microsoft bases this behavior on Section 3.3 of RFC2617 (see `http://www.faqs.org/rfcs/rfc2617.html` for details).

Pre-authentication is just another method of authenticating the client. However, instead of using the challenge/response system, the client simply acknowledges the need to authenticate at the outset and sends the required credentials. Instead of three trips, the process only requires one trip across the wire. Listing 9.1 shows one method of using the pre-authentication technique within a client application making a request to a Web server. You'll find this example in the \Chapter 09\C#\AuthManager and \Chapter 09\VB\AuthManager folders of the source code located on the Sybex Web site.

Listing 9.1   **Using the *AuthenticationManager* Class for Pre-Authentication**

```csharp
private void btnTest_Click(object sender, System.EventArgs e)
{
    IEnumerator              RMods;    // A list of registered modules.
    IAuthenticationModule    AuthMod;  // Current authentication module.
    StringBuilder            ModOut;   // Pre-authentication module list.
    WebRequest               WebReq;   // Contains the Web request.
    NetworkCredential        Cred;     // Authentication Credentials
    Authorization            Auth;     // Authorization if successful.

    // Setup the output string.
    ModOut = new StringBuilder();
    ModOut.Append("Registered Authentication Modules\r\n");

    // Create the Web request.
    WebReq = WebRequest.Create(txtURL.Text);
    WebReq.Method = "Get";
    WebReq.PreAuthenticate = true;

    // Create the credentials.
    Cred = new NetworkCredential(txtName.Text, txtPassword.Text);
    WebReq.Credentials = Cred;

    // Get the registered module list.
    RMods = AuthenticationManager.RegisteredModules;

    // Try to pre-authenticate against each module.
    while (RMods.MoveNext())
    {
        // Get the module name.
        AuthMod = (IAuthenticationModule)RMods.Current;
        ModOut.Append("\r\n" + AuthMod.AuthenticationType);

        // Determine if it allows pre-authentication.
        if (AuthMod.CanPreAuthenticate)
        {
            // The module does allow pre-authentication.
            ModOut.Append("\t\tYes");

            try
            {
                // Get the authorization.
                Auth = AuthMod.PreAuthenticate(WebReq, Cred);

                // Display the authorization information.
                if (Auth.Complete)
                    ModOut.Append("\t" + Auth.Message);
```

```
        }
        catch
        {
            // The authorization didn't work.
            ModOut.Append("\tNot Authorized");
        }
    }
    else
        // The authorization module doesn't allow pre-authentication.
        ModOut.Append("\t\tNo");
}

// Display the authentication module types.
MessageBox.Show(ModOut.ToString(), "Registered Modules",
            MessageBoxButtons.OK, MessageBoxIcon.Information);
}
```

The code begins by creating several objects, including a WebRequest and a NetworkCredential object. The WebRequest object is important because it holds the identity of the specific network object that you'll access using the NetworkCredential object. Notice that you must set the access method using the WebReq.Method property. Failure to tell IIS how you want to access the resource will result in an authorization failure. You must also tell the code to send the required pre-authorization headers with the request by setting the WebReq.PreAuthenticate to true.

> **NOTE**   The Web request header requirement actually appears at the protocol level. The client must send a WWW-authenticate header with the request or the server won't recognize the pre-authenticate requirements (which means the authorization will fail). See the WebClientProtocol.PreAuthenticate property description at http://msdn .microsoft.com/library/en-us/cpref/html/frlrfSystemWebServicesProtocols-WebClientProtocolClassPreAuthenticateTopic.asp.

The AuthenticationManager has a number of interesting features, including the RegisteredModules property. The code uses this property to initialize an IEnumerator object, RMods. The code enumerates each authentication module in turn and converts it to an IAuthenticationModule. The AuthMod.AuthenticationType property contains the name of the authentication module and the CanPreAuthenticate property determines whether the authentication module can pre-authenticate a request.

At this point, the code finally makes use of the Web request and credentials created earlier in the example to call the AuthMod.PreAuthenticate() method. You must perform this task within a try...catch block because there's a chance the call will fail. The resulting error message simply says there's a null object reference somewhere without specifying where or which object. The .NET documentation is less than clear on this subject (it doesn't tell you what the error message means at all and none of the example code shows the try...catch block in use). It turns out that the null object reference is the Authorization object, Auth. The catch portion of the block simply states that the code couldn't produce an authorization because that's all you know. When the authorization is successful, however, you can determine whether the authorization is complete and access the authorization message. Figure 9.4 shows a sample of the output of this example.

FIGURE 9.4:

Determining the ability of various authentication modules to use pre-authentication

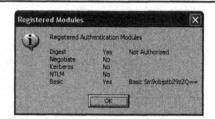

The results you obtain will vary from the ones shown in Figure 9.4. You might have different authentication modules installed on your system. In addition, the IIS setup determines the output of the various authentication modules and defines whether an authorization attempt is successful.

Working with HTTP-Specific Classes

You might have reason to work directly with a few of the HTTP-specific classes. For example, you might want to control the flow of data between your application and the client more directly than standard programming techniques will allow. Here's the list of HTTP-specific classes you should consider for protocol-level authentication purposes:

- HttpWebClientProtocol
- HttpSimpleClientProtocol
- HttpGetClientProtocol
- HttpPostClientProtocol
- HttpWebRequest

A number of these classes include special properties and methods for authentication purposes. For example, most of these classes include a PreAuthenticate (determines whether the pre-authentication feature is enabled) and a Credentials (contains the caller's credentials) property. Listing 9.1 shows how to use these two special properties to create an application that is not only secure, but also more efficient than many applications.

The base class, HttpWebClientProtocol, includes a special property, UnsafeAuthenticated-ConnectionSharing, which enables or disables connection sharing when the caller logs in using

Window NT LAN Manager (NTLM) authentication. All of the derived classes in this chapter also include this property, as well as the SoapHttpClientProtocol and DiscoveryClientProtocol classes discussed in Chapter 11. The documentation is unclear about using this property, but essentially, it turns off the need for the Web server to authenticate the caller for each request and simply keeps the connection open instead.

The UnsafeAuthenticatedConnectionSharing property comes into play in a high performance scenario. Normally, the HttpWebClientProtocol class (and all its subclasses) relies on HTTP 1.1 standard calling with the Connection: KeepAlive header in place. This is an efficient setup when you have multiple unique requests from individual clients. However, what if you have multiple similar requests (such as requesting quotes for a car insurance program) and want to optimize those requests using a pool of connections that you can control through timeouts, maximum number of connections, and other settings? In this case, you'd use the ConnectionGroupName property to ensure that the calls use the same connection pool. Unfortunately, this property disallows authenticated connections unless you also set the UnsafeAuthenticatedConnectionSharing property to true.

WARNING   You can create situations that are even more dangerous by setting properties that work well on their own to specific settings in conjunction with the UnsafeAuthenticatedConnection-Sharing property. For example, setting the useDefaultCredentials value in an application configuration file to true also sets the useAuthenticatedConnectionSharing property to true. The combination of these properties essentially removes most protections from your system, even when the Web server requires authentication. See Microsoft Knowledge Base article Q323490 at http://support.microsoft.com/default.aspx?scid=kb;[LN];323490 for additional details.

Once you set these two properties, you can create a high-performance setup that uses connections quite efficiently. However, using the UnsafeAuthenticatedConnectionSharing property also incurs a security penalty. Normally, IIS authenticates the caller for each request. Using this property keeps the connection open. User B (the cracker) could gain access to the connection originally opened by User A by obtaining access to the User A credentials. In short, it's possible to create a security breach using this technique. Given the current state of technology, however, the risk is very low and most crackers will opt for easier exploits. In addition to the usual secure coding practices, you should take the following precautions:

- Use the pooled connections for different users to avoid opening the door to use of the connection pool by non-authenticated applications.

- Run the application in a protected environment to avoid possible connection exploits.

- Use the Windows Integrated Authentication option to reduce the chance of outside credential stealing using a simple username and password.

Authorization Techniques

From previous chapters you know that *authorization* is the act of giving a caller access to specific resources and services for specific purposes. This step always occurs after authentication, so it's your second line of defense. You use the authenticated identity of the caller to verify their right to access a resource or service. Most Web servers provide an error message when someone tries to access a resource or service that they shouldn't. In many cases, the server should cut off the communication at this point and log the error. However, unless you build this functionality into your application, the Web server will continue to allow a potential cracker continued access to the account and associated access rights.

The .NET Framework and CLR do provide you with some help in the area of authorization. When using Windows NT security, a caller has the same access rights from an Internet connection as they do from the local desktop. This free range of access is usually unacceptable because the caller normally needs just enough rights to work with Web applications, not to perform every task associated with desktop access. Fortunately, .NET provides context-specific rights that are controlled based on the caller's context—an Internet caller will have fewer rights than the same caller from a desktop location.

Flexible authentication is useful if you want to maintain a strict environment without making things difficult on the user. Listing 9.2 shows one method you can use to build on the authorization technique shown in Listing 9.1. In this case, pre-authorization helps the routine build a fast authentication setup that lets the user obtain access to data the first time and with greater efficiency. You'll find this example in the \Chapter 09\C#\GetResource and \Chapter 09\VB\GetResource folders of the source code located on the Sybex Web site.

> **Listing 9.2** **Accessing a Secured Web Source**

```
private void btnTest_Click(object sender, System.EventArgs e)
{
    NetworkCredential Cred;        // Authentication credentials.
    Authorization     Auth;        // URL authorization.
    String            AuthType;    // Type of credential cache to create.
    CredentialCache   CredCache;   // Cached credential information.
    HttpWebRequest    Req;         // Resource request.
    WebResponse       Resp;        // Response to the request.
    Stream            DataStream;  // The file data.
    StreamReader      SR;          // The I/O stream.

    // Create the credentials.
    Cred = new NetworkCredential(txtName.Text, txtPassword.Text);

    // Validate the authorization.
    Auth = GetAuthorized(txtURL.Text, Cred);
    if (Auth == null)
    {
        MessageBox.Show("You don't have access to this resource.",
```

```
                    "Connection Error",
                    MessageBoxButtons.OK, MessageBoxIcon.Error);
        return;
    }

    // Define the authorization type.
    AuthType = Auth.Message.Substring(0, Auth.Message.IndexOf(" "));

    // Use the credential to get content.
    Req = (HttpWebRequest) WebRequest.Create(txtURL.Text);
    CredCache = new CredentialCache();
    CredCache.Add(new Uri(txtURL.Text), AuthType, Cred);
    Req.Credentials = CredCache;

    // Get the response.
    Resp = Req.GetResponse();

    // Get the data and display it.
    DataStream = Resp.GetResponseStream();
    SR = new StreamReader(DataStream);
    MessageBox.Show(SR.ReadToEnd());

    // Close the communication.
    Resp.Close();
}

private Authorization GetAuthorized(String URL, ICredentials Cred)
{
    IEnumerator            RMods;    // A list of registered modules.
    IAuthenticationModule  AuthMod;  // Current authentication module.
    WebRequest             WebReq;   // Contains the Web request.
    Authorization          Auth;     // Contains authorization.

    // Create the Web request.
    WebReq = WebRequest.Create(new Uri(URL));
    WebReq.Method = "Get";
    WebReq.PreAuthenticate = true;
    WebReq.Credentials = Cred;

    // Get the registered module list.
    RMods = AuthenticationManager.RegisteredModules;

    // Try to pre-authenticate against each module.
    while (RMods.MoveNext())
    {
        // Get the current module.
        AuthMod = (IAuthenticationModule)RMods.Current;

        // Determine if it allows pre-authentication.
        if (AuthMod.CanPreAuthenticate)
        {

            try
```

```
        {
            // Get the authorization.
            Auth = AuthMod.PreAuthenticate(WebReq, Cred);

            // Return the authorization to the caller.
            return Auth;
        }
        catch
        {
            // Don't do anything.
        }
    }
}

// The authorization failed.
return null;
}
```

The example begins by building a credential that it uses to obtain pre-authorization for the selected Web resource. The `GetAuthorized()` method is a modified version of the code in Listing 9.1. However, in this case, the code returns the authorization to the calling routine. This technique is extremely helpful because it searches for the correct authentication technique and verifies access before the caller goes through the longer process of requesting a resource. Because of the short message, authentication is nearly instantaneous, even when using a dial-up connection.

Once the code verifies that the caller has the proper rights to access the resource and it determines the authentication method, it uses the `Auth.Message` property to provide the authentication method to the caller. The caller uses this value to build a `CredentialCache` object containing just one authentication method, which reduces the authentication time when getting the resource. The server only has to check one credential and you already know that the credential will work because the code has already tested it.

To get a resource, the code has to build an `HttpWebRequest` object (or it can use a simple `WebRequest` object if desired. The code uses the `Req.GetResponse()` method to obtain the actual resource and place it in a `WebResponse` object. Normally, you'd perform some kind of processing at this point. The example simply places the information in a `StreamReader` object and displays the information it contains on screen by using the `SR.ReadToEnd()` method.

Obviously, this isn't the only way to obtain authorization to use a particular resource, but it does demonstrate how you can combine various .NET features to make the process as fast as possible. The user will know almost immediately whether the access will fail because that part of the process is separate from the act of actually accessing the resource.

Communication with Other Servers

A new security issue for many Web developers is the fact that you normally use more than one server. Desktop applications that rely on a LAN often use a single server because the environment is more secure. The application accesses the server in a secure environment, so you don't need to move your data behind a defensive wall. Web applications often place the business logic and Database Management System (DBMS) behind a wall to provide an additional level of protection. Consequently, you now need to consider communication between servers with different levels of security as part of your application. Because of the relationship between the Web server and the back end systems, you can actually consider this multiple server setup as another line of defense—another chance to get security for your application right.

Administering the Server

Many developers are clueless about any of the responsibilities of administering a server. The reasoning is that a good developer can write secure programs without learning these administration tasks by using good coding practices. The fact that many of the security tools in use today don't work and many applications circumvent reasonable security measures points to the fact that this line of reasoning is absurd. A good developer not only employs the best coding practices, but also understands how the application and its security features work in the Web environment. In short, you don't have to be a perfect administrator, but you have to know the tools an administrator uses and understand how they work. This section provides an overview you can use for further exploration of the administration side of your Web server.

> **TIP**
>
> The numbers of types of threats to Web servers increases daily. The task of classifying these threats so that you can do something about them can quickly get out of hand. Microsoft provides a convenient method of classifying most server threats using the acronym STRIDE (Spoofing, Tampering, Repudiation, Information disclosure, Denial of service, and Elevation of privilege). Learn more about this technique at `http://msdn.microsoft.com/library /en-us/vbcon/html/vbconOverviewOfWebApplicationSecurityThreats.asp`.

Microsoft is attempting to provide tools and checklists that network administrators and developers can use to secure their systems. Part of the problem is that many of those who are responsible for maintaining security don't know the tools exist, don't know how to use them, or don't use them often enough to make a difference. Of course, the other part of the problem is that Microsoft often fails to admit to bugs in their products and refuses to acknowledge security problems until the issue is painfully obvious to everyone. However, Microsoft does provide a list of tools and checklists that you should consider at `http://www.microsoft.com/technet /security/tools/tools.asp`.

Using the Microsoft Baseline Security Analyzer

The Microsoft Baseline Security Analyzer (MBSA) helps you locate, categorize, and track security problems on your server or development machine. This tool can scan one or more machines during a single session. Microsoft has mixed new functionality with existing tools in this product and performed the task well. You can find MBSA at `http://www.microsoft.com/technet/security/tools/tools/mbsahome.asp`.

When you start MBSA, the tool will ask whether you want to scan a single or multiple machines. Figure 9.5 shows a typical example of the single machine scanning setup. To scan a single machine, you choose a specific machine name or enter an IP address. It's also important to check the scanning options. It's usually best to scan for all vulnerabilities because the check on a single machine doesn't take very long.

FIGURE 9.5:

Select the identity and scanning options for the test system.

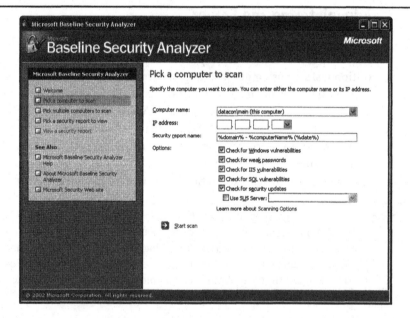

Scanning multiple machines means telling MBSA specifically what you want to scan. For example, you can type a domain name or a range of IP addresses. Typing a domain name means that MBSA will scan every machine in the domain, which can require a substantial amount of time. Selecting an IP address range is reasonable only if you know the current addresses of the machine—depending on how you set your server up, these addresses could change. If I'm only concerned about the two machines I'm using for development, I normally perform two single scans. Once you choose the identity of the machines that you want to check, you can select from the same options shown in Figure 9.5. It's often more efficient to select specific options when scanning multiple machines, rather than perform the entire test.

After you select the machine identity and options you want, click Start Scan to begin the scanning process. Figure 9.6 shows typical output from this program. You might be surprised at the number of security problems your development server and workstation have.

FIGURE 9.6:

Typical output from MBSA after a security scan

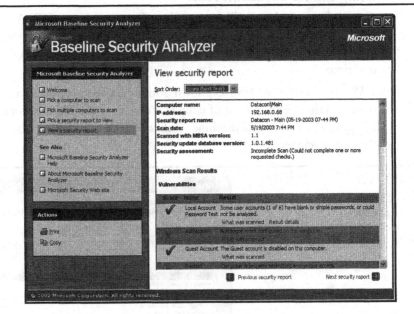

MBSA also includes a command line interface through MBSACli.EXE so you can use it within scripts. The default setup uses command line features that emulate the standard MBSA interface. If you don't select a particular feature, then MBSA will choose defaults. For example, if you type **MBSACli** alone, the program will perform a complete check of the local system.

NOTE   MBSA tries to download a copy of the MSSecure.XML every time you start the program. If MBSA can't find an Internet connection or it can't contact the Microsoft Web site for some reason, the program will still work, but the results could be outdated. The best policy is to run the scans from a machine with an active Internet connection so MBSA can provide the latest results.

In many respects, MBSA overlaps the functionality provided by another tool, HFNetChk (see http://www.microsoft.com/technet/security/tools/tools/hfnetchk.asp for details). If you want to emulate the behavior of the older HFNetChk tool, you can use **MBSACli /hf** in the script file. MBSA can use any HFNetChk command line option, which means MBSA is extremely flexible.

Using the IIS Lockdown Tool

One of the tools that you'll see mentioned as part of your MBSA scan is the IIS Lockdown Tool. This tool helps you reconfigure your system for maximum security. It uses a number of templates to automate the task, or you can choose to perform the process by answering questions.

When you start the IIS Lockdown Tool, it asks you to agree to the usual licensing statement and then displays a list of templates similar to the ones shown in Figure 9.7 if it detects a copy of IIS on the local machine. Unlike MBSA, you must run the IIS Lockdown Tool on the host machine.

FIGURE 9.7:

The IIS Lockdown Tool uses templates to make the configuration process easier.

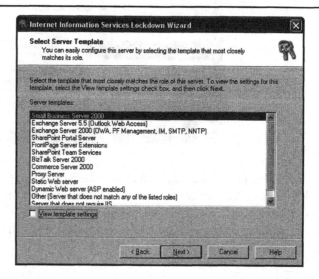

Notice the View Template Settings option at the bottom of the dialog box in Figure 9.7. It usually pays to check this option so you can validate that the template settings are going to work for your system. When you select this option, you see a series of screens such as the one shown in Figure 9.8. The screens take a while to read and verify, but you'll receive better results from the configuration if you take the required time.

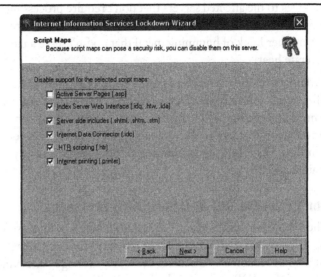

The IIS Lockdown Tool also offers to install URLScan (see `http://www.microsoft`
`.com/technet/security/tools/tools/urlscan.asp` for details). Essentially, this tool uses
a rule base to block harmful requests from reaching the server. In general, if you install
URLScan on your production systems, you should also include it on your development
machine. The fact that this tool blocks certain requests means that you could run into situations where an application works fine on a development machine, but doesn't work at
all on the production system. An URLScan problem can prove difficult to find because
the tool blocks the request before it reaches the Web server. Consequently, many of the
troubleshooting techniques you normally use won't work (including remote debugging).

Once you decide on the various settings (including the URLScan installation), the IIS
Lockdown Tool displays a summary of the tasks that it will perform on your system. Use the
Back button to change any settings that don't appear to fit within the security guidelines for
your company. Click Next to begin the lockdown process. The IIS Lockdown Tool displays
status information as it completes the task. At some point, the process will complete—simply
follow the prompts to finish the process.

Avoiding Distributed Denial of Service (DDOS) Attacks

The DDOS attack is one of the most devastating attacks that a Web server can experience.
Zombie computers (those infected with a special virus that gives the cracker full control of the
system) attack from all over the world. The essence of a DDOS attack is to send high priority

messages to the affected servers that don't require processing. Such an attack wastes processing cycles. What the user sees is an inability to contact the server. In short, your server becomes just another hunk of humming metal that doesn't serve a particular useful function other than generate heat.

Many developers have the misconception that they can't do anything about DDOS attacks. The attack comes from other machines where the administrator failed to exercise proper control and the thought is that the local administrator can change server settings and set up firewalls for protection. Turning off features such as Telnet can help, but it's not a complete solution. The following sections discuss coding practices you can enforce to help in the fight against DDOS.

Don't Process Out-of-Band (OOB) Messages

The "Working with Sockets" section of Chapter 8 discussed how sockets work. In fact, Listing 8.1 shows how to use the SocketPermission class to restrict access to this important feature. That section also discusses the OOB message—essentially an error message for sockets. Because the OOB message is higher priority than the standard socket message, crackers can use it to start a DDOS attack on your system. In short, your application could become the focus of a DDOS attack, even if it works as intended and has the proper security features in place.

The standard practice for applications is to check for errors and react to them as needed. Consequently, you might think that processing OOB messages is a prerequisite for good computing. However, look at the example in Listing 8.1 and you'll notice there isn't a single line of code that checks for the OOB message because this application doesn't have a need for this level of error checking. In fact, most applications don't have a need to process OOB messages. Leaving OOB message processing out of your application may not seem like a good idea, but consider first what you'll do with the information. If, like many applications, you aren't going to do anything with it, then don't process the OOB messages and leave yourself open to attack.

However, what happens when you do need to check for OOB messages for some reason? In this case, setting a performance counter can be helpful. If you reach a specific threshold, turn off OOB message processing. The goal, in this case, is to react to normal levels of error reporting without allowing avalanches of error messages to bring processing on the server to a halt.

Using the Performance Counter Approach

The important thing to remember about DDOS is that the attack is on the server's ability to process requests. As long as the cracker is successful in shutting the server down, causing it to crash, or at least reducing its ability to process legitimate messages, the attacker has won the DDOS battle. It's important to concentrate on the concept of overloading the server in some way. This means the attack could take a form as simple as passing bad requests to your application. After all, the cracker doesn't need to know anything about the application to pass it a bad request—the simple act of passing bad data is enough.

Creating a performance counter in the Win32 API environment is nothing short of a nightmare, so many developers avoid performing this task. However, the .NET environment makes the task of creating a custom performance counter relatively easy. All you need to do is create a custom performance counter that tracks the number of bad requests to your application. When the number reaches a specific threshold, you know that something is wrong—it could be a DDOS.

Listing 9.3 shows an example of a performance counter approach for detecting DDOS or other error overflow conditions on a server. You'll find this example in the \Chapter 09\C#\ PerfCounter and \Chapter 09\VB\PerfCounter folders of the source code located on the Sybex Web site.

Listing 9.3   Using a Performance Counter Approach for Detecting DDOS

```
// A collection of counters.
CounterCreationDataCollection CounterCollect;
// The error counter.
CounterCreationData           ErrorCount;
// Determines random error.
Random                        EventVal;
// Error performance counter.
PerformanceCounter            PerfCount;

public frmMain()
{
   // Required for Windows Form Designer support
   InitializeComponent();

   // Create the collection and error counter.
   CounterCollect = new CounterCreationDataCollection();
   ErrorCount =
      new CounterCreationData(
         "Error_Count",
         "Contains the application error count.",
         PerformanceCounterType.RateOfCountsPerSecond32);

   // Add the counter to the collection.
   CounterCollect.Add(ErrorCount);

   // Create a custom counter category.
   PerformanceCounterCategory.Create(Application.ProductName,
                              "Error checking counter.",
                              CounterCollect);

   // Create the performance counter.
```

```
    PerfCount = new PerformanceCounter(Application.ProductName,
                              "Error_Count",
                              false);

    // Create the random number generator.
    EventVal = new Random(DateTime.Now.Second);
}

private void btnTest_Click(object sender, System.EventArgs e)
{
    // Set the number of events per second.
    EventGen.Interval = Convert.ToInt32(1000 / txtTimerVal.Value);

    // Start the timer.
    EventGen.Start();
}

private void EventGen_Tick(object sender, System.EventArgs e)
{
    // Generate a random error event.
    if (EventVal.Next(5) <= 1)
        PerfCount.Increment();
}

private void frmMain_Closing(object sender,
                       System.ComponentModel.CancelEventArgs e)
{
    // Destroy the counter.
    PerformanceCounterCategory.Delete(Application.ProductName);
}
```

I used a standard Windows application for the example, but the same technique works fine in a component or any other kind of application you want to create. The constructor begins by initializing the counter. This example shows a very simple counter. The code begins by creating a counter and a counter collection to hold it. It then uses the PerformanceCounterCategory .Create() method to add the collection to Windows. The collection can contain any number of counters and you can create counters of various types. You can read more about the various performance counter types at http://msdn.microsoft.com/library/en-us/cpref/html /frlrfSystemDiagnosticsPerformanceCounterTypeClassTopic.asp.

Creating a performance counter for Windows doesn't provide access to it. The code creates a new PerformanceCounter object using the name of the counter category and the individual counter. Notice that you must set the ReadOnly argument to false or you won't be able to generate new data for the counter.

The one element in the constructor that you don't need to create, in most cases, is the Random object, EventVal object. This object generates random errors in this example. In a production environment, you'd only want to know about the real errors.

The btnTest_Click() method sets the timer interval and starts the timer. Once the timer starts, it generates ticks at the rate specified by the Interval property. Each call to the EventGen_Tick() event handler is the result of a tick. The code checks the current random number value. If it's less than or equal to 1, the code increments the performance counter using the PerfCount.Increment() method.

Because this is a temporary counter, you should destroy it before you exit the application. The frmMain_Closing() method accomplishes this task. All you need to supply is the name of the counter category.

Start the program at this point, so you can test it. Use the following procedure to view the output of this application:

1. Open the Performance console located in the Administrative Tools folder of the Control Panel. You'll see the Performance console consisting of the System Monitor and Performance Logs and Alerts snap-ins.

2. Select the System Monitor snap-in. The right pane now contains a graphic display of some type.

3. Add a new counter to the display by clicking the Add button (looks like a plus sign). Select the application name, PerfCounter, Performance Object field, and Error_Count from the Select Counters from List field.

4. Click Add, and then Close.

5. Click Test. The program will begin generating random error events. Figure 9.9 shows typical output.

FIGURE 9.9:

Use a performance counter to help detect DDOS attacks.

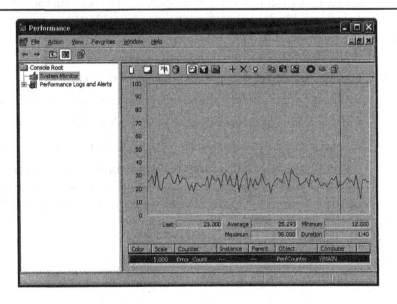

Detection is a good first step in dealing with a DDOS attack. Obviously, you need to remedy the problem once you detect it, which could be the topic of another book (or at least a very long article). Most companies find ways to increase Web server capacity during a DDOS and then filter packets coming from the zombies attacking the server. Generally, you'll find that you need to work with a network administrator during the remedy phase to ensure that the DDOS attack doesn't bring your system down. Because there are so many possible solutions, I won't discuss the remedy phase in detail in this book.

Overcoming Apparent Communication Errors

A communication error occurs whenever someone tries to send data to your server or receive information from your server and the data doesn't arrive at all or it becomes damaged in some way. Generally, the server handles communication errors by resending the data behind the scenes or as the result of a user request to refresh the data. However, apparent communication errors are different from the naturally occurring type. In this scenario, a cracker tampers with the data in some way or tries to request a refresh of data that the cracker shouldn't access at all.

Tampering is the most frequent problem. A cracker could send a script as input to one of the fields of a form. As part of the process of trying to interpret what appears as data, the server ends up running the script. Chapter 3 covered these issues in the "Preventing Data Entry Errors" section. Tampering as a means of creating an apparent communication error is a significant issue because the cracker can gain access to your system.

Most developers think that the data transfer error is the only communication problem they'll ever have. However, developers need to broaden their definition of communication. Some sites actually end up causing security problems by communicating poorly with the user. For example, when a developer asks for information from the user, the request needs to have these characteristics:

- Clearly stated so the user understands what you mean.
- Grammatically correct so the user doesn't stumble over the text.
- All words spelled correctly so the user understands specific terms.
- Short, so the developer doesn't stretch the user's attention span to the limit.

Communication in all its forms is a secure computing requirement. All types of data transfer must take place without error or you're going to have more security problems than you expect. Look for user problems in addition to the usual data transfer problems.

Using Web-based Application Testing Techniques

We've already discussed much of what you need to know in order to configure a system for Web-based application testing. The "A Case for Using Multiple Machines" section at the beginning of the chapter discusses the need to set up a two-machine network as a minimal testing setup. Failure to perform this setup means that you'll probably end up spending more time diagnosing errors when you move the application to a production setup because users won't have the luxury of using a single machine setup.

Unfortunately, using a multiple machine setup can create new problems for the developer. For example, the "Enabling Authentication for Debugging" section of the chapter covers some of the problems that you'll run into with remote debugging. Of course, your debugger isn't the only problem. When you use a LocalHost setup, everything needed to run the application is on a single machine. Using a separate server means additional cost, setup time, and problems during development. Unless the two machines are side by side (a configuration I recommend), you'll also spend more time running between your desktop machine and the server. However, the additional problems are worth overcoming because you have a much better chance of creating a good application with all the required functionality the first time.

When you test your application, you'll normally begin with manual testing, and then move on to automated testing as the project progresses and you can develop a test suite. In general, automated testing looks for expected responses to data input requests and application events. Unfortunately, most automated testing does little to check the security of your application. Security testing means checking for unexpected input. Crackers rely on unexpected input to cause application crashes and let them gain access to back doors. When you want to perform automated security testing, you normally have to create a custom test suite specifically for that purpose.

NOTE   A number of consulting agencies specialize in hacker testing of your Web site. For example, the Secure Web Online site at http://www.securewebonline.com/services.htm discusses this type of service. You can also find an interesting Aberdeen Group report on the topic of automated security testing for Web sites at http://www.aberdeen.com/2001/research/07020009.asp. (You have to register with the Web site to review the report.) Note that this is one of those reports that states developers lack time to perform security testing—you always have time to perform security testing because testing is always less expensive than cleaning up after a virus or a cracker. It's also helpful to check out product reviews from high profile consulting companies such as PricewaterhouseCoopers. For example, you can find a review of AppShield and AppScan at http://www.pwcglobal.com/extweb/manissue.nsf/DocID/4728487E7DAD27D985256C790071619B.

When you do decide to perform security testing for your application, make sure you spend time researching the current exploits for your system using written documentation (such as security reports) and technical updates (such as the techniques found on some Web sites). In some cases, these security reports can provide you with everything needed to perform a good test. The Microsoft Knowledge Base articles usually fall into this first category. In other cases, you'll find techniques that you should perform for every Web application. The email exchange on the SecurityFocus site at `http://www.der-keiler.de/Mailing-Lists/securityfocus/secprog/2001-07/0001.html` is an example of this second category. In this case, the author shows how you can use a few simple additional characters in the fields of a form to fool SQL Server into giving you complete access to the data on a Web site. The extreme ease of this technique should prompt every developer to perform the range and data type checks discussed in the "Preventing Data Entry Errors" section of Chapter 3.

Developing a Secure Web-based Application Installation

The concept of the flawless Web-based application installation is a myth. If you secure the application according to every guideline, some user will leave their name and password lying around for the nearest cracker to find. Removing every vulnerability in your application only means that your application is more secure—all of the vulnerabilities left by product vendors are in place. In addition, crackers are usually able to come up with a new vulnerability. Adding firewalls and layers of security will slow a cracker down, but not stop them completely. Having an external hacker consultant test your application will help you find the flaws that hacker is able to find, but you'll eventually come across a cracker who can find the one hole the hacker didn't. Training and education reduce security risks, but don't prevent them, and this assumes the user is even interested in using the training. Most military experts will tell you that you win wars by exploiting the lack of diligence on the part of the opponent—as a defender you require an extra measure of diligence.

However, you can create a secure application installation by looking for the obvious. Crackers are patient; they have hours on end to look for the smallest hole in your security, but like anyone else, they'll eventually look for an easier target if your Web site proves too difficult to crack. Unfortunately, even this assumes that you haven't made some outrageous claim about the security of your Web site or done something else to attract attention. In general, it's best to keep your security strategy as quiet as possible and not attract attention to it.

Simple solutions often mean looking at vulnerability lists output by the leading security experts. For example, the article entitled, "Open Source Group Issues Top Ten Web Vulnerabilities" at `http://www.internetnews.com/dev-news/article.php/1568761` provides a checklist you can use to check your applications. I often combine the lists of several organizations to create my own security checklist. Yearly updates ensure that my checklist doesn't get too far out-of-date, but means that I don't spend an inordinate amount of time creating a checklist, rather than performing useful work. Here are some other Web sites you should consider checking:

SANS / FBI Top 20 List   `http://www.sans.org/top20/`

Russ Harvey Consulting Services
`http://www.russharvey.bc.ca/rhc/websecurity.html`

The Top 10/20 Internet Security Vulnerabilities—A Primer
`https://courseware.vt.edu/marchany/NS2000/top10a.ppt`

The Open Web Application Security Project   `http://www.owasp.org/guide/`

Some of these sites also provide advice on how to eliminate the security threats now that you know about them. For example, the SANS site at `http://www.sans.org/top20/top10.php` tells how you can eliminate the 10 most critical Internet application security threats. Don't discount advice provided for other operating systems either. Most of that advice works fine for your ASP.NET application.

TIP   The trade press does a good job of covering the latest virus or significant threat. However, you might want to catch up on some of the more subtle threats from time to time. Online newsletters such as Internet Security Review (`http://www.isr.net/`) can give you a decided advantage when it comes to learning about the next major security threat.

Summary

This chapter has demonstrated some of the techniques you can use to maintain a safe environment for your Web server. All of these techniques relate to Web servers or Web programming in some way. Remember that these techniques are in addition to the techniques you use at the desktop and the LAN. The most important bit of information you can take with you from this chapter is that the hype surrounding Web security is just that. You can create a secure environment, but it requires preparation, maintenance, and vigilance.

Now that you have some new tips and techniques for maintaining Web server security at your fingertips, it's time to put them into action. One of the first things I do when I start a new consulting job is create a threat summary. It's a good practice to create and maintain a threat summary that reflects your risks. Make sure you include internal risks. Some of those users who look stupid really aren't—they're trying to ruin your day by damaging your network in some way.

Chapter 10 discusses an area of special importance for Web developers—your data. Yes, data is important to everyone, but Web applications can use data in ways that increase security risks. In many cases, the data source was designed for a LAN environment and doesn't have the added security needed for a Web environment. For example, many Database Management Systems (DBMSs) provide adequate security, but they aren't secure because the Database Administrator (DBA) is used to a LAN environment where the risks are fewer. Discover what you can do to reduce your data risks in Chapter 10.

Web Data Security

- Creating and Using Database Connections

- Stopping Information Leaks

- Adding Data Encryption to an Application

- Using Remoting and Data Encryption

- Creating Applications that Rely on SSL for Requests and Responses

C hapter 9 discussed the importance of keeping your server safe. The server is the container for your data and that use spells out the value of keeping the server safe. After you consider every other aspect of security, the ability to manipulate and use data safely is the cornerstone of the process. The result of creating a safe environment is data that you can rely on for business needs.

This chapter moves beyond the server—the container for the data—and examines the data itself. The chapter begins by discussing a data manipulation, presentation, and storage application—the database. Many Web pages still rely on static data and others use manual programming techniques, but the database is becoming an ever greater part of the data picture for Web sites—just as it has for every other business need.

The next several sections of the chapter discuss data protection. For example, you need to consider the problem of data leaks—information that you want to stay within the enterprise, company, workgroup, or other area of control but ends up leaking into other locations. Every company has data leak problems, but you can minimize them. The chapter also discusses data encryption techniques for Web applications. Make sure you understand the cryptography techniques discussed in Chapter 7 before you move on to these sections. As part of the data protection strategy, you'll also need to consider using Secure Sockets Layer (SSL) features.

Defining the Database Connection

The Database Management System (DBMS) was one of the first applications developed for computer systems once computer technology moved beyond calculations. A DBMS provides the management capability, accessibility, and security required to handle large quantities of data. Databases (the containers that hold the data managed by the DBMS and accessed by the caller) serve many purposes when it comes to Web applications. The most common use of the database now is as a means of serving up current data for a requestor. Instead of seeing the same static report that you saw yesterday, you could now see the latest report with the most current data. Many business Web sites make use of database functionality for this purpose—at least where they see a need for dynamic data display.

A database can also act as input to a program that serves up the Web pages. Instead of forcing everyone who contributes to a Web site to write the required code, the author provides the content in the form of a database record. The program reads the record and creates the page based on the content of that record. Instead of a server directory full of Web pages, the developer ends up with a single template page and a lot of content. In theory, such a strategy reduces the space requirements for the Web site and makes it easier to maintain.

The following sections discuss some of the special considerations of making database access secure when working with .NET applications over the Internet. This isn't a complete primer of database strategies, but it does discuss the main Web-based application security issues in detail.

NOTE   This book focuses on security issues. You can learn about general database techniques from my book *Visual C# .NET Developer's Handbook* (Sybex, 2002), *Visual Basic .NET Developer's Handbook* by Evangelos Petroutsos and Mark Ridgeway (Sybex 2003), and *Mastering C# Database Programming* by Jason Price (Sybex, 2003).

Securing the DBMS

One of the problems with creating a Web application using a desktop mentality is that you can fall into logic errors. For example, when a user accesses a database from the desktop, they have already logged into the server. Consequently, some administrators use just the security provided with the DBMS, which often equates to the database administrator (DBA) and everyone else. In other words, the administrator often protects the database by relying on the server's security, rather than using the server built into the DBMS itself. Newer versions of products such as SQL Server can use Windows authentication, rather than a separate username and password, which can make the situation worse.

The problem with this strategy is that it can fall short when a developer exposes the database to the Internet through an application. Now, the component that the developer uses to exchange information is the logged in element—the entity logged into Windows for access purposes. Unless the DBMS provides additional security, a cracker could potentially gain access to the database through the component using the component's credentials. Unfortunately, this kind of exploit has already occurred with devastating results. The InformIT article at `http://www.informit.com/isapi/product_id~%7B9AF62809-408D-401A-9144-B0A695B72424%7D/content/index.asp` describes common SQL Server exploits that rely on SQL language deficiencies and security holes. For another example of how this exploit can occur, read the Wired article at `http://www.wired.com/news/infostructure/0,1377,57897,00.html`.

Some application developers simply hard code the access information for SQL Server directly into the component or application. This technique is the same as leaving the DBMS without any protection at all because the protection is effectively disabled. The first input you should ask of any caller seeking access to the database is their credentials. Only allow access to the database once the DBMS verifies the credentials independently of any access built into your component for internal needs. Because of the nature of Web-based applications, you need to set up a cookie or other means of determining when a user makes a second request. Otherwise, you would need to ask the user for their credentials for every access—something that most users would find less than appealing.

You learned about the Internet Information Server (IIS) Lockdown tool in the "Using the IIS Lockdown Tool" section of Chapter 9. One of the screens you won't see unless you choose the View Template Settings option is Additional Security as shown in Figure 10.1. The Microsoft Advanced Data Connector (MSADC) works with Remote Data Services (RDS) to provide database support for remote clients. RDS is an interesting technology because it places part of the burden of processing database requests on the client through RDS client components. However, the technology also opens a huge security hole and probably doesn't offer enough of a performance boost to make securing the technology worth the effort. Consequently, most Web-based applications that provide database access don't use the RDS technology. Unless you specifically use RDS in an application, you should check the MSADC option on the Additional Security dialog box shown in Figure 10.1. You can learn more about this technology at `http://msdn.microsoft.com/library/en-us/iisref/htm/RemoteDataBindingwithRemoteDataService.asp`.

FIGURE 10.1:

Ensure you eliminate the MSADC folder on your server unless you actually need it.

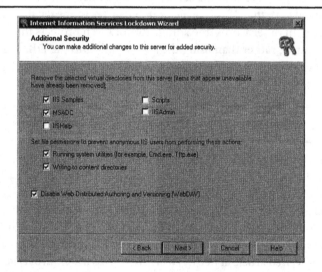

Unfortunately, there's little you can do about some exploits except ensure your copy of SQL Server includes all of the required patches. For example, the Slammer virus (see the CERT advisory at `http://www.cert.org/advisories/CA-2003-04.html` for details) is a problem with SQL Server itself and not a worm you can prevent through configuration alone. The fact that Slammer embarrassed Microsoft because some of the DBAs on their staff didn't install the required patch shows that securing the DBMS is a task that everyone has to perform. According to a CNET article (`http://news.com.com/2100-1001-982305.html`), Microsoft failed to install the patches required to keep Slammer at bay.

Developing a Database Application

One of the most common exploits for any Web application that relies on forms is to trick the form into doing something the originator didn't envision. The "Preventing Data Entry Errors" section of Chapter 3 discusses the need to verify and validate data entries before you use them. However, unlike a desktop application, Web applications often prove difficult to monitor. The reasons include the use of text for all entries, the lack of strong data typing, and the problems of forcing scripts to perform tasks normally associated with full-fledged programming languages. Fortunately, ASP.NET provides validators to make it easier to maintain security by ensuring the user can only input values that you want to use.

NOTE   This example relies on the ExistingMovies database. The \Chapter 10\MyData folder located on the Sybex Web site contains scripts for creating the ExistingMovies database and importing data for it. These scripts assume that you have a D drive with a MyData folder on it. If you want to use some other drive and folder, you'll need to modify these entries in the scripts. Use SQL Query Analyzer or a similar tool to run the MovieGuide.SQL script first, and the ImportRecords.SQL script second. The MovieGuideData.DAT and MovieGuideData.FMT files must appear in the folder defined in the MovieGuide.SQL script or SQL Server will complain that it can't find the files.

An Overview of Validators

Chapter 3 shows techniques for validating user input when working with a desktop application. In general, you'll use inline code to perform the task using any of a number of simple procedures. Validating Web applications isn't quite so easy, so Microsoft provides validators. A validator is a special control that ensures the user enters the right type of data and in the proper range. Each kind of validator performs a specific check, so you might use several validators together to provide full data entry coverage for your application.

Although validators vary in functionality, all validators require an error message found in the Text property that the user will see and use to correct the error on the Web page. For example, when a user types a value that's outside the correct range, the RangeValidator displays the error message in the Text property. In addition, all validators provide a ControlToValidate property that you use to associate the control with the validator. (Some validators might require two controls as input.) Visual Studio .NET supports several validator types, but here are the four types you'll commonly use for applications.

CompareValidator   The CompareValidator accepts two controls as input and then compares the value of each control. If the two controls don't match the condition you specify, the CompareValidator displays an error message. The name of the second control appears in the `ControlToCompare` property. The `Operator` property defines the comparison between the two controls. For example, if you choose the `GreaterThan` option, the value of the control listed in the `ControlToValidate` property must be greater than the value of the control listed in the `ControlToCompare` property. A `Type` property ensures the second control contains data of the correct type, but this is almost superfluous because the two controls won't compare if their types don't match.

RangeValidator   The `RangeValidator` ensures the input in a control falls within a range of values. The `MinimumValue` and `MaximumValue` properties contain the limit of values the user can input. You'll use the `Type` property to determine what type of data the control will accept. The `RangeValidator` accepts common types including string, integer, double, date, and currency. If the input doesn't fall within the selected range of values or is of the wrong type, the control will display an error message.

RegularExpressionValidator   The `RegularExpressionValidator` uses an expression consisting of a specially formatted string that defines the kind of input required to validate the content or format of the input. For example, you could use an expression that evaluates input for all numeric entries or all character entries. You'll find that the Microsoft help topics tend to focus on the format of the expression, as do the built-in expressions. However, the example in this section will show you how to build an expression that defines the content of the expression. The expression used for comparison with the input of the target control appears in the `ValidationExpression` property. Click the ellipses in this property to display the Regular Expression Editor dialog box shown in Figure 10.2.

FIGURE 10.2:

The Regular Expression Editor helps you choose a predefined expression or create one of your own.

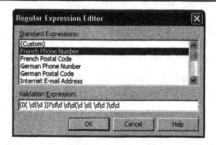

RequiredFieldValidator   This is the easiest of validators to understand. If the target control is blank, the validator displays an error message. Some developers will use an asterisk in place of the error message and simply display one error message for all required fields. However, the use of a custom error message for each controls means that you can provide example input for each field.

Notice that I haven't mentioned any need for application code. All four validators perform their job without any coding on your part. The only work you need to perform is configuring the validator as described in the list. The validator performs the rest of the work for you at that point. (See the example in the "Building the Validated Database Application" section for further details.)

All of the validators provide client-side support. This feature will force the client to fix any errors in the form before the browser will send it to the server. Using a validator means your server will have to react to fewer poorly formatted messages and will work more efficiently. Of course, validators can only check for specific problems.

You can use multiple validators on one field to ensure the application detects as many problems as possible. In addition, the CustomValidator enables you to create special validators that can react to some unique conditions. Unfortunately, the CustomValidator requires you create code to make it functional, which makes a CustomValidator the custom programming solution for special situations.

Implementing the Security Setup

The "Using the IIS Lockdown Tool" section of Chapter 9 discusses the IIS Lockdown Tool. This too really can save your server from prying eyes. However, it can also cause a great deal of confusion if you don't fully understand the implications of what this tool does. Once you lock down your server, you'll find that some programs will suddenly experience errors and some won't work at all. Database applications tend to fall in the latter category. In fact, if you see the mysterious message shown in Figure 10.3, you're the victim of an IIS Lockdown Tool generated error—or, more precisely, you're the victim of a configuration error that you didn't know about.

FIGURE 10.3:

IIS errors such as this one become common after an IIS Lockdown Tool session.

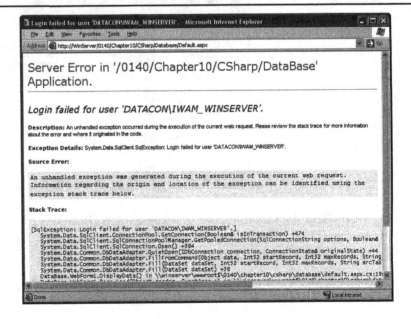

None of the documentation you'll find explains this problem and there's even a dearth of information on the topic on the Internet. At the time of this writing, I found seven obscure references to the problem using Google. You need to perform three steps to fix this problem.

1. Add one or more groups to your security setup using a utility such as the Active Directory Users and Computers console. The example in the "Building the Validated Database Application" section relies on four security groups (each of which offers a higher level of security than the previous group in the list): MovieViewer (read-only), MovieUser (read/write), MovieSupervisor (read/write, insert, and delete), and MovieOwner (all rights).

2. Assign each user that will access the database application to one of the groups you've just created. Again, you'll need to use a utility such as the Active Directory Users and Computers console. You must include the IWAM group in this list. I suggest assigning the IWAM group the minimum possible rights to ensure the database remains safe. Web Application Management Interface (IWAM) is defined in the next section, "Building the Validated Database Application."

3. Use the SQL Server Enterprise Manager to add these groups to the target database (MovieGuide for this example). The scripts used to create the database don't include this step—it's something you need to perform for your server. Simply locate the Users folder shown in Figure 10.4 and add the groups as users of the database.

FIGURE 10.4:

Make certain you add the groups you create to SQL Server.

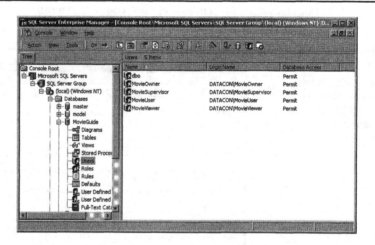

The IWAM group is important because it lets IIS launch processes, sometimes anonymously. That's why you have to give this group some rights, but you also want to keep those rights to a minimum.

IIS loads and caches your application in most cases. Caching seems to affect security as well. If you want to see the true effects of a security change, close all copies of Internet Explorer and restart IIS. In addition, you might also need to restart the local machine to see a change in local settings (logging out and back in is usually enough, but might not clear memory and could cause the error to return).

Building the Validated Database Application

This example includes several unique security features. First, it uses validators to ensure the user can only enter the correct data. Second, the application uses role-based security to determine the availability of features. Combined, these two features make it difficult for a cracker to gain access to your system.

NOTE The Web examples in this book always come in two parts. The first part contains the code that you should place on your development machine. The second part has (Server) added to the folder name. Place this code on your Web server. For example, the server code for this example appears in the \Chapter 10\C#\DataBase (Server) and \Chapter 10\VB\DataBase (Server) folders of the source code located on the Sybex Web site. Move this code to your server and remove the (Server) part of the folder name, so the folder name now matches the name of the folder on your development machine. You'll also need to modify the project file using a pure text editor such as Notepad. Open the Database.SLN (or other) project file and you'll notice a Web site reference near the top. Change this Web site reference to match the URL on your development system.

The first part of this example shows how to use attributes and demonstrates role-based programming techniques that modify the appearance of output. Listing 10.1 contains the Web page rendering code for this program. This listing isn't complete—it only shows the security-related code for the example. You'll find the complete source for this example in the \Chapter 10\C#\DataBase and \Chapter 10\VB\DataBase folders of the source code located on the Sybex Web site.

Listing 10.1   **Using Role-Based Security to Modify Page Rendering**

```
[SqlClientPermissionAttribute(SecurityAction.Demand,
    ConnectionString = "integrated security=SSPI;" +
                       "data source=WINSERVER;" +
                       "persist security info=True;" +
                       "initial catalog=MovieGuide")]
private void DisplayData()
{
```

```
DataRow      CurRow;              // Current database row.
Object       CurColumn;           // Current column in the row.
HttpCookie   RowCookie;           // Determines the current record.
Int32        RowCookieValue;      // The numeric value of the cookie.

if (HttpContext.Current.User.IsInRole("DataCon\\MovieOwner"))
{
   // Enable new buttons and fields.
   btnUpdate.Visible = true;
   btnAdd.Visible = true;
   btnDelete.Visible = true;
   btnRunScript.Visible = true;
   Label12.Visible = true;
   Label13.Visible = true;
   Label14.Visible = true;
   txtIsIn.Visible = true;
   txtFormat.Visible = true;
   txtDatePurchased.Visible = true;

   // Check the password.
   CheckPassword();
}
if (HttpContext.Current.User.IsInRole("DataCon\\MovieSupervisor"))
{
   // Enable new buttons and fields.
   btnUpdate.Visible = true;
   btnAdd.Visible = true;
   btnDelete.Visible = true;
   Label12.Visible = true;
   Label13.Visible = true;
   txtIsIn.Visible = true;
   txtFormat.Visible = true;

   // Check the password.
   CheckPassword();
}
if (HttpContext.Current.User.IsInRole("DataCon\\MovieUser"))
{
   // Enable new buttons and fields.
   btnUpdate.Visible = true;
   Label12.Visible = true;
   Label13.Visible = true;
   txtIsIn.Visible = true;
   txtFormat.Visible = true;

   // Check the password.
   CheckPassword();
}

// Fill the dataset with data.
```

```
sqlDataAdapter1.Fill(dataSet11);

// Determine whether there is a cookie to use.
if (Request.Cookies["RowNumber"] == null)
    // If not, set the row to 0.
    CurRow = dataSet11.ExistingMovies.Rows[0];
else
{
    // Set the row value according to the cookie setting.
    RowCookie = Request.Cookies["RowNumber"];
    RowCookieValue = Int32.Parse(RowCookie.Value);
    CurRow = dataSet11.ExistingMovies.Rows[RowCookieValue];
}

// Display the individual fields.
CurColumn = CurRow["InventoryID"];
txtInventoryID.Text = CurColumn.ToString();
... Lots of other Fields ...
CurColumn = CurRow["DatePurchased"];
txtDatePurchased.Text = CurColumn.ToString();
}
```

One of the security problems you'll discover when working with SQL Server is that the system doesn't have the required permission. Some applications will perform a lot of work before they discover this fact. The example uses the [SqlClientPermissionAttribute] attribute to avoid this problem. The program will generate an exception and send an error message to the user before it performs any significant work. Notice that the attribute demands that the application user have the right to use a particular connection string. The ConnectionString argument is the same one that the sqlConnection1 control uses, so this permission determines that the caller has the required minimum rights.

The DisplayData() method begins by performing a series of role-based security checks. Many developers assume that role-based security only fulfills permission needs. However, this example demonstrates that role-based security affects every aspect of a program. In this case, the code uses role-based security to determine how ASP.NET renders the display. Callers with more rights see additional buttons (to perform additional tasks) and a larger number of data fields. The code also calls the CheckPassword() method, which appears in Listing 10.2 (discussed later in this section). Note that these rendering changes take place before ASP.NET creates the Web page code, so the caller with fewer privileges doesn't even know the other options exist.

Only after the code checks the user's security does it fill the sqlDataAdapter1 control with data. The data adapter contains the entire recordset, rather than just a single record. The code relies on the RowNumber cookie to provide the record it should display. If this cookie doesn't appear, the code uses a default value. This code points out an important security consideration for Web applications—try to provide a default value whenever possible so your code can't fail. The remaining code displays the data on screen.

One of the problems with the Security Support Provider Interface (SSPI) is that it can be extremely difficult and frustrating to work with. When a caller requests a Web page from IIS, it uses the credentials the user provides to perform any in-process tasks such as serving up the Web page, which is why the code in Listing 10.1 works as it does. The problem with IIS is that it runs every out-of-process server (including applications) using the Web Application Management Interface (IWAM) account. This account has the server name attached, so on my server it appears as IWAM_WINSERVER. The term IWAM comes from the `IWAMAdmin` interface that Visual C++ developers use to interact with IIS. The point is that this account should have minimal rights, so when the application calls SQL Server with `integrated security=SSPI` in the connection string, IIS sends the credentials for the IWAM account, which might not even be enabled after you run the IIS Lockdown Tool. Consequently, the application fails to perform as anticipated.

TIP

The Microsoft documentation has a general lack of SSPI information and programming examples. One of the better places to find SSPI specific code is Keith's Security Sample Gallery (http://www.develop.com/kbrown/security/samples.htm). This site has a number of interesting tools you can use to make your SSPI experience easier. Of special importance is the SSPI Workbench—a tool you can use to explore SSPI authentication.

Listing 10.2 shows one way to overcome this problem. This solution has risks because someone could discover passwords if they poke around in memory. However, the solution doesn't expose any passwords on disk, which is where most crackers will look for information. Note that this portion of the example relies on SSL for encryption, so you must set up your server to use SSL. See the "Adding SSL Support to a Server" section for details.

Listing 10.2   Setting the SQL Server Password

```
private void CheckPassword()
{
    HttpCookie  ReturnCookie;    // Return URL for this page.
    String      PasswordUrl;     // URL of the Password screen.
    String      UserName;        // The user's name.
    String      UserPassword;    // The user's password.

    // Create a return cookie.
    ReturnCookie = new HttpCookie("ReturnUrl",
        "http://" + this.Server.MachineName + "/" +
        this.TemplateSourceDirectory + "/" + "Default.ASPX");
    Response.AppendCookie(ReturnCookie);

    if (Request.Cookies["UserName"] == null)
    {
```

```
    // Display the password screen.
    PasswordUrl = "https://" + this.Server.MachineName + "/" +
        this.TemplateSourceDirectory + "/" + "Password.ASPX";
    Response.Redirect(PasswordUrl, true);
}
else
{
    // Get the name and password.
    UserName = Request.Cookies["UserName"].Value.ToString();
    UserPassword = Request.Cookies["UserPassword"].Value.ToString();

    // Create a new connection string for the database.
    sqlConnection1.ConnectionString =
        "packet size=4096;integrated security=false;" +
        "data source=WINSERVER;persist security info=True;" +
        "initial catalog=MovieGuide;User ID=" + UserName +
        ";Password=" + UserPassword;
}
}
```

The example begins by creating a "call home" cookie in the form of `ReturnUrl`. Some developers create a separate login screen for every purpose. Developing a good login screen that supports the call home cookie saves time and makes it easier to perform security updates. Notice again that the code provides separate paths for times when the cookie exists and when it doesn't. In this case, the code calls on the Password Web page described in Listing 10.3 when the cookie doesn't exist to allow the user to log into the system.

When the cookie does exist, the code uses it to create a new `sqlConnection1`.`ConnectionString` value. This new string doesn't rely on SSPI. Instead, it turns off the integrated security and relies on a username and password instead. This solution exposes the username and password in memory, so this solution isn't as safe as using integrated security in one respect because the information could become available to crackers. However, because the average caller will use the integrated security and the example sets integrated security with minimal rights, this solution is actually safer than giving everyone equal access to SQL Server. In addition, by using a different username and password for SQL Server, the caller would need to know more information to gain the required access.

The Password Web page shown in Figure 10.5 demonstrates use of validators. If you allow the user to perform any kind of data entry on a Web page, you should include validators as well. In this case, each field uses two validators. The upper validator in both cases is a `RegularExpressionValidator`, while the lower validator is a `RequiredFieldValidator`.

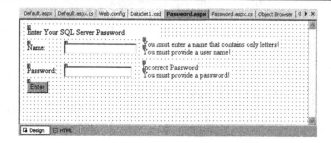

The RegularExpressionValidator requires a ValidationExpression property entry to define how to validate the field entry. The txtName field is relatively easy because it only requires a name of a particular length. The ValidatorExpression entry in this case is [ABCDEFGHIJKLMNOPQRSTUVWXYZabcdefghijklmnopqrstuvwxyz]{3,15}. The user can enter any name that is 3 to 15 characters long. The name can't contain anything but letters.

It's possible to get too explicit when you create a ValidatorExpression entry. For example, if you normally use two words separated by a special symbol or a number for passwords, you might be tempted to create a validator like this one (note that even though this expression appears on multiple lines in the book, it actually appears on one line in your code):

```
[ABCDEFGHIJKLMNOPQRSTUVWXYZ]{5,10}[1234567890!#$%%^&]{1}[ABCDEFGHIJKLMNOPQRSTUV
WXYZ]{5,10}
```

This ValidatorExpression entry defines a password that contains a word, followed by a special symbol, followed by a word. The problem is that this entry gives the cracker too much information. Remember not to volunteer information the cracker could use against you. The actual ValidatorExpression entry for this example looks like this:

```
[ABCDEFGHIJKLMNOPQRSTUVWXYZabcdefghijklmnopqrstuvwxyz1234567890!#$%%^&]{5,20}
```

Although this ValidatorExpression entry is less specific, it prevents the user from entering a long string or using special symbols that crackers commonly use for exploits. The best part about using this form of protection is that, other than the validator expression, you don't have to perform any special coding.

Listing 10.3 shows the Password Web page code for this example. All that the Web page really needs to do is package the name and password, and then return control to the caller.

Listing 10.3   **Getting the Password**

```
private void btnEnter_Click(object sender, System.EventArgs e)
{
    HttpCookie  UserName;       // User name cookie.
    HttpCookie  UserPassword;   // User password cookie.
```

```
String      ReturnUrl;      // Return location.

// Store the cookies.
UserName = new HttpCookie("UserName", txtName.Text);
Response.AppendCookie(UserName);
UserPassword = new HttpCookie("UserPassword", txtPassword.Text);
Response.AppendCookie(UserPassword);

// Return to the original location.
if (Request.Cookies["ReturnUrl"] != null)
{
    ReturnUrl = Request.Cookies["ReturnUrl"].Value.ToString();
    Response.Redirect(ReturnUrl);
}
}
```

The code begins by creating cookies to package the information. Because the caller uses SSL to request this page, you don't need to worry about the cracker learning about the content of the cookies while the information is in transit.

After the code packages the cookies, it requests the return URL from the `ReturnUrl` cookie. This is one situation where it would be difficult to provide a secondary course of action if the caller failed to provide the `ReturnUrl` cookie. The problem is that you can't return control anywhere without potentially creating a security hole. Consequently, the page doesn't return anywhere if the `ReturnUrl` cookie is missing.

Stemming the Tide of Leaking Information

Your Web site has a data leak. It doesn't matter how well you secure the site or whether the people using it are trustworthy, the data leak is there. Many developers discount the problem of data leaks because they think they have followed every security procedure. However, data leaks occur not because of a programming problem, but because of an implementation problem. Displaying any information at all on a Web site causes an information leak for your organization. Of course, since the purpose of a Web site is to provide information to viewers, your application wouldn't be worth very much without at least a small information leak. In addition, some kinds of information leaks are actually good for your organization, such as when you announce a new product.

Part of your responsibility as a developer is ensuring your design doesn't leak data that is better left private. For example, make sure your template contains only the information it needs to contain. Of course, the template still has to provide functionality, so you can't leave it blank. Make sure that you don't confuse protected company information with essential user information. You still have to make the Web page accessible and it still requires good help to avoid confusing the user.

Data leak protection can take other forms. For example, your organization might rely on a database to supply information for Web pages. At some point, your program will need to access the required database record, extract the data, apply it to a page, and output the result. This setup provides a perfect opportunity to scan for forbidden words, such as the name of a new secret project, during the extraction phase using regular expression parsing. The "Keeping Unnecessary Characters Controlled" section of Chapter 3 explains how to use data parsing for data input needs—the same principle applies to parsing content for Web pages. Obviously, this form of data leak protection won't fulfill every need—a smart user that is determined to leak information will find some other words to do it. This limitation is the same reason that spam filters are only partially successful.

Many people complain that digital rights management is a bad thing and it can be a bad thing when used for the wrong purposes. This book doesn't discuss matters legal, philosophical, or ethical, except when it comes to working with code. Information leaks occur when someone passes data from your Web site to a second person that shouldn't view it. The data transferal can occur as part of covert information sharing or as an accidental data release as part of an email. If you want to maintain the secrecy of proprietary company information that you must make available on the Internet, make sure you use digital rights management. Even if someone obtains a copy of the file, it's useless without the password required to open it for viewing.

After you decide to protect the file using some type of encryption (such as password protection for Adobe Acrobat files), you should also use data encryption to transfer the data. The "Implementing Data Encryption" section of the chapter discusses techniques for performing this task in a Web environment. (We discussed the desktop environment in Chapter 7—it helps to read this chapter before you start working with the Web environment.)

Ensuring no one can access your data without permission and then guarding the data through encryption doesn't accomplish much if you don't protect the means for obtaining it. The "Creating a Simple `System.Web.Security` Namespace Program" section of Chapter 13 discusses authentication techniques that especially affect Web applications. For example, "Defining File Security Using the `FileAuthorizationModule` Class" section, also in Chapter 13, discusses the special requirements for protecting file downloads—an essential part of keeping data leaks under control.

Implementing Data Encryption

Chapter 7 demonstrates that the .NET Framework provides a number of ways to encrypt and decrypt data. You have a number of choices to make, such as the use of symmetric or asymmetric encryption. Remember that the asymmetric technique found in the `System.Security.Cryptography.AsymmetricAlgorithm` class relies on a public/private key pair, making it the logical choice for Web communications because you can trust others with the public key, while keeping the private key safe on your system. The use of two keys makes it possible to work with others in a secure manner without exposing yourself to needless risk.

Encryption also relies on an encryption technique and a specific hash algorithm. When working with Web-based algorithms, you need to consider the likes, dislikes, and requirements of the other participants in a data exchange. The most common encryption technique in use today is Rivest, Shamir, and Adleman (RSA). You can find this algorithm in the RSA class and the implementation in the `RSACryptoServiceProvider` class. The example in the "Using Asymmetric Cryptography" section of Chapter 7 demonstrates the basics of working with this technology.

Some developers see data encryption as an all or nothing undertaking. The facts are less clear. You actually have multiple encryption choices and strategies to choose from when working with Web applications. However, you can group these approaches into whole message or individual element categories. When you use SSL to create an application, the system encrypts the entire message. (See the "Creating an SSL Application" section for details.) Encryption and decryption time is one reason why SSL communication takes so much time. Likewise, you can implement channel sinks to perform the task if you don't want to rely on a pure SSL approach (see the "Understanding Remoting and Code Access Security" section for details). A channel sink lets you maintain control over the communication.

Encryption always increases the size of the message, consumes additional processing time, and generally slows everything down. Consequently, the smart developer uses enough encryption to ensure sensitive data remains safe, but not so much encryption that the system slows to an unacceptable speed. Desktop applications have faster communication channels, so full message encryption isn't quite as much a burden as with Web applications. Partial message encryption is much faster and resource efficient when working with Web applications. You can see an example of one approach to this problem in the example in the "Understanding Remoting and Data Encryption" section.

Understanding Remoting and Data Encryption

Remoting is the act of accessing an object in another process. The object can appear on another machine, on the same machine in a different application, in a different application domain (see the "Relying on the `AppDomain` for Managed Code" section of Chapter 6 for an explanation of the application domain), or any other process that is different from the current process. This technology is an essential part of certain types of distributed applications. You can create applications that cross machine and domain boundaries using remoting—even if the boundary is the Internet.

The .NET Framework places certain boundaries on remoting. For example, you can't use it as a replacement for Web services, in many cases, because your application has to know that the component and the corresponding object exist. (It isn't necessary to know where they exist, just the fact that they do exist is sufficient.) When using a Web service application you can use Discovery of Web Services (DISCO) or Universal Description, Discovery, and Integration (UDDI) to locate a service from an unknown source. In addition, remoting doesn't necessarily provide the ease of using a Simple Object Access Protocol (SOAP) message to encapsulate data. Yes, you can use SOAP as one of the interoperability options and you can even expose the object through IIS, but you have to perform all of the work required to locate and use the resource manually.

All remoting applications consist of three parts: component with remoting capabilities, host application that acts as a request listener, and a client application that makes remoting requests. This chapter doesn't provide a full discussion of remoting. You can discover the basics of remoting at `http://msdn.microsoft.com/library/en-us/cpguide/html/ cpconbuildingbasicnetremotingapplication.asp`.

The following sections describe the security requirements for a remoting application. This discussion includes some information about low-level functionality such as deserialization of data. In addition, the example code concentrates on the security features you need to build into the three parts of a remoting application.

Understanding Automatic Deserialization

Whenever the application communicates with the remote components that it uses, it needs to serialize the data (package the data for transmission) at the sender and deserialize it (remove the data from the package) at the recipient. Serialization doesn't incur much of a security risk because you have full control over the content of the package. However, deserialization does incur a security risk because the cracker could use the short time the process exposes the data to corrupt or change it in some way. In addition, the cracker could change the package in transit so that it contains data elements not found in the original package. Consequently, Microsoft devised a method to reduce the deserialization risk that includes two levels of deserialization.

The default deserialization (called the low deserialization level) only allows the package to contain certain data types and information. By reducing the amount and type of information the package can carry, the .NET Framework can reduce the potential security risk. Generally, you can use the low deserialization level because it includes all standard value and reference types, in addition to some custom object types (explained in detail later in the section). In essence, the .NET Framework makes the problem smaller so that the variables are easier to control.

Unfortunately, you can't solve every remoting problem using the security settings in place with the low deserialization level. The .NET Framework also provides the full deserialization level, which allows the recipient to access all of the data in the package without filtering it first. The most important addition for developers is the ObjRef object passed as a parameter.

> **TIP** This section provides an overview of the data serialization and deserialization considerations for remoting. You can find out more about the deserialization levels that the .NET Framework supports at http://msdn.microsoft.com/library/en-us/cpguide/html/cpconautomaticdeserializationinnetremoting.asp.

An ObjRef object is literally a reference to a remote object. From a COM perspective, the ObjRef object is the proxy the server uses to converse with the client. If you pass an object to the remote location as part of a method call, what CLR really passes is an ObjRef object. However, don't confuse an ObjRef type with other reference types. For example, you can build a custom object, mark it with the [Serializable] attribute (without implementing the ISerializable interface), and still pass it to the remote location using the low deserialization level. (See the example in the "Creating a Permission Assembly" section of Chapter 5 for details on using the [Serializable] attribute.)

You also need the full deserialization level to work with objects that interact with partially trusted code (including unmanaged code). The objects that allow this kind of access have the [assembly: AllowPartiallyTrustedCallersAttribute] attribute. By default, only fully trusted assemblies can access any assembly with a strong name, which includes all of the assemblies in the Global Assembly Cache (GAC). The normal effect of accessing an assembly with a strong name is having a permission attribute attached with the SecurityAction.LinkDemand = FullTrust argument. Using the [assembly: AllowPartiallyTrustedCallersAttribute] attribute lets partially trusted code access the assembly. You can still add the full trust requirement to individual classes, methods, properties, fields, and other elements. All that this element offers is a little calling flexibility. (See the "Working with Methods that Require Full Trust" section of Chapter 15 for additional examples of how the [assembly: AllowPartiallyTrusted-CallersAttribute] attribute works with the .NET Framework and CLR).

Understanding Remoting and Code Access Security

One of the biggest security problems with remoting is that it disables code access security. CLR can't access the call stack in another process or on another machine. When your code uses remoting to call on an object in another process, CLR essentially ignores any required permissions. The code can't assert or deny a permission if CLR can't check the call stack.

The consequence of this problem with code access security is that any component that derives from the MarshalByRefObject class must take responsibility for security to ensure the managed application environment remains secure. In other words, the remoting component must provide some type of security for three major concerns: caller authentication, data encryption, and wire integrity. When a component doesn't implement security that answers these three requirements, it isn't safe to use in the Internet environment.

Fortunately, you don't have to program every aspect of these three security needs. Using SSL with an HTTP channel (see the "Using HttpChannel Security" section) takes care of the wire security. Likewise, you can rely on IIS to authenticate the caller. (You can also take care of the authentication using the techniques shown in Chapter 9.)

Data encryption is the remaining requirement and the reason I chose the name for this section of the chapter. You have two choices for meeting the data encryption requirement: internal data encryption or using a channel sink. A channel sink is a special class that intercepts a message and performs some type of work with it, such as formatting the data or getting it ready for transport to the remote system. Remoting normally relies on multiple channel sinks for every communication and channel sinks normally come in pairs. Whatever you do to the message as it leaves the client, you have to undo as it arrives at the server.

> **NOTE**   Data encryption, especially in distributed applications, stirs controversy because there are so many issues to consider. On the one hand, you have human rights groups and others who use cryptography for good uses that save human lives. On the other hand, you have people with less than honorable goals who use cryptography to hide their activities from the authorities. The bottom line for a developer is that you need to consider the laws in effect at the time you place an application into production to ensure your use of cryptography complies with the laws of every country (or even state) that receives the application. For a recent news story that highlights the issue, see the InfoWorld article at http://www.infoworld.com/article/03/05/21/HNpdapgp_1.html.

The first method, internal data encryption, is the easiest and provides enough security when combined with user authentication and wire security to meet most needs. A major advantage of this technique is that the component remains self-contained so you don't have to perform any odd setups on either client or server. The disadvantage of this technique is that it only encrypts the data, not the entire message.

The second method, using a channel sink, requires that you write a special class that intercepts the message, performs the required security task, and then sends it to the next channel sink. Channel sinks derive from the IClientChannelSink or IServerChannelSink classes. You must register the channel sink with CLR and provide linkage to the next channel sink in line. Consequently, the major disadvantage of this technique is that it's complex to implement.

Creating a Remoting Component

The remoting component in this example is the same MathFunctions class used for other examples in the book. This version differs in a number of ways, however, to accommodate remoting and encryption requirements. Although the basic task of performing a match function is the same, the example has to consider security requirements as mentioned in the "Understanding Remoting and Code Access Security" section. It also derives from the MarshalByRefObject class.

> **TIP** The natural way to approach the problem of adding encryption to an application consisting of a server and a client is to add the code to the individual elements, and then test it for functionality. The easier method is to create the encryption and decryption as separate routines and use a single test application to test all of the routines at one time. The biggest advantage to this technique is that you can debug all of the crucial routines on a single machine and then move them to your client and server modules for further testing. You can find an example of such an application in the \Chapter 10\C#\EncryptionDemo and \Chapter 10\VB\EncryptionDemo folders of the source code located on the Sybex Web site. This chapter doesn't contain this example because the code is similar to the actual application shown here. One interesting feature of the original test is that I used a MemoryStream, rather than a Byte[] array to transfer data between endpoints. You can't transfer a MemoryStream across boundaries, so the Byte[] array is the obvious answer. This test therefore points out some of the limitations of using a local test as well as showing the benefits.

Listing 10.4 contains the source code you need for this example. This listing isn't complete—it includes the code for just the add math operation. You'll find the complete source for this example in the \Chapter 10\C#\RemotingClient and \Chapter 10\VB\RemotingClient folders of the source code located on the Sybex Web site.

Listing 10.4   Simple Remoting Component Example

```
public class MathFunctions : MarshalByRefObject
{
    private RSACryptoServiceProvider RSACrypto;   // The key pair.

    public MathFunctions()
    {
        String         KeyPath;      // The location of the key.
        FileStream     KeyFile;      // Key disk storage.
        Byte[]         KeyConv;      // Converted key data.
        StringBuilder  KeyString;    // Key data as a String.
        Int32          Counter;      // Loop counter.

        // Create the key path string.
```

```
      KeyPath = "SpecialKey";

      // Detect the presence of a key pair file.
      if (!File.Exists(KeyPath))
      {
         throw(new FileLoadException("Cannot Find Application Key"));
      }
      else
      {
         // Open the key file for reading.
         KeyFile = File.Open(KeyPath, FileMode.Open);
         KeyConv = new Byte[KeyFile.Length];
         KeyFile.Read(KeyConv, 0, (Int32)KeyFile.Length);
         KeyFile.Close();

         // Convert the key file.
         KeyString = new StringBuilder(KeyConv.Length);
         for (Counter = 0; Counter < KeyConv.Length; Counter++)
            KeyString.Append(Convert.ToChar(KeyConv[Counter]));

         // Create the key.
         RSACrypto = new RSACryptoServiceProvider(2048);
         RSACrypto.FromXmlString(KeyString.ToString());
      }
   }

   public Byte[] DoAdd(Byte[] Input)
   {
      Int32    Value1;  // The first input value.
      Int32    Value2;  // The second input value.
      Int32    Result;  // Result of the computation.
      Byte[]   DataOut; // The output information.

      // Decrypt the data.
      DecryptInput(Input, out Value1, out Value2);

      // Perform the computation.
      Result = Value1 + Value2;

      // Encrypt the result as a stream.
      EncryptOutput(Result, out DataOut);

      // Return the result.
      return DataOut;
   }

   private void DecryptInput(Byte[] Input,
                             out Int32 Value1, out Int32 Value2)
   {
      Byte[]   Decrypted;     // Decrypted byte array.
```

```csharp
    Int32    Counter;      // Loop counter variable.
    Int32    CurCounter;   // Loop counter position bookmark.
    Char[]   ConvChar;     // Converted data in array form.
    String   ConvString;   // Individual value in string form.

    // Decrypt the input data.
    Decrypted = RSACrypto.Decrypt(Input, false);

    // Retrieve the first input value.
    ConvChar = new Char[Decrypted[0]];
    for (Counter = 0; Counter < Decrypted[0]; Counter++)
       ConvChar[Counter] = Convert.ToChar(Decrypted[Counter + 1]);
    ConvString = new String(ConvChar);
    Value1 = Int32.Parse(ConvString);

    // Retrieve the second input value.
    CurCounter = Counter + 1;
    ConvChar = new Char[Decrypted[CurCounter]];
    CurCounter++;
    for (Counter = 0;
         Counter < Decrypted.Length - CurCounter; Counter++)
       ConvChar[Counter] =
           Convert.ToChar(Decrypted[Counter + CurCounter]);
    ConvString = new String(ConvChar);
    Value2 = Int32.Parse(ConvString);

    return;
}

private void EncryptOutput(Int32 Input, out Byte[] Output)
{
    Char[]    InputData;   // Input data in Char array form.
    Int32     Counter;     // Loop counter variable.
    Byte[]    ConvData;    // Unencrypted output data.

    // Convert the input data.
    InputData = Input.ToString().ToCharArray();

    // Convert the data to a Byte array.
    ConvData = new Byte[InputData.Length];
    for (Counter = 0; Counter < InputData.Length; Counter++)
       ConvData[Counter] = Convert.ToByte(InputData[Counter]);

    // Encrypt the data.
    Output = RSACrypto.Encrypt(ConvData, false);

    return;
}
}
```

The program begins by creating an RSACryptoServiceProvider object. The first task is to locate the key for the encryption. The client and server use either the public or the private key as needed. If the code doesn't find the key file, it throws a FileLoadException exception. When the code does find the key, it converts it to a string and then uses it to initialize the RSACryptoServiceProvider object, RSACrypto.

The DoAdd() method takes on a different look for this example. Notice that it passes data in and out as a Byte[] array. You might wonder why the example doesn't use some type of stream. The fact is that using a stream causes a security error. The ObjRef object discussed in the "Understanding Automatic Deserialization" section won't allow the use of a data stream, in most cases, because the data stream could contain information that you don't want the other party to see. A data stream is a security breach waiting to happen, but a Byte[] array contains just the information. The process the DoAdd() method uses is to decrypt the data, perform the required operation, and then encrypt it immediately. Clearing the local variables as a last step would tend to reduce the risk of someone gaining access to local memory and finding the data (this technique doesn't remove the possibility of memory snooping completely).

The DecryptInput() method accepts the Byte[] array as input. This Byte[] array could contain any value and some reference types. However, the example uses a structured string. The string can contain any number of values of any length (within the confines of the .NET architecture). The DecryptInput() method begins by decrypting the Byte[] array. The first entry in the decrypted Byte[] array is the length of the first string element. The code uses this information to retrieve the first input value. Notice that the code first converts the Byte[] array to a Char[] array, which acts as input for creating a string. The code parses the string into an Int32 value. The code retrieves the second value using the same technique. As before, the first Byte[] array entry contains the length of the string, followed by the string itself.

The EncryptOutput() method begins by converting the Int32 input value into a Char[] array. The next step is to create a Byte[] array that the RSACrypto.Encrypt() method can encrypt. The decrypted array is relatively small, so the example doesn't have to worry about the size of the input data. The output in this case is always a 256-byte array.

Creating a Remoting Host Application

The host application, or listener, is the easiest part of the application to build. In fact, it's quite possible that you'll build just one of these applications and use it for every need. The host application relies on a configuration file to provide information about the component. Consequently, if you want to change how the host application works, you modify the configuration file, not the host application.

NOTE This chapter doesn't even begin to explore the configuration options that remoting provides. The configuration file discussed in this section is actually quite simple and you can use a variety of other options including SOAP interoperability. However, you have to build all of these features into the configuration file manually using the remoting settings schema. You can find an outline of this schema complete with element explanations at `http://msdn.microsoft.com/library/en-us/cpgenref/html/gnconremoting-settingsschema.asp`.

Listing 10.5 shows the remoting host source code. You'll find this example in the `\Chapter 10\C#\RemotingHost` and `\Chapter 10\C#\RemotingHost` folders of the source code located on the Sybex Web site.

Listing 10.5   Simple Remoting Host Example

```
static void Main(string[] args)
{
    RemotingConfiguration.Configure("RemotingHost.EXE.CONFIG");
    Console.WriteLine("Listening for requests. Press Enter to exit...");
    Console.ReadLine();
}
```

The remoting host configures the remoting functionality for your application by calling the `RemotingConfiguration.Configure()` method. Notice the name of the configuration file. Files with other names will load, but CLR tends to ignore their content, which means the host won't actually listen for component requests. The remoting host continues to listen until you press Enter at the command line. The moment the remoting host application ends, the remoting functionality also ends and CLR closes the channel. Listing 10.6 shows the configuration file used for the remoting host.

Listing 10.6   Typical Remoting Host Configuration File

```
<?xml version="1.0" encoding="utf-8" ?>
<configuration>
    <system.runtime.remoting>
        <application>
            <service>
                <wellknown
                    displayName="RemotingApplication"
                    mode="Singleton"
                    type="RemotingComponent.MathFunctions,
                        RemotingComponent"
                    objectUri="RemotingComponent.DLL"
                />
```

```
            </service>
            <channels>
                <channel ref="http" port="8989"/>
            </channels>
        </application>
    </system.runtime.remoting>
</configuration>
```

The configuration file begins with the usual declaration for XML files. The .NET environment doesn't appear to require this declaration, but adding it lets you view the configuration file in any of a number of XML utilities. Every remoting configuration file will contain the `<system.runtime.remoting>`. You normally add the `<application>` as well. The host always uses the `<service>` tag, while the client always uses the `<client>` tag.

When you use the `<service>` tag, you need to describe the service. The .NET Framework provides a number of methods to perform this task. The example specifically relies on direct access to the RemotingComponent.DLL. This DLL could contain any number of classes, but the example configuration file only accesses the `RemotingComponent.MathFunctions` class. Note that this is the namespace followed by the class name. The second parameter is the name of the assembly, which could be different from the namespace, so you need to exercise caution. I always include a `displayName` attribute value. The .NET Framework doesn't use this value, but it does appear in the .NET Framework Configuration tool, so adding this value can help you locate the component as needed. (See the "Using the .NET Framework Configuration Tool" section of Chapter 4 for details on using this tool.)

The `<channel>` element is especially important when it comes to security. You can choose either `ref="http"` or `ref="tcp"` in the current .NET configuration. Other protocols could become available in the future. However, it's essential that you choose `ref="http"`from a security perspective for now because this setting affords you channel level security given specific setup conditions. See the "Using HttpChannel Security" section for details. In addition to choosing the HTTP channel, make sure you choose a unique port. Unlike some technologies, remoting only relies on a single port, but CLR doesn't tie it to the standard HTTP port 80 used for Web requests. Using a single port means that you can monitor a specific port for incoming requests. However, this technique also means you have to open yet another hole in your firewall security. Overall, the superior monitoring capability does provide enough advantages that remoting could be superior to using other data communication techniques as long as you actually monitor the port.

Creating a Remoting Client Application

This section discusses the remoting client application. When you run a remoting client, it redirects requests from the local environment to the remote object. Like the host application, you can either define the redirection programmatically or use a configuration file, with the configuration file providing the more flexible option. The point is that the client tells the remoting system to use the remote object, rather than the local object.

You still need some type of object reference when you build the application. The reference doesn't have to contain the full implementation of the object—all it really needs are the declarations so that Visual Studio .NET features such as IntelliSense work as anticipated. The declaration file must have the same name as the full featured file though, so it often helps to create a Declaration folder beneath the folder containing the actual DLL. Using the declaration file is important because it also contains remoting references the code needs to make remoting work properly.

Once you have everything set up, you need to generate a file that contains the declaration using the SoapSuds (or similar) utility. Open a command prompt in the folder that holds the component DLL, type **SoapSuds -ia:RemotingComponent -oa:Declaration\ RemotingComponent.DLL**, and press Enter. SoapSuds will generate a declaration file based on the assembly you provide as input using the -ia switch (make sure you exclude the assembly file extension). The -oa switch defines the output assembly name. The resulting DLL is significantly smaller than the original DLL. When you create the client, use this declaration assembly as the reference for the application. You can find the declaration component for this example in the \Chapter 10\RemotingComponentDeclaration folder of the source code located on the Sybex Web site.

Listing 10.7 shows the code required to build a remoting client. Unlike other clients you might have built in the past, this one encrypts the data before placing it on the wire and decrypts it on return. The listing isn't complete—it doesn't include the initialization code for the cryptographic service provider. This code appears in the form constructor and is precisely the same as the code that appears in Listing 10.4 for the component. You'll find the complete source code for this example in the \Chapter 10\C#\RemotingClient and \Chapter 10\VB\RemotingClient folders of the source code located on the Sybex Web site.

Listing 10.7   **Simple Remoting Client Example**

```
private RSACryptoServiceProvider RSACrypto;  // The key pair.

private void btnTest_Click(object sender, System.EventArgs e)
{
   MathFunctions  MyObject;      // The target object.
   Byte[]         DataTransmit;  // The data tranmission stream.
   Int32          Result;        // Computation result.

   // Create the object.
   MyObject = new MathFunctions();

   // Encrypt the input.
```

```
        EncryptRequest(1, 2, out DataTransmit);

        // Perform the calculation.
        DataTransmit = MyObject.DoAdd(DataTransmit);

        // Decrypt the result.
        DecryptResult(DataTransmit, out Result);

        // Display the result of an addition.
        MessageBox.Show(Result.ToString(), "Results of Addition",
                    MessageBoxButtons.OK, MessageBoxIcon.Information);
    }

    private void EncryptRequest(Int32 Value1,
                            Int32 Value2, out Byte[] Data)
    {
        Char[]   SValue1;    // Holds the first input value.
        Char[]   SValue2;    // Holds the second input value.
        Int32    Counter;    // Loop counter variable.
        Int32    CurCounter; // Loop counter position bookmark.
        Byte[]   ConvData;   // Unencrypted output data.

        // Convert the input values to Char arrays.
        SValue1 = Convert.ToString(Value1).ToCharArray();
        SValue2 = Convert.ToString(Value2).ToCharArray();

        // Set the size of the conversion array.
        ConvData = new Byte[SValue1.Length + SValue2.Length + 2];

        // Convert the first input value to a byte array.
        ConvData[0] = Convert.ToByte(SValue1.Length);
        for (Counter = 0; Counter < SValue1.Length; Counter++)
            ConvData[Counter + 1] = Convert.ToByte(SValue1[Counter]);

        // Convert the second input value to a byte array.
        Counter++;
        ConvData[Counter] = Convert.ToByte(SValue2.Length);
        CurCounter = Counter + 1;
        for (Counter = CurCounter; Counter < SValue2.Length + CurCounter;
            Counter++)
            ConvData[Counter] =
                Convert.ToByte(SValue2[Counter - CurCounter]);

        // Encrypt the byte array.
        Data = RSACrypto.Encrypt(ConvData, false);

        return;
    }

    private void DecryptResult(Byte[] Input, out Int32 Result)
    {
```

```
Byte[]   Decrypted;      // Decrypted byte array.
Int32    Counter;        // Loop counter variable.
Char[]   ConvChar;       // Converted data in array form.
String   ConvString;     // Individual value in string form.

// Decrypt the input data.
Decrypted = RSACrypto.Decrypt(Input, false);

// Convert the input value to a string.
ConvChar = new Char[Decrypted.Length];
for (Counter = 0; Counter < Decrypted.Length; Counter++)
   ConvChar[Counter] = Convert.ToChar(Decrypted[Counter]);
ConvString = new String(ConvChar);

// Define the result.
Result = Int32.Parse(ConvString);

return;
}
```

The example program begins in the form constructor where it creates the RSACrypto object. The code also loads a configuration file similar to the one shown for the remoting host application in Listing 10.6. The configuration file performs the same task—it redirects requests for the RemotingComponent class to the remote machine. The user's interaction begins with the btnTest_Click() method. This method begins by instantiating a new copy of the MathFunctions class. However, because of the redirection provided by the RemotingConfiguration.Configure() method, the client doesn't actually use the local copy of the component that it used during design—it calls on the remote component instead.

The code then encrypts the input values for the remote object using the EncryptRequest() method. The object is actually executing on the remote machine—not the local machine, so encrypting the data that will go over the wire is important. The code calls the MyObject.DoAdd() method as usual. However, it calls the method using the encrypted data and receives an encrypted response. The code calls the DecryptResult() method to decrypt the result. Finally, the code displays the result using a message box.

The EncryptRequest() method accepts the two Int32 values as input and returns an encrypted Byte[] array. The code converts the two inputs to Char[] array values. It obtains the length of the first Char[] array and uses that value as the first entry into the Byte[] array, ConvData. The code then places the first Char[] array value into ConvData. The code adds the second Byte[] array using the same technique so that it follows the first in ConvData. What you have now is a Byte[] array that contains both sets of values. The final step is to encrypt ConvData and place the result in Data.

The DecryptResult() method begins by decrypting Input, which is a Byte[] array. Because there's only one value in the array, conversion is relatively simple. The converted data appears in a Char[] array, which acts as input for a String, and is finally parsed into an Int32 value.

Like the remoting host, the client requires a configuration file to know where to find the remote object. The fact that you're using a configuration file means that you can change the location of the remote object without recompiling the application. Listing 10.8 shows the configuration file for the client.

Listing 10.8   **Typical Remoting Host Configuration File**

```xml
<?xml version="1.0" encoding="utf-8" ?>
<configuration>
   <system.runtime.remoting>
      <application>
         <client>
            <wellknown
               type="RemotingComponent.MathFunctions,
                  RemotingComponent"
               url="http://WinServer:8989/RemotingComponent.DLL"
            />
         </client>
      </application>
   </system.runtime.remoting>
</configuration>
```

As you can see, the client configuration file contains many of the same elements as the remoting host configuration file. In this case, the configuration file contains the <client> tag. The <wellknown> tag contains attributes that describe the namespace, class name, and assembly name of the component. It also includes the location of the component. Note that you can use LocalHost if you want to test on a local machine, rather than using a remote machine as I did. You'll need to change the name of the server to match your server (unless you also named your remote server WinServer).

When you click Test the first time, it will appear that nothing happened. After a lengthy delay, you'll finally see the result. While writing this example, I finally started listening for the hard drive on the server—it takes that long. However, click Test a second time and you'll notice the response is quite speedy (almost instantaneous). Nothing has changed except the component is loaded in memory. An unbelievable number of tasks must take place before the component can perform encrypted data transfer.

Of course, it's easy to assume that you're not engaging in a remote conversation between two machines. At the listener prompt, press Enter. The listener will stop at this point and unload itself from memory. Click Test again and you'll see the error message shown in

Figure 10.6. This is your proof that the remoting is working as advertised. No listener means no component access.

Test the reality of using remoting by turning the listener off and clicking Test on the client.

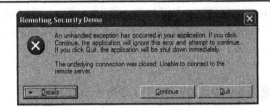

Using HttpChannel Security

In the "Using the `AuthenticationManager` Class" section of Chapter 9, you learned about the technique used to authenticate a user on IIS (see Listing 9.1). The example in that section relied on the `PreAuthenticate()` method to check the authentication of a caller by using a Web request and one or more credentials in a cache. You also know from the example in this section of this chapter that you can pass requests to a remoting listener directly or through IIS using any of a number of protocols such as SOAP. The `HttpChannel` class provides access to the low-level communication that occurs when you use remoting through an IIS connection.

The `HttpChannel` class provides access to the transport protocol used to transfer the information from one point to another. One of the `HttpChannel` class properties is credentials, which works precisely like the credentials discussed in Listing 9.1. In fact, the `HttpChannel` object passes the credentials to the `AuthenticationManager` object, which passes them to the server.

The main reason you would want to use the `HttpChannel` class and its associated properties is control. Adding the credentials at this level, rather than using the `AuthenticationManager` directly, is a matter of convenience. Using this class lets you control every aspect of the channel and therefore the communication session. Control requires additional code, testing time, and programming effort. However, by exercising control over the channel, you also gain opportunities to check and validate security.

For this technique to work, you must also configure IIS to provide SSL support. See the "Adding SSL Support to a Server" section of this chapter for details on performing this task. The URL you provide in the configuration files must use HTTPS, rather than the standard HTTP transport. In addition, you must set up the application's virtual directory to provide some type of authentication: Basic, Digest, Cookie, or Windows Integrated.

You can always verify the security status of a connection before you use it. First, gain access to the `HttpRequest` object using the `HttpContext.Request` property. Second, once you have access to an `HttpRequest` object, use the `IsSecureConnection()` method to determine the current connection security status.

Note that the TcpChannel class doesn't provide the same low-level support as the HttpChannel class. The main reason is that the TcpChannel class bypasses IIS, which means you don't have access to the SSL support the IIS provides. When you create a remoting application that transfers information over the Internet from a client to a Web server, you should always use the HTTP channel. See Listing 10.6 and 10.8 for the application configuration settings that you need to make.

Using SSL to Communicate Credentials

SSL is the method that most Web sites use to secure communication because it's standardized, relatively easy to implement, and safe. One option that you don't see too often is the exchange of credentials between client and server. The server normally presents credentials, but the application doesn't expect the client to provide any. The problem is that many clients don't have credential to provide, making a two-way credential exchange difficult on public Web sites.

Fortunately, private Web sites can use this solution to keep the exchange of text data to a minimum. You must set the server up to accept the client certificate (see the "Adding SSL Support to a Server" section for details). When you want to use the certificate as part of an authentication strategy in place of the one shown in Listings 10.1 through 10.3, you must also create a certificate to Windows account mapping. The "Creating an SSL Application" section shows how to access the certificate information.

Adding SSL Support to a Server

Once you lock down your Web server, you'll find that many of the programs that used to work don't any longer. In general, the changes force you to use a secure connection strategy such as SSL to ensure a cracker can't monitor your communications. Unfortunately, Microsoft can't ship IIS with SSL support installed because the server requires a certificate. You can obtain a certificate from a third party source or you can generate one of your own using the procedure in the "Getting Your Own Certificate" section of Chapter 7. After you add a certificate to your system, you can follow the steps below to add SSL support.

NOTE   You might need to perform this procedure at the server console, rather than use a remote connection. In some cases, a remote connection won't allow access to the server certificate, which is a requirement for installing SSL support. When this occurs, the Server Certificate button on the Directory Security tab of the target Web site's Properties dialog box is disabled.

1. Open the Internet Information Services Console.
2. Right-click the target Web site entry in the hierarchy and choose Properties from the context menu. Select the Directory Security tab and you'll see a Web site Properties dialog box similar to the one shown in Figure 10.7.

FIGURE 10.7:

Make sure you can add SSL from the current location by looking at the Server Certificate button.

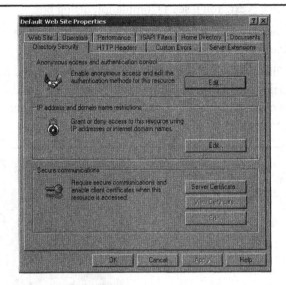

3. Click Server Certificate. You'll see the Welcome to the Web Server Certificate Wizard.

4. Click Next. You'll see the Server Certificate dialog box.

5. Select the Assign an Existing Certificate option. Click Next. You'll see an Available Certificates dialog box.

6. Select one of the available certificates. Generally, you'll see more than one certificate. To choose the correct certificate, look in the Intended Purpose column for a certificate with the Client Authentication feature, such as the one shown in Figure 10.8. Click Next. You'll see a Certificate Summary dialog box.

FIGURE 10.8:

Select a client authentication certificate.

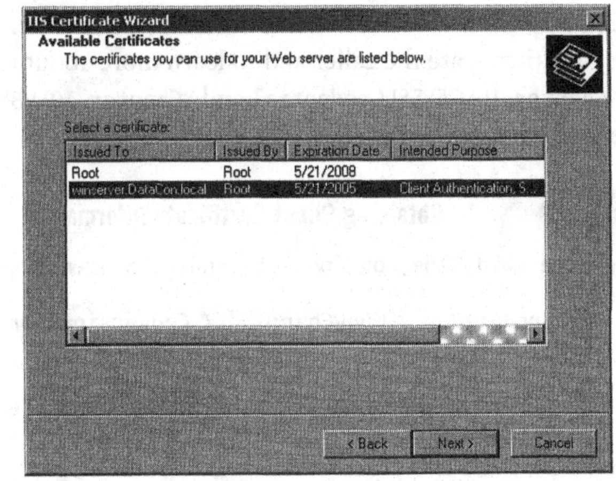

7. Click Next. You'll see a Completion dialog box.

8. Click Finish. The wizard will end and you'll return to the Directory Security tab of the Web site's Properties dialog box.

9. Click Edit in the Secure Communications section. You'll see a Secure Communications dialog box shown in Figure 10.9. Notice that this dialog box lets you set up features such as client certificate mapping, which associates client certificates with specific Windows accounts.

FIGURE 10.9:

Choose the client authentication option.

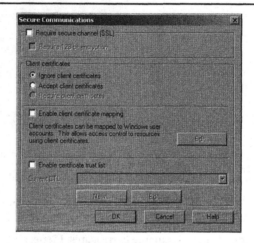

10. Select the Accept Client Certificates option. Click OK. This step ensures the server can determine the identity of clients accessing the Web site.

Creating an SSL Application

Listing 10.9 shows how to obtain information from a certificate. In general, you'll use certificates to authenticate the caller and to learn more about the caller. You'll find this example in the \Chapter 10\C#\SSLCredential and \Chapter 10\VB\SSLCredential folders of the source code located on the Sybex Web site.

Listing 10.9   Obtaining Client Certificate Information

```
private void Page_Load(object sender, System.EventArgs e)
{
    StringBuilder   ConvChar;   // Conversion for public key.
    Int32    Counter;    // Loop counter.

    // Determine whether the certificate is present.
    if (Request.ClientCertificate.IsPresent)
```

```
    {
        // Convert the public key.
        ConvChar = new StringBuilder();
        for (Counter = 0;
            Counter < Request.ClientCertificate.PublicKey.Length;
            Counter++)
            ConvChar.Append(
                Request.ClientCertificate.PublicKey[Counter].ToString("X2") +
                " ");

        // Get each of the statistics.
        txtIssuer.Text =
            Request.ClientCertificate.Issuer.ToString();
        cbValid.Checked =
            Request.ClientCertificate.IsValid;
        txtKeySize.Text =
            Request.ClientCertificate.KeySize.ToString();
        txtPublicKey.Text =
            ConvChar.ToString();
        txtSerialNumber.Text =
            Request.ClientCertificate.SerialNumber.ToString();
        txtServerIssuer.Text =
            Request.ClientCertificate.ServerIssuer.ToString();
        txtServerSubject.Text =
            Request.ClientCertificate.ServerSubject.ToString();
        txtSubject.Text =
            Request.ClientCertificate.Subject.ToString();
        txtValidFrom.Text =
            Request.ClientCertificate.ValidFrom.ToLongDateString();
        txtValidTo.Text =
            Request.ClientCertificate.ValidUntil.ToLongDateString();
    }
    else
        // There is no certificate.
        txtIssuer.Text = "No Certificate Supplied";
}
```

All of the values for a certificate appear within the `Request.ClientCertificate` property. However, this property is `null` if the client doesn't provide a certificate, so you need to make this check first. The `Request.ClientCertificate.IsPresent` property always defines the presence or absence of a certificate.

Once it knows the client has supplied a certificate, the code begins by converting the `Request.ClientCertificate.PublicKey` property to a string. The code then displays the various values on screen using the property values shown in the listing. The example shows a few of the properties—the certificate provides a wealth of additional information. Figure 10.10 shows typical output from this application.

FIGURE 10.10:

Typical certificate
information you can
use to validate a Web
site caller.

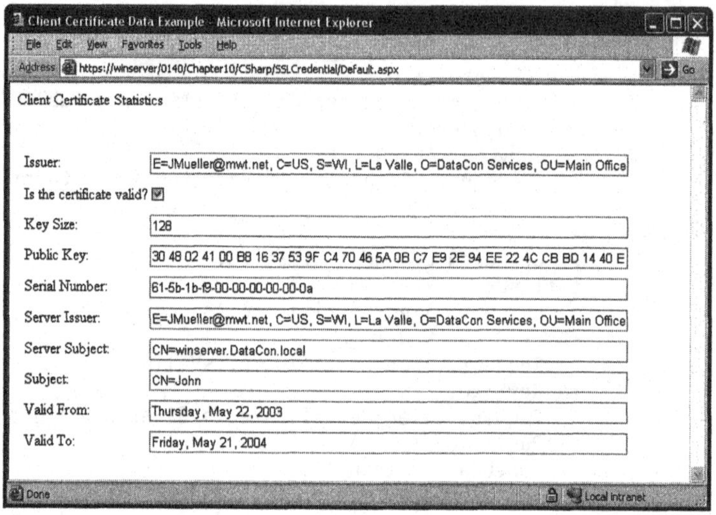

Summary

This chapter discussed the data portion of security for Web applications. It's important to consider that every piece of information, no matter how small or unimportant, that you place on a public Web site is available to everyone at some point. Even if you password protect the Web site and grant access only to a privileged few, the data is going to leak. You also need to protect data as you move it from one location to another. This requirement normally means that you have to encrypt the data in some way, either manually or automatically as part of some other process. Finally, you need to consider the ramifications of using messaging queuing with your application. Yes, it's a nice feature, but you need to consider the costs associated with the Windows message queuing feature.

Now it's time to take action for the sake of your data. Begin by looking at the security policies for your company. Do you have a policy in place that not only governs the dissemination of data by employees, but the presentation of that data by applications? The application developer is in a good position to reduce the vulnerability of data to outside influences. You'll also need to consider whether you need additional data security in place. A good way to look at data transferal across the Internet is to consider how much damage that data would cause if you printed it in the local newspaper.

Chapter 11 discusses one of the most popular Web applications in use today, the Web service. It's not always a good idea to buy into all of the hype surrounding this technology. In addition, you need to choose the correct technology for a specific need. Using some technologies for a Web service can leave your server and your data completely open to attack.

CHAPTER 11

Securing XML and Web Services

- Developing Secure Web Services

- Understanding the `System.Security.Cryptography.Xml` Namespace

- Working with the Global XML Architecture (GXA)

- Developing Applications with WS-Security

- Using the eXtensible Access Control Markup Language (XACML)

- Developing Applications with the Visual Studio .NET Passport Features

- Adding XML Digital Signatures to an Application

- Developing a Web Service Application Using COM+ 1.5

W eb services hold a lot of promise for businesses. Because Web services use standardized ports, standards-based communication strategies, and pure text for content, they can cross boundaries thought unassailable by developers using older technologies such as DCOM and CORBA. However, the very strengths that help make Web services technologies such as SOAP so compatible also cause significant security problems. Do you really want to transmit secret information using a text-based SOAP message that anyone can read? This chapter demonstrates that Web services are inherently less secure than other technologies you use. However, the chapter also discusses strategies you can use to decrease the security problems and address the necessary monitoring requirements.

Part of the strategy for protecting your Web services investment is to use standardized security approaches. The .NET-specific approach is the `System.Security.Cryptography.Xml` namespace. In a larger sense, you also need to consider generalized Microsoft technologies such as those found in GXA. It's also important to consider using standardized approaches such as WS-Security and XACML.

Web services don't focus on just corporate data. As users begin interacting with your applications, you also need to consider the issue of privacy and personal data management. When you lose a piece of corporate data, the consequences can be dire, but they're normally limited to your company and perhaps corporate partners. Personal data management incurs an additional level of burden that could cause problems well beyond simple data loss. Passport and the Liberty Alliance Project are two of several promising technologies for personal information management. Although the chapter discusses the Microsoft-supported Passport extensively because support for this technology appears in the .NET Framework, both technologies are valuable to a company that needs to manage personal information.

The next section of the chapter discusses XML digital signatures. Web services suffer from a lack of identification, as well as a lack of security. You don't really know that a Web service comes from a specific source unless the underlying application is signed using a digital signature. This section of the chapter discusses how you can add a digital signature so others know the Web service they're using actually comes from your company and not a cracker.

The final section discusses a special feature of COM+ 1.5. You can actually create a Web service application by checking a few simple options. Of course, developing a Web service application using this technique leaves all kinds of questions unanswered, such as whether the process is even safe.

NOTE This chapter assumes that you already know how to work with Web services and want to learn techniques for creating a secure environment. You can learn more about using Web services with the .NET Framework from *.NET Web Services Solutions* (Sybex, 2003) by Kris Jamsa, which provides code examples in both VB.NET and C#, and my book *Visual C# .NET Developer's Handbook* (Sybex, 2002), which discusses both desktop and mobile device development strategies for .NET. If you want a complete overview of SOAP, including SOAP products from various vendors and SOAP testing strategies, my book *Special Edition Using SOAP* (Que, 2001) can help you. This book doesn't offer .NET-specific information, but is still very useful for the other insights it provides. For example, it tells you how to overcome compatibility problems between the Microsoft implementation of SOAP and the implementation provided by Apache.

Securing Web Services

It helps to know a little about the reasons behind the development of Web services before you delve into the security issues associated with this technology. You can use technologies such as DCOM and CORBA in an Internet environment. In fact, these technologies offer many features that Web service technologies such as SOAP don't offer. DCOM can automatically encrypt your communication so that it isn't readable by anyone else. It also provides the support needed to validate the data and authenticate the user. DCOM and CORBA are both inherently more secure than any Web service communication, even with the latest security features for Web services installed on your system. In addition, both DCOM and CORBA are heavily tested and mature technologies that developers understand well. The fact that developers truly understand these technologies also helps make them more secure—you can't create a secure application if you don't understand the underlying technology.

The problem with using DCOM and CORBA is that they're incompatible. An application that relies on DCOM can't communicate with an application that uses CORBA. In addition, both technologies are binary. Even if you can locate the data stream, it's unlikely that any virus scanning software could find a hidden virus because the data stream is unreadable. It's also impossible to use a firewall. DCOM requires so many open ports that any firewall you set up is going to be useless. In short, even though DCOM and CORBA are secure from a data perspective, they have problems that a developer can't easily fix in a distributed application environment.

TIP   Microsoft is obviously interested in promoting their new Web services, so their marketing machine is pumping out the usual flood of interesting documents. Cutting through the hype can be difficult. However, you'll find a technically solid article on the topic entitled, "Using Web Services Instead of DCOM" at http://msdn.microsoft.com/library/en-us/dndotnet/html/webservicesdcom.asp.

Web services are secure to a point. You can use a single standardized port for communication, which means firewalls remain effective. Web services rely on pure text data transmission, so you don't have to consider weird programming strategies to ensure compatibility. The use of standardized communication tends to make the application more secure as a whole. However, the text-based nature of Web service communication leaves your data completely unprotected. The lack of data security, user authentication, validation, and other security needs all conspire to make Web service solutions inherently non-secure. The following sections describe these problems in greater detail and offer solutions for resolving them.

XML and Security

XML is an important part of the security efforts for distributed applications. The need for security is greater in distributed applications than in desktop or LAN applications, yet security efforts have lagged in the distributed application arena. Many companies cite the lack of good security as one of the main reasons their distributed application plans are on hold, so, obviously, the computer industry has to do something to address the problem.

The Worldwide Web Consortium (W3C) and Internet Engineering Task Force (IETF) released the XML Signature specification as an industry standard shortly after the release of Visual Studio .NET. This means you won't find this important security feature as part of Visual Studio .NET until Microsoft adds it as a service pack or part of a subsequent release.

XML security is an important issue because the standard XML transmission relies on pure text, which means data is open to the casual observer. Using an XML Signature means that the recipient can validate the XML data sender and verify that the data is unmodified. Look for third party vendors to offer products that add XML Signature support to Visual Studio .NET. You can read about this standard at http://www.w3.org/TR/2002/REC-xmldsig-core-20020212/. The W3C and IETF are still working on two other XML security standards: XML Encryption and XML Key Management.

The use of biometrics is also becoming an important part of local application security. Biometrics make it difficult for a third party to steal passwords because the password is based on a body feature such as a fingerprint, facial component, voiceprint, or the construction of the iris. Previous biometric encoding techniques relied on binary technology, which doesn't work well with XML—a text-based technology designed to overcome the limits of binary data transfer. The XML Common Biometric Format (XCBF) is a new standard designed to make biometrics accessible to XML communication. You can see an overview of this technology at `http://www.eweek.com/article/0,3658,s=1884&a=23693,00.asp`, `http://www.infoworld.com/articles/hn/xml/02/03/07/020307hnoasis.xml?0308fram`, and `http://www.internetnews.com/dev-news/article/0,,10_987001,00.html`. You can find a more comprehensive discussion of this topic at `http://www.oasis-open.org/committees/xcbf/`.

Web Service Proxy Security Considerations

A Web service works like the other remote code strategies that came before it in one important way—the component executes on the host machine, not the client machine. The client machine receives a proxy—a representation—of the Web service to use locally. The host machine has a stub—a representation of the caller—to use in most cases. Consequently, you aren't working with an actual object on your system when you perform a Web service call.

TIP   If you wonder how the security of the Web service functionality provided by the .NET Framework compares to other platforms, at least one study on the subject is in. According to an eWeek article (`http://www.eweek.com/article2/0,3959,1113313,00.asp`) an @Stake study confirms that the features provided by the .NET Framework are a little better than those provided by IBM's Websphere. The article states that neither company had any input into the test to ensure @Stake conducted the test in the fairest manner possible. Although this speaks highly of Microsoft's efforts, it's always important to consider the basis for such tests and whether they reflect the realities of your installation.

Both the client and the server experience some level of risk when using a proxy/stub setup to perform communication. In fact, it doesn't matter which technology you use for communication—the risks are the same. However, the probability of a security breach due to these risks is much greater in a Web services environment due to the use of a text-based communication media. Here are the security risks you should consider.

Query Contamination

Web services are self-describing—your program sends a request and the Web service returns an XML document that describes the service. You can list many benefits to this approach, such as the ability to locate and use a component even when the component lacks registry information on the local machine. DCOM required such information, making the technology less than useful in a distributed environment of the kind provided by the Internet. However, the self-describing nature of Web services can also cause security problems. To learn about the component, an application must send a query. The act of making a query and allowing return information opens the door to cracker attack.

WARNING Some developers have the misinformed opinion that viruses can't reside in XML because XML is just text. Actually, XML is formatted text—it includes tags and other information. Yes, you can read XML, but most people use a parser to interpret the tags and present the information in a more readable form. The moment you use a parser on any text, you add the potential for a virus. For example, Rice University has a Web site containing its latest virus to test student code for the COMP 314 course where they learn to write an XML parser (`http://www.owlnet.rice.edu/~fnjord/output/article17.html`). In fact, the addition of XML support to products such as Office 2003 could slow adoption of these products according to a ComputerWeekly.com article (`http://www.cw360.com/Article120453.htm`). Even Microsoft acknowledges that viruses in XML are a significant threat and provides a free XML filter for their Internet Security and Acceleration (ISA) Server (`http://www.microsoft.com/presspass/features/2002/feb02/02-18xmlfilter.asp`). To put the threat into perspective, a Network World Fusion article states that at least one virus already targets .NET applications through Web services (`http://www.nwfusion.com/news/2002/0110donut.html`). In short, running Web services represents a significant security threat that you must consider carefully.

Data Security and Data Validation

Text-based communication means that there's no way to ensure the data is the same data that the other party transmitted. Everything from acts of nature to a cracker's intervention could modify the data. Consequently, you can't trust any data you receive unless you provide some type of security of your own. Yes, using Secure Sockets Layer (SSL) does help, but the flaw is in the data itself. This use of text means a Trojan or virus on either machine will remain undetected (or is at least harder to detect).

Channel Security

A cracker's best hope of remaining undetected is to intercept the data between sites. Intercepting the data isn't as hard as you might think. All the cracker needs is a relatively inexpensive packet sniffer and an IP address. It doesn't take long for the cracker to determine which port to use, which means your data is completely exposed. SSL is a good deterrent for channel problems and you should always use it with Web services.

User Authentication

Chapter 10 discussed a number of user authentication issues and strategies. For example, the "Using SSL to Communicate Credentials" section discusses how you can learn more about a caller by checking the SSL credentials. The problem with this approach is that it assumes the caller has credentials—many don't. In addition, it also relies on your trusting both the Credential Authority (CA) and the caller possessing the credentials. In short, even with credentials, user authentication can become difficult. Of course, standard user authentication assumes you know the caller—it's quite possible with a Web service that you won't know anything at all about the caller, which makes authentication nearly impossible.

Caller Location

Sometimes the best checks are the ones that you can implement with the fewest number of problems and the least amount of code. The "Using Principal and Identity Objects" section of Chapter 4 shows how to check the caller's zone (or location). If you expect a caller to make a request from the intranet and suddenly a request comes from the Internet, you have to question the sudden change. You can verify this information using the `ZoneIdentityPermission` attribute—a single statement can save you some security headaches.

Third Party Intervention

Third parties are an increasing threat for Web services. A third party could simply listen to the conversation and record everything for future blackmail. In fact, an InfoWorld article (`http://www.infoworld.com/article/03/05/23/21secadvise_1.html`) points out that cracking is now one of the strategies organized crime uses. Third parties can also modify the data, erase it completely, interfere with its transmission, and perform other nasty deeds. Given the number of third party threats, it's amazing that Web services work at all.

Most developers don't work with third party Web services today. The developers who do work with third party Web services usually know the third party and can trust them. If Web services continue in their current direction, you might not know the third party in the future. The problem with this lack of knowledge becomes clear when you consider what happens when you connect to another machine looking for a Web service to use. Visual Studio .NET creates a proxy of that Web service on your local machine using your trusted user's account. Any virus code or Trojan that the third party installs in the Web service could also affect your machine. Always exercise caution when creating a reference to a third party Web service in your application.

Working with *SoapHttpClientProtocol* Class Security

The Visual Studio .NET IDE performs a lot of the work required to create a Web service for you. For example, in the "Creating a Simple COM+ Test Application" section of the chapter, you'll create a client application that calls a Web service that accesses a COM+ 1.5 application. When you create the Web reference to that Web service, the Visual Studio .NET IDE automatically builds a `Reference.CS` file for you. Contained within this file is a `MathFunctionsService` class definition that derives from the `System.Web.Services .Protocols.SoapHttpClientProtocol` class. Look in the `\Chapter 11\C#\COMPlusTest\ Web References\main` or `\Chapter 11\VB\COMPlusTest\Web References\main` folder of the source code located on the Sybex Web site for a detailed view of this class.

The fact that Visual Studio .NET performs all of this work for you is nice—it's convenient, reduces development time, and can reduce errors. However, you need to consider just what type of code Visual Studio .NET generates for you. Most people won't experience problems with the code, but you should at least look at it since this code is part of your application. For example, even the release version of your code will contain the `System.Diagnostics` `.DebuggerStepThroughAttribute` attribute for the `MathFunctionsService` class. When developing native code, most developers remove all debugging features from the release version. Not only does this step enhance performance, but it also makes it more difficult for the user to reverse engineer the code—a prerequisite for learning about any security holes in your code. To make matters worse, the Microsoft documentation is especially terse for this attribute—it's hard to know why it's included at all. Experimentation shows that you do need the `DebuggerStepThroughAttribute` attribute to ensure you can set a breakpoint within the proxy.

TIP   It's important to consider some of the hidden security threats that can occur when working with Web services. For example, Microsoft Knowledge Base article 322866 (`http://support.microsoft.com/default.aspx?scid=kb;[LN];322886`) presents an interesting security issue. In this case, the developer might see a particular error message if the Web service lacks access to the \Temp folder. On the face of things, it would seem like a small problem that's easily resolved. However, you have to wonder why a Web service would require access to your drive and what other areas the Web service can access. The Microsoft documentation doesn't list this particular requirement anywhere, nor does it tell you about the security implications of providing access to this part of the system. The point is that you must monitor the activity of your Web service applications to ensure they remain within their designated areas and don't begin looking in other areas of your system.

Let's say that you really don't want to keep this debugging feature in place when you release your product. Nothing says that you must use the Visual Studio .NET IDE method of providing a reference to your Web service. You can just as easily generate the proxy manually or you can use the WSDL utility to generate the class and modify it as needed. To generate the proxy class manually, open a command prompt and type **WSDL -out:MathProxy.CS http://Main/MathFunctionsMethod/COMPlusComp.MathFunctions.soap?WSDL**. You'll need to substitute the URL for your server. The file WSDL outputs looks remarkably similar to the file generated by a Web reference. The only difference is that you can modify the source code as needed to meet security needs. Of course, the IDE doesn't update anything automatically using this technique. When you change the component, you also need to generate this file again or add the changes manually.

NOTE WSDL assumes that you use C#. If you use another language that WSDL supports, you need to specify it as part of the command line syntax. For example, Visual Basic users will need to type **WSDL -out:MathProxy.VB -language:VB http://Main/MathFunctionsMethod/ COMPlusComp.MathFunctions.soap?WSDL** at the command prompt to get a Visual Basic version of the proxy. Again, you'll need to substitute the URL for your server as part of the input.

The client code for this example is precisely the same as the client code shown in Listing 11.7. (You'll find the complete source code for this example in the \Chapter 11\C#\COMPlusTest2 and \Chapter 11\VB\COMPlusComp2 folders of the source code located on the Sybex Web site.) The only difference is that you don't need to add a reference to the proxy with the using statement because you created the proxy yourself. However, the most important difference is that you can edit the proxy code as needed to meet specific security requirements.

To see the effect of removing the DebuggerStepThroughAttribute attribute, try this experiment. Comment the entry out, as shown here,

```
using System.Web.Services;
```

```
// Comment this attribute to improve performance and
// reduce security problems.
//[System.Diagnostics.DebuggerStepThroughAttribute()]
[System.ComponentModel.DesignerCategoryAttribute("code")]
```

compile the application, and run it. You'll notice that the code is smaller, uses a few less resources, and runs slightly faster.

You can try a number of other changes too. For example, WSDL assumes that you'll run your Web service on port 80 of the Web server. You can choose other ports in the interest of security. All you need to do is change the constructor shown here.

```
public MathFunctionsService()
{
// Change this URL to use other ports.
this.Url =
    "http://main:80/MathFunctionsMethod/COMPlusComp.MathFunctions.soap";
}
```

One of the more interesting security problems with the generated proxy is that it doesn't include any permissions checks. You don't know that the caller has permission to make the request. For example, you can add the UrlIdentityPermission attribute to the code to verify the caller has permission to make the required proxy call. Proxies also make a good place to include custom permissions and to verify the caller is in a specific role.

Using a manually generated proxy also lets you decide how the user will call the Web service. Microsoft assumes that you want to include both synchronous and asynchronous access techniques—using a custom proxy lets you make all access synchronous or asynchronous as needed. The automatically generated proxy also includes every public method the Web service exposes. You might create a custom proxy that only exposes the methods you want the client to see. Some methods might only exist for in-house use. In general, reducing access to just the features a client needs improves security.

It's important to remember that your proxy derives from the `SoapHttpClientProtocol` class. This class also includes a `Credentials` property you can use in the same way other classes in the book use this feature. Look at Listing 11.7 and you'll notice that the client uses the `MathFunctionsService.Credentials` property that's included automatically with your proxy. However, you can also override the default property and provide custom handling in your proxy (and call the base class to perform the default handling later).

Working with *DiscoveryClientProtocol* Class Security

Discovering services is important—it's the first step in using a Web service you need for your application. However, like other Web service discussions so far, you need to consider who's using the Web service, how they use it, and where they access it. In short, you need to provide some form of security. The technique for discovering the Web service varies, but in this section, you'll learn the manual process that relies on the `DiscoveryClientProtocol` class. The Visual Studio .NET IDE also provides means for accessing the Web service using the IDE (the "Creating a Simple COM+ Test Application" section of the chapter discusses the automated method).

Previous chapters have discussed the issue of using attributes versus inline code for checking permissions. Web services are definitely one case where using attributes can become a problem. Consider the simple Web service shown in Listing 11.1.

Listing 11.1 • A Web Service Using Security Attributes

```
namespace MathComp
{
    public class MathFunctions : System.Web.Services.WebService
    {
        public MathFunctions()
        {
            // Perform default action.
            InitializeComponent();
        }

        [WebMethod,
         ZoneIdentityPermission(SecurityAction.LinkDemand,
```

```
        Zone=SecurityZone.Intranet)]
    public Int32 DoAdd(Int32 Value1, Int32 Value2)
    {
        return Value1 + Value2;
    }

    ... Other Web Methods ...

    }
}
```

Notice that this Web service uses the `ZoneIdentityPermission` attribute to ensure the caller comes from the `SecurityZone.Intranet` zone. However, the attribute doesn't work as expected in this case. Figure 11.1 shows the WSDL for this component—notice it doesn't include a single method.

FIGURE 11.1:

Attributes don't work very well for Web service security needs.

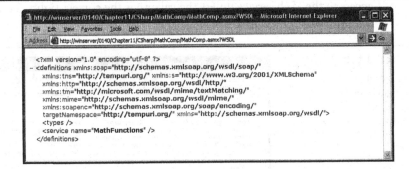

If you attempt to use this version of the component for Web services, no one will access them. The use of the security attribute appears to keep everyone, even local users, from accessing the Web service. However, the new version in Listing 11.2 does work as anticipated and accomplishes the same task. You'll find this example in the \Chapter 11\C#\MathComp and \Chapter 11\VB\MathComp folders of the source code located on the Sybex Web site.

Listing 11.2   A Web Service Using Imperative Security

```
namespace MathComp
{
    public class MathFunctions : System.Web.Services.WebService
    {
        public MathFunctions()
        {
            // Perform default action.
            InitializeComponent();
        }

        [WebMethod]
```

```
public Int32 DoAdd(Int32 Value1, Int32 Value2)
{
    // Validate the user has permission.
    ZoneIdentityPermission  ZIP;
    ZIP = new ZoneIdentityPermission(SecurityZone.Intranet);
    ZIP.Demand();

    // Return the requested value.
    return Value1 + Value2;
}

... Other Web Methods ...

}
}
```

Using this technique permits the discovery phase to proceed as normal, yet doesn't allow access to the Web service unless the caller has the correct rights. Figure 11.2 shows the output from this version of the component.

FIGURE 11.2:

Use imperative security as needed to address Web service requirements.

Now that the Web service is working and more secure, let's look at the client making the request using the DiscoveryClientProtocol class. First, you need to understand that using this class is the beginning of the journey, not the end. You receive the same information you receive when viewing the WSDL directly with a Web browser. The difference is that you can now manipulate the data with ease. Second, you'll actually work with a document that contains the WSDL in the form of collections. This book won't show you all the ins and outs of working with the collections because it focuses on security, but the information you can retrieve is substantial. Listing 11.3 shows the client portion of this example. You'll find this example in the \Chapter 11\C#\MathCompTest and \Chapter 11\VB\MathCompTest folders of the source code located on the Sybex Web site.

Listing 11.3   **Using the *DiscoveryClientProtocol* Class**

```
private void btnTest_Click(object sender, System.EventArgs e)
{
    DiscoveryClientProtocol DCP;       // Web service discovery protocol.
    NetworkCredential       NetCred;   // Credential for current user.
    CredentialCache         Cache;     // Cached credentials.
    DiscoveryDocument       Doc;       // Results of the query.
    StringBuilder           Output;    // Contains the discovery data.
    ContractReference       ConRef;    // The Web service contract.

    // Create the credentials.
    NetCred = new NetworkCredential(txtName.Text, txtPassword.Text);
    Cache = new CredentialCache();
    Cache.Add(new Uri(txtURL.Text), "Basic", NetCred);
    Cache.Add(new Uri(txtURL.Text), "Digest", NetCred);
    Cache.Add(new Uri(txtURL.Text), "NTLM", NetCred);
    Cache.Add(new Uri(txtURL.Text), "Kerberos", NetCred);

    // Initialize the discovery protocol.
    DCP = new DiscoveryClientProtocol();
    DCP.Credentials = Cache;

    // Make the query.
    Doc = DCP.DiscoverAny(txtURL.Text);

    ConRef = new ContractReference();
    foreach (Object Temp in Doc.References)
       ConRef = (ContractReference)Temp;

    // Build an output string.
    Output = new StringBuilder();

    // Get the Bindings.
    Output.Append("Bindings:\r\n");
    foreach (System.Web.Services.Description.Binding Bind in
       ConRef.Contract.Bindings)
    {
       Output.Append("\r\n");
       Output.Append(Bind.Name);
    }

    // Get the Messages.
```

```
Output.Append("\r\n\r\nMessages:\r\n");
foreach (System.Web.Services.Description.Message Msg in
   ConRef.Contract.Messages)
{
   Output.Append("\r\n");
   Output.Append(Msg.Name);
}

// Display the results.
txtOutput.Text = Output.ToString();
}
```

One of the essentials for this example is that you must build a `CredentialCache` object specifically for the Web service. Don't build a `CredentialCache` object for the application Web site or the example won't work. For example, the URL for my Web site is `http://winserver/0140/Chapter11/CSharp/MathComp/MathComp.asmx?WSDL`. Notice that I've included the WSDL in my URL—you'll need to include it as well. Each `NetworkCredential` includes a username and password as a minimum. You can also include a domain when required. Notice that the `CredentialCache` object is not only specific to the WSDL URL, but it also contains one entry for each type of authentication to ensure the program will make a connection. You can probably reduce it to one or two authentication methods for a local application because you'll know how the administrator set the Web server up.

Using the `DiscoveryClientProtocol` object is relatively easy. The code creates a new instance of the object, adds the `CredentialCache` object, and then uses the `DCP.DiscoverAny()` method to obtain the data. The resulting `DiscoveryDocument` object contains all of the information you normally see in your browser and all of the hidden headers. At this point, you could lose the connection with the server and the application would still work because all of the data appears within the `DiscoveryDocument` object. View this object with the debugger and you'll immediately see it several levels down in the hierarchy.

The problem is that you can't access any of this information directly—it's all contained in collections. The code shows how to retrieve a few pieces of information, such as the bindings used to create the connection. The `Message` objects describe the various SOAP messages you can create (and therefore the methods the Web service exposes for use). The final step is to output the information to a textbox on screen so you can see the data.

Using the *System.Security.Cryptography.Xml* Namespace

Cryptography is an extremely important part of data communications, especially as companies move into the Internet environment to communicate with partners and customers better.

Chapter 7 discusses many of the issues surrounding cryptography. The problem is that many cryptographic techniques would prove difficult to use with XML because XML is structured text—not pure text. The structure is important to the interpretation of the data XML provides. Consequently, the .NET Framework provides the special System.Security.Cryptography.Xml namespace to make working with XML easier.

When you look at the cryptographic examples in Chapter 7, you'll notice that the data is unreadable. You could use this method to transmit an XML document that didn't require immediate processing on the other side. XML is structured data, so readability is important when immediate interpretation is required. Consequently, signing the document so that tampering is immediately obvious is the next best choice. No, signing won't protect your data, but it does make it less likely that someone will change the data or even add a virus to it. The cryptographic techniques in Chapter 7 will work just as well for XML as they will for any other file when data hiding is important. The technique in this section of the chapter demonstrates how to sign a file so that tampering is immediately apparent. You could use this technique to ensure the integrity of transactions, such as those created by an application that relies on SOAP.

The following sections help you understand the role of the System.Security.Cryptography.Xml namespace better. These sections describe what makes this namespace different from other cryptographic functionality discussed earlier in the book. However, if you don't already know how to use cryptographic techniques, you'll want to read Chapter 7 first.

Understanding the *System.Security.Cryptography.Xml* Namespace

The System.Security.Cryptography.Xml namespace looks somewhat complicated until you start to break it into pieces. The important thing to remember is that this namespace augments the functionality provided by the System.Security.Cryptography namespace. For example, when you need a key to compute a signature, you'll use a standard RSACryptoServiceProvider object, just like what's shown in the examples in Chapter 7 (see Listing 7.4 for the first example of how to use such a key). You can easily divide the classes in this namespace into three areas.

Key Management   Cryptography in all its forms relies on keys. When you work with Web services, you need some method of managing keys with parties that you might never meet. As you'll see in the example, the key management features in classes such as KeyInfo and Reference make it possible to work with third parties in a secure manner.

Data Management   At some point, you'll need to modify the original data to include a signature. The data management features of classes such as SignedXml make it possible to generate, maintain, and output a signed document without affecting the content of the original document.

Data Transformation   You'll use one of several transforms to add the signature to the document. The transform defines the appearance of the signature within the document. Use a different transform and the signature will have a different appearance. Most of the transforms provided with the .NET Framework follow the World Wide Web Consortium (W3C) guidelines.

Creating and Verifying XML Digital Signatures

The example in this section performs two tasks. First, it reads a standard XML file from disk, calculates a signature for it, and writes the resulting signed document to disk. Second, it reads the signed XML file from disk, verifies the signature, and reports whether the document remains unchanged or not. Listing 11.4 shows the essential code for both tasks. However, this listing isn't complete. You'll find the complete source code for this example in the \Chapter 11\C#\XMLCrypto and \Chapter 11\VB\XMLCrypto folders of the source code located on the Sybex Web site. The \Chapter 11\Sample XML Data folder contains the sample data for this example.

Listing 11.4   **Signing and Verifying an XML File**

```
private void btnSign_Click(object sender, System.EventArgs e)
{
    XmlDocument                              Doc;         // The XML document.
    SignedXml                                SignedDoc;   // Signed document.
    Reference                                RefDoc;      // Reference doc.
    Transform                                Trans;       // Doc Tranform.
    XmlDsigEnvelopedSignatureTransform       EnvTrans;    // Env Transform.
    KeyInfo                                  KeyData;     // RSA Key Data.
    XmlElement                               XmlSig;      // XML Signature.
    XmlTextWriter                            Writer;      // XML File Writer.

    // Create the document and load the file.
    Doc = new XmlDocument();
    Doc.Load(new XmlTextReader(txtInput.Text));

    // Create the signed document.
    SignedDoc = new SignedXml(Doc);

    // Add the key to the signed document.
    SignedDoc.SigningKey = RSACrypto;

    // Create the reference document.
    RefDoc = new Reference();
    RefDoc.Uri = "";
    Trans = new XmlDsigC14NWithCommentsTransform();
    RefDoc.AddTransform(Trans);
    EnvTrans = new XmlDsigEnvelopedSignatureTransform(true);
    RefDoc.AddTransform(EnvTrans);
```

```csharp
    // Add the reference to the signed document.
    SignedDoc.AddReference(RefDoc);

    // Add key information to the signed document.
    KeyData = new KeyInfo();
    KeyData.AddClause(new RSAKeyValue((RSA)RSACrypto));
    SignedDoc.KeyInfo = KeyData;

    // Compute the signature value and add it to an element.
    SignedDoc.ComputeSignature();
    XmlSig = SignedDoc.GetXml();

    // Add the element to the document.
    Doc.DocumentElement.AppendChild(Doc.ImportNode(XmlSig, true));

    // Remove the XML declaration if necessary.
    if (Doc.FirstChild is XmlDeclaration)
        Doc.RemoveChild(Doc.FirstChild);

    // Save the document to disk.
    Writer = new XmlTextWriter(txtSigned.Text, new UTF8Encoding(false));
    Doc.WriteTo(Writer);
    Writer.Close();
}

private void btnValdiate_Click(object sender, System.EventArgs e)
{
    XmlDocument Doc;        // The XML document.
    SignedXml   Signed;     // Holds the signed XML.
    XmlNodeList SignNode;   // Contains the signature node.

    // Create the document and load the file.
    Doc = new XmlDocument();
    Doc.Load(txtSigned.Text);

    // Define a signed XML object.
    Signed = new SignedXml(Doc);

    // Get the signed node.
    SignNode = Doc.GetElementsByTagName("Signature");
    Signed.LoadXml((XmlElement)SignNode[0]);

    // Verify the signature.
    if (Signed.CheckSignature())
        MessageBox.Show("The Signature is Verified",
                    "Check Signature",
                    MessageBoxButtons.OK,
                    MessageBoxIcon.Information);
    else
```

```
MessageBox.Show("Error in Signature",
                "Check Signature",
                MessageBoxButtons.OK,
                MessageBoxIcon.Error);
}
```

Signing the document is a lot more complicated than verifying the signature. The `btnSign_Click()` method begins by loading the document into memory using an `XmlTextReader`. It then uses the original document found in `Doc` to create a `SignedXml` object. This section object performs data manipulation tasks such as calculating the signature value for the input document shown in Figure 11.3.

FIGURE 11.3:

The input document is
a basic XML file.

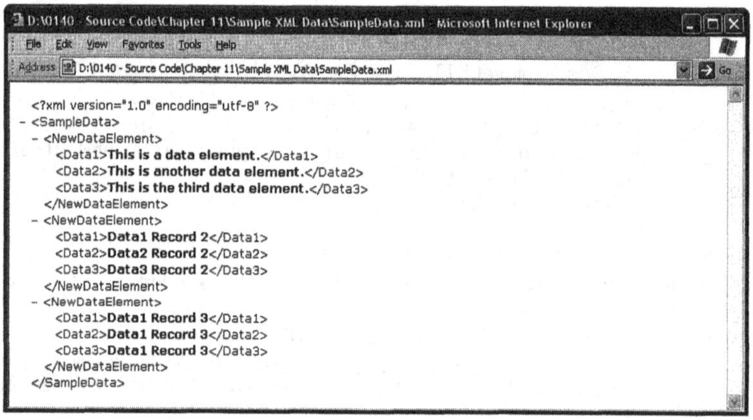

The code creates a `Reference` object next. You can look at the `Reference` object in a number of ways, but the easiest method is as a reference document—essentially a guide the program will use to create the signature. The code begins by defining an empty `Uri` property value. It's possible to set a URI as a definition document, but the example builds the information from scratch. Make certain you set the `Uri` property to an empty value or you'll end up with odd null reference error messages. The code defines two transforms for the signature. The first, `XmlDsigC14NWithCommentsTransform`, defines the canonicalization or data presentation transform. The second, `XmlDsigEnvelopedSignatureTransform`, defines the data envelope. The code adds the Reference object to `SignedDoc` for use in generating the signature.

At this point, the code has defined rules for creating a signature. It now adds a key for generating the signature. This is the same key used in Chapter 7 for asymmetric cryptography.

The public key will appear as part of the signed document so that any third party can verify the signature. You can also make the public key available in a public place so third parties can verify that no one has changed keys and signed the document a second time.

The code generates a signature, at this point, and adds it to the original document in memory. The code removes the XML declaration to show that this document no longer follows the standard XML format (it contains a signature) and writes the data to disk. Figure 11.4 shows the output of the program.

FIGURE 11.4:

Creating a signed document means no one can change the content without also changing the signature.

The original data is still intact. However, notice that the file now contains signature information. The btnValidate_Click() method validates this code—a simple procedure. Any change to the file in Figure 11.4 at all will cause the validation to fail. In addition, the file contains the public key value, making it possible to check the key as well for modification.

The code begins by loading the signed XML document. It uses this document to create a SignedXml object similar to the one used to create the original signature. The code also loads the signature element and places it in the SignedXml object. The code completes the process by calling the Signed.CheckSignature() method. A true return value means that the file is unchanged.

Global XML Architecture

At some point, you're going to hear Microsoft talk about *Global XML Architecture* (GXA). At first, you might think this is yet another in a long line of Microsoft technologies such as *Distributed Network Architecture* (DNA) that could affect application development at a conceptual level. However, all that Microsoft has done is package the Web technologies discussed in this book into a more convenient form.

From a security perspective, GXA doesn't add anything new you need to consider as part of your application development strategy. The same security holes discussed in other parts of the chapter for other Web technologies also appear in GXA. You'll also find that .NET will work the same from a security perspective as it does with any other Web technology. (The chapter doesn't consider the productivity, reliability, or other benefits that GXA does provide.)

You can see an overview of GXA at `http://msdn.microsoft.com/library/en-us/dngxa/html/gloxmlws500.asp`. Don Box provides another, more technical, view of GXA at `http://msdn.microsoft.com/library/en-us/dngxa/html/understandgxa.asp`. If you'd like to see some typical case studies for GXA, try the Got Dot Net site at (`http://www.gotdotnet.com/team/XMLwebservices/gxa_overview.aspx`). For a list of GXA related links, check out `http://msdn.microsoft.com/webservices/understanding/gxa/`.

Working with WS-Security

When it comes to SOAP security, the SOAP standard doesn't provide much in the way of guidance. The standard essentially says that you're on your own and need some form of extension (see `http://www.w3c.org/TR/2003/PR-soap12-part1-20030507/#secconsiderations` for details). Many developers use encryption to secure sensitive data. They send the encrypted data as a Base64 encoded payload in the SOAP message.

TIP   The SOAP Security Extensions can provide essential security and are a good alternative to WS-Security. It's important to know about this option as you consider the security of your Web services application. You can learn more about the W3C SOAP Security Extensions at `http://www.w3.org/TR/SOAP-dsig/`.

Fortunately, Microsoft provides the necessary extension in the form of the Web Services Development Kit (WSDK). You may also see the Microsoft Web sites use Web Services Enhancements (WSE) in place of WSDK. Because WSE seems to be the most popular name as of this writing, the chapter will use WSE. No matter what Microsoft is calling this product this week, you can download it at `http://msdn.microsoft.com/webservices/building/wse/default.aspx`. After you install the product on your machine, you'll have a new `Microsoft.WSDK` namespace on your system that encapsulates a number of technologies, including WS-Security. Note that you can download an associated settings tool at `http://microsoft.com/downloads/details.aspx?familyid=E1924D29-E82D-4D9A-A945-3F074CE63C8B&displaylang=en`.

You have to make two separate downloads to gain access to this tool. First, you need to download and install WSE. Second, you need to download and install the WSE Settings Tool. Once you spend some time with the WSE Settings Tool, you'll understand why it's a required addition and wonder why Microsoft didn't make it part of the main download.

After you perform the installation, start a new project. The WSE Settings Tool documentation isn't very clear on where the tool comes into play, but you can use it on any project that relies on a Web service. This includes desktop applications. To activate the tool, open your Web services project, right-click the project name in Solutions Explorer, and choose WSE Settings from the context menu. You'll see the Web Services Enhancements Settings dialog box shown in Figure 11.5.

FIGURE 11.5:

Use the Web Services Enhancements Settings dialog box to make configuring WSE easier.

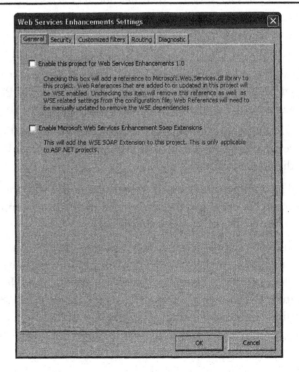

You'll also notice there's a decided lack of documentation—nothing appears on the Start menu, nor is it available within Visual Studio .NET. Look in the \Program Files\ Microsoft WSE\v1.0.2312\Unsupported\WseSettings folder of your machine and you'll find an innocuous looking README.HTM file. This file provides you with a complete description of all the pages on the Web Services Enhancements Settings dialog box.

Working with the eXtensible Access Control Markup Language

The eXtensible Access Control Markup Language (XACML) is an important new standard in the making from the Organization for the Advancement of Structured Information Standards (OASIS) (http://www.oasis-open.org/committees/tc_home.php?wg_abbrev=xacml). This standard lets developers add specialized XML tags to their code that defines the security policy for something like a Web service. Many developers view XACML as the next step beyond Security Assertions Markup Language (SAML). In fact, XACML is a high-level protocol that relies on SAML to perform many of the low-level tasks. In both cases, the process follows a four-step process for most callers:

1. The caller requests access to a resource from an authentication server, rather than directly from the Web server. The caller doesn't necessarily realize the difference, and the two servers might reside on the same physical machine, but the difference between the two servers is real.

2. The authentication server requests a name and password from the user. It uses this information to look up the user's credentials in a secure store such as Active Directory using a language such as the Lightweight Directory Access Protocol (LDAP). At some point, the server either authenticates the caller or ejects the caller from the system.

3. The authentication opens a session with the destination (Web) server. It provides the user request and credentials. The Web server provides a Uniform Resource Identifier (URI) to the authentication server.

4. The authentication server presents the caller with the URI from the Web server. At this point, the caller and the Web server are in direct communication and the authentication server drops out of the conversation.

The advantage of using XACML is that the developer need not worry about multiple protocols to implement a security solution. Using one set of markup tags enables the developer to control security for a Web application. Note that this is a Web application solution and probably won't affect your desktop application development strategies. You can find a relatively technical description of precisely how XACML and SAML work together at http://sunxacml.sourceforge.net/guide.html.

The current version of Visual Studio .NET doesn't provide direct XACML support. In fact, there isn't any evidence that Microsoft plans to provide this support in the near future. However, it's an option to consider as third parties develop add-ons for Visual Studio .NET that provide this capability. Currently, one training company shows how to develop XACML solutions using the .NET Framework. Learn more about this course at http://www .objectinnovations.com/CourseOutlines/418.html.

Using the Visual Studio .NET Passport Features

Most of the resources you read will view Passport from the perspective of user identification and authentication. In fact, the essential focus of this section is on both identification and authentication. However, vendors didn't design Passport and technologies like it (see the "A Quick Overview of the Liberty Alliance Project" sidebar) for simple identification and authentication. These technologies store and manage a caller's personal information, so they're personal identification management technologies.

> **NOTE** While the .NET Framework does provide the hooks required to use Passport, it doesn't provide all of the software you need. At a minimum, you must download the Passport SDK from http://msdn.microsoft.com/downloads/list/websrvpass.asp. In some cases, you might need additional software to make Passport work on your system. Your server must fully support SSL and have a certificate installed to use the Passport SDK. The current version of the Passport SDK works with Windows 2000 Server (not Professional), Windows XP Professional, and Windows 2003 Server. Microsoft warns against using older Passport versions (especially the 1.4 version) with the .NET Framework and testing shows that heeding the warning is a good idea.

When a user stores credit card or address information as part of their Passport settings, Passport becomes a convenience tool for the user as well as a means for a third party to identify and authenticate the user. The goal is to identify and authenticate the user in a way that doesn't transfer sensitive user information over the wire. A user can make a purchase online without revealing secret (personal) information, yet the vendor gains access to information to make the sale. This perspective of the services that Passport offers is important because it changes the way businesses use the technology and consequently changes the way you develop applications using Passport.

The following sections discuss the security features that Passport provides. I'm not providing a complete view of all Passport functionality because the goal of this section is to discuss ways you can use Passport to make your application more secure. Be aware, however, that you'll probably use Passport for purposes other than identification and authorization at some point.

A Quick Overview of the Liberty Alliance Project

Using a Microsoft product means that you normally use Microsoft development strategies, unless, of course, you're willing to do a lot of extra work to accomplish a specific task using a different strategy. Fortunately, you do have alternatives when it comes to personal identification management in the form of the Liberty Alliance Project. Many developers have questioned which technology to use and the media has followed suit (see the eWeek article at `http://www.eweek.com/article2/0,3959,266840,00.asp`.) The .NET Framework doesn't include any support for the Liberty Alliance project, but you can add support using third party add-ons such as SourceID (`http://www.sourceid.org/?SourceID.NET`). The appearance of these third party alternatives leaves the decision of which technology to use up to you.

You need to consider a number of issues when determining which technology to use. The Liberty Alliance Project is open source and used mainly on Unix systems (including Linux) right now. Many developers point to the fact that Passport came out well before the Liberty Alliance Project and that Passport has a lead in testing and functionality. In fact, the Liberty Alliance recently released the second phase of their specification, which is the Identity Web Services Framework (ID-WSF). You can learn more about this specification in the InfoWorld article at `http://www.infoworld.com/article/03/04/15/15appnews_1.html` and the Specifications link on the Liberty Alliance Web site at `http://www.projectliberty.org/`.

The differences in strategy will ultimately affect the functionality of both technologies. The single company view the tightly controlled Passport provides means you won't suffer the problems of "designed by committee" software. However, the design of the Liberty Alliance Project technology makes it more flexible. In fact, this technology already appears on more platforms than Passport does. Consequently, if you work in a mixed platform environment such as Linux and Windows, then the Liberty Alliance Project technology might be your only viable option. The InternetNews article at `http://www.internetnews.com/bus-news/article.php/973001` discusses additional strategic differences between the two products.

Passport and the Liberty Alliance Project have essential differences. Even the technique used to move the identification token from one site to another differs. While Passport uses a proprietary schema, the Liberty Alliance Project uses the Security Assertions Markup Language (SAML) (you can learn more about SAML from the Organization for the Advancement of Structured Information Standards, OASIS, site at `http://www.oasis-open.org/committees/tc_home.php?wg_abbrev=security`). However, a recent eWeek article (`http://www.eweek.com/article2/0,3959,890520,00.asp`) points out that the Liberty Alliance is working on a strategy where a third party Web site would act as an intermediary between the two technologies, giving developers at least some sense of interoperability.

Passport Features in the *System.Web.Security* Namespace

The System.Web.Security namespace provides access to most of the Passport features you need. The goal of using Passport is to obtain a ticket that identifies a particular user. The ticket doesn't provide any confidential information about the user—it simply states that the server has authenticated the user. In short, the identity saves an application time authenticating a caller and the caller time providing credentials. The PassportIdentity class provides access to this ticket.

WARNING Passport is still a young technology. Although Microsoft has made great strides in creating a useful and secure verification mechanism, problems still abound (as they will with any new technology). For example, a recent InfoWorld article states that a bug in Passport could reveal user information (http://www.infoworld.com/article/03/05/08/HNpassportflaw_1.html). Hardly a week passes without some mention of a Passport problem. Microsoft is quick to fix these problems, but the newness of the technology is definitely a problem. Make sure you consider the potential problems in using Passport for mission critical applications.

You normally use the PassportIdentity class directly to create the initial login. However, much of the actual work takes place indirectly through the PassportAuthenticationModule class. You can intercept the actual authentication event by adding an event handler to the Authenticate event of the PassportAuthenticationModule class. When you do intercept the authentication schedule, you'll receive a PassportAuthenticationEventArgs object that includes information such as the username and identity. Note that the Identity property, in this case, is the Passport identity, not a local identity.

A Simple Passport Example

This section includes a simple Passport example consisting of two Web pages. The first page appears when the user selects the site. This page contains only the Passport logon button. When the user clicks this button, the Passport logon dialog appears. The user must enter their Passport email address and password. Once Passport authenticates the user, it redirects the call to the second page. This page logs on the user as long as the user has a ticket. The page then displays the logged on status. Listing 11.5 contains the code for the first page. You'll find this example in the \Chapter 11\C#\PassportTest and \Chapter 11\VB\PassportTest folders of the source code located on the Sybex Web site.

Listing 11.5   **Logging in with Passport**

```
// Contains an <Img> tag for the Passport Login.
protected String LogoTag;

private void Page_Load(object sender, System.EventArgs e)
{
    PassportIdentity  PI;    // The Passport Identity.

    // Create a new identity.
    PI = new PassportIdentity();

    // Tell the user to log in.
    LogoTag = PI.LogoTag2("LoggedIn.ASPX",  // Return URL
                    3600,           // Time to wait.
                    0,              // Don't force login.
                    null,           // No co-branding site.
                    -1,             // Use default language.
                    1,              // Non-secure page.
                    "",             // Passport namespace.
                    -1,             // Children's privacy policy.
                    0);             // Use secure authorization.

    // If the user is successful, provide the Passport
    // User ID with the return value.
    if (PI.IsAuthenticated)
        Response.Write(PI.HexPUID);
}
```

The code begins by creating a `PassportIdentity` object. It uses this object to call the `LogoTag2()` method, which does more than the document states. Supposedly, all of this information will create a piece of HTML code that displays a Passport icon. In fact, this code indirectly generates the call to the Passport service for authentication. Of course, this begs the question of how the Passport icon appears on screen. Notice that the `LogoTag` variable is global to the namespace. A little code in the HTML portion of the example, as shown here, takes care of the rest.

```
<form id="Form1" method="post" runat="server">
    <%=LogoTag%>
</form>
```

The remainder of the code verifies the authenticated state of the caller. If Passport authenticated the caller, then the code writes the Passport Unique Identifier (PUID) to the response stream. At this point, the Passport service redirects the user to the LoggedIn.ASPX page. Listing 11.6 shows the code for this page.

Listing 11.6   **Displaying the Logged In Status**

```
// Contains an <Img> tag for the Passport Login.
protected String LogoTag;

private void Page_Load(object sender, System.EventArgs e)
{
    PassportIdentity  PI;    // The Passport Identity.

    // Create a new identity.
    PI = new PassportIdentity();

    // Log the user into this page.
    if (PI.HasTicket && !PI.IsAuthenticated)
        PI.LoginUser("LoggedIn.ASPX");

    // Display the Passport status.
    if (PI.IsAuthenticated)
        LoggedStatus.Text = "You're Logged In!";
    else
        LoggedStatus.Text = "You Didn't Log In.";
}
```

This page begins by creating a PassportIdentity object again. However, this time the code verifies that the user has a ticket. If the user has a ticket and isn't authenticated for this page, the code silently logs the user back into the system. The code ends by displaying the user's logged in status.

Using the Web Service Features of COM+ 1.5

One of the more interesting new features you'll find in COM+ 1.5 is the ability to create a SOAP setup for your COM+ application. For the purposes of discussion, this section relies on the COMPlusComp.DLL file originally presented in the "Working with COM+" section of Chapter 8. You'll find the version of this example used for this chapter in the \Chapter 11\ C#\COMPlusComp and \Chapter 11\VB\COMPlusComp folders of the source code located on the Sybex Web site. See the Listing 8.5 and the associated write-up for an explanation of this example.

The example in this section will only work on platforms that support COM+ 1.5 such as Windows XP and the Windows .NET 2003 server. This example won't work on earlier versions of Windows, including Windows 2000. Create the COM+ application by manually defining an application and adding the component to it in the Component Services console found in the Administrative Tools folder of the Control Panel, rather than the RegSvcs utility. The RegSvcs utility technique creates a COM+ 1.0 application, even on platforms that support COM+ 1.5. The example in this section uses TestCOMPlus as the COM+ application name. You'll find an MSI file to install this application in the `\Chapter 11\ COMPlusApp\` folder of the source code located on the Sybex Web site.

Performing the Application Setup

You'll begin the project by creating a COM+ application named TestCOMPlus and installing the COMPlusComp component. Right-click the TestCOMPlus icon in the Component Services console and choose Properties from the context menu. Select the Activation tab. Figure 11.6 shows the SOAP configuration setting on the Activation tab of the TestCOMPlus Properties dialog box. Notice that the figure shows the Uses SOAP option checked and MathFunctionsMethod entered in the SOAP VRoot field.

FIGURE 11.6:

Adding support for SOAP to your COM+ application is relatively easy.

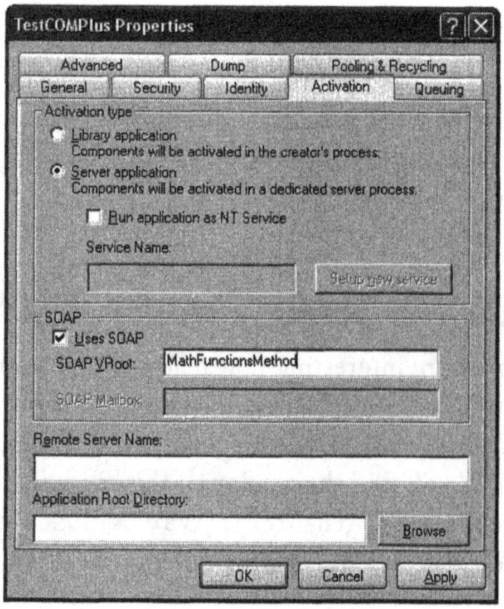

When you click Apply, COM+ creates several files for you that become accessible from Internet Information Server (IIS) as an application. Figure 11.7 shows the results of this process. As you can see, the application includes several files and a bin folder.

FIGURE 11.7:

Setting the SOAP
support options
automatically creates
some application files
for your IIS setup.

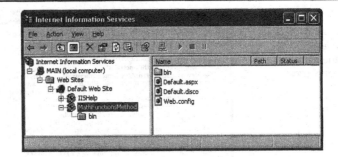

The first problem you'll notice when you look at the settings for this application is that it
lacks security settings. When you enable anonymous access for any location on your Web
site (even the root directory), the application allows anonymous access too. Follow this procedure to secure your application:

1. Right-click the MathFunctionsMethod entry in the Internet Information Services console and choose Properties. IIS displays the MathFunctionsMethod Properties dialog box.

2. Select the Directory Security tab, and then click Edit in the Anonymous Access and
   Authentication Control section. IIS displays the Authentication Methods dialog box.

3. Clear the Anonymous Access option and click OK. Clearing this option ensures the caller
   has to present some type of credential to the server before gaining access to the application.
   If your program will transmit confidential data and you have a server certificate installed,
   you'll want to perform a few additional steps.

4. Click Edit in the Secure Communications section of the Directory Security tab. IIS displays
   the Secure Communications dialog box.

5. Select the Require Secure Channel (SSL) option. This step forces the caller to use SSL to
   access the application.

The second problem is that the application doesn't expire the content. Not only does this
mean that copies of your application data will hang around on client hard drives forever, but
it means clients could receive old data. Select the HTTP Headers tab. Check the Enable
Content Expiration option and choose the Expire Immediately radio button. Click OK to
make the changes to the application permanent.

Now that you've secured the application a little better, you can try it out. This application
displays a simple Web page containing the name of the SOAP application. When you click
the COMPlusComp.MathFunctions.soap?WSDL link, you'll see the Web Services Description
Language (WSDL) output generated for this application, as shown in Figure 11.8. The
WSDL describes the COMPlusComp.MathFunctions class and the services it provides.

FIGURE 11.8:

The WSDL output of the Web page describes the class and the functionality it provides.

You can obtain this same output using the SoapSuds utility initially discussed in the "Creating a Remoting Client Application" section of Chapter 10. This utility accepts a number of inputs and generates output using a number of techniques. For this example, it's most convenient to obtain the required information directly from the Web site and place it in an XML file. Simply open a command line, type **soapsuds -url:http://Main/MathFunctionsMethod/COMPlusComp .MathFunctions.soap?WSDL -os:MathFunctions.XML**, and press Enter. You'll also find the SoapSudsGen.BAT file in the \Chapter 11\COMPlusWSDL folder of the source code located on the Sybex Web site. Note that you'll have to change the name of the server to match your server.

Look through the MathFunctions.XML file in the \Chapter 11\COMPlusWSDL folder and you'll notice that it contains a complete description of the Web service. Using a Web service represents a tradeoff. The WSDL output of the IIS request or the SoapSuds utility represents information that you're giving away. A cracker could use this information to learn more about your application and eventually break into it. Consequently, securing the Web site so that only authorized applications users can access it is essential. In general, this means adding some type of secure data transmission for the WSDL information such as the example in the "Understanding Remoting and Data Encryption" section of Chapter 10.

Creating a Simple COM+ Test Application

Once the Web application is in place, using it is easy. All you need to do is start a new project and create a Web reference by right-clicking the References folder in Solution Explorer and choosing Add Web Reference from the context menu. When you browse to the location that holds the MathFunctionsMethod application (`http://Main/MathFunctionsMethod/Default .ASPX` on my system), you'll see a list of discovery services for that server (you can also view the DISCO file if desired). Click the `COMPlusComp.MathFunctions.soap?WSDL` link and you'll see a display like the one shown in Figure 11.9. Click Add Reference and your application will have access to this COM+ application through SOAP and the IIS server.

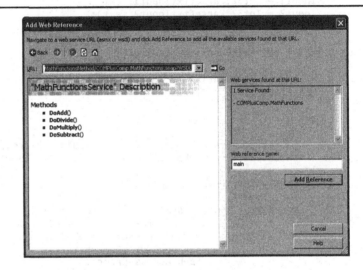

FIGURE 11.9:

The Add Web Reference dialog box can help you locate and use services.

The transformation of your COM+ application to a SOAP application can bring some unexpected surprises. You might intend that your COM+ application provide only direct synchronous service. However, given the nature of the Web, Microsoft assumes that you also want asynchronous service. Listing 11.7 demonstrates that the COM+ application from Chapter 8 now sports both a synchronous and an asynchronous interface. The problem with this assumption is that it could cause security breaches on your system. It's important to test both the synchronous and asynchronous setup to ensure your COM+ application continues to work as anticipated and doesn't crash. In some cases, you might need to include a hand tuned WSDL file that excludes the asynchronous operation within the IIS application directory to ensure a cracker can't use the security hole to gain access to your system. You'll find this example in the `\Chapter 11\C#\COMPlusComp` and `\Chapter 11\VB\COMPlusComp` folders of the source code located on the Sybex Web site.

Listing 11.7   The SOAP Quick Test Application

```
private void btnSynchronous_Click(object sender, System.EventArgs e)
{
    Int32              Input1;  // First input value.
```

```
Int32               Input2;  // Second input value.
MathFunctionsService MFS;    // Remote object.
ICredentials        MyCred;  // Credentials for the current user.

// Create the network credential.
MyCred = new NetworkCredential("YourName", "YourPassword");

// Get the input.
Input1 = Int32.Parse(txtInput1.Text);
Input2 = Int32.Parse(txtInput2.Text);

// Create the MathFunctionsService object.
MFS = new MathFunctionsService();

// Add the credential to the service reference.
MFS.Credentials = MyCred;

try
{
   // Perform a synchronous add and display the result.
   txtOutput.Text = MFS.DoAdd(Input1, Input2).ToString();
}
catch (System.Net.WebException WE)
{
   MessageBox.Show("Message: " + WE.Message +
              "\r\nSource: " + WE.Source +
              "\r\nResponse: " + WE.Response +
              "\r\nStatus: " + WE.Status,
              "Web Access Error",
              MessageBoxButtons.OK,
              MessageBoxIcon.Error);
}
}

private void btnAsynchronous_Click(object sender, System.EventArgs e)
{
   Int32               Input1;  // First input value.
   Int32               Input2;  // Second input value.
   MathFunctionsService MFS;    // Remote object.
   ICredentials        MyCred;  // Credentials for the current user.

   // Create the network credential.
   MyCred = new NetworkCredential("YourName", "YourPassword");


   // Get the input.
   Input1 = Int32.Parse(txtInput1.Text);
   Input2 = Int32.Parse(txtInput2.Text);

   // Create the MathFunctionsService object.
   MFS = new MathFunctionsService();
```

```
    // Add the credential to the service reference.
    MFS.Credentials = MyCred;

    // Perform a synchronous add and display the result.
    MFS.BeginDoAdd(Input1,
                   Input2,
                   new System.AsyncCallback(MyCallback),
                   null);
}
public void MyCallback(IAsyncResult ar)
{
    // Create the MathFunctionsService object.
    MathFunctionsService MFS;
    MFS = new MathFunctionsService();

    // Obtain the result of the operation.
    txtOutput.Text = MFS.EndDoAdd(ar).ToString();
}
```

Both of the pushbutton event handler routines begin by creating a credential using the ICredential interface. This single credential can include the name, password, and domain of the caller, but the sample uses just the name and password. You must add this credential to the MFS.Credentials property or the application will always fail—a Web service application can't negotiate security information with the server. It also helps to set the Web services application to use Windows integrated security, rather than digest or basic security.

As you can see from the btnSynchronous_Click() method listing, making a synchronous call isn't much different from making a direct call to the COM+ application. You instantiate the MathFunctionsService object, and then call the DoAdd() method to add the two input numbers. Obviously, the .NET Framework has made it quite easy to make SOAP calls without worrying about the SOAP coding that used to take place.

Notice that the btnSynchronous_Click() method includes a try...catch block. The "Verifying the Application Is Safe" section describes why this check is necessary. However, the btnAsynchronous_Click() doesn't include this check. An asynchronous call simply won't return when a security error occurs, so the try...catch block is unnecessary. However, the lack of feedback points out one reason why you shouldn't use asynchronous calls and should avoid them whenever possible.

The asynchronous call is still simple, but not quite as straightforward as the synchronous call. The code still begins by instantiating the MathFunctionsService object. In this case, the code calls the BeginDoAdd() method with the name of the callback method as the third parameter. The MyCallback() method follows the format of the System.AsyncCallback delegate. The fourth parameter is an optional asynchronous state object that you can pass to the callback method—you don't need it in this situation.

The MyCallback() method receives an IAsyncResult variable, ar. This variable actually contains a significant amount of information about the call. However, all you need for this example is the result of the addition. Notice that the code begins by instantiating the MathFunctionsService object again. It calls the EndDoAdd() method with the IAsyncResult variable and converts the result to text for display.

Verifying the Application Is Safe

Don't assume that the Web server is your first and last level of security when working with a COM+ application. One of the better reasons to use COM+ is that the same role-based security features discussed in Chapter 8 are still in effect when using COM+ as a Web service. In fact, when you run this program the first time, it will very likely fail with the error information shown in Figure 11.10.

FIGURE 11.10:

Web services set up through COM+ retain COM+ security features.

The "Implementing the Security Setup" section of Chapter 10 points out the problems with the IWAM group. Unfortunately, the same problems will plague your COM+ application. You'll need to work out the same issues that the "Building the Validated Database Application" section of Chapter 10 discusses for your COM+ application. In many cases, you might want to provide very limited access for the IWAM group to the component.

Summary

Web services are an upcoming technology of strategic importance to most companies—ignoring them will put your company at a strategic disadvantage. Many companies are experimenting with Web services, but haven't committed to using them for critical applications for one reason—security. This chapter has demonstrated that Web services today are extremely difficult and perhaps impossible to secure. However, companies such as Microsoft are developing strategies to deal with this problem. In short, you should get a balanced view of Web services security from this chapter.

The issue now is applying the warnings and techniques in this chapter to your own company. You need to consider issues such as the amount of information you're willing to risk to a Web services application. Once you define the data requirements for the application, you need to consider what kind of security to use. Every strategy has significant tradeoffs you need to consider. Unfortunately, the difficulty of creating secure Web service applications that still provide the information exchange functionality that most companies require is going to remain difficult despite the advances Microsoft has made in the current version of the .NET Framework.

Chapter 12 moves on to a new topic, Active Directory, which is the central information store that many companies use today. Active Directory not only contains security information, it also contains specifics about the machines connected to the network and personal information about the people using it. In many cases, developers now use Active Directory to store custom settings, such as those used by applications. In short, securing Active Directory is an essential task that all companies must undertake to ensure core information remains private.

PART IV

Other Security Topics

CHAPTER 12

Active Directory Security

- Working with the ADSI Viewer Utility

- Storing Information in Active Directory instead of the Registry

- Using Domain Trust Relationships

- Developing Active Directory Aware Applications

At one time, many companies avoided using Active Directory. The problem wasn't one of security; rather, it was one of administration. Microsoft simply didn't provide enough information about Active Directory to make it an attractive tool for network administrators or developers. However, as companies have learned more about Active Directory, the merits of storing information in it, rather than in the registry or other locations, have become apparent. Generally, Active Directory provides a more secure environment for data storage than any other location on your network. In addition, the centralized location means users can float between machines as needed to perform work without having to have duplicate settings on each machine.

Working with Active Directory is still a complex undertaking—as is working with any of the directory services. The hierarchical storage technique that Active Directory uses means you can't rely on the orderly fields, rows, and tables of a relational database—you have to spend a little more time looking for what you need. In addition, there's no guarantee that a specific item will appear in Active Directory, so you have to consider the null dataset. Active Directory is expandable—you can add new data elements as required, so it's a perfect solution for many hardware, software, and user configuration setting needs.

> **NOTE** This chapter assumes that you already know how to manage and access Active Directory. You can learn more about working with Active Directory from *Mastering Active Directory for Windows Server 2003* (Sybex, 2003) by Robert R. King.

This chapter discusses Active Directory from a security perspective. However, the chapter does include a few nontypical security topics. For example, many developers don't really know how to use the ADSI Viewer—an essential tool for learning what your Active Directory setup actually includes. Knowing that you have specific resources is an important part of safeguarding them, so the chapter does discuss this utility. Once you get past access and discovery concerns, the chapter discusses .NET Framework–specific classes you can use to secure your installation. For example, you can deny access to Active Directory using the `DirectoryServicesPermissionAttribute`.

Monitoring Active Directory

When you're working with any networked operating system, the data that defines that network is extremely sensitive. Active Directory is the main store of information for your network. It includes the names of all the network users, the machines that connect to the network, the domain controllers, and even the applications you use on the network. It's possible to add information stores to Active Directory so that you can store other information that it originally didn't possess, such as the user settings for your custom application. It's impossible to calculate the value of Active Directory to you as a developer.

In the grand scheme of things, Active Directory is relatively secure. Even Windows includes safeguards that make it difficult for just anyone to break into Active Directory and steal its secrets. The use of replication and multiple copies tends to reduce the risk of contamination—multiple stores means redundancy that keeps Active Directory safe. However, no matter how safe you think a network resource is, it still requires monitoring because crackers can usually find a way around your security measures. With this in mind, the following sections describe techniques you can use to monitor your setup.

Using the ADSI Viewer Utility

The Active Directory Services Interface (ADSI) Viewer enables you to see the schema for Active Directory. From a security perspective, the ADSI Viewer helps you detect changes in both the schema and content of Active Directory. The schema controls the structure of the database. Knowing the schema helps you to work with Active Directory, change its contents, and even add new schema elements. In order to control the kinds of data stored for the applications you create, you must know the Active Directory schema. Otherwise, you could damage the database (given sufficient rights) or at least prevent your application from working correctly.

> **NOTE**   If you're using the original version of Visual Studio .NET, you'll find the AdsVw application in the \Program Files\Microsoft Visual Studio .NET\Common7\Tools\Bin folder. Visual Studio .NET 2003 might not come with this tool. However, you can obtain it as part of any of the Windows operating system Resource Kits or as part of the Platform SDK. (See http://msdn.microsoft.com/library/en-us/sdkintro/sdkintro/obtaining_the_complete_sdk.asp for instructions on obtaining the entire Platform SDK.) If you want to download just the tool, try the Core SDK download site at http://www.microsoft.com/msdownload/platformsdk/sdkupdate/.

When you first start ADSI Viewer, you'll see a New dialog box that allows you to choose between browsing the current objects in the database or making a specific query. You'll use the browse mode when performing research on Active Directory schema structure. The query approach provides precise information fast when you already know what you need to find.

In most cases, you'll begin your work with Active Directory by browsing through it. This means you'll select Object Viewer at the New object dialog box. Once you do that, you'll see a New Object dialog box like the one shown in Figure 12.1. Notice that this dialog already has the LDAP path for my server entered into it. If you're using Windows 2000, you can also use a WinNT path.

FIGURE 12.1:

The New Object dialog box enables you to create a connection to the server.

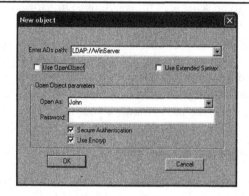

This figure shows a sample ADs Path entry. You'll need to supply Active Directory path information, which usually means typing LDAP:// followed by the name of your server (WinServer, in my case). If you're using Windows 2000 to access Active Directory, you'll want to clear the Use OpenObject option when working with an LDAP path and check it when using a WinNT path.

Once you've filled in the required information in the New Object dialog box, click OK. If you've entered all of the correct information and have the proper rights to access Active Directory, then you'll see a dialog box similar to the one shown in Figure 12.2. (Note that I've expanded the hierarchical display in this figure.)

FIGURE 12.2:

Opening a new object browser allows you to see the Active Directory schema for your server.

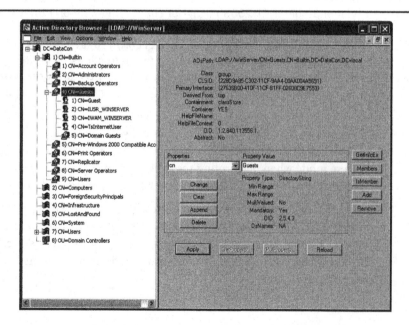

This is where you'll begin learning about Active Directory. On the left side of the display is the hierarchical database structure. Each of these elements is an Active Directory object. Clicking the plus signs next to each object will show the layers of objects beneath. Highlighting an object displays detailed information about it in the right pane. For example, in Figure 12.2, you're seeing the details about the Guests user group object for the server. The heading for this display includes object class information, help file location, and whether the object is a container used to hold other objects.

Below the header are the properties for the object. You can choose one of the properties from the Properties list box and see its value in the Property Value field. Active Directory is extensible, which means that you can add new properties to an existing object, change an existing property, or delete properties that you no longer need. If you want to add a new property, all you need to do is type its name in the Properties list box and assign it a value in the Property Value field, then click Append. This doesn't make the change final; however, you still need to click Apply at the bottom of the dialog box. Deleting a property is equally easy. Just select it in the Properties list box, and then click Delete. Clicking Apply will make the change final.

Leaf properties often have additional features that you can change. For example, the user object shown in Figure 12.3 helps you to change the user password and determine user group affiliation. When working with a computer object, you'll can determine the computer status and even shut it down if you'd like.

FIGURE 12.3:

Some containers and leaf objects provide special buttons that help you perform tasks.

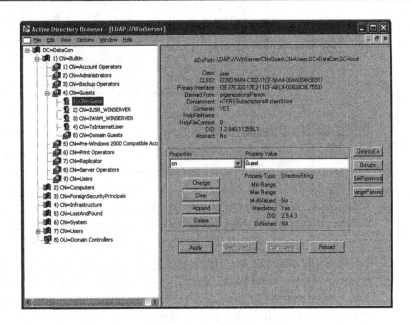

The method you use to access Active Directory affects the ADSI Viewer display. For example, Figure 12.4 shows the information for the same server using WinNT instead of LDAP for access. Notice that you garner less information in the left pane using WinNT. You'll also find that the WinNT method produces fewer property entries. The advantage of using the WinNT path is that more of the information appears in human readable form. For example, if you want to check the date the user last logged in under LDAP, you'd better be prepared to convert a 64-bit timer tick value to the time and date. The WinNT version provides this value in human readable form.

FIGURE 12.4:

Use the WinNT path to access hard to read information.

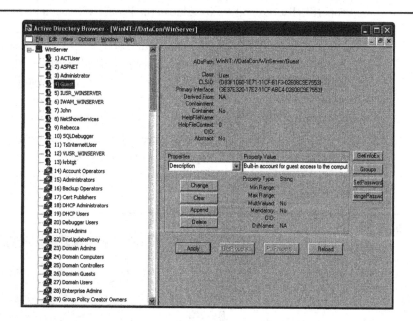

Other Active Directory Tools

Microsoft provides a wealth of Active Directory tools—the only problem is finding them. You can find a list of the most important tools at http://www.microsoft.com/windows2000/ en/advanced/help/sag_ADcmdTools.htm. Most of these tools appear as part of the Windows Resource Kit (the Web site shows the Windows 2000 Resource Kit, but other resource kits have similar tools). In some cases, the tools also appear as links in Microsoft Knowledge Base articles, as separate downloads for Visual Studio, or as part of another package.

One of the more interesting tools is ASDIEdit—an MSC snap-in you can download separately or obtain as part of the Windows Resource Kit. Figure 12.5 shows a typical view of this tool. As you can see, it provides an Explorer interface with the hierarchical presentation of Active Directory on the left pane and the details in the right pane.

FIGURE 12.5:

A typical view of the
ADSIEdit tool

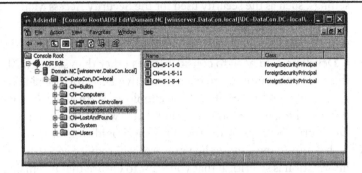

You can easily use this tool as a substitute for the ADSI Viewer. In fact, some developers prefer this tool because it's easier to use. However, the ADSIEdit tool lacks some of the flexibility of the ADSI Viewer—you can't make queries against Active Directory as an example. In addition, you might find that this tool skips some of the details. Even so, it's a particularly good tool to have for quick monitoring because you have less setup to consider. To change any particular entry in the list, right-click the entry and choose Properties from the context menu. You'll see a Properties dialog box with capabilities similar to those found in ADSI Viewer.

TIP   Microsoft often hides tool updates in service packs. For example, you can find both the ADSIEdit and the SDCheck tool in the Windows 2000 SP3 Support Tools download at `http://www.microsoft.com/windows2000/downloads/servicepacks/sp3/supporttools.asp`.

Another interesting tool to consider if you're having security issues with an application is SDCheck. This tool verifies that all user rights have propagated throughout the system correctly. In addition, it verifies the inheritance status of the various rights to ensure that the user has the correct permissions. Using this tool can save you hours of troubleshooting time when you think that an application error could have its roots in an incorrect security setting.

Using Active Directory in Place of the Registry

The main topic of this book is security. From a strictly security perspective, there isn't any better place to store sensitive settings than Active Directory. Storing settings on the local machine invites crackers to peek. For that matter, some users can't wait to modify the registry so that Windows better suits some perceived need. In some cases, user preference doesn't affect security, but, in other cases, it does. For example, you don't want the user changing Windows so it no longer requires a password to deactivate the screen saver. Although you can secure registry settings, such as the security used for the Security Access Manager (SAM) settings, you can't guarantee that the user won't fiddle with the settings you miss. When information is stored in Active Directory, it remains safe because Windows itself protects the data store.

Developers do need to consider issues other than security. Although security is the focus of this book, it's important to consider Active Directory outside of the security issues so you gain a fuller appreciation of this technology. With all of the functionality that Active Directory provides, it's tempting to think that it will replace the registry. In some respects, Active Directory does replace the registry. You should consider using it wherever an application has global importance, more than one user will require access to a single set of settings, or the information is so critical that you want to ensure that it remains safe. However, placing all your data within Active Directory also presents some problems that you need to consider.

> **TIP**   You don't have to write a complete program to meet every ADSI programming requirement. Any environment that lets you access objects will work fine. For example, Microsoft produces a scripting tool that generates the code required to perform basic ADSI operations quickly. You can learn more about this tool at http://www.microsoft.com/downloads/details .aspx?familyid=39044e17-2490-487d-9a92-ce5dcd311228&displaylang=en.

Active Directory is a poor choice for local settings for applications that only matter to the user. For example, no one else is concerned with the user's settings for a word processor. You gain nothing in the way of shared resource management or data security by storing these settings on the server. In fact, using Active Directory could mean a performance hit, in this case, because the application will need to access the server every time it needs to change a stored setting.

The performance hit for server access is relatively small for a LAN. However, consider the global nature of networks today. A user on the road is going to be out of communication for some time, which means Active Directory setting changes will languish on the local machine. In short, the registry is a better choice in many situations where the user data is noncritical, even though that data is more secure when stored in Active Directory.

A secondary performance consideration is one of managed versus unmanaged code and data. When you work with Active Directory, you'll often need to work with unmanaged data and code. Active Directory applications require some access to the native COM components provided as part of the ADSI interface. Every time the application makes a transition between managed and unmanaged environments, the application suffers a performance penalty. In addition, unmanaged code requires special handling if you want to maintain a safe environment (read the "Extending the AppDomain to Unmanaged Code" section of Chapter 6 for details).

Using the registry is also easier than using Active Directory. The example applications in this chapter demonstrate that working with Active Directory is akin to working with a complex database. The registry is smaller and easier to understand. It's less likely that you'll experience major bugs when working with the registry because all of the registry manipulation functionality you need is contained within the .NET Framework. Because CLR performs extensive checks on managed code, you'll find that it also catches more potential problems with your code.

Understanding Domain Trust Relationships

Domain trust relationships are a necessary part of Active Directory. These trust relationships essentially define a condition where one domain trusts the security mechanisms of another domain. The two domains are still separate; they simply trust the work performed by the other domain.

The following sections describe domain trust issues. For example, it's important to consider the difference between authentication and permission when working with multiple domains. You'll also see an example of how to work with the domain controller directly. Although you won't have to perform this task very often, the need is usually critical when you do. The example concentrates on providing you with good sample code for the most commonly used directory services and Win32 API functions.

Defining the Domain Trust Issues

It's easy to get confused about the relationship between authentication and permission when working with domain trust relationships. A caller trusted and authenticated by one domain is trusted and authenticated by the trusting domain. However, don't assume that trust automatically equates to access. A caller is still subject to the security requirements of the trusting domain and doesn't automatically receive access to resources. The only security right granted is authentication. Consequently, a domain could authenticate a caller on the trusting domain, but the caller still might not have any access to resources. Active Directory acts as the repository for all of the trust relationship information, so it plays a very active role in creating and maintaining trust relationships. This chapter won't discuss the architectural details of trust relationships, but you can read about them in the article entitled "Trust Relationships" at `ms-help://MS.MSDNQTR.2003FEB.1033/w2krk/html/dsbb_act_kxlx.htm`.

TIP   The NetDiag tool can help you discover information about domains on your system. For example, you can use it to locate a specific domain or to enumerate domain accounts. You can also verify primary domain details such as the domain globally unique identifier (GUID) and security identifier (SID).

It's important to note that there's one architectural detail of significant importance for the security setup of your .NET application. When working with Windows NT, all trust relationships are one way. One domain trusts another, but the reverse might not be true. Even when Windows NT establishes two-way trust, it's the result of two one-way trusts. Windows 2000 uses a domain tree setup where all trust relationships are two way. A parent that trusts a child domain will also have the child domain's trust. Consequently, when you write applications that rely on domain trust relationships, you need to consider the target platform and ensure that the correct domain trust relationships are in place. Otherwise, you might have to solve odd security problems where User A can access a resource from Machine A, but not from Machine B. Unfortunately, the .NET Framework doesn't make detection of such problems easy, so they normally look like an application bug or at least a setup error.

NOTE   You may run into situations where the domain trust security features of an application don't work properly because the network administrator has used the incorrect procedure for working with the domains. For example, the Microsoft Knowledge Base article Q112372 (http://support.microsoft.com/default.aspx?scid=kb;[LN];112372) discusses what can happen when a network administrator uses the incorrect procedure to split a domain. Because the security identifier (SID) remains that same, trust relationships can fail. Unfortunately, the .NET Framework doesn't provide good feedback on these issues, making it very difficult to locate the error. The best way to approach the problem is to verify that network administrators know the correct procedures to ensure that the error doesn't occur in the first place.

Working Directly with the Domain Controller

The .NET Framework provides a number of tools to search Active Directory. For example, you can use a DirectoryEntry or a DirectorySearcher object to work with Active Directory entries. In fact, the example in the "Using Imperative Active Directory Security" section shows how to work with a DirectoryEntry object. However, if you want to work directly with the domain controller, you'll need to resort to using Win32 API calls—those that help you work with directory services. This seeming omission is by design. For example, look at the DirectorySearcher.SearchRoot property documentation and you'll notice that Microsoft mentions using the DsGetDcName() function to find the global catalog. Unfortunately, Microsoft doesn't supply any example code that shows how to perform this task.

TIP The list of directory service functions isn't very long—you can normally perform any task you need to with a few calls. You'll find a list of standard directory services functions at `http://msdn.microsoft.com/library/en-us/netdir/ad/directory_service _functions.asp`. Make sure you also check out the domain controller and replication management functions at `http://msdn.microsoft.com/library/en-us/netdir/ad/dc_and _replication_management_functions.asp`. These two lists don't include some supplementary functions, but they do contain the main functions you'd call.

Listing 12.1 shows how to perform a number of domain controller–related tasks using directory service–related functions. This section relies on the PInvoke functionality provided by the .NET Framework to access the Win32 API. We'll pursue the topic of Win32 API access for security needs in detail in Chapters 14 and 15. This chapter also tells you how you can get more information about using PInvoke in general. The example code shown in Listing 12.1 isn't complete, but it does contain the essential code needed to perform the required tasks. You'll find the complete source code for this example in the \Chapter 12\C#\DomainAccess and \Chapter 12\VB\DomainAccess folders of the source code located on the Sybex Web site.

Listing 12.1   **Using Win32 API Calls for the Domain Controller**

```
// Define the method used to retrieve the computer name.
// This first version accepts a domain GUID.
[DllImport("NetAPI32.DLL", CharSet=CharSet.Ansi, SetLastError=true)]
public static extern Int32 DsGetDcName(
    String ComputerName,
    String DomainName,
    Guid DomainGuid,
    String SiteName,
    DsGetDcNameFlags Flags,
    ref IntPtr DomainControllerInfo);

// This second version doesn't require a domain GUID.
[DllImport("NetAPI32.DLL", CharSet=CharSet.Ansi, SetLastError=true)]
public static extern Int32 DsGetDcName(
    String ComputerName,
    String DomainName,
    IntPtr DomainGuid,
    String SiteName,
    DsGetDcNameFlags Flags,
    ref IntPtr DomainControllerInfo);

// This data structure contains the domain controller
// information on return from the call.
public struct DOMAIN_CONTROLLER_INFO
{
    public String              DomainControllerName;
```

```
    public String              DomainControllerAddress;
    public DCAddressType       DomainControllerAddressType;
    public Guid                DomainGuid;
    public String              DomainName;
    public String              DnsForestName;
    public DCInfoReturnFlags   Flags;
    public String              DcSiteName;
    public String              ClientSiteName;
}

// This function binds the current application to a directory services
// session. In essence, it begins a remote procedure call to the domain
// controller so your application can make queries.
[DllImport("NTDSAPI.DLL", CharSet=CharSet.Ansi, SetLastError=true)]
public static extern Int32 DsBind(String DomainController,
                                  String DnsDomainName,
                                  out IntPtr phDS);

// This function releases the handle created by the DsBind() function.
[DllImport("NTDSAPI.DLL", CharSet=CharSet.Ansi, SetLastError=true)]
public static extern Int32 DsUnBind(IntPtr phDS);

// This function obtains information about the domain controller.
[DllImport("NTDSAPI.DLL", CharSet=CharSet.Ansi, SetLastError=true)]
public static extern Int32 DsGetDomainControllerInfo(
    IntPtr hDs,
    String DomainName,
    Int32 InfoLevel,
    out Int32 pcOut,
    out IntPtr ppInfo);

// This data structure contains the information retrieved with
// the DsGetDomainControllerInfo() function. You actually have a
// choice of using two data structures; this is the more complex
// of the two.
public struct DS_DOMAIN_CONTROLLER_INFO_2
{
    public String  NetbiosName;
    public String  DnsHostName;
    public String  SiteName;
    public String  ComputerObjectName;
    public String  ServerObjectName;
    public Boolean fIsPdc;
    public Boolean fDsEnabled;
    public Boolean fIsGc;
    public Guid    SiteObjectGuid;
    public Guid    ComputerObjectGuid;
    public Guid    ServerObjectGuid;
    public Guid    NtdsDsaObjectGuid;
}

// This function frees the domain controller data structure created by
```

```
// the DsGetDomainControllerInfo() function.
[DllImport("NTDSAPI.DLL", CharSet=CharSet.Ansi, SetLastError=true)]
public static extern void DsFreeDomainControllerInfo(Int32 InfoLevel,
                                                     Int32 cInfo,
                                                     IntPtr pInfo);

private void btnQuery_Click(object sender, System.EventArgs e)
{
    DOMAIN_CONTROLLER_INFO  Output;       // Domain output structure.
    IntPtr                  OutputRef;    // Domain Structure Reference.
    IntPtr                  BindHandle;   // Domain bind handle.
    Int32                   DCDataLen;    // Domain data length.
    IntPtr                  DCDataRef;    // Domain data reference.
    DS_DOMAIN_CONTROLLER_INFO_2[] DCData; // Domain Controller Data.
    StringBuilder           DCDataOut;    // Final information output.

    // Initialize the domain information data structure.
    Output = new DOMAIN_CONTROLLER_INFO();

    // Allocate memory from the global heap to hold the domain data
    // structure reference.
    OutputRef = Marshal.AllocHGlobal(Marshal.SizeOf(Output));

    // Get the domain information for the default domain.
    DsGetDcName(null,
                "",
                IntPtr.Zero,
                "",
                DsGetDcNameFlags.DS_NONE,
                ref OutputRef);

    // Convert the reference pointer to the associated data structure.
    Output = (DOMAIN_CONTROLLER_INFO)Marshal.PtrToStructure(
        OutputRef, typeof(DOMAIN_CONTROLLER_INFO));

    // Free the memory used by the data structure reference.
    Marshal.FreeHGlobal(OutputRef);

    // Bind the application to the directory services instance.
    DsBind(Output.DomainControllerName,
           Output.DomainName,
           out BindHandle);

    // Get the domain controller information.
    DsGetDomainControllerInfo(BindHandle,
                              Output.DomainName,
                              2,
                              out DCDataLen,
                              out DCDataRef);

    // Size the domain controller information array.
```

```
    DCData = new DS_DOMAIN_CONTROLLER_INFO_2[DCDataLen];

    // Place the information in the array.
    DCData[0] =
        (DS_DOMAIN_CONTROLLER_INFO_2)Marshal.PtrToStructure(
            DCDataRef,
            typeof(DS_DOMAIN_CONTROLLER_INFO_2));

    // Free the controller information pointer.
    DsFreeDomainControllerInfo(2, DCDataLen, DCDataRef);

    // Unbind the application from the directory services instance.
    DsUnBind(BindHandle);

    // Display the information on screen.
    DCDataOut = new StringBuilder();
    DCDataOut.Append("Computer Object Name: ");
    DCDataOut.Append(DCData[0].ComputerObjectName);
... A lot of other data output. ...
    DCDataOut.Append("\r\nSiteObject GUID: ");
    DCDataOut.Append(DCData[0].SiteObjectGuid.ToString());
    if (DCData[0].fDsEnabled)
        DCDataOut.Append("\r\nDomain Services are Enabled");
    if (DCData[0].fIsGc)
        DCDataOut.Append("\r\nThis is the global catalog server.");
    if (DCData[0].fIsPdc)
        DCDataOut.Append("\r\nThis is the Primary Domain Controller.");
    MessageBox.Show(DCDataOut.ToString(), "Domain Controller Data",
        MessageBoxButtons.OK, MessageBoxIcon.Information);
}
```

The code begins by declaring all of the Win32 API functions used in the example. The [DllImport] attributes for this example always include three features. First, you must provide the name of the Win32 DLL that contains the function you want to use. Second, you must tell the CLR which character set to use: Unicode or ANSI. Third, you must set the SetLastError to true. Otherwise, you can't use the Marshal.GetLastWin32Error() method to obtain extended error information.

The DsGetDcName() function presents a special problem because it requires a GUID as input. When working with C/C++, you can simply set this entry to null (Nothing in Visual Basic) and expect the code to work. However, .NET applications can't set a Guid value to null because CLR returns an error. Consequently, the code creates an overload that accepts an IntPtr as input for the Guid value. The DsGetDcName() function returns a DOMAIN_CONTROLLER_INFO data structure. This data structure calls for the use of UInt32 values, which presents a problem for Visual Basic developers (Visual Basic doesn't support unsigned integers directly). The code gets around this problem by using enumerated values for the two UInt32 values. Not only does this technique overcome the unsigned integer problem, but it also makes the resulting code easier to read.

NOTE The code in Listing 12.1 lacks error trapping for the sake of clarity. You normally need to trap function return values, as well as use the `Marshal.GetLastWin32Error()` method to locate errors. In many cases, the .NET Framework won't tell you what's wrong because it doesn't know—you have to rely on Win32 API error trapping. The sample code includes a full set of return errors as an enumeration that you can use in your own code.

The `DsBind()` function creates an RPC session between the requesting application and the domain controller. This function returns a handle to the RPC session that the code uses with other function calls. The handle identifies the RPC session. Notice that this function declaration uses an `out IntPtr`, rather than the `ref IntPtr` used by the `DsGetDcName()` function. The `DsGetDcName()` function uses memory allocated by CLR, while the `DsBind()` function uses memory allocated by the Win32 API. Consequently, the `DsBind()` function receives an un-initialized `IntPtr` that the code frees using the `DsUnBind()` function. In general, if the Win32 API function automatically allocates memory for you, then you must use the technique shown for the `DsBind()` function.

The `DsGetDomainControllerInfo()` function presents a few problems. First, you can't call it until you call a number of the other functions because the code won't have the required information. Almost every input argument derives from one of the other functions described in this section. Second, you must decide on how much information to request. This function can actually accept one of two data structures as input. The example shows how to create the more complicated of the two data structures, `DS_DOMAIN_CONTROLLER_INFO_2`. You indicate which data structure to use with the `InfoLevel` argument. Third, this function returns an array of data structures, which means the code has to perform additional handling to obtain the correct information. Because the `DsGetDomainControllerInfo()` function returns an array of data structures, you can't allocate memory so you must rely on the `DsFreeDomainControllerInfo()` function to free the memory.

At this point, you can start looking at the `btnQuery_Click()` method. The code begins by initializing a `DOMAIN_CONTROLLER_INFO` data structure. This initialization process doesn't initialize the internal variables—just the data structure itself. The initialization process is necessary so that you can use the `Marshal.SizeOf(Output)` method to determine the size of the data structure. The output from this method lets you allocate memory from the global heap for the data structure reference, `OutputRef`, using the `Marshal.AllocHGlobal()` method. Any memory you allocate manually won't get garbage collected properly, so you must deallocate it using the `Marshal.FreeHGlobal()` method.

Now that the code has some memory to use, it calls the `DsGetDcName()` function to obtain preliminary information about the domain controller. The example shows how to obtain information for the default domain controller. Consequently, you don't need to know anything about the host system. This technique always returns a domain controller if one exists (error trapping is essential if you use this on systems where the presence of a domain controller is in doubt). The DsGetDcName() function returns a pointer to a data structure, not the data structure itself. The code uses the Marshal.PtrToStructure() method to convert the pointer to a data structure you can use.

The code now has enough information to start a conversation with the domain controller, so it uses the DsBind() function to create an RPC session. Notice how this function relies on information retrieved from the Output data structure.

After the code begins a conversation with the domain controller, it uses the DsGetDomain-ControllerInfo() function to request information about the domain controller. This isn't the standard server information, but the actual domain controller (the software server on the physical machine) information. The DsGetDomainControllerInfo() function, like many directory services functions, requires a bind handle as input so that it knows which RPC session to use. The DCDataLen output from this function states the number of array elements pointed at by the DCDataRef pointer.

The issue of how to handle arrays is important. Notice the first piece of the puzzle comes next. The code initializes DCData to hold the correct number of DS_DOMAIN_CONTROLLER_INFO_2 array elements. The code then uses the Marshal.PtrToStructure() method to place these array elements into DCData starting with the first array entry.

At this point, the program has the data needed to identify the server. The next two steps free the DS_DOMAIN_CONTROLLER_INFO_2 array pointer and close the RPC session with the server. You must perform these two steps or your program will have a significant data leak. The final lines of code display the information in the first element of the DS_DOMAIN_CONTROLLER_INFO_2 array. Figure 12.6 shows the output from this program.

FIGURE 12.6:

Using PInvoke can help you learn a lot about the domain controller.

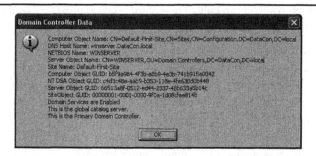

As you can see from the figure, this application provides a wealth of information about the domain controller that you can't obtain using strict .NET Framework functionality. However, you often need this information to invoke security on the domain controller and perform security-related tasks. For example, if you want to move security information from one machine to another, you need the `DsAddSidHistory()` function. Many of the .NET Framework methods also rely on information provided by the functions in this example. Finally, this example demonstrates that you can partially secure your server simply by denying the user access to unmanaged code.

Managing Directory Services

Although the "Understanding Domain Trust Relationships" section demonstrates that access to your domain controller information is relatively hard to come by when using a .NET application, working with Active Directory itself is relatively easy. All you need is access to either the `DirectoryEntry` or `DirectorySearcher` controls as appropriate. Consequently, you have to manage access to Active Directory using permissions.

The following sections show how to use permissions to manage directory service access in a number of ways. The examples also demonstrate types of Active Directory access. This information is essential because you might need to modify the security for a group or individual user as part of an application. The code in these sections shows how to access individual values and modify them as needed. The example doesn't modify properties that could make your system inaccessible—I decided not to include this code as an example because the techniques for modifying these dangerous values are the same as the techniques used to modify values with fewer negative consequences.

Using Declarative Active Directory Security

Previous chapters have stressed how you can use declarative and imperative security to secure your code. Generally, the examples have used one form or the other based on the requirements of the application. Active Directory is one place where using a combination of declarative and imperative security is helpful, especially if the program relies on multiple access levels.

The example in this, the "Using Imperative Active Directory Security," and the "Defining Write Access to Active Directory" sections rely on a combination of imperative and declarative security to verify minimum and required access needs. This section uses the declarative security provided by the `DirectoryServicesPermissionAttribute` class to establish minimum requirements because Active Directory access is optional for most users. For example, the `MainForm` class declaration includes the following attribute.

```
[DirectoryServicesPermissionAttribute(
    SecurityAction.Demand,
    PermissionAccess=DirectoryServicesPermissionAccess.Browse)]
public class MainForm : System.Windows.Forms.Form
```

To use this program, the user must have the right to browse Active Directory. If the user doesn't have this right, there's little point in continuing the program. The sole purpose of this program is to look at Active Directory and optionally perform modifications on it.

The DetailForm class also uses this declarative security. However, the user can use this form to write information to Active Directory, so the DirectoryServicesPermissionAccess.Browse permission only signifies one level of access the user could need. In this case, the declarative security acts as a basic filter, rather than an access determination.

Using Imperative Active Directory Security

Ensuring that the user has rights to browse Active Directory is a good first step, but you still don't know where the user will browse. At this point, you need to use imperative security to ensure that the user doesn't go beyond the bounds set by the network administrator. Listing 12.2 shows the main browsing form for the example application. This form relies on imperative security to ensure that the user has rights to browse the specified path. This listing isn't complete, but it does contain the essential elements for this discussion. You'll find the complete source code for this example in the \Chapter 12\C#\Monitor and \Chapter 12\VB\Monitor folders of the source code located on the Sybex Web site.

Listing 12.2   **Accessing Active Directory**

```
private void btnQuery_Click(object sender, System.EventArgs e)
{
   // Active Directory Permission.
   DirectoryServicesPermission              DSP;
   // A single Directory Service Permission.
   DirectoryServicesPermissionEntry         []DSPEntry;

   // Define a permission entry for the requested path.
   DSPEntry = new DirectoryServicesPermissionEntry[1];
   DSPEntry[0] = new DirectoryServicesPermissionEntry(
      DirectoryServicesPermissionAccess.Browse, txtQuery.Text);

   // Set security for the program.
   DSP = new DirectoryServicesPermission(DSPEntry);
   DSP.Demand();

   // Clear the previous query (if any).
   lvUsers.Items.Clear();

   // Add the path information to the DirectoryEntry object.
   ADSIEntry.Path = txtQuery.Text;

   // The query might fail, so add some error checking.
```

```
try
{

    // Process each DirectoryEntry child of the root
    // DirectoryEntry object.
    foreach (DirectoryEntry Child in ADSIEntry.Children)
    {
        // Look for user objects, versus group or service objects.
        if (Child.SchemaClassName.ToUpper() == "USER")
        {
            // Fill in the ListView object columns. Note that the
            // username is available as part of the DirectoryEntry
            // Name property, but that we need to obtain the
            // Description using another technique.
            ListViewItem lvItem  = new ListViewItem(Child.Name);
            lvItem.SubItems.Add(
                Child.Properties["Description"].Value.ToString());
            lvUsers.Items.Add(lvItem);
        }
    }
}
catch (System.Runtime.InteropServices.COMException eQuery)
{
    MessageBox.Show("Invalid Query\r\nMessage: " +
                    eQuery.Message +
                    "\r\nSource: " + eQuery.Source,
                    "Query Error",
                    MessageBoxButtons.OK,
                    MessageBoxIcon.Error);
}
}
```

The application begins with the btnQuery_Click() method. At this point, the application knows which Active Directory path to search, so it's time to verify that the user actually has the required access. The code begins by creating a DirectoryServicesPermissionEntry array. This is the first time that the book uses such a technique. You might think that you actually need a DirectoryServicesPermissionEntryCollection object, but the constructor for the DirectoryServicesPermission class only accepts a DirectoryServicesPermissionEntry array. Size the array to hold all of the permissions you need, but no more. Empty array elements tend to cause problems such as unexplained security errors. Each array element contains a DirectoryServicesPermissionEntry object that consists of an access level and an Active Directory path.

After you create the DirectoryServicesPermission object, you can look at the Permission-Entries property in the debugger to see the DirectoryServicesPermissionEntryCollection. This is the only time that .NET appears to use the collection form of the DirectoryServices-PermissionEntry class.

At this point, application security for the main form is in place. The program has cleared the user to browse a specific Active Directory path. Now the code begins defining the view. The example uses a `ListView` control to display the output of the query, so the first task is to clear the items in the `ListView` control. Notice that you specifically clear the items, not the entire control. This prevents corruption of settings such as the list headings.

You can configure all elements of the `ADSIEntry` (`DirectoryEntry`) control as part of the design process except the path. The application provides an example path in the `txtQuery` textbox that you'll need to change to meet your specific server configuration. You can obtain the correct path from the `ADsPath` field for the ADSI Viewer application—the application will allow you to copy the path to the clipboard using the Ctrl+C key combination. See the "Using the ADSI Viewer Utility" section for details.

The `ADSIEntry.Children` property is a collection of `DirectoryEntry` objects. The application won't fail with a bad path until you try to access these `DirectoryEntry` objects, which is why you want to place a portion of the code in a `try...catch` block. Notice how the code uses a property string as an index into each `DirectoryEntry` object. Even if the property is a string, you must use the `ToString()` method or the compiler will complain. This is because .NET languages view each `DirectoryEntry` value as an object, regardless of object type.

The output of this portion of the code can vary depending on the path string you supply. Figure 12.7 shows the output for a WinNT path. The actual `DirectoryEntry` values change to match the path type, so using an LDAP path will produce different results. This means you can't depend on specific `DirectoryEntry` values within your code, even if you're working with the same Active Directory entry. The return value issues can lead to security problems if your code design doesn't handle them. In general, it isn't safe to assume much about the format of the data coming from Active Directory.

FIGURE 12.7:

The WinNT path tends to produce easy-to-read `DirectoryEntry` values.

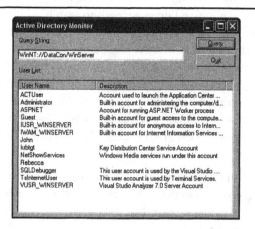

Defining Write Access to Active Directory

This example lends itself to demonstrating one security principle that you won't run into often, but will need to handle. Generally, you can provide protection for an application by hiding menus or simply not making the information available. Many of the applications in this book use that approach to keeping data secure—the best way to keep a secret is not to tell anyone. However, in this example, the code must allow everyone to see the information, but must prevent some users from changing it. Hiding is no longer an option.

Most of the activity for the details form occurs in the constructor. The constructor accepts the username, description, and path as inputs so it can create a detailed query for specific user information. Listing 12.3 shows the constructor code for this part of the example. This listing isn't complete, but it does contain the essential elements for this discussion. You'll find the complete source code for this example in the \Chapter 12\C#\Monitor and \Chapter 12\VB\Monitor folders of the source code located on the Sybex Web site.

Listing 12.3   **The Details Form Displays Individual User Information**

```csharp
public DetailForm(string UserName, string Description, string Path)
{
    // The current domain.
    AppDomain                    MyDomain;
    // The current user information.
    WindowsPrincipal             WP;
    // Active Directory Permission.
    DirectoryServicesPermission        DSP;
    // A single Directory Service Permission.
    DirectoryServicesPermissionEntry []DSPEntry;
    // Path to the user object.
    string                       UserPath;
    // LDAP provides more information.
    bool                         IsLDAP;

    // Required for Windows Form Designer support
    InitializeComponent();

    // Set the principal policy for this application.
    MyDomain = Thread.GetDomain();
    MyDomain.SetPrincipalPolicy(PrincipalPolicy.WindowsPrincipal);

    // Obtain the current user information.
    WP = (WindowsPrincipal)Thread.CurrentPrincipal;

    // Detect the user's role.
    if (WP.IsInRole(WindowsBuiltInRole.Administrator))
    {

        // Define permission entries for the requested path.
```

```
      DSPEntry = new DirectoryServicesPermissionEntry[1];
      DSPEntry[0] = new DirectoryServicesPermissionEntry(
         DirectoryServicesPermissionAccess.Write, Path);

      // Set security for the program.
      DSP = new DirectoryServicesPermission(DSPEntry);
      DSP.Demand();
   }
   else
   {
      // Make the user note information read-only.
      txtNotes.ReadOnly = true;

      // Get rid of the Update button.
      btnUpdate.Enabled = false;
      btnUpdate.Visible = false;
   }

   // Set the username and description.
   lblUserName.Text = "User Name: " + UserName;
   lblDescription.Text = "Description: " + Description;

   // Determine the path type and create a path variable.
   if (Path.Substring(0, 4) == "LDAP")
   {
      IsLDAP = true;

      // LDAP requires some work to manipulate the path
      // string.
      int CNPosit = Path.IndexOf("CN");
      UserPath = Path.Substring(0, CNPosit) +
              UserName + "," +
              Path.Substring(CNPosit, Path.Length - CNPosit);
   }
   else
   {
      IsLDAP = false;

      // A WinNT path requires simple concatenation.
      UserPath = Path + "/" + UserName;
   }

   // Set the ADSIUserEntry Path and get user details.
   ADSIUserEntry.Path = UserPath;
   ADSIUserEntry.RefreshCache();

   // This information is only available using LDAP
   if (IsLDAP)
   {
      // Get the user's title.
      if (ADSIUserEntry.Properties["Title"].Value == null)
```

```
            lblTitleDept.Text = "Title (Department): No Title";
        else
            lblTitleDept.Text = "Title (Department): " +
                ADSIUserEntry.Properties["Title"].Value.ToString();

        // Get the user's department.
        if (ADSIUserEntry.Properties["Department"].Value == null)
            lblTitleDept.Text = lblTitleDept.Text + " (No Department)";
        else
            lblTitleDept.Text = lblTitleDept.Text + " (" +
                ADSIUserEntry.Properties["Department"].Value.ToString()
                + ")";
    }

    // This information is common to both WinNT and LDAP, but uses
    // slightly different names.
    if (IsLDAP)
    {
        if (ADSIUserEntry.Properties["lastLogon"].Value == null)
            lblLogOn.Text = "Last Logon: Never Logged On";
        else
        {
            LargeInteger        Ticks;      // COM Time in Ticks.
            long                ConvTicks;  // Converted Time in Ticks.
            PropertyCollection  LogOnTime;  // Logon Property Collection.

            // Create a property collection.
            LogOnTime = ADSIUserEntry.Properties;

            // Obtain the LastLogon property value.
            Ticks = (LargeInteger)LogOnTime["lastLogon"][0];

            // Convert the System.__ComObject value to a managed
            // value.
            ConvTicks = (((long)(Ticks.HighPart) << 32) +
                        (long) Ticks.LowPart);

            // Release the COM ticks value.
            Marshal.ReleaseComObject(Ticks);

            // Display the value.
            lblLogOn.Text = "Last Logon: " +
                DateTime.FromFileTime(ConvTicks).ToString();
        }
    }
    else
    {
        if (ADSIUserEntry.Properties["LastLogin"].Value == null)
            lblLogOn.Text = "Last Logon: Never Logged On";
        else
            lblLogOn.Text = "Last Logon: " +
```

```
                    ADSIUserEntry.Properties["LastLogin"].Value.ToString();
    }

    // In a few cases, WinNT and LDAP use the same property names.
    if (ADSIUserEntry.Properties["HomeDirectory"].Value == null)
        lblHomeDirectory.Text = "Home Directory: None";
    else
        lblHomeDirectory.Text = "Home Directory: " +
            ADSIUserEntry.Properties["HomeDirectory"].Value.ToString();

    // Get the text for the user notes. Works only for LDAP.
    if (IsLDAP)
    {
        if (ADSIUserEntry.Properties["Info"].Value != null)
            txtNotes.Text =
                ADSIUserEntry.Properties["Info"].Value.ToString();

        // Enable the Update button.
        btnUpdate.Visible = true;
    }
    else
    {
        txtNotes.Text = "Note Feature Not Available with WinNT";
    }
}
```

The code begins by obtaining the WindowsPrincipal object for the current user. Remember that you must use the SetPrincipalPolicy() method to configure the thread information first. Once the code obtains the WindowsPrincipal object, it detects the user's current role.

If the user is an administrator, the code adds a new DirectoryServicesPermissionEntry permission using the same technique as for the main form. You might wonder why the code doesn't also set the DirectoryServicesPermissionAccess.Browse permission. The details form inherits this permission from the main form, so you don't need to set it again. In fact, if you try to set it, CLR will raise an error. However, this fact brings up an important issue—permissions flow from form to form, so you need to add or revoke permissions as appropriate.

Any user who isn't an administrator doesn't have permission to write to Active Directory. Even if you don't do anything else at this point, the directory entries are safe. However, the example makes txtNotes read-only and removes btnUpdate to keep confusion to a minimum. In addition, this form of data hiding is important because otherwise the user would know that an update option exists.

The process for adding the path to the DirectoryEntry control, ADSIUserEntry, is the same as for the main form. In this case, the control is activated using the RefreshCache() method. Calling RefreshCache() ensures that the local control contains the property values for the user in question.

LDAP does provide access to a lot more properties than WinNT. The example shows just two of the additional properties in the form of the user's title and department name. While WinNT provides access to a mere 25 properties, you'll find that LDAP provides access to 56 or more. Notice that each property access relies on checks for null values. Active Directory uses null values when a property doesn't have a value, rather than set it to a default value such as 0 or an empty string.

WinNT and LDAP do have some overlap in the property values they provide. In some cases, the properties don't have precisely the same name, so you need to extract the property value depending on the type of path used to access the directory entry. Both WinNT and LDAP provide access to the user's last logon, but WinNT uses LastLogin, while LDAP uses lastLogon.

WinNT normally provides an easy method for accessing data values that CLR can understand. In the case of the lastLogon property, LDAP presents some challenges. This is one case when you need to use the COM access method. Notice that the lastLogon property requires use of a LargeInteger (defined in the ACTIVEDS.TLB file). If you view the property value returned by the lastLogon property, you'll see that it's of the System.__ComObject type. This type always indicates that CLR couldn't understand the value returned by COM. Notice that the code converts the COM value to a managed type, then releases the COM object using Marshal.ReleaseComObject(). If you don't release the object, your application will have a memory leak—so memory allocation problems aren't quite solved in .NET, they just don't occur when using managed types. The final part of the conversion process is to change the number of ticks into a formatted string using the DateTime.FromFileTime() method.

As previously mentioned, the sample application shows how to present and edit one of the user properties. The Info property is only available when working with LDAP, so the code only accesses the property if you're using an LDAP path. The code also enables an Update button when using an LDAP path so you can update the value in Active Directory. Here's the simple code for sending a change to Active Directory.

```
private void btnUpdate_Click(object sender, System.EventArgs e)
{
    // Place the new value in the correct property.
    ADSIUserEntry.Properties["info"][0] = txtNotes.Text;

    // Update the property.
    ADSIUserEntry.CommitChanges();
}
```

The application uses a double index when accessing the property to ensure that the updated text from txtNotes appears in the right place. All you need to do to make the change permanent is call CommitChanges(). Note that the change will only take place if the user has sufficient rights to make it. In most cases, COM will ignore any update errors, so you won't know the change took place unless you actually check the entry. Figure 12.8 shows the LDAP output for the sample application.

FIGURE 12.8:

The LDAP output is more complete than the WinNT output, but requires more work as well.

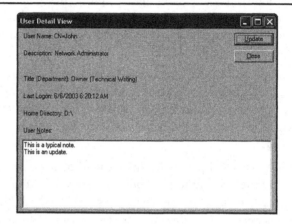

Summary

This chapter has demonstrated access, discovery, and security features of Active Directory. Although it doesn't provide a full treatment of many Active Directory tasks, you do know how to make Active Directory the kind of secure environment that protects your most sensitive data completely. You also know of a new use for the ADSI Viewer—as a monitoring tool. Many network administrators are unaware of the full capabilities of this particular tool—how it can help locate and track potential security problems.

Now that you know more about the security needs of Active Directory, it's time to put them into practice. One of the first tasks you should perform is to audit your Active Directory installation. You might find entries that you never knew existed (most of which will contain legitimate configuration information). It's also time to plan secure extensions for Active Directory (as needed) and to secure access to this essential database by adding the proper permissions to your applications.

Chapter 13 discusses a topic that's received a lot of press: wireless device security. The problem with wireless devices is that they transmit information into the open air, making it possible for anyone to listen in on the conversation. However, the problem is more severe than you might imagine. Some industry pundits are describing wireless as the biggest disaster that could ever hit your network. However, the .NET Framework provides options to make your wireless application more secure and they're covered in Chapter 13.

Wireless Device Security

- Defining .NET Compact Framework Security Issues

- Developing Wireless Programs That Work in Two Environments

- Understanding the Effects of Security Policy on Mobile Applications

- Understanding Component Calling Limitations

- Working with the Simple `System.Web.Security` Namespace

Wireless devices have stirred more than a little controversy in the workplace. Some people are addicted to their gadgets; others find them a nuisance that makes any thought of freedom a pipe dream (your boss can now find you anywhere that provides the proper connection). Corporations currently question the viability of using wireless solutions in some areas, but try to implement the solutions anyway to avoid losing a perceived technical advantage. The computer industry is already questioning the viability of some wireless businesses such as Wi-Fi hotspots (see the InfoWorld article at `http://www.infoworld.com/article/03/06/02/HNwifistudy_1.html`). Many developers look at wireless as a source of extra work. Network administrators view wireless as the biggest security hole in the organization and a source of support headaches.

> **NOTE** This chapter isn't the definitive guide to building wireless applications, nor will you learn how to solve every support issue with these devices. In fact, the chapter won't even touch on some security issues because there isn't any means to solve them in the .NET Framework. For example, the .NET Framework doesn't provide a solution to the person who spreads spam on the Internet by making a wireless connection to your network. (Carlton Vogt wrote an interesting series of articles for InfoWorld on this problem starting with the October 2, 2002 issue of Ethics Matter that you can find at `http://www.infoworld.com/article/02/10/02/021004opethics_1.html`.)

What you do get out of this chapter is information about what the .NET Compact Framework can do for you. The .NET Compact Framework is a smaller version of the .NET Framework that Microsoft designed especially to meet the needs of certain mobile devices such as the Pocket PC. You might be surprised to learn that many of the security features discussed for the .NET Framework in this book also work with the .NET Compact Framework. The help files supplied with Visual Studio .NET clearly mark the functionality that works in both environments. I'll be sure to discuss some of the more important crossovers, but be sure to check other elements as you need them.

The chapter does discuss a few configuration issues you need to consider as part of the development for your application. First, you need to identify the environment in which the application will operate correctly. An application designed specifically for the Pocket PC that doesn't rely on a Web connection is always more secure than a Web application designed for a number of platforms. Second, you need to consider the effect of security policies on your application. There's a chance that a security policy that looks fine for desktop applications will leave large holes when used for Web-based applications, especially those that work with wireless devices.

The next section of the chapter discusses a few additional precautions you need to consider when using your components with wireless applications. In some cases, you can resolve the problems by using a few additional roles. However, in other cases, you might decide that the risk is too high and not make the functionality provided by the component available to wireless devices.

Finally, the chapter discusses the System.Web.Security namespace. This namespace contains a few classes that are especially important to wireless device developers that rely on Web-based applications. Sometimes the best solution to a problem is to ensure that you lock things down at both ends and assume that someone will try to listen in. Wireless devices transmit their data into open air—they're inherently nonsecure devices.

> **NOTE** This chapter assumes that you've worked with the .NET Compact Framework 1.1 and features found in Visual Studio .NET 2003 for mobile device development. This new environment contains better security features and is easier to use for wireless device development environments, such as the Pocket PC.

.NET Compact Framework Security Considerations

The .NET Compact Framework is Microsoft's attempt to bring the functionality you enjoy when working with a desktop, LAN, or Internet application to the Pocket PC. You can use the .NET Compact Framework to produce a wide variety of applications for devices such as the Pocket PC, SmartPhone compatible devices, and some embedded applications. Theoretically, your next home security system could have the .NET Compact Framework installed. Web-based application programming extends the range of application types and platforms to most wireless devices that can support a Web browser interface. For example, if you need to support both the Pocket PC and the Palm, you'd use a Web-based application to do it.

The following sections describe the security implications of working with wireless devices using the .NET Compact Framework. These sections don't discuss other wireless security issues in very much detail. You'll also learn a quick way to determine which classes the .NET Compact Framework supports. By using careful programming strategies, you can often reduce the amount of work required to produce a secure application that works with little recoding on a wireless device. Finally, you'll see a simple programming example with a few of the security measures you'll need to implement. This programming example shows functionality provided by Visual Studio .NET 2003 (the first version that has embedded .NET Compact Framework support), so it probably won't work with older version of Visual Studio .NET, even if you've added .NET Compact Framework support.

Understanding Wireless Security Issues

It's important to understand that at best the .NET Compact Framework can secure the data within the application you create. It can't secure the wire (which includes all of the connectivity between two machines) because the wire isn't physical. Using wireless transmission leaves the communication path open. Even Wired Equivalent Privacy (WEP) has limitations that make it less than a perfect solution for wireless security. (See the 802.11 Planet article at http://www.80211-planet.com/tutorials/article.php/2106281 for details.) Some users make the wireless problem worse by not changing the default Service Set Identifier (SSID) or using the SSID as part of the WEP encryption key.

Wireless data interception isn't a new problem—everyone who has ever used radio to transmit secret data has had the same problem. For example, many people imagine that spies obtain the secret information used to fight wars, but most modern wars (including World War II) have relied on breaking the enemy's radio codes and using that information to listen in on the enemy's conversations. Any data transferred over the air is susceptible to interception and interpretation by someone else.

The .NET Compact Framework also can't secure the transfer point between the wireless connection and the physical network (part of the access point). Current systems translate the data at this connection point, which means decrypting the data, performing the translation, and encrypting it again. This particular area is the point where many crackers break into the system. The lack of processing power for wireless devices makes it harder to use strong encryption, which only makes the problem worse. (Read the eWeek article at `http://security.ziffdavis.com/article2/0,3973,1115544,00.asp` to learn how you can control rogue access points.)

When you couple these special wireless application problems with the problems of a laptop or desktop system (such as stupid user tricks and inept enterprise policies), you have a significant security threat that the .NET Compact Framework can't address. In short, anyone who relies on wireless technology to protect the innermost secrets their company possesses is in for a surprise. The .NET Compact Framework can help you make the data more secure, but these external issues make it impossible for any .NET developer to guarantee the security and data integrity of a wireless application.

Advances in Mobile Device Security

Mobile device vendors understand that security is a significant issue for their products. Most vendors are working on new security features that make security easier. For example, according to InfoWorld, ARM is adding hardware-based security to their processors (`http://www.infoworld.com/article/03/05/27/HNarmsecure_1.html`). An interesting concept to take from this story is that no security scheme seems to fulfill everyone's needs. Although a hardware-based security setup would tend to keep crackers at bay, at least for awhile, many people are concerned that vendors will use the security feature to enforce digital rights management (DRM). The same technology that lets you lock up an application could allow someone else to lock up data or the off-the-shelf application your company purchased. Another vendor making the push into hardware-based security is Cisco. You can read this story at `http://www.infoworld.com/article/03/05/21/HNciscosecure_1.html`. The point is that you will need to design your wireless application with security from other sources in mind.

The problems with wireless security get worse. In some respects, wireless security flaws are a matter of developer attitude toward the devices. Many developers find wireless devices a nuisance because they normally require separate coding. Even using the .NET Compact Framework or Web-based applications is only a partial solution because desktop users also demand full functionality from their applications—most wireless device applications have fewer features than do their desktop counterparts because they have less capacity. As a result, some wireless applications are rushed and not fully secured because they aren't fully tested.

Another problem that you'll have to face is user demand. Users who don't fully appreciate the significant security threats posed by wireless devices are asking for more applications. If wired device vendors have their way, users might soon request applications that are difficult to secure and could be illegal depending on how you interpret the law. Consider the InfoWorld story on biotechnology at `http://www.infoworld.com/article/03/04/24/HNbiotech_1.html`. On the surface, such new applications are laudable. However, given the current state of wireless security and the requirements of the Health Insurance Portability and Accountability Act of 1996 (HIPAA), it's reckless for a developer to consider creating such an application even if the vendor provides the proper tools. You can learn more about HIPAA on the Health and Human Services site at `http://www.hhs.gov/ocr/hipaa/` and the HIPAA.ORG site at `http://www.hipaa.org/`.

As you can see, the security problems of wireless applications are significant and you can't do anything to make security even approach a reasonable level of reliability. For this and many other reasons, it's probably a good idea to restrict any data you transfer using a wireless connection significantly. Although the .NET Compact Framework can help you secure the transmission a little, it simply isn't enough to make security good enough for critical data.

Discovering Which Classes Apply to Both Environments

The .NET Compact Framework isn't the same as the .NET Framework you normally use—you'll notice differences between the two. Most of the differences are due to environment. All of the wireless devices you use have limited capability—although some industry pundits predict that the Personal Digital Assistant (PDA) will eventually catch up with the desktop. For now, however, you need to consider the capacity limitations and understand how they affect .NET functionality. Microsoft just couldn't make the two environments the same.

Fortunately, Microsoft makes it relatively easy to perform a comparison as long as you have a newer version of MSDN to use. The Class Library Comparison Tool provides a color-coded list of the .NET Framework classes and shows which classes the .NET Compact Framework implements. This tool appears at `ms-help://MS.MSDNQTR.2003FEB.1033/dv_spchk/html/NET _Compact_Framework.htm`. When you first open this tool, you see a list of display options similar to the ones shown in Figure 13.1.

FIGURE 13.1:

Use the display option settings to filter the output of the Class Library Comparison Tool.

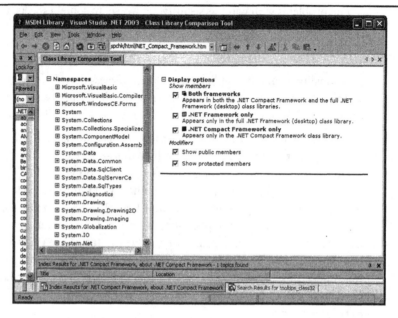

Once you choose some display settings, you can start looking at the classes that interest you. Just click through the hierarchical list as usual. For example, Figure 13.2 shows the System.Collections.ArrayList class comparison.

FIGURE 13.2:

Display an individual class and you see how the two frameworks compare.

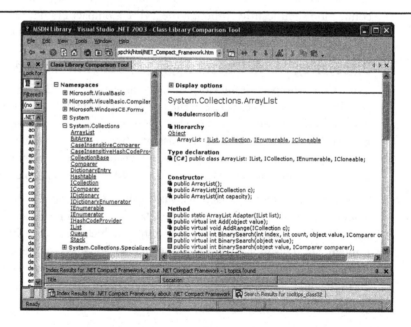

The color-coding does make the list a lot easier to see than the image in the book. Fortunately, each entry uses a different icon as well. For example, both frameworks support all of the constructors. They also support the `Add()` and `AddRange()` methods. However, you can only use the `BinarySearch()` method with the .NET Framework—wireless devices won't support this method.

Unfortunately, some exceptionally important security classes are missing. For example, notice that the entire `System.Security.Permissions` namespace is missing. This omission makes simple security measures such as imperative (Listing 1.2) and declarative (Listing 4.4) security impossible. The `System.Security.Principal` namespace is also missing. This means you can't create a `WindowsPrincipal` object (Listing 1.1) to verify a user's role.

Interestingly enough, the .NET Compact Framework has a few features that the .NET Framework doesn't. You can find a complete list of these features in the Classes Exclusive to the .NET Compact Framework help topic at `ms-help://MS.MSDNQTR.2003FEB.1033/ dv_evtuv/html/etconclassesexclusivetonetcompactframework.htm`. These new classes fall into three categories.

Infrared Data Association (IrDA) Support   These classes help you communicate with the IrDA port on your wireless device (if it has one). I wish that Microsoft had chosen to make these classes available earlier and make them available to the desktop. The problem is that Microsoft doesn't provide good support for IrDA devices on desktop machines, so you might find yourself resorting to older Win32 API programming techniques to develop a complete solution.

SQL Server CE Support   SQL Server CE is a special version of SQL Server for wireless devices. Many developers complain about its lack of functionality. In general, it is a limited solution for very special needs—I haven't found any yet and haven't heard about good uses for this product from other developers either, so the need is very special.

`Microsoft.WindowsCE.Forms` Classes   The support provided by these classes wouldn't have a place anywhere on the desktop, so you should become familiar with this group of classes immediately. It's interesting to note that these classes provide a level of application control that does fit within the realm of security. For example, you can choose to enable or disable the `InputPanel` as needed to ensure safe operation of your application.

Developing a Simple .NET Compact Framework Program

One of the first concerns many developers have with wireless devices is the safety of their applications. A cracker could tamper with an application and many users wouldn't notice until the virus has so corrupted their data that any attempt at recovery is futile. Unfortunately, attempting to protect the application using other techniques in this book won't work for the most part. Yes, you can sign the file, but as demonstrated in the "Validating Your Code" section of Chapter 6, smart crackers can still get around your security measures. Unfortunately, the Pocket PC doesn't provide quite as many resources for solving this problem, but you can still do it.

NOTE   The .NET Compact Framework can work with a wide variety of devices to create a broad range of applications. For example, the default Visual Studio .NET installation includes both Windows CE and Pocket PC platform support for the Smart Device Application Wizard. Both of these platforms support a Windows application, class library, non-graphic (console) application, and an empty project. In short, this chapter won't cover all of the project types—I chose projects based on how they could present security issues, rather than application programming technique.

Listing 13.1 shows a technique for checking the hash code of an assembly. The method isn't quite as refined as the desktop version shown in Listing 6.1, but it does work well enough that most crackers won't try to circumvent it. (You can find this example in the \Chapter 13\C#\SimpleSecurity or \Chapter 13\VB\SimpleSecurity folder of the source code located on the Sybex Web site.)

Listing 13.1   Application Security Technique

```
private void btnTest_Click(object sender, System.EventArgs e)
{
    Assembly    Asm;        // Assembly reference.
    FileStream  FStrm;      // File holding data.
    String      HashOut;    // Hash value in string form.
    Char[]      Converter;  // Conversion array.
    Byte[]      Output;     // Output data.
    Int32       Counter;    // Loop counting variable.

    // Get the current assembly.
    Asm = Assembly.GetExecutingAssembly();

    // Check for the hash file.
    if (File.Exists(@"Settings.TXT"))
    {
        // Open the file.
        FStrm = File.Open(@"Settings.TXT", FileMode.Open);

        // Determine the file length and read it.
        Output = new Byte[FStrm.Length];
        FStrm.Read(Output, 0, Output.Length);

        // Convert the output to a string.
        Converter = new Char[Output.Length];
        for (Counter = 0; Counter < Output.Length; Counter++)
            Converter[Counter] = Convert.ToChar(Output[Counter]);
        HashOut = new String(Converter);

        // Close the file stream.
```

```
        FStrm.Close();

        // Perform the comparison.
        if (HashOut == Asm.GetHashCode().ToString())
            MessageBox.Show("The code is safe.", "Application Status");
        else
            throw new SecurityException("Unsafe Application");
    }
    else
    {
        // Create a new file to contain the hash code.
        FStrm = File.Create(@"Settings.TXT");

        // Get the hast code and convert it to a Byte array.
        HashOut = Asm.GetHashCode().ToString();
        Output = new Byte[HashOut.Length];
        Converter = HashOut.ToCharArray();
        for (Counter = 0; Counter < Converter.Length; Counter++)
            Output[Counter] = Convert.ToByte(Converter[Counter]);

        // Write the hash code to disk and close the file.
        FStrm.Write(Output, 0, Output.Length);
        FStrm.Close();

        // Display a success message.
        MessageBox.Show("Hash value successfully written!",
                        "Data Output");
    }
}
```

The code begins by getting the current assembly using the `Assembly.GetExecutingAssembly()` method. The desktop version of the `Assembly` object contains a number of useful features, including the `Evidence` property. The .NET Compact Framework lacks support for this feature, but it does include the `GetHashCode()` method, which the example uses to check the validity of the code.

Once the code obtains the assembly information, it checks for the hash file using the `File.Exists()` method. The first time the application runs, the file won't exist, so the code uses the `File.Create()` method to create a new file. It then uses the `Asm.GetHashCode()` method to obtain the current hash value and converts it to a `Byte[]` array. The `FStrm.Write()` places the data on disk and the `FStrm.Close()` method closes the file.

Note that the example uses a simple text file for storage to make it easy for you to check the application results and remove the file when you get finished working with the example. In a real world implementation, you should choose a file with a unique name, store it in a unique location, and protect it as much as possible. You could also encrypt the content of the file to make it difficult to modify the content.

When the hash file exists, the code opens the file using the `File.Open()` method. The code converts the input data to a string. It then uses the string contained in `HashOut` to compare the current hash value with the `Asm.GetHashCode().ToString()` method. Notice that you can throw a `SecurityException` exception if the hash values don't match.

To test this program, try clicking Test twice. The first time you'll see the "Hash value successfully written!" message. The second time you'll see the "The code is safe." message. Open the File Explorer found in the Programs folder of the emulator (not on your desktop machine). Locate the `Settings.TXT` file in the `MyDevice` folder, as shown in Figure 13.3. Open the file and change the hash value to something else.

> **NOTE**   Although every wireless application in this chapter is tested using a Pocket PC, all of the screenshots in this chapter rely on the emulator. They may vary slightly from the images you see on screen. Differing screen resolutions and device capabilities affect the appearance of the test applications on screen.

FIGURE 13.3:
Locate the
`Settings.TXT`
file in the MyDevice
folder so you can
change the hash
value.

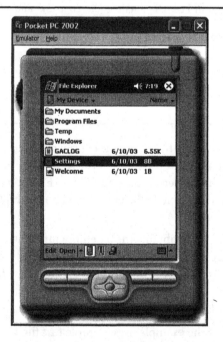

Now that the program is set up for a failure, click Test. You should see an error message appear after a waiting period (normally a few seconds). Figure 13.4 shows a typical security exception when you use the emulator from the debugger.

FIGURE 13.4:

Throwing a security exception when the hash values don't match alerts the user to the problem.

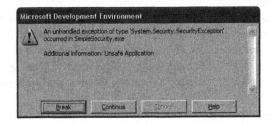

As you can see, this error message looks very similar to the ones you receive when you work with desktop applications. I pointed this out because Microsoft has tried hard to make the development environment friendly (and, in this case, it shows). You could try to catch the exception, but, in this case, the output is more dramatic and likely to catch the user's attention the first time. Figure 13.5 shows typical output from the emulator when you run the application without the debugger.

FIGURE 13.5:

The wireless device user will see a message similar to this one when an application hash error occurs.

TIP If you see a deployment error when you try to run the program from the debugger, verify that the application isn't already running on the emulator. When the application runs, the emulator locks the file and makes it impossible to deploy the application. The debugger won't run until it can deploy the latest version. Closing the existing copy of the application on the emulator usually solves the problem and lets you run the debugger.

Generally, I try to make the user's life as easy as possible because it's poor programming practice not to catch errors and handle them if possible. In this case, the error message occurs before the application is running (you might even include the check as part of the constructor), so displaying the actual error message isn't such a big problem. Obviously, there isn't any way to fail gracefully if the application has a security error that demonstrates some kind of tampering. The best practice is to inform the user immediately and end the program before it has a chance to load any data.

The Two Environments of Wireless Programs

The emphasis of many wireless development efforts today is the Web. However, most mobile devices support both a local (or desktop) environment and a Web environment. It's easy to come up with a number of reasons for the emphasis on Web development. Many developers consider the Windows CE toolkits one of the harder IDEs to use for development. In addition, Web-based applications commonly work with more than one platform. A single Web-based application could meet the needs of a cellular telephone, a Pocket PC, and a Palm. In fact, given enough time, a developer could create a single application that would meet all of these wireless needs and the needs of desktop users too. In short, you can find many reasons to use Web-based applications to the exclusion of everything else.

However, the desktop environment has a certain appeal as well. First, the user doesn't require a connection to anything to use the application. Second, an application designed for local use can rely on the special features provided by the device. Finally, the local environment is more secure simply because you eliminate the problems of using a wireless connection. In short, both environments have something to offer.

NOTE Application testing is complex. Testing desktop and Web-based applications that need to work together is more complex. Adding wireless to the equation makes testing even more complex— some say nearly impossible. Complexity breeds security problems because complex issues often require a level of analysis that few developers can provide. One InfoWorld column by Wayne Rash (`http://www.infoworld.com/article/03/05/16/20secadvise_1.html`) reminded me that even the industry pundits have a hard time figuring out what to test, much less how to test it. In this case, the columnist asks readers not only to help him discover which security devices to test, but to offer input on how to test them.

When you write applications to the lowest common denominator, you usually give something up. This book won't go into all of the flexibility and performance issues that Web-based applications can incur. However, the following sections do discuss security issues you need to consider. Each environment incurs security penalties that you need to consider as part of your development effort. Combine these limitations with the lack of security functionality in the .NET Compact Framework and you'll see the need to discover creative solutions to security problems.

Overcoming Direct Execution Problems

This section discusses the PDA. Unless technology changes significantly, cellular telephones will remain connected to the Internet as their only significant means of application communication (that is, they can only use the Web environment). In addition, the Smart Device Application template currently provided with Visual Studio .NET 2003 doesn't include support for anything other than the Pocket PC (you can't even work with the Palm).

For the most part, wireless applications don't exist in a secure environment, even when you use the Smart Device Application project to build a Windows application. However, the desktop environment is more secure than the Web environment simply because you have more control over application execution and data handling. Standalone applications are the most secure because you don't have to deal with the vagaries of transmitting information over a wireless connection.

Of course, the assumption is that you'll always use a wireless connection for your application. However, you have to consider whether this is a valid assumption. You can synchronize to a host machine by placing the PDA in the cradle (or using some other hard-wired connection). When you don't need a live connection, using the synchronization feature works well. A service on the host machine can detect data changes and take the appropriate action.

Live connections don't necessarily mean a nonsecure environment. You can add a network card to your PDA that allows a direct connection. (I currently have a Kingston model CIO10T, but there are likely other products on the market.) Unfortunately, this means you have a physical connection to the network again, and many people like their PDA because it frees them from the limitations of a physical connection. Even so, requiring a physical network connection to transfer sensitive data can reduce your risk substantially. You can ensure that the user uses a network connection by checking for the network adapter in your code and using that connection with members of the System.Net.Sockets namespace. (See Listing 8.1 for one example of how to use sockets within an application—the associated explanation details some of the security issues you need to consider for an application that relies on a socket connection.) Use a TcpClient object on the PDA and a TcpListener object on the server to create a direct connection.

Another alternative is to use the Infrared Data Association (IrDA) connection. You implement this solution by creating an `IrDAClient` object on the PDA and an `IrDAListener` object on the host. The advantage of this method is that you don't have to worry about a wire. In addition, IrDA doesn't transmit in every direction as wireless does, so it's more secure than wireless. Unfortunately, although it's portable, you need a line-of-sight connection to the host because IrDA uses light transmission to make the connection. You can find a discussion about using IrDA for communication purposes at `http://dotnet247.com/247reference/msgs/27/137277.aspx`.

Avoiding Browser-Based Application Issues

At some point, you'll have to consider using a Web-based application to meet specific needs. Web-based applications normally run with some type of wireless connection when you use a cellular telephone or a Palm. A Pocket PC can theoretically make a connection to the Internet through a host using a standard network connection (see the "Overcoming Direct Execution Problems" section for details on this solution). The point is that you'll access the application using a browser.

While you can use Secure Sockets Layer (SSL) to secure the communication when the mobile device browser supports it, generally, mobile browsers will access the application using only the functionality provided by the wireless connection. The reason is simple—an application that runs slowly on a desktop using SSL will be nearly unusable with a mobile device such as a cellular telephone. The speed of the device becomes a hindrance in securing the application using this simple technique.

More about Web-Based Security

One of the more interesting places to learn about Web-based security threats is Internet Security Systems (ISS) (`https://gtoc.iss.net/issEn/delivery/gtoc/index.jsp`). The main page tells you about the current security state of the Internet, which is valuable to a developer planning an application deployment. ISS does sell security services and it provides articles on the latest security threats. You can view this information at `http://xforce.iss.net/`. Most developers will benefit most from the Internet Risk Impact Summary—a report you can download at `https://gtoc.iss.net/documents/summaryreport.pdf`. For example, this report will tell you that 33 percent of all security incidents happen on Friday and Saturday. You'll also discover that many attackers prefer ports 135, 137, 138, 139, and 445. The selection of these ports is interesting. For example, Microsoft Exchange clients use port 135 to communicate with the server. You can see Microsoft Knowledge Base article 176466 (`http://support.microsoft.com/default.aspx?scid=kb;[LN];176466`) for details on Exchange port usage.

Fortunately, it's relatively easy to detect the kind of device that's requesting services from a Web application. The ASP.NET Mobile Web Application template provides built-in functionality for determining the device type. The initial goal of this support is to help you build applications that scale to specific devices—it helps you size the screen to meet the needs of the device. You can also use this information to consider the effect of the device on security. For example, a cellular telephone is going to be a lot less secure than a desktop machine connecting to the same application. Consequently, you can leave specific features out of the cellular telephone version of the application.

One of the easiest ways to leave information out of a less secure mobile version of an application is to use filtering. All of the controls and forms supported by ASP.NET include an (`AppliedDeviceFilters`) property. Click the ellipses button for this property and you'll see an Applied Device Filters dialog box similar to the one shown in Figure 13.6.

FIGURE 13.6:

Use filters to define custom setups based on the caller type.

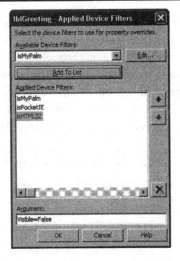

Notice that Figure 13.6 includes a number of device types. Visual Studio .NET 2003 includes a number of default filters that handle most situations. You can also click Edit to create a custom filter or adjust the settings of an existing filter. The point is that you have a way to detect the client and modify the information you present. This capability lets you secure the application based on the caller's ability to maintain a secure connection.

What isn't apparent in Figure 13.6 is that you're adding HTML tags to the application. It also isn't apparent that you can modify these tags to perform specific tasks. For example, you can set the filter for a specific device to make the associated control invisible. To set these properties, click the ellipses next to the (`PropertyOverrides`) property. You'll see a Property Overrides dialog box similar to the one shown in Figure 13.7.

FIGURE 13.7:
Use property overrides
to change the page
appearance and
functionality.

The Applied Device Filter list only contains those devices that you added to the list in
Figure 13.6. In this case, the code changes the `lblGreeting.Text` property to read Pocket IE
Client. However, the client won't actually see the greeting because the `Visible` property is false.
You can still interact with the information in code, so it's essential to set the values as needed.
Listing 13.2 shows how these changes affect the tags for the ASPX page. (You can find this
example in the `\Chapter 13\C#\ClientCapabilities` or `\Chapter 13\VB\ClientCapabilities`
folder of the source code located on the Sybex Web site.)

Listing 13.2   Tag Changes Based on Filter Settings

```
<mobile:Label id="lblGreeting" runat="server">
    <DeviceSpecific>
        <Choice Filter="isPocketIE"
                Argument="Visible=False"
                Visible="False"
                Text="Pocket IE Client">
        </Choice>
        <Choice Filter="isMyPalm"
                Argument="Visible=False"
                Visible="False"
                Text="Palm Client">
        </Choice>
        <Choice Filter="isHTML32"
                Argument="Visible=True"
                Text="HTML32 Client">
        </Choice>
    </DeviceSpecific>
Hello</mobile:Label>
```

The <DeviceSpecific> tag sets off a list of device choices. Notice that each of the <Choice> tags contains settings for a particular device, so you have good control over the property settings. The server doesn't tell the client about controls that lack information or are invisible. As far as the client is concerned, the lblGreeting label doesn't exist if you set its Visible property to False. Data hiding is an essential part of maintaining security when you have to work with wireless devices. Only tell the client what it needs to know in order to perform specific functions.

Fortunately, you can also manipulate the controls from within your code. When working with a database application, you might choose to send a subset of the information to a wireless client. You can't perform this task using the <Choice> tag, so you have to perform the filtering in code. Listing 13.3 shows an example of how you can access information about the current client using the DeviceSpecific property.

Listing 13.3   Using the DeviceSpecific Property

```
private void btnTest_Click(object sender, System.EventArgs e)
{
    // Display the device specific information.
    txtOutput.Text = "The device specific data is:" +
        "\r\nCount: " +
        lblGreeting.DeviceSpecific.Choices.Count.ToString() +
        "\r\nArgument: " +
        lblGreeting.DeviceSpecific.SelectedChoice.Argument +
        "\r\nFilter: " +
        lblGreeting.DeviceSpecific.SelectedChoice.Filter;
}
```

The DeviceSpecific property lets you access what amounts to an undocumented object, System.Web.UI.MobileControls.DeviceSpecific. (You can view the current documentation for this object at http://msdn.microsoft.com/library/en-us/mwsdk/html/mwlrfDeviceSpecificClass.asp.) Some of the features of this object appear in the TemplateControl class. The two most important features of this object are the Choices collection and the SelectedChoice property. The Choices collection tells you about the device choices currently enabled for the page, while the SelectedChoice property contains a DeviceSpecificChoice object that contains the current device properties.

Use the Choices collection to add new DeviceSpecificChoice objects to the page and to check on the current choices. This collection works the same as any other you've used with Visual Studio .NET. It includes an enumerator you can use to list the choices, an Add() method, and a Remove() method.

You might wonder what would keep a cracker from attempting to change the device settings to obtain additional rights to the page. First, your CLR compiles your application and loads it into memory, so the cracker would have to perform something akin to a buffer overload exploit. Second, the various objects include a `GetHashCode()` method. This method enables you to use a technique similar to the one shown in Listing 13.1 to verify the integrity of your code at any point.

Effects of Security Policy on Mobile Applications

You've accomplished what most developers only dream of doing—your application is completely secure. All sensitive data is hidden from the prying eyes of mobile users, you have all of the proper security measures in place, check every user's identity, encrypt data as needed, and even worked with the administrator to ensure that the firewall and other protection are in place. The fact that you have both a written and a configured security policy in place makes you feel as if your application could take on a world of crackers and come out on the winning end. You're in the most dangerous position that any developer can be in because it's too easy to become complacent when everything seems to be going your way.

Here's one example from a real company (name withheld for the obvious reasons). The company had all of the proper security measures in place, including data hiding for their mobile applications. The lack of information frustrated User A, who depended on his cellular telephone for almost every communication possible. User B decided to help User A by forwarding the sensitive data to User A's email. The email automatically forwarded the information to User A's cellular telephone. The security breach could have gone on for years, but the company performed email audits regularly and caught the problem before it became an issue. Theoretically, neither User A nor User B did anything wrong. The company had no policy in place that prohibited one user from sending data to another user in the company's email. Likewise, the company had no policy in place for forwarding email to a mobile device such as a cellular telephone. The company no longer allows email forwarding—an employee has to take care of company email from within the confines of the company. However, the security breach could have become significant due to the lack of a simple policy—one that no one thought the company actually needed.

Policies, both written and configured, must work with your code to ensure the integrity of your applications and data. Fortunately, developers and network administrators don't have to do all of the work in this area. Organizations such as the SANS Institute have already compiled template information for policies that you should implement along with your mobile application. See the SANS Security Policy Project (`http://www.sans.org/resources/policies/`) for details.

Once you have a policy in place, you need to implement best practices for configuration and setup to ensure that your application remains as safe as possible (realizing, of course, that a wireless application is never truly secure). Microsoft has put together an impressive collection of security resources in a white paper titled "Protecting Your Network: Wireless, Firewall, and Perimeter Security" at `http://www.microsoft.com/technet/security/prodtech/network/default.asp`. These resources discuss issues that I haven't discussed in this chapter, such as the use of Internet Protocol Security (IPSec) and how to limit your security risk when using Windows features such as Internet Connection Sharing (ICS).

Component Calling Limitations

Components are valuable because they encapsulate code you can reuse without adding it to your current application. You can access components with a mobile device in a number of ways. The method that ensures maximum compatibility relies on a Web page. Simply add the component to the Web project as you would any component. Any device with an appropriate browser can use the component and you can control access to the data using the data hiding techniques, shown in Listing 13.2 and 13.3.

However, it's not always possible to work with a component using a Web page, due to performance or data handling factors. In this case, you might have to turn to alternative methods that could incur a higher security risk. For example, you can employ the component as a Web service, as in the COM+ example in Chapter 8 (Listing 8.5). In this case, you might find yourself using a third party product such as PocketSoap (`http://www.pocketsoap.com/`) to gain access to the component. Listing 13.4 shows a typical example of how this product works. In this case, the mobile device accesses a component with a method named GetCompName().

Listing 13.4 **Accessing Web Services Using SOAP**

```JScript
<SCRIPT LANGUAGE="JScript">
function cmdGetSingleName_Click()
{
    var SOAPEnv;      // SOAP envelope
    var Transport;    // SOAP transport
    var Param;        // Parameter list
    var SOAPParam;    // SOAP method call parameters.
    var RecData;      // Received data holder

    // Create the envelope.
    SOAPEnv = new ActiveXObject("pocketSOAP.Envelope");
    SOAPEnv.MethodName = "GetCompName";
    SOAPEnv.URI = "https://tempuri.org/message/";

    // Create a parameter to place within the envelope.
```

```
Param = SOAPEnv.CreateParameter("NameType",
    window.document.SampleForm1.comboName.value, "");

// Send the request and receive the data.
Transport = new ActiveXObject("pocketSOAP.HTTPTransport");
Transport.SOAPAction =
    "https://tempuri.org/action/NameValuesProc.GetCompName"
Transport.Send(
    "https://WinServer/soapexamples/ComputerName/CompNameProc.WSDL",
    SOAPEnv.Serialize());
RecData = Transport.Receive();
SOAPEnv.Parse(RecData);

// Display the result.
RecData = SOAPEnv.Parameters.Item(0);
window.document.SampleForm1.Results.value = RecData.Value;
}
</SCRIPT>
```

This example uses a five-step process to access the component. First, the code creates an envelope. Second, the code places data within the envelope. Third, the code initializes the data. Fourth, the code sends and receives the data. Finally, the code displays the data on screen.

Aside from the fact that this is an interesting way to use a Web service from a Pocket PC, notice that the URLs all use the HTTPS protocol. This application uses SSL rather than the standard straight text data transfer, which makes it a lot more secure than using a simple Web page. This technique only works with the Pocket PC, but it's an important technique to consider when the data provided by your component is too sensitive for other data transfer techniques and you must support some form of wireless device. Note that PocketSoap is one of the few products that will support SSL transfer for a Pocket PC.

Using the *System.Web.Security* Namespace

The System.Web.Security namespace is the one that you'll use for the majority of your Web security needs—no matter what type of application you want to create. For example, this namespace contains the PassportIdentity class demonstrated in Listing 11.5. Some of the classes provide general functionality that you could use in both wireless and desktop application. When you want to use the classes in a general way, you need to implement the functionality on the server, rather than on the client. The following sections describe these three classes of interest.

TIP Web security takes a number of forms. While the classes in the System.Web.Security namespace can help you keep your data safe locally (to a large extent) and remotely (to a lesser extent), most applications will still require additional security measures such as the WS-Security standard (http://www-106.ibm.com/developerworks/webservices /library/ws-secure/). You can read about a number of products on the market today to help developers make the most of the potential of WS-Security in the InfoWorld article at http://www.infoworld.com/article/03/04/15/15appnews_1.html.

Defining File Security Using the *FileAuthorizationModule* Class

The FileAuthorizationModule class doesn't look like very much from the description in the help files. However, this class is exceptionally important because it's one of the few distinct links between Windows security and the security employed by the .NET Framework. Whenever a caller requests a resource such as a file, the FileAuthorizationModule class authenticates the caller against the Windows Access Control List (ACL). This isn't the role-based or code access security that a .NET application normally relies on to authenticate a caller.

The tie-in with older Windows technology is important. For example, without this link, ASP.NET impersonation (the use of a default account in place of the standard user account to access a resource) wouldn't work. This class also provides a way for you to restrict access to certain resources such as a file to specific callers using standard security measures. This means that someone who accesses the site using a PDA will have the same rights to that file as if they were accessing it from their desktop—a good feature when used to deny or grant access to a resource based on credentials, rather than other factors.

An alternative to using the FileAuthorizationModule class is to rely on the Url AuthorizationModule class. Although this option might seem more in line with the .NET way of working with security, you must manually enter the information used for authorizations purposes in the Web.CONFIG file. Here's an example of an authorization entry:

```
<authorization>
    <allow users="John"/>
    <allow roles="Administrators"/>
    <deny users="Guest"/>
    <deny roles="Guests"/>
</authorization>
```

In this case, the user named John and anyone in the Administrators role would gain access to the resource, but CLR would deny the user named Guest and anyone in the Guests role access. The problem with this technique is that it doesn't necessarily work well with all callers (including wireless devices where the username or role is ambiguous at times) and it keeps the authorization information in plain text form on the Web server. In short, using the `FileAuthorizationModule` class method is the more secure choice in this case. CLR uses the `FileAuthorizationModule` class automatically when you fail to include an `<authorization>` section in the `Web.CONFIG` file. You can learn more about the various roles of these two classes in security in Microsoft Knowledge Base article 306590 at `http://support.microsoft.com/default.aspx?scid=kb;[LN];306590`. Note that using the `FileAuthorizationModule` class can result in errors due to a bug in the .NET Framework implementation. See Knowledge Base article 317955 at `http://support.microsoft.com/default.aspx?scid=kb;[LN];317955` for details.

Defining Form Security Using the *FormsAuthentication* Class

The `FormsAuthentication` class can help you overcome some of the issues with authenticating clients who can't use the more secure Windows login. For one thing, it helps you create an environment in which ASP.NET authenticates the caller, but it doesn't matter quite as much who the caller is, where the caller is located, or what device the caller is using. This form of authentication relies on special server configuration, application configuration, and a few programming tricks. Listing 13.5 shows the first part of this application. (You can find this example in the \Chapter 13\C#\FormAuth or \Chapter 13\VB\FormAuth folder of the source code located on the Sybex Web site.)

Listing 13.5   **Defining the Login Page**

```
private void btnLogin_Click(object sender, System.EventArgs e)
{
   HttpCookie  AuthCookie; // Authorization cookie.

   // Initialize forms authentication.
   FormsAuthentication.Initialize();

   // Verify the user has proper access.
   if (!FormsAuthentication.Authenticate(txtName.Text,
                             txtPassword.Text))
      throw new SecurityException(txtName.Text +
                             " is not authorized!");

   // If the user is authenticated, generate a cookie.
   AuthCookie = FormsAuthentication.GetAuthCookie(txtName.Text, true);

   // Place the cookie in the response.
   Response.Cookies.Add(AuthCookie);

   // Redirect to the default page.
   Response.Redirect("Default.ASPX");
}
```

The code begins by initializing the FormsAuthentication object using the Initialize() method. Always initialize the authentication environment; otherwise, you could get some strange results. The code calls on the FormsAuthentication.Authenticate() method next to authenticate the user against the data stored in the Web.CONFIG file. This method of authentication doesn't rely on the standard Windows names and passwords—a caller must appear in a separate credential database to access the page.

At this point, ASP.NET has authenticated the user or the application has generated a SecurityException and the caller hasn't gained access to anything. The code stores the authentication information in a cookie and redirects the caller to the target page.

You can't ask for forms authentication and not provide any data to support it. The Web.CONFIG file requires additional entries to make this type of authentication work. Listing 13.6 shows the changes you'll need to make.

Listing 13.6   Modifying the *Web.CONFIG* File

```
<!-- Use the Login.ASPX form for authentication. -->
<authentication mode="Forms">
  <forms loginUrl="Login.ASPX" requireSSL="true">

    <!-- Create a list of credentials. -->
    <credentials passwordFormat="SHA1">
      <user name="John"
            password="AAF4C61DDCC5E8A2DABEDE0F3B482CD9AEA9434D" />
    </credentials>

  </forms>
</authentication>

<!-- Deny access to users who aren't authenticated. -->
<authorization>
    <deny users="?" />
</authorization>
```

You need to pay careful attention to several features of this configuration file. First, notice the requireSSL="true" attribute. It's extremely dangerous not to include this entry because the user's name and password appear in plain text otherwise. You should also set the server to use SSL by changing the Secure Communications entry on the Directory Security tab of the application Properties dialog in the Internet Information Services console. (You could also change just the entry for the particular file, but securing the entire application is better.)

Second, notice the passwordFormat="SHA1" attribute. All of the passwords in the credentials list are hashed using the SHA1 encryption standard. Listing 13.7 shows one technique you can use to obtain the required information. Because the cracker could access the configuration file, you want to keep all sensitive data encrypted.

Third, notice the `<authorization>` element now contains a `<deny>` child. This entry specifically denies access to any unauthenticated callers.

Once ASP.NET authenticates the user, the application redirects them to the `Default.ASPX` page. In this case, the page shows several of the other `FormsAuthentication` object features. Listing 13.7 shows the code for this portion of the example.

Listing 13.7   Generating Forms Authentication Statistics

```
private void Page_Load(object sender, System.EventArgs e)
{
    // Get the information for the current user and display it.
    lblOutput.Text = "Forms Cookie Name: " +
        FormsAuthentication.FormsCookieName +
        "<BR/>Forms Cookie Path: " +
        FormsAuthentication.FormsCookiePath +
        "<BR/>Is SSL Required? " +
        FormsAuthentication.RequireSSL;

    // Hash a password for storage in the configuration file.
    lblHashPwd.Text = "Hashed Password for hello:<BR/>" +
        FormsAuthentication.HashPasswordForStoringInConfigFile(
            "hello", "SHA1");

    // Sign out.
    FormsAuthentication.SignOut();
}
```

The code begins by listing a few statistics for the page. Notice that you can determine the SSL status of the page before you do anything. Always check the `FormsAuthentication.RequireSSL` property to ensure that the application uses SSL. The code uses the `FormsAuthentication.HashPasswordForStoringInConfigFile()` method to generate a hash for the password for user John using the SHA1 standard. Finally, the application logs off using the `FormsAuthentication.SignOut()` method.

Summary

This chapter has discussed many of the .NET issues regarding wireless security. It has also taken a quick look at other wireless security issues, but not discussed them in depth. The bottom line for developers is that you need to consider many more security factors when working with wireless. Not only do you have the problems normally associated with desktop, LAN, and Internet communication to consider, but you also have the natural problems of wireless to consider. Any time you transmit data using radio waves, the data is openly available to anyone within listening range.

Part of your testing strategy as a developer has to include wireless security issues. You might want to check how well someone can receive data from your application outside the company walls. Spend time looking for potential holes in your code based on the operating conditions you find. For example, crackers can and will try to find holes in your data encryption. They'll look for places where your application leaves data in the open. Once you begin testing the application thoroughly, you might find it easier to build a case for not allowing the application to run on wireless than to try to secure this communication method.

Chapter 14 begins a discussion of the requirement to use the Win32 API to perform some security tasks. This chapter demonstrates how to access the Win32 API using PInvoke. Many developers are convinced that the code access and role-based security implemented by the .NET Framework will answer every need. While this form of security is far superior to anything Microsoft has produced in the past, the fact remains that you still need to access older code and that means understanding the security that code uses. In addition, as demonstrated by the example in the "Working Directly with the Domain Controller" section of Chapter 12, you must perform some tasks using the Win32 API because the .NET Framework doesn't provide the proper functionality.

CHAPTER 14

Win32 API Overview

- Defining Win32 API Usage Requirements

- Determining How to Use the Windows Security API

- Understanding How Access Problems Affect the Win32 API

- Working with the Access Control Editor

- Working with the Security Configuration Editor

- Creating an Application That Uses SIDs

- Developing Applications That Use the DACL and ACE Directly

Writing a managed application means that you rely on the .NET Framework to provide essential application functionality. The managed environment brings with it features such as memory management that developers have always wanted in the Windows programming environment. However, you can't write every application you want using pure managed code today. The Win32 API is huge. It includes functionality that no one is supposed to use anymore because Microsoft has introduced better features over time. In addition, some Win32 API features are so obscure that Microsoft felt that most developers wouldn't use them. Finally, because the .NET Framework is so young, Microsoft simply hasn't had time to implement every possible feature from the Win32 API. For all these reasons and more, you occasionally need to use the Win32 API directly within your application.

NOTE   This chapter assumes you have some knowledge of how to use the Win32 API. In addition, it only provides information on the security uses of the Win32 API. You can learn more about the Win32 API and its uses in my book .NET Framework Solutions: In Search of the Lost Win32 API (Sybex, 2002).

This book first demonstrated a use for the Win32 API in the "Working Directly with the Domain Controller" section of Chapter 12. However, Chapter 12 doesn't really discuss the situations in which you would use the Win32 API for security because that chapter focuses on working with Active Directory. This chapter discusses situations in which you'll find the Win32 API particularly helpful. In addition, it helps you understand which Win32 API functions you should avoid to maintain application security. The chapter then tells you about specific functions that you'll find helpful and others you must use to accomplish specific tasks.

Many developers don't realize that the Windows interface provides a number of tools that help check the results of security changes. The next two sections of the chapter discuss the most essential of these security tools, the Access Control Editor and the Security Configuration Editor. Using these tools to check security results can ensure that the security measures you think are in place actually work as anticipated. Unlike code access security and role-based security, the results of using a Win32 API call aren't always clear.

The remaining sections of the chapter demonstrate various common security tasks. You'll learn how to work with security identifiers (SIDs), the Security Access Control List (SACL), the Discretionary Access Control List (DACL), and Access Control Entries (ACEs). These four elements form the basis of Win32 API security, so you need to understand all four in order to maintain some level of application security.

Knowing When to Use the Win32 API

There's a good reason why the Win32 API topics appear at the end of this book—you should view them as the option of last resort. It's not that the Win32 API is inherently difficult to use (although that's one reason to avoid it), but the fact that you have considerable resources you can rely on in the .NET Framework. You should exhaust all of the other options before you attempt to use the Win32 API to solve a security problem. However, some situations do call for the Win32 API. Here's a list of the common tasks you'll perform.

- Interoperability with older Win32 applications

- Working with Active Directory

- Managing some types of COM+ applications

- Accessing messages in Microsoft Message Queuing Services (MSMQ)

- Filling a security gap not supported by the .NET Framework

> **TIP** One of the issues you must consider as a developer is when the Win32 API is an appropriate alternative to using .NET Framework security features. However, many developers don't consider the third solution—hardening the server to make it less likely that a cracker will gain entry without significant effort. According to an InfoWorld article (http://www.infoworld.com/article/03/04/29/HNmsguide_1.html), Microsoft is creating guides that demonstrate how to harden a server. You can find the Windows 2003 Server version of the guide at http://www.microsoft.com/technet/security/prodtech/windows/win2003/w2003hg/sgch00.asp. The Windows 2000 Server version of the guide appears at http://www.microsoft.com/technet/security/prodtech/windows/win2khg/default.asp.

Win32 API and .NET Framework Differences

The Win32 API has several advantages in its favor that the .NET Framework simply can't duplicate. For example, the Win32 API has an advantage in speed—security checks are nearly instantaneous. Even on a fast machine, some .NET Framework checks can incur a noticeable delay in seconds. When you ask a technology to do more, it requires more resources to answer the request.

It's also important consider the complexity and the simplicity of the Win32 API. From a coding perspective, the Win32 API requires a lot of code and most of it's hard to understand.

For the most part, the .NET Framework makes programming considerably easier once you know what you want to do and how you want to do it. However, the Win32 API has a simpler security model. All you really need to understand is that every caller has a SID. This SID appears on a resource's access list or it doesn't. When a SID doesn't appear on the access list, the caller doesn't have the right to use the resource. The .NET Framework model means you not only have to track both code access and role-based security requirements, but you also need to decide which method to use for implementing that security, imperative or declarative. The Win32 API is simultaneously easier and harder to use than the .NET Framework.

Avoiding Dangerous APIs

One of the security issues with the Win32 API is that the code is unmanaged. When an application needs memory, it requests the memory from Windows and then returns the memory to the pool when finished—at least if everything works as anticipated. The Win32 API doesn't perform any type checking, so it's possible to make dangerous data coercions and create an environment where buffer overruns are difficult to avoid. Fortunately, Windows does perform some error checking and CLR performs some management checks when working with unmanaged code, so you don't have to worry that every function is a security time bomb ready to explode in your face.

The sections that follow describe features that make an API dangerous from a security perspective. You should treat functions and function classes that fall into these categories with special care. It's still possible to use them safely, but you have to be aware of the limitations these functions have when working with them and include additional security checks to avoid possible problems.

Using Old Functions

Microsoft has expanded the Win32 API over the years to meet specific needs, to adapt to changing conditions, and to fix errors. In most cases, Microsoft gave the updated function a new, but similar, name. In many cases, Microsoft simply added a number or the word *Ex* to the function name. For example, you might see MyFunction(), MyFunctionEx(), and MyFunction3() listed in the Win32 API. Whenever a new function offers significantly different functionality, Microsoft attempts to keep the old function in place and simply gives the new function the expanded name.

Because Microsoft doesn't document why it added the new function, in most cases, you need to consider the old versions as less safe from a security perspective than the newer function. The new function could add functionality that you need to maintain a secure environment—the older version of the function might work fine in the desktop environment, but could cause problems on a LAN. In some cases, developers became so used to the broken operation of a function that Microsoft retained the broken function and added a new one that fixed the problem. Obviously, you don't want to add a broken function to your code.

NOTE Some developers might argue that Microsoft has tested the older function better and therefore the older function contains fewer security holes. This argument doesn't hold up well in light of Microsoft's policy of not changing broken functions for fear of also damaging code that relies on the faulty function.

Using Unsafe Code

Only C# developers need to worry about unsafe code—at least in the way this section uses the term. The best definition for unsafe code is unmanaged code that appears within a managed environment. Any code that relies on the use of manual pointers (* symbol) or addresses (& symbol) is unsafe code. Whenever you write code that uses these symbols, you also need to use the unsafe keyword in the method declaration as shown in Listing 14.1. (You can find this example in the \Chapter 14\C#\Unsafe folder of the source code located on the Sybex Web site.)

Listing 14.1   **Using Unsafe Code in a C# Program**

```
unsafe private void btnTest_Click(object sender, System.EventArgs e)
{
    int   Input = Int32.Parse(txtInput.Text); // Input string.

    // Convert the input value.
    DoTimeIt(&Input);

    // Display the result
    txtOutput.Text = Input.ToString();
}

unsafe private void DoTimeIt(int* Input)
{
    int   Output;  // Output to the caller.

    // Display the current minute.
    txtMinute.Text = System.DateTime.Now.Minute.ToString();

    // Create the output value.
    Output = *Input;
    Output = Output * System.DateTime.Now.Minute;

    // Output the result.
    *Input = Output;
}
```

This is a simple example that you create using other methods, but it demonstrates a principle you'll need to create applications that rely on the Win32 API. The btnTest_Click() accesses the input value, converts it to an int, and supplies the address of the int to the DoTimeIt()

method. Because the code relies on an address rather than the value, any change in the supplied value by DoTimeIt() will remain when the call returns.

The DoTimeIt() method accesses the current time, multiplies it by the value of the input string, and then outputs the value. Notice the use of pointers in this method to access the values contained in the Input and Output variables. The reason this code is unsafe is that the compiler can't check it for errors. For example, you could replace the last line with Input = &Output; and the compiler would never complain, but you also wouldn't see the results of the multiplication.

From a security perspective, the inability to check for errors is a disaster in the making. Whenever you lose the ability to verify the integrity of the data you're working with, you give crackers an opportunity to change that data. Even if you later verify that the data is of the right type and correct length, and contains the proper information, you have no way of knowing whether an external force compromised the data or the surrounding memory when you weren't able to view the pointer.

Generally, you should avoid using unsafe code whenever possible—if for no other reason than to get as much help as possible from the compiler. The "Using Pointer Alternatives" section tells you about managed alternatives that mimic pointers. In short, while unsafe code is a necessity when working with the Win32 API, you should avoid it whenever possible.

Using Pointer Alternatives

One of the first issues that you'll face when working with the Win32 API is the use of pointers—the Win32 API uses them by the gross. The Win32 API uses pointers as function arguments: they appear within data structures, and you even find them nested within each other. The problem with pointers is that they aren't objects—they really aren't anything. A pointer is an abstraction, an address for something real. As a real world example, the pointer to your house is the street address found on letters and packages. The .NET Framework refrains from relying on pointers (from a developer's perspective) and uses the actual object whenever possible. The pointers are still there; CLR simply manages them for you. You can use this fact to your advantage in avoiding pointers by making use of pointer alternatives.

The first pointer alternative to consider is that pointers aren't always necessary. Avoid pointers, whenever possible, by verifying the need to use them. In many situations, you can simply pass a value to the Win32 API when your application doesn't require a return value. CLR still converts the value to a pointer for you—the point is that the conversion occurs in a managed environment and all of the details are taken care of for you. Passing a value is safe from a security standpoint because your code won't receive any contamination on return from the call.

A second pointer alternative to consider is the use of the out or the ref keywords in C#. When you use these keywords, CLR automatically creates a pointer to the object, data structure, or value for you. (When using the out keyword, you let the function you call initialize the memory.) Visual Basic supports the ref keyword using the ByRef keyword. However, it doesn't have a direct substitute for the out keyword, which can make things a little difficult. In many cases, you can substitute the [OutAttribute] attribute as part of the function declaration, but this feature doesn't always work and you might find that you get an error return from the Win32 API function. Of the two options, using the ref keyword is the most secure because your code controls the memory. However, the ref keyword is also the most work because your code is also responsible for allocating and freeing the memory from the global heap.

Using an IntPtr (essentially a managed pointer) is a third option. An IntPtr easily handles a variety of tasks, including a pointer to a pointer (such as void** used in Visual C++). In fact, you can place this use of an IntPtr in your rules of thumb book. Generally, you can replace any pointer to a pointer (such as a handle) with an IntPtr for all Win32 API calls. The IntPtr is problematic from a security perspective because you have less control over it than you do using any other technique discussed in this section.

Sometimes you must use a pointer—there simply isn't any way around the issue. For example, you'll often find that COM calls require pointers to pointers, such as when you want to work with an interface. In this situation, you might find it impossible to develop a substitute for pointers. When this problem occurs, try to localize the pointer code to a special function, even if it might not make sense to create a separate function from a program flow perspective. Placing the pointer in its own function makes it easier to work with the pointer, reduces the probability of missed pointer errors, and makes it easier to debug the application later. Most importantly, by isolating the problem code, you increase the chance that you'll catch security issues before they become a problem.

Understanding the Windows Security API

The Win32 API contains a set of functions that help you perform various security tasks. Each set of functions addresses a specific area, such as a caller access token or an access control list (the SACL or DACL). This section of the chapter provides a quick overview of the most important functions. You can find a complete list of authorization functions at http://msdn .microsoft.com/library/en-us/security/security/authorization_functions.asp.

The user (or caller) access token is a key to a resource. When a user access token appears in the list of access granted tokens for a particular resource, the caller can access that resource. Table 14.1 contains an overview of the most common API functions that you'll normally use to change the user's access token. I used features that you commonly need, but can't access from the

.NET Framework, as a criterion. For example, you can't easily determine whether the system is auditing the actions of a caller without using the GetAuditedPermissionsFromAcl() function.

NOTE   The entries in the Function Name column in Tables 14.1, 14.2, 14.3 and 14.4 are single function names, even though the name may appear on more than one line. The use of multiple lines helps make the function name fit within the confines of the book. See the example source code in Chapters 14 and 15 for examples of the full function names in use.

TABLE 14.1: Common User Access Token Function Overview

Function Name	Description
AdjustTokenGroups	Allows you to adjust one or more group flags that control group usage within the access token. For example, you can use this function to replace the group's owner.
AdjustTokenPrivileges	Allows you to adjust one or more privileges within the access token. This function enables or disables an existing privilege; you can't add or delete privileges from the access token.
BuildExplicitAccessWithName	Creates an EXPLICIT_ACCESS data structure for the named trustee. This data structure defines the trustee's ACL information. Use this data structure with API functions like SetEntriesInAcl to define a trustee's access level to objects. The EXPLICIT_ACCESS data structure can affect either the SACL or DACL depending on the access mode you set for it.
BuildTrusteeWithName	Creates a TRUSTEE data structure used to identify a specific trustee. You supply a trustee name and Windows fills the other data structure elements with default values. You'll need to modify the data structure before using it.
BuildTrusteeWithSid	Creates a TRUSTEE data structure that relies on a SID, rather than a trustee name. Windows modifies the default data structure values appropriately.
CheckTokenMembership	Determines whether a SID appears within an access token. This can help you to determine if a user or process belongs to a particular group.
GetAuditedPermissionsFromAcl	Returns a list of ACL entries that result in an audit log entry for the specified trustee. This includes ACL entries that affect the trustee as well as groups to which the trustee belongs. You get a complete list of all audit-generating access events, not just those associated with the trustee. Windows returns the audited access in an ACCESS_MASK data structure.
GetEffectiveRightsFromAcl	Returns a list of ACL entries that list the effective rights for the specified trustee. Windows returns the effective rights in an ACCESS_MASK data structure.

Continued on next page

TABLE 14.1 CONTINUED: Common User Access Token Function Overview

Function Name	Description
GetExplicitEntriesFromAcl	Returns an array of EXPLICIT_ACCESS data structures that define the level of access each ACE within an ACL grants the trustee. The data structure provides information like the access mode, access rights, and inheritance setting for each ACE.
GetTokenInformation	Returns a data structure containing complete information about the access token. This includes the token's user, groups that appear within the token, the owner of the token, the imperson-ation level, and statistics associated with the token.
GetTrusteeName	Returns the name associated with a name trustee. If the TRUSTEE data structure that you provide is for a SID or object, Windows returns a NULL value.
GetTrusteeType	Returns a constant from one of the TRUSTEE_TYPE enumeration values for a trustee. In most cases, the constants indicate whether the trustee is a user, group, domain, or alias. There are also values to show deleted or invalid trustees.
IsTokenRestricted	Detects whether the access token contains one or more restricting SIDs.
LookupPrivilegeDisplayName	Converts a privilege name listed in WINNT.H to human readable form. For example, SE_REMOTE_SHUTDOWN_NAME might convert to "Force shutdown from a remote system."
LookupPrivilegeName	Allows you to convert a privilege name specified by a LUID to one of the constant forms listed in WINNT.H.
OpenProcessToken	Opens a token associated with a process (application). Like a file, you need to specify level of access to the token. For example, the TOKEN_ALL_ACCESS constant gives you complete access to the token.
OpenThreadToken	Opens a token that's associated with a thread within an application. As with a process token, you need to request a specific level of access when making the request.
SetEntriesInAcl	Creates a new ACL by merging new access control or audit con-trol information into an existing ACL. You can use this function to create an entirely new ACL using the ACL creation function, BuildExplicitAccessWithName.

In general, you can obtain access to user information without using a SID. However, you do need SIDs to perform useful work. For example, certain Windows objects have static SIDs that you can use to access their security settings. (See the list of well-known SIDs at http://msdn .microsoft.com/library/en-us/security/security/well_known_sids.asp.) Active Directory also relies on SIDs for a number of tasks (see the example in the "Working Directly with the Domain Controller" section of Chapter 12 to see how to work with Active Directory using PInvoke). Table 14.2 contains a list of the most common SID-related functions.

TABLE 14.2: Common SID-Related Function Overview

Function Name	Description
AllocateAndInitializeSid	Creates and initializes a SID with up to eight subauthorities.
ConvertSidToStringSid	Converts a SID to a string in human readable format. This format consists of values in the form S-R-I-SA, where S designates the string as a SID, R is the revision level, I is the identifier authority value, and SA is one or more sub-authority values. Note the dashes between SID values are always part of the SID string.
ConvertStringSidToSid	Converts a specially formatted string into a SID.
FreeSid	Deallocates the memory used by a SID previously created using the AllocateAndInitializeSid function.
GetSidIdentifierAuthority	Returns a pointer to a SID_IDENTIFIER_AUTHORITY data structure that contains an array of six bytes that specify the SID's top-level authority. Predefined authorities include NULL (0), local (1), world (2), creator (3), and Windows NT/Windows 2000 (5).
InitializeSid	Sets the identifier authority of a SID structure to a known value using a SID_IDENTIFIER_AUTHORITY data structure. Sub-authority values aren't set using this function. Use the AllocateAndInitializeSid function to initialize a SID completely.
IsValidSid	Determines the validity of a SID structure's contents. This function checks the revision number and ensures that the number of sub-authorities doesn't exceed the maximum value.
LookupAccountName	Retrieves the SID (and accompanying data) for a specific account. You must supply an account and system name.
LookupAccountSid	Retrieves the name and machine associated with a given SID. It also returns the name of the SID's first domain.

Once Windows determines a caller's rights, it must match those rights to the access requirements of the system resource. This means working with security descriptors. A security descriptor is a lock on the object or other system resource. The key (access token) fits the lock or it doesn't. Windows grants or denies access when the key fits the lock. Table 14.3 is an overview of the security descriptor API functions.

NOTE   The entries in the Function Name column are single function names, even though the name may appear on more than one line. The use of multiple lines helps make the function name fit within the confines of the book. See the example source code in Chapters 14 and 15 for examples of the full function names in use.

TABLE 14.3: Security Descriptor Function Overview

Function Name	Description
ConvertSecurityDescriptor-ToStringSecurityDescriptor	Converts a security descriptor to string format. Flags determine the level of information returned in the string. A complete string contains the owner SID, the group SID, a DACL flag list using coded letters, a SACL flag list using coded letters, and a series of ACE entries.
ConvertStringSecurityDescriptor-ToSecurityDescriptor	Converts a specially formatted string into a security descriptor.
GetNamedSecurityInfo	Returns the security descriptor for the named object provided as input. Flags determine what kind of information to retrieve.
GetSecurityDescriptorControl	Returns the security descriptor control information and revision number for the security descriptor structure provided as input.
GetSecurityInfo	Returns the security descriptor for an object that specified using an object handle. Windows 2000 provides flags that determine which security descriptor entries to retrieve.

By now, you should have some idea of how to work within the security portion of the Win32 API. The divisions I set up within the tables are artificial; they're for description purposes to make the functions easier to comprehend and use. In a real world application, you'll combine elements of all three tables to create a complete security picture.

Considering Access Problems with the Win32 API

The structure and setup of the Win32 API make it possible to create security holes without realizing it. In some cases, a perfectly good setup will fail because you didn't test all of the user categories completely. Other situations may cause a failure when you don't understand a nuance of Windows security. Too many people accessing the same security information and making changes independently of each other can cause problems too. The following sections discuss potential access problems for developers working with the Win32 API.

Using the Run As Windows Feature

This section isn't actually about an access problem—it's an access solution. When you want to test the security of an application, you have several choices. The first choice is to log out and back on as the user you want to check. However, this can prove time consuming if you need to test several user types.

The second choice is to send a copy of the beta software to a testing group and let them check it. Unfortunately, this technique isn't very practical if you're an independent developer or if the change you want to test is small enough that you don't want to bother the testing group. Besides, if you perform the test yourself, you can ensure that you test all of the security features.

The third option is actually the most efficient. After you compile the program, right-click the executable and select Run As from the context menu. You'll see a Run As dialog box. Choose The Following User option. Select the user from the drop-down list and type their password. The application starts using that user's credentials. Using this technique can save considerable time because you can start the application with a test user's credentials without logging in or out of the system.

Understanding Resources Both Granted and Denied

Once you know how Windows evaluates the ACEs in the DACL, you'll discover a few problem areas—problems that the Windows utilities address automatically but your code won't. These potential security issues are the reasons you might want to consider just reading the security information using application code and use utilities as needed to modify the security information. Unfortunately, it's not always possible to follow this advice, so this section discusses the access pitfalls.

Order is an important consideration when working with Windows security because Windows uses a very basic method for determining how to evaluate the security elements. You'll need to program around these problems to derive the same result found in the various Windows utilities. The SACL has the same problem, but it only affects auditing, so the effect is less severe from the system security standpoint.

Windows evaluates the ACEs in an ACL in the order in which they appear. At first, this might not seem like a very big deal. However, it could become a problem in some situations. For example, what if you want to revoke all of a user's rights to one resource, but his or her list of ACEs includes membership in a group that allows access to that resource? If you place the access-allowed ACE before the access-denied ACE in the list, the user would get access to the resource. When the access-denied ACE appears first, the user loses access to the resource. The ACEs are the same—only their order is different. The bottom line is that you should place all your access-denied ACEs in the list first, to prevent any potential breach in security.

Also, use care in the ordering of group SIDs. Rights that a user acquires from different groups are cumulative. This means a user who appears in two groups, one that has access to a file and another that doesn't, will have access to the file if the group granting the right appears first on the list. In addition, if one ACE grants read rights and another write rights to a file, and the user is asking for read and write rights, Windows will grant the request.

Obviously, you could spend all your time trying to figure out the best arrangement of groups. As the number of groups and individual rights that a user possesses increases, the potential for an unintended security breach does as well. That's why it's important to create groups carefully and limit a user's individual rights. It's also essential that you actually test various user scenarios using impersonation—see the "Using the Run As Windows Feature" section for details.

Using the Access Control Editor

The Access Control Editor is a COM control that helps you to add a standard interface to your application—allowing administrators to set application security as needed. These are the same property pages that Microsoft uses within Windows 2000 to set security. The Access Control Editor uses two sets of property pages. The user will normally see a simple property page dialog. However, the Administrator will normally use the advanced property page shown in Figure 14.1. You can access this page by right-clicking any object (a drive works best) in Windows Explorer and choosing Properties from the context menu. Select the Security tab. Click Advanced.

FIGURE 14.1:

The Advanced features of the Access Control Editor provide the administrator with full access control.

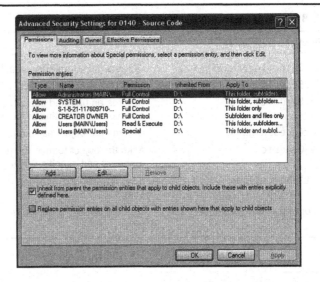

Both property pages allow the administrator to work with the security settings for an application with relative ease. However, the advanced dialog provides complete controls for setting every security aspect for this particular object. The Permissions tab sets the DACL, the Auditing tab the SACL, and the Owner tab the owner information. The only missing element is the group information, which isn't important at the user level in many cases. Notice that most of the entries in the Permission Entries List in Figure 14.1 have human-readable names. However, the third entry uses a SID, rather than a name. Sometimes the Access Control Editor displays a SID rather than a name.

Now that we've seen the Access Control Editor user interface, let's consider development issues. You create Access Control Editor property sheets using the ISecurityInformation interface. There are two main methods used to call on this interface: CreateSecurityPage() and EditSecurity(). The CreateSecurityPage() method adds a Security tab to an existing property sheet. You can use the PropertySheet() function or the PSM_ADDPAGE message to add the resulting property page to the existing property sheet. The EditSecurity() method displays the Security property page on a property sheet that's created specifically to display the Access Control Editor.

Some two-way communication takes place between your application and the Access Control Editor. The Access Control Editor doesn't know anything about your application when you first start it, so you have to supply this information. This means implementing several methods of the ISecurityInformation interface within your application. Table 14.4 provides a very brief description of these functions.

TABLE 14.4: *ISecurityInformation* Interface Member List

Function	Description
GetObjectInformation	Obtains the information to initialize the Access Control Editor.
GetSecurity	Obtains the object security descriptor.
SetSecurity	Returns an updated security descriptor to the object after the user completes the editing process in the Access Control Editor dialog.
GetAccessRights	Obtains the object access rights.
MapGeneric	Asks the object to map the generic rights in an access mask to the standard and specific rights equivalents.
GetInheritTypes	Asks how child objects can inherit the ACEs owned by the requesting object.
PropertySheetPageCallback	Tells the object that Windows is about to create or destroy the property page.

TIP   The Access Control Editor provides you with control over the security environment it creates. In fact, you can set one of the flags to allow the user to view only the object security information. This means a user could look at what rights they had to an object in your application, then request help from an administrator if needed.

The `GetObjectInformation()` method implementation is important. You create an `SI_OBJECT_INFO` data structure and pass it to Access Control Editor. The data structure includes security dialog configuration information. For example, you can choose which features the user will see. You can also disable the Advanced button, making it impossible to change auditing options or the object owner. In addition, this data structure defines property page elements like the title bar contents, the name of the object, and the name of a server that Access Control Editor uses to look up object security information.

Using the Security Configuration Editor

The Microsoft Security Configuration Editor is an administration tool that reduces both security management and analysis time. Initially you'll use this tool to configure the operating system security parameters. Once these parameters are in place, you can use the Security Configuration Editor to schedule periodic tests.

NOTE   Windows 2000 and Windows XP divide the Security Configuration Editor into two parts. The Security Configuration and Analysis MMC snap-in helps you configure the security database, while the Security Templates MMC snap-in helps you work with the security configuration files. All of these operating systems provide similar functionality. Windows 2000 and Windows XP do provide some advanced features. The screenshot in this section of the chapter depicts the Windows XP setup.

The overall goal of the Security Configuration Editor is to provide a single place to manage all of the security concerns for a network. However, it doesn't actually replace the tools you used in the past—the Security Configuration Editor augments other security tools. The Security Configuration Editor also provides auditing tools that Windows has lacked in the past.

One of the unique ideas behind the Security Configuration Editor is that it's a macro-based tool. You'll create a set of instructions for the Security Configuration Editor to perform and then allow it to perform those instructions in the background. Obviously, this saves a lot of developer time since the developer doesn't have to wait for one set of instructions to complete before going to the next set. You can also group tasks, which saves input time.

Creating a security setup begins when you choose an existing template or when you create a new one using the Security Templates MMC snap-in. If you want to use an existing template as a basis for creating a new one, you can right-click on the desired template and use the Save As command found on the context menu. Microsoft supplies a variety of templates designed to get you started in creating this security database.

Microsoft designed each of the security templates for a different purpose (which is indicated by the name). The one I'll use in this section is the compatibility workstation template (compatws), but all of the other templates work about the same as this one. All of the templates contain the same basic elements shown in Figure 14.2.

FIGURE 14.2:

Each of the security templates contains the same security elements.

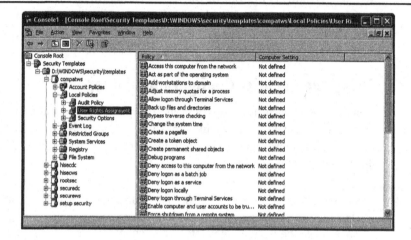

Each of these elements plays an important part in the overall security configuration for a system. Table 14.5 describes each of these elements.

TABLE 14.5: Security Template Elements

Element Name	Description
Account Policies	Defines the password, account lockout, and Kerberos policies for the machine. Password policies include items like the minimum password length and the maximum time the user can use a single password. The account lockout policy includes the number of times a user can enter the wrong password without initiating a system lockout. Kerberos policies feature elements like the maximum user ticket lifetime.
Local Policies	Defines the audit policy, user rights assignment, and security options. Audit policies determine the types of data you collect. For example, you could audit each failed user logon attempt. User rights assignments are of special interest since this policy affects the rights you can assign to a user (the access token). The security options policy contains the elements that determine how the security system will react given a set of circumstances. For example, one policy will log a user off when their usage hours expire.
Event Log	Defines how the event log stores data and for how long. These policies also determine maximum event log size and event log viewing rights.

Continued on next page

TABLE 14.5 CONTINUED: Security Template Elements

Element Name	Description
Restricted Groups	Defines groups that can't access the workstation or server at all, or restricts the amount of access they can obtain.
System Services	Displays a list of the system services on the target machine. Double-clicking a service displays a dialog that allows you to set the policy for that service and allows you to adjust the startup mode for the service. Normally, you'll leave the icons in this policy alone. However, you can safely change any system service DLLs you create.
Registry	Contains all of the major registry hives. Double-clicking a branch displays a dialog you use to set the security for that branch. In addition, you can choose the method of security inheritance by children of this branch.
File System	Contains protected file system entries. You can add new files to the list or modify exiting entries. Double-clicking a file system entry displays a dialog you use to set the security level for that file system member. In addition, you can choose the method of security inheritance by children of this file system entity (applies only to folders).
Active Directory Objects	This entry is only available if you have Active Directory enabled (which means you must have a domain controller set up). It allows you to edit the security settings for any Active Directory objects, including users and groups.

Working with SIDs

Sometimes you know the name of a well-known account, such as Administrators, but you don't know anything else about it. The Win32 API provides an answer to this dilemma. You can create a SID for the account without knowing anything about it, and then look up the information for that account. This technique proves handy for a number of uses. For example, if you know that you want to create a new user that has starting rights that are the same as a well-known account, you can begin by obtaining information about the well-known account SID. Listing 14.2 shows the essential code you'll need for this example—the listing doesn't include items like the function declarations. (You can find the complete source code for this example in the \Chapter 14\C#\LookUpSID or \Chapter 14\VB\LookUpSID folders of the source code located on the Sybex Web site.)

Listing 14.2   Converting a SID to Human Readable Form

```
private void btnTest_Click(object sender, System.EventArgs e)
{
    Int32       SIDSize;    // Size of the returned SID.
    IntPtr      GuestSID;   // SID of the Guest account.
    int         LastError;  // Last error produced by an API call.
```

```
Int32           NameSize;   // Size of the account name.
Int32           DomainSize; // Size of the domain name.
StringBuilder   Name;       // Account name.
StringBuilder   Domain;     // Domain name.
SID_NAME_USE    Use;        // Account use.

// Allocate memory for the SID.
GuestSID = Marshal.AllocHGlobal(SECURITY_MAX_SID_SIZE);

// Create the SID.
SIDSize = SECURITY_MAX_SID_SIZE;
if (!CreateWellKnownSid((WELL_KNOWN_SID_TYPE)cbSelect.SelectedIndex,
                        IntPtr.Zero,
                        GuestSID,
                        ref SIDSize))
{
    // Get the last error.
    LastError = Marshal.GetLastWin32Error();

    // Display an error message and exit if not successful.
    MessageBox.Show("Error creating the account SID." +
                    "\r\nLast Error: " + LastError.ToString(),
                    "Application Error",
                    MessageBoxButtons.OK,
                    MessageBoxIcon.Error);

    // Free the memory we allocated.
    Marshal.FreeHGlobal(GuestSID);

    // Exit the routine.
    return;
}

// Obtain the size of the Name and Domain strings.
NameSize = 0;
DomainSize = 0;
Use = SID_NAME_USE.SidTypeAlias;
LookupAccountSid(null,
                GuestSID,
                null,
                ref NameSize,
                null,
                ref DomainSize,
                ref Use);

// Allocate memory for the strings.
Name = new StringBuilder(NameSize);
Domain = new StringBuilder(DomainSize);

// Obtain the SID information.
if (!LookupAccountSid(null,
                    GuestSID,
```

```
                        Name,
                        ref NameSize,
                        Domain,
                        ref DomainSize,
                        ref Use))
    {
        // Get the last error.
        LastError = Marshal.GetLastWin32Error();

        // Display an error message and exit if not successful.
        MessageBox.Show("Error obtaining the account SID data." +
                        "\r\nLast Error: " + LastError.ToString(),
                        "Application Error",
                        MessageBoxButtons.OK,
                        MessageBoxIcon.Error);
    }
    else
    {
        // Display the account information.
        MessageBox.Show("Obtained the SID Account Information" +
                        "\r\nName: " + Name.ToString() +
                        "\r\nDomain: " + Domain.ToString() +
                        "\r\nUse: " + Use.ToString(),
                        "Application Output",
                        MessageBoxButtons.OK,
                        MessageBoxIcon.Information);
    }

    // Free the memory we allocated.
    Marshal.FreeHGlobal(GuestSID);
}
```

Windows provides a wealth of well-known SIDs—predefined SIDs that every machine can use. The CreateWellKnownSid() function will create a SID for a well-known value such as the World. All you need to supply is an enumerated SID type, a pointer to a buffer to hold the SID, and the size of the SID buffer. The domain SID is optional. However, supplying this value will enable you to look up SIDs on other machines. There are 51 enumerated SID types to choose from and the example application lets you test them all. (Some of the well-known SIDs might not work on your machine if you don't have the required support installed.)

The LookupAccountSid() function accepts a SID as input. It doesn't matter where you get the SID, as long as the SID is valid. If the call to this function fails, you can assume the SID was invalid—even if it's a well-known SID. The LookupAccountSid() function returns the name and domain information for the SID, along with the SID usage as indicated by the SID_NAME_USE enumeration.

One of the first tasks the code has to perform is allocating memory for the SID. When working with a .NET application, it's best to use the Marshal.AllocHGlobal() function.

This function returns an `IntPtr` to the allocated memory, which you must deallocate later using the `Marshal.FreeHGlobal()` function. The `SECURITY_MAX_SID_SIZE` constant defines the maximum size of the SID.

We've used a number of techniques for gaining access to error information. This example uses the Microsoft recommended technique of setting the `SetLastError` argument of the `[DllImport]` attribute to `true`, and then using the `Marshal.GetLastWin32Error()` function to return the error number. Note that the .NET Framework doesn't provide any means for converting this number into a human-readable form. You still need to use the Win32 API `FormatMessage()` function to perform the conversion.

Once the code obtains the desired SID, it uses the `LookupAccountSid()` function to determine the SID information. However, the code requires two calls to the `LookupAccountSid()` function to perform this task. The first call returns the size of the strings used to contain the account name and domain information. The code uses this information to allocate two `StringBuilder` variables. The second call returns the actual information.

Accessing an ACE Directly

This example describes how to work with the ACEs that make up the SACL and the DACL. By working with an ACE, you also learn how to use the SACL and DACL. Because you're most likely to work with the DACL, this example emphasizes access over auditing. However, working with the ACEs in either structure is about the same. Listing 14.3 contains the essential elements that show how you'd access the ACEs for a file—the listing doesn't include items like the function declarations. (You can find the complete source code for this example in the `\Chapter 14\C#\GetGroupAccess` or `\Chapter 14\VB\GetGroupAccess` folders of the source code located on the Sybex Web site.)

Listing 14.3   **Gaining Access to the ACEs Means Reading the ACL**

```
private void btnTest_Click(object sender, System.EventArgs e)
{
    Boolean         DACLPresent;   // Is the DACL present?
    Boolean         Defaulted;     // Is the DACL defaulted?
    IntPtr          DACL;          // Pointer to the DACL.
    Int32           Result;        // Result of a call.
    UInt32          ACECount;      // Number of ACEs in DACL.
    EXPLICIT_ACCESS []ACEList;      // An array of ACE entries.

    // Obtain a security descriptor containing the DACL.
    if (!GetFileSD(txtFile.Text,
        SECURITY_INFORMATION.DACL_SECURITY_INFORMATION))
        return;

    // Obtain the DACL.
```

```
DACLPresent = false;
Defaulted = false;
if (!GetSecurityDescriptorDacl(SecurityDescriptor,
                               ref DACLPresent,
                               out DACL,
                               ref Defaulted))
{
   // Display an error message.
   MessageBox.Show("Unable to retrieve the DACL.",
                   "Application Error",
                   MessageBoxButtons.OK,
                   MessageBoxIcon.Error);

   // Free the memory we allocated.
   Marshal.FreeHGlobal(SecurityDescriptor);

   return;
}

// Make sure there is a DACL to display.
if (!DACLPresent)
{
   // If not, tell the user there is no DACL.
   MessageBox.Show("There is no DACL.",
                   "Processing Report",
                   MessageBoxButtons.OK,
                   MessageBoxIcon.Information);

   // Free the memory we allocated.
   Marshal.FreeHGlobal(SecurityDescriptor);

   return;
}

// Obtain the array of ACEs from the DACL.
ACECount = 0;
Result = GetExplicitEntriesFromAcl(DACL,
                                   ref ACECount,
                                   out ACEList);

// Check the results.
if (Result != ERROR_SUCCESS)
{
   // Display an error message.
   MessageBox.Show("Unable to retrieve the ACEs.",
                   "Application Error",
                   MessageBoxButtons.OK,
                   MessageBoxIcon.Error);

   // Free the memory we allocated.
   Marshal.FreeHGlobal(SecurityDescriptor);

   return;
```

```
  }

  // Display the number of ACEs.
  MessageBox.Show("The file has " + ACECount.ToString() +
                  " ACEs attached to it.",
                  "Number of ACEs",
                  MessageBoxButtons.OK,
                  MessageBoxIcon.Information);

  // Free the memory we allocated.
  Marshal.FreeHGlobal(SecurityDescriptor);
}
```

The code begins with a simple define—a reminder that the various Win32 API functions return different values. In this case, the GetExplicitEntriesFromAcl() function returns a value of ERROR_SUCCESS if successful or an error value if unsuccessful. You compare the return value with constants to determine the cause of the error.

Notice that the GetExplicitEntriesFromAcl() function is also unique in that it requires an array as input. You don't define a specific number of array elements—just the fact that the return value is an array. The call will still work, in this case, whether you provide an IntPtr or a single EXPLICIT_ACCESS structure value. The difference is that you won't actually be able to use the return value if you don't use an array.

The EXPLICIT_ACCESS structure is relatively complex. It includes both an enumerated value and another structure, TRUSTEE. The other two values are flags—you have to go through a complicated comparison routine to determine what the flag values mean.

While the TRUSTEE structure looks relatively simple, it can become complex because it also includes enumerated values that determine what each of the fields in the structure mean. For example, the ptstrName variable only has meaning if the TRUSTEE_FORM enumeration value is TRUSTEE_IS_NAME. Matters are further complicated by hidden rules. The MULTIPLE_TRUSTEE_OPERATION should always equal NO_MULTIPLE_TRUSTEE because Microsoft hasn't implemented this feature yet, or at least they haven't documented it.

The GetSecurityDescriptorDacl() obtains the DACL. You should never change the security descriptor directly because other applications might try to access it at the same time. This function has an odd return value until you consider that most parts of the security descriptor are optional. The lpbDaclPresent tells you if the DACL is present in the security descriptor. The call can succeed even if the security descriptor doesn't contain a DACL, so you need to know this additional information.

In general, the `btnTest_Click()` method doesn't contain too many surprises. Of course, the first major call is to `GetSecurityDescriptorDacl()` because we have to check the security descriptor created with the `GetFileSD()` function for a DACL. If there's no DACL, the application hasn't actually experienced an error—it's simply found an unprotected file. Consequently, you need to handle the return as a type of legitimate return value. It simply might not be the return value you were expecting.

The next call is to `GetExplicitEntriesFromAcl()`. Theoretically, the `ACECount` variable could contain a 0 on return, so you should check it. Again, it's not an actual application error—the DACL could simply be empty. It's unlikely that you'll ever see this happen unless the `GetExplicitEntriesFromAcl()` function experiences some type of error.

Summary

This chapter has provided an overview of Win32 API security features. It's important to understand that these features represent basic security and that Win32 API security can become more complex. You should take knowledge of the two basic security tools (Access Control Editor and Security Configuration Editor) and the four basic security elements (SID, SACL, DACL, and ACE) from this chapter. In addition, you should have a better idea of when to use Win32 API security and when to avoid it.

What you need to consider now is whether you require Win32 API security for a current project. In most cases, the answer is going to be no, you can use the security features that the .NET Framework provides. However, as you begin interacting with unmanaged code, require special features, need access to Active Directory, or perform other complex tasks, the need to use Win32 API security increases. Planning for this security need is the best way to ensure that everything works as intended and the security features interact as you expect.

Chapter 15 is actually the second part of this chapter. The reason I divided the two parts is that many people only need the Win32 API features presented in this chapter. When you begin working in Chapter 15, you'll notice that many of the features work directly with a network or perform low-level tasks that you won't commonly perform. For example, Chapter 15 demonstrates a method for locking registry keys so that users can't access them easily and your application settings remain safe.

Win32 API Advanced Techniques

- Developing Applications with the SACL

- Developing Applications with the DACL

- Making Controls and Components More Secure

- Making Files More Secure

- Developing Applications that Rely on Registry Functions

- Using Remote Unmanaged Components

This is the second half of the Win32 API coverage for the book. Chapter 14 discusses some of the basics you need to make Win32 API applications work and demonstrates the most common security procedures. This chapter covers a few of the less used security procedures from a .NET Framework perspective. All of the examples perform tasks that you can't easily perform using the .NET Framework, and you won't use these features as often because you can use other techniques in a .NET application. For example, you can use Discretionary Access Control List (DACL) entries to secure a file on your hard drive, but you can just as easily rely on the FileIOPermission class to perform the same task (see Listing 1.2 for details). However, you might need to use the DACL to ensure compatibility with an existing Win32 API application. It's important to use the security model that best fits with your existing infrastructure to ensure you don't accidentally create security holes.

Once the chapter shows you how to work with the Security Access Control List (SACL) and DACL, it moves on to common tasks you can perform. One of the more important tasks is learning to secure the registry. You can't perform this task using the .NET Framework. Securing the registry is important if you want to use techniques to secure your applications, such as the one shown in Listing 6.1. The chapter also discusses such important issues as securing unmanaged components and controls you access from your managed code.

Working with the DACL

Most developers are familiar with using security to grant or deny permission to perform a task or use a resource. However, you can use the DACL to perform other tasks as well. The example in this section discusses one of the more important tasks you can perform—verifying a permission's state. Many Win32 API functions won't work if the application doesn't have the correct permission. For example, you can't easily set data in the SACL without the SeSecurityPrivilege in all cases and the SeAuditPrivilege in some cases. You can find a list of these privileges (28 in all) in the WinNT.H file (located in the \Program Files\Microsoft Visual Studio .NET 2003\Vc7\PlatformSDK\Include folder of your hard drive). Listing 15.1 shows how to work with the DACL directly to obtain privilege information for the current process. This listing is incomplete—it doesn't include the Win32 API function declarations and some of the error handling found in the complete program. (You can find the complete source code for this example in the \Chapter 15\C#\GetTokenData and \Chapter 15\VB\GetTokenData folders of the source code located on the Sybex Web site.)

Listing 15.1   **Obtaining Permission Information**

```
private void btnTest_Click(object sender, System.EventArgs e)
{
   Int32          LastError;        // Last Win32 API error.
   IntPtr         ProcessHandle;    // Current process.
```

```
IntPtr           ProcessTokenHandle; // Process access token.
IntPtr           TokenPriv;          // Token privileges pointer.
Int32            TokenPrivLen;       // Length of the token data.
Int32            RequiredLen;        // Required structure length.
TOKEN_PRIVILEGES TokenStruct;        // Access token data.
StringBuilder    Output;             // Output information.

// Open the process token.
ProcessHandle = GetCurrentProcess();
if (!OpenProcessToken(ProcessHandle,
   TokenAccessFlags.TOKEN_ADJUST_PRIVILEGES |
   TokenAccessFlags.TOKEN_QUERY,
   out ProcessTokenHandle))
{
    // Get the last error.
    LastError = Marshal.GetLastWin32Error();

    // Display an error message and exit if not successful.
    MessageBox.Show("Couldn't obtain process token handle." +
                "\r\nLast Error: " + LastError.ToString(),
                "Application Error",
                MessageBoxButtons.OK,
                MessageBoxIcon.Error);

    // Close the process handle and return.
    CloseHandle(ProcessHandle);
    return;
}

// Determine the length of the data field.
TokenPriv = new IntPtr(0);
GetTokenInformation(ProcessTokenHandle,
                TOKEN_INFORMATION_CLASS.TokenPrivileges,
                TokenPriv,
                0,
                out RequiredLen);

// Get the access token information.
TokenPriv = Marshal.AllocHGlobal(RequiredLen);
TokenPrivLen = RequiredLen;
GetTokenInformation(ProcessTokenHandle,
                TOKEN_INFORMATION_CLASS.TokenPrivileges,
                TokenPriv,
                TokenPrivLen,
                out RequiredLen);

// Convert the data to a usable form.
TokenStruct = new TOKEN_PRIVILEGES();
TokenStruct = (TOKEN_PRIVILEGES)Marshal.PtrToStructure(
   TokenPriv, typeof(TOKEN_PRIVILEGES));

// Free the memory.
```

```
Marshal.FreeHGlobal(TokenPriv);

// Close the handles.
CloseHandle(ProcessTokenHandle);
CloseHandle(ProcessHandle);

// Process the information...

// Display the information on screen...

}
```

It doesn't take long to figure out that the Win32 API uses handles for everything. A handle allows you to access the object in question. Consequently, the first task the code performs for this program is to locate the handle for the current process using the GetCurrentProcess() function. Once the code has a handle to the current process, it uses the handle to get a process token handle using the OpenProcessToken() function. Notice that you must tell Windows how you intend to use the process token handle—the application asks permission to adjust the privileges and query the token for information. You must prepare for failure when you work with these functions because neither the Win32 API nor CLR will handle the errors for you. A function could fail and you wouldn't know about it until you tried to use the result as input to another function. The example shows one of the many forms of error handling used by the Win32 API.

Many of the Win32 API functions use variable length data. When working with variable length data, you normally need to make two calls. The first call tells you how much memory to allocate to retrieve the data, while the second call obtains the data. The example uses this two call procedure with the GetTokenInformation() function. Notice that in the first call, the fourth argument is 0—this number indicates that the code doesn't know how much memory to allocate. The RequiredLen argument contains the length of the required buffer on return from the call. In this case, the code asks for the token privileges for the current process by using the ProcessTokenHandle value and the TOKEN_INFORMATION_CLASS.TokenPrivileges enumeration member. Also notice that the code allocates memory from the global heap using the Marshal.AllocHGlobal() method. This method allocates unmanaged memory for use with Win32 API calls. Because CLR doesn't know anything about unmanaged memory, you must make all the calls.

The pointer you receive from the GetTokenInformation() function isn't very useful because you can't access the data it points at. The next step is to create a managed structure in which to place the data. You use the Marshal.PtrToStructure() method to move the data pointed to in unmanaged memory by TokenPriv to the managed TokenStruct data structure. This process can fail in a number of ways, none of which appears in the documentation. The most common problem is making the data structure too complex by including arrays or other indeterminate features. The code will compile, but you'll see any number of odd runtime errors that seem to have nothing to do with the actual problem. The best practice is to make the data structure as simple as possible—a difficult task given the complexities of Win32 API data structures.

At this point, you have the data you need, so there's no point in keeping all that unmanaged memory in use. The code uses the `Marshal.FreeHGlobal()` method to free the unmanaged memory allocated from the heap. Likewise, the code uses the `CloseHandle()` function to free both the handles it used to obtain access to the process access token. The code goes on to create an output string and display it on screen. See the source code for the details of this process. Figure 15.1 displays the results of this example on my machine—your machine will likely differ.

FIGURE 15.1:

Windows NT–based systems can support up to 28 privileges.

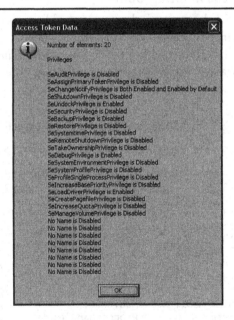

Although the `WinNT.H` file lists 28 possible privileges, you'll seldom find that a machine has them all turned on. When you run into a problem getting an application to work, make sure you have all the proper permissions turned on and enabled. The code presented in this example could reside in a debug library file that you automatically add to all of your programs to make this check. Notice that although my machine has the `SeAuditPrivilege` turned on, it doesn't have the privilege enabled. The "Working with the SACL" section discusses why this fact is important.

Working with the SACL

The SACL helps you perform application auditing. You can tell Windows to monitor an application or a file and make Event Log entries each time a caller does something with it. Auditing is a feature that the .NET Framework doesn't provide—you need to use the Win32 API when you want to perform auditing. Using auditing can help you track the activities of crackers and make it less likely that someone can do anything on your system without notice.

Unfortunately, auditing is one of the least used Windows security features because most network administrators don't want to wade through the security entries that auditing creates. However, it's an important tool for your security arsenal and you need to know how to use it.

Writing the Auditing Code

Listing 15.2 shows a typical example of adding a SACL entry to a managed application. This listing is incomplete—it doesn't include the Win32 API function declarations and some of the error handling found in the complete program. (You can find the complete source code for this example in the \Chapter 15\C#\AuditFile and \Chapter 15\VB\AuditFile folders of the source code located on the Sybex Web site.)

Listing 15.2	Adding a SACL Entry to an Application

```
private void btnTest_Click(object sender, System.EventArgs e)
{
    IntPtr              SecurityDescriptor;   // File security information.
    Int32               LastError;            // Last Win32 API error.
    IntPtr              UserSID;              // User security identifier.
    Int32               UserSIDSize;          // Size of the user SID.
    StringBuilder       DomainName;           // User's domain.
    Int32               DomainNameSize;       // User's domain name length.
    SID_NAME_USE        AccountUse;           // The type of account.
    IntPtr              SACL;                 // Audit information.
    Int32               SACLSize;             // Size of the SACL needed.
    ACL                 SACLStruct;           // Used for size calculation.
    SYSTEM_AUDIT_ACE    AuditACE;             // Holds the audit ACE.
    IntPtr              ProcessHandle;        // The current process.
    IntPtr              ProcessTokenHandle;   // Process access token.
    LUID                SecurePriv;           // Security privilege LUID.
    LUID                AuditPriv;            // Audit privilege LUID.
    TOKEN_PRIVILEGES    NewPriv;              // New process privileges.
    Int32               NewPrivLen;           // Size of NewPriv buffer.

    // Determine the variable sizes for the audited user.
    UserSID = new IntPtr(0);
    UserSIDSize = 0;
    DomainName = new StringBuilder();
    DomainNameSize = 0;
```

```
LookupAccountName(null,
                  @txtUserName.Text,
                  UserSID,
                  ref UserSIDSize,
                  DomainName,
                  ref DomainNameSize,
                  out AccountUse);

// Get the audited user SID.
UserSID = Marshal.AllocHGlobal(UserSIDSize);
if (!LookupAccountName(null,
                       @txtUserName.Text,
                       UserSID,
                       ref UserSIDSize,
                       DomainName,
                       ref DomainNameSize,
                       out AccountUse))
{
   // Get the last error.
   LastError = Marshal.GetLastWin32Error();

   // Display an error message and exit if not successful.
   MessageBox.Show("Error getting User SID." +
      "\r\nLast Error: " + LastError.ToString(),
      "Application Error",
      MessageBoxButtons.OK,
      MessageBoxIcon.Error);

   // Release the memory and exit.
   Marshal.FreeHGlobal(UserSID);
   return;
}

// Calculate the size of the SACL.
SACLStruct = new ACL();
AuditACE = new SYSTEM_AUDIT_ACE();
SACLSize = Marshal.SizeOf(SACLStruct) + Marshal.SizeOf(AuditACE) -
   Marshal.SizeOf(UserSIDSize) + UserSIDSize;

// Initialize the SACL.
SACL = Marshal.AllocHGlobal(SACLSize);
if (!InitializeAcl(SACL, SACLSize, ACL_REVISION_DS))
{
   Handle error...
}

// Add the ACE to the SACL
if (!AddAuditAccessAceEx(
   SACL,
   ACL_REVISION_DS,
   AceFlags.SUCCESSFUL_ACCESS_ACE_FLAG |
   AceFlags.FAILED_ACCESS_ACE_FLAG,
```

```
        AccessMaskFlags.GENERIC_ALL |
        AccessMaskFlags.SPECIFIC_RIGHTS_ALL |
        AccessMaskFlags.STANDARD_RIGHTS_ALL,
        UserSID,
        true,
        true))
{
    Handle error...
}

// Initialize the security descriptor.
SecurityDescriptor =
    Marshal.AllocHGlobal(SECURITY_DESCRIPTOR_MIN_LENGTH);
if (!InitializeSecurityDescriptor(SecurityDescriptor,
                                  SECURITY_DESCRIPTOR_REVISION))
{
    Handle error...
}

// Set the SACL into the security descriptor.
if (!SetSecurityDescriptorSacl(SecurityDescriptor,
                               true,
                               SACL,
                               false))
{
    Handle error...
}

// Get the LUID for the security privilege.
if (!LookupPrivilegeValue(null,
                          "SeSecurityPrivilege",
                          out SecurePriv))
{
    Handle error...
}

// Get the LUID for the audit privilege.
if (!LookupPrivilegeValue(null, "SeAuditPrivilege", out AuditPriv))
{
    Handle error...
}

// Open the process token.
ProcessHandle = GetCurrentProcess();
if (!OpenProcessToken(ProcessHandle,
    TokenAccessFlags.TOKEN_ADJUST_PRIVILEGES |
    TokenAccessFlags.TOKEN_QUERY,
    out ProcessTokenHandle))
{
    Handle error...
```

```
        }

        // Create the token privileges data structure.
        NewPriv = new TOKEN_PRIVILEGES();
        NewPriv.PrivilegeCount = 2;
        NewPriv.Privileges = new LUID_AND_ATTRIBUTES[2];
        NewPriv.Privileges[0].Luid = AuditPriv;
        NewPriv.Privileges[0].Attributes =
            PrivilegeFlags.SE_PRIVILEGE_ENABLED;
        NewPriv.Privileges[1].Luid = SecurePriv;
        NewPriv.Privileges[1].Attributes =
            PrivilegeFlags.SE_PRIVILEGE_ENABLED;
        NewPrivLen = Marshal.SizeOf(NewPriv);

        // Assign the new privilege to the process.
        if (!AdjustTokenPrivileges(ProcessTokenHandle,
                                   false,
                                   ref NewPriv,
                                   NewPrivLen,
                                   IntPtr.Zero,
                                   IntPtr.Zero))
        {
            Handle error...
        }

        // Verify that the AdjustTokenPrivileges() call actually adjusted
        // the privileges.
        LastError = Marshal.GetLastWin32Error();
        if (LastError != ERROR_SUCCESS)
            MessageBox.Show("Error in setting privileges, the application " +
                            "may fail.\r\nError is: " + LastError.ToString(),
                            "Error Setting Privilege",
                            MessageBoxButtons.OK,
                            MessageBoxIcon.Warning);

        // Close the handles.
        CloseHandle(ProcessHandle);
        CloseHandle(ProcessTokenHandle);

        // Save the resulting security information.
        if (!SetFileSecurity(txtFile.Text,
                             SECURITY_INFORMATION.SACL_SECURITY_INFORMATION,
                             SecurityDescriptor))
        {
            Handle error...
        }

        // Free the memory we allocated.
        Marshal.FreeHGlobal(UserSID);
        Marshal.FreeHGlobal(SACL);
        Marshal.FreeHGlobal(SecurityDescriptor);
}
```

This application demonstrates one of the reasons that many developers appreciate the .NET form of security management. Even cutting out the error handling and function declarations, this program runs several pages. Some security exercises for the Win32 API are lengthy and there aren't any good methods for getting around the problem.

When you assign auditing to a particular object, you have to associate the audit entry with an object and a caller. The caller can be a group, a person, another server—any entity that could request access to the object, resource, or service. Consequently, the code begins by using the `LookupAccountName()` function to obtain a SID for the account that you provide. This function also returns the domain name for the caller. It's a handy feature for validation purposes in your code to ensure the caller doesn't belong to another domain. This code also shows a simple form of the error handling the example uses. Notice that you must free memory before the application exits or the application will develop a memory leak.

At this point, the code knows which caller to associate with an auditing entry, so it begins to build the SACL. This SACL only exists in memory for the moment, so the code needs to know how much memory to allocate for it. Unfortunately, Windows can't tell the code how much memory to provide, so the code has to calculate the value. The example shows a typical calculation. The SACL must include space for the SACL structure, the audit ACE, and the caller's SID. However, due to an oddity in the way Windows stores the data, you must subtract the size of a DWORD (Int32) from the calculation. Once the code knows how much memory to allocate, it uses the `Marshal.AllocHGlobal()` method to perform the task and initializes the SACL using the `InitializeAcl()` function. You must perform the initialization or the code will report odd errors when you attempt to use the SACL. The most common error is that the SACL version number is wrong. Never attempt to modify the SACL directly.

An empty SACL isn't very useful, so the code adds an ACE to it next using the `AddAuditAccessAceEx()` function. The flags for this function are exceptionally important because they determine how the ACE affects the SACL and consequently, the security settings. The example provides the empty SACL as the first entry, the ACE revision number as the second entry, the kind of ACE entries to create as the third entry, the rights that these ACE entries will affect as the fourth entry, and the caller's SID as the fifth entry. These five entries define how auditing occurs on the system. The example will monitor all access to the target file for the selected user. See the source code and the `AddAuditAccessAceEx` help topic for a complete listing of flag values.

A SACL appears as part of a security descriptor that also includes owner, group, and DACL information. As with the SACL, never modify the security descriptor directly. The code creates a minimum length security descriptor and then initializes it using the `InitializeSecurityDescriptor()` function. Notice that this action adds a security descriptor revision number to the structure. The next step is to add the SACL to the security descriptor using the `SetSecurityDescriptorSacl()` function. At this point, the security descriptor is ready to add to the target file.

There's only one problem. The application doesn't have permission to add an auditing entry to anything. Unlike security settings, Windows doesn't assume that programs should have rights to make SACL entries. Consequently, the next set of steps gives the example permission to perform this step. (Make sure your security policy allows such an action.)

The code begins by obtaining the locally unique identifiers (LUIDs) for the two rights needed to add an auditing entry, `SeSecurityPrivilege` and `SeAuditPrivilege` using the `LookupPrivilegeValue()` function. A LUID is about the same as a GUID, except that Windows doesn't retain a LUID after the current session.

The code not only needs the kind of permission in the form of a LUID, it also needs to apply that permission to a specific object. For example, you could give the caller permission to perform the act, but that wouldn't do much good, in this case, because the process is performing the change, not the caller. The code obtains the process token using a combination of the `GetCurrentProcess()` and `OpenProcessToken()` functions. The code builds a `TOKEN_PRIVILEGES` that contains the two LUIDs obtained earlier and the associated permission. It then uses the `AdjustTokenPrivileges()` function to give the process permission to add the audit entry to the selected file.

You need to be aware of an odd problem that can occur when you call the `AdjustToken-Privileges()` function. The function can succeed, without making any change to the process's privileges. The call did succeed—it didn't run into any memory or other errors, but the security change can fail. To overcome this problem, Windows records any security errors. However, to obtain these errors, you must call the `Marshal.GetLastWin32Error()` method after the call. A 0 return value means that the call succeeded and Windows changed the privileges. Unlike an actual call failure, your program could still work if the security update fails, but you still need to consider the fact that it won't—that's why the example displays a warning message.

The code has created the security descriptor that includes the auditing changes to the file and the process has permission to apply it. At this point, the code can finally call the `SetFileSecurity()` function to make the change permanent. Notice that the code ends by clearing up all of the memory items created to perform this task.

Running the Application

Running this example could still present a few surprises. It's easy to run into a 1314 error, "A required privilege is not held by the client." when working with this program. The program normally indicates that it couldn't set the security policy by first displaying a 1300 error, "Not all privileges referenced are assigned to the caller." When you see this combination of errors, check the local or domain security policy to ensure you have the correct privileges. Verify the Replace a Process Level Token right found in the User Rights Assignment folder of the appropriate MMC console (such as the Local Security Settings console) lists you as one of the entities that can perform this task.

After the program runs, you'll need to verify that it actually added the entry by checking the security settings for the file. To check the security settings, right-click the file and choose Properties from the context menu to display the file's Properties dialog box. Select the Security tab and you'll see a list of common security settings. Click Advanced, select the Auditing tab, and you'll see a new entry for the user you selected similar to the one shown in Figure 15.2.

FIGURE 15.2:

Verify the program worked by checking the advanced security settings for the selected file.

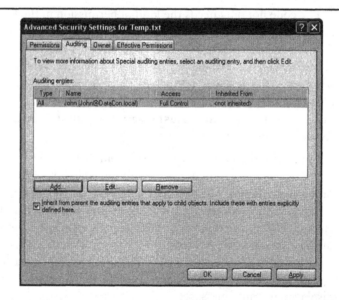

You also need to perform a second check. The fact that you have an audit in place doesn't mean that the system is set up to allow entry of the events in the Event Log. Open and close the file several times to generate audit events. Open the Event Log and select the Security log. You should see a series of entries for the selected file. If you don't see these entries, make sure you have the local or domain security policy set to provide an audit policy.

Considering a Security Setting Alternative

Not every object is a file, so you can't always use the SetFileSecurity() function to set security. Fortunately, the Win32 API supplies a generic alternative that works about the same as the

SetFileSecurity() function. Listing 15.3 shows how to use the SetNamedSecurityInfo() function. The example application in the \Chapter 15\C#\AuditFile and \Chapter 15\VB\Audit-File folders of the source code located on the Sybex Web site also contain this code so you can see the program in action.

Listing 15.3   An Alternative Method for Setting Security

```
LastError = SetNamedSecurityInfo(@txtFile.Text,
    SE_OBJECT_TYPE.SE_FILE_OBJECT,
    SECURITY_INFORMATION.SACL_SECURITY_INFORMATION,
    IntPtr.Zero,
    IntPtr.Zero,
    IntPtr.Zero,
    SACL);
if (LastError != ERROR_SUCCESS)
    MessageBox.Show("Error setting the security descriptor." +
                    "\r\nLast Error: " + LastError.ToString(),
                    "Application Error",
                    MessageBoxButtons.OK,
                    MessageBoxIcon.Error);
```

Notice that the SetNamedSecurityInfo() function accepts each of the four security descriptor entries separately, so you don't have to create a security descriptor to hold them. You do have to tell the function what types of entries you want to make using the SECURITY_INFORMATION enumeration. Unlike the SetFileSecurity() function, the SetNamedSecurityInfo() function returns error values directly, so you need to use a slightly different technique for handling errors, as shown in the listing.

Securing Controls and Components

The security information contained in the "Working with the DACL" and "Working with the SACL" sections of this chapter apply to just about any kind of object you can imagine. The fact that the examples rely on a file doesn't make much of a difference. However, components and controls do require some changes in the way you handle certain security features.

The first consideration is the need to use the Win32 API at all. You can make a good case for using the Win32 API when an application uses a component as an in-process server. Because the client and the component share the same memory and resources, it's important to coordinate their security efforts as well. However, when working with an out-of-process server, it's easier to use security that suits the component, rather than the host application because the application and component might not even appear on the same machine. Always provide control security that works with the client. In some cases, this might mean providing separate versions of the control for managed and unmanaged code are needed if you can't create a security solution that works properly for both environments.

Another consideration is the caller. The application-oriented examples in the previous sections of the chapter assumed that the current process is making all of the changes and that the current process is trustworthy. When designing component and control security of the Win32 API environment, you must consider that the current process isn't likely to make the changes—the calling application will. In addition, because you know nothing about the calling application, it isn't safe to assume that it's trustworthy.

You also have to consider the communication environment. For example, when working in a LAN environment, you may need to use DCOM to maintain compatibility with older applications. The "Working with DCOM" section of Chapter 8 shows how to code an example to use DCOM properly. See the "Working with Remote Unmanaged Components" section of this chapter for a discussion of how to configure a component once you create secure code for it. The bottom line is that transparent communication is essential.

A final consideration for the Win32 API environment is that you don't have as many choices as you do when working with .NET security. The emphasis is on what the caller can do. In addition, you can't consider context as part of the security solution—a user who calls from the Internet will have the same rights as when calling from a local machine. It's essential to consider these factors when developing your component and provide some form of administrator-level control over how the component resolves security issues. Make sure you also use conservative settings for the component setup.

Securing Files

One of the problems that many developers have noted with the .NET Framework security is a lack of access to file (and other object) security information. For example, it's hard to tell who owns a file without using the Win32 API calls. That's where the `GetFileSecurity()` function comes into play. It enables you to retrieve file security information in the form of a security descriptor. From the theoretical discussion earlier in the chapter, you know that the security descriptor contains just about every piece of security information that Windows can supply. The example shown in Listing 15.4 shows how to obtain the owner identification for a file. However, the same techniques can help you obtain the SACL, DACL, and other security elements. The source in Listing 15.4 isn't complete—it only contains the material not discussed in other areas and lacks the Win32 API function declarataions. (You can find the complete source code for this example in the `\Chapter 15\C#\FileSecurity` and `\Chapter 15\VB\FileSecurity` folders of the source code located on the Sybex Web site.)

Listing 15.4   **One Technique for Accessing File Security Information**

```csharp
private void btnTest_Click(object sender, System.EventArgs e)
{
    IntPtr         SecurityDescriptor;  // File security information.
    Int32          SDSize;              // Security descriptor size.
    Int32          SDSizeNeeded;        // Required security desc. size.
    int            LastError;           // Last Win32 API error.
    IntPtr         OwnerSID;            // SID of the owner account.
    Boolean        IsDefault;           // Is this a defaulted account?
    Int32          NameSize;            // Size of the account name.
    Int32          DomainSize;          // Size of the domain name.
    StringBuilder  Name;                // Account name.
    StringBuilder  Domain;              // Domain name.
    SID_NAME_USE   Use;                 // Account use.

    // Determine the size of the security descriptor.
    SecurityDescriptor = new IntPtr(0);
    SDSizeNeeded = 0;
    GetFileSecurity(@txtFile.Text,
                    SECURITY_INFORMATION.OWNER_SECURITY_INFORMATION,
                    SecurityDescriptor,
                    0,
                    ref SDSizeNeeded);

    // Allocate the memory required for the security descriptor.
    SecurityDescriptor = Marshal.AllocHGlobal(SDSizeNeeded);
    SDSize = SDSizeNeeded;

    // Get the security descriptor.
    if (!GetFileSecurity(@txtFile.Text,
                    SECURITY_INFORMATION.OWNER_SECURITY_INFORMATION,
                     SecurityDescriptor,
                     SDSize,
                     ref SDSizeNeeded))
    {
        // Get the last error.
        LastError = Marshal.GetLastWin32Error();

        // Display an error message and exit if not successful.
        MessageBox.Show("Error obtaining the security descriptor." +
                    "\r\nLast Error: " + LastError.ToString(),
                    "Application Error",
                    MessageBoxButtons.OK,
                    MessageBoxIcon.Error);

        // Free the memory we allocated.
        Marshal.FreeHGlobal(SecurityDescriptor);

        // Exit the routine.
```

```
        return;
    }

    // Obtain the owner SID for the file.
    IsDefault = false;
    if (!GetSecurityDescriptorOwner(SecurityDescriptor,
                                    out OwnerSID,
                                    ref IsDefault))
    {
        // Get the last error.
        LastError = Marshal.GetLastWin32Error();

        // Display an error message and exit if not successful.
        MessageBox.Show("Error obtaining the owner SID." +
                        "\r\nLast Error: " + LastError.ToString(),
                        "Application Error",
                        MessageBoxButtons.OK,
                        MessageBoxIcon.Error);

        // Free the memory we allocated.
        Marshal.FreeHGlobal(SecurityDescriptor);

        // Exit the routine.
        return;
    }

    // Code to obtain the user information from the SID and some display
    // code appears in this area. See Listing 14.2 for an example of how to
    // convert a SID to a name.

}
```

The GetFileSecurity() function retrieves a security descriptor for the file requested by lpFileName. However, the function doesn't retrieve a complete security descriptor. It instead asks you to supply a SECURITY_INFORMATION enumeration value that chooses one of several pieces of a standard security descriptor. This means that the call must match the data you want to work with later. You must also provide a buffer pointer and the buffer length. The GetFileSecurity() function returns the security descriptor that you requested and the amount of buffer space needed to store the information.

Remember that you should never work with the security descriptor directly, but instead use the Win32 API supplied functions. The GetSecurityDescriptorOwner() function will retrieve owner information from a security descriptor if such information exists. Other functions such as GetSecurityDescriptorDacl() and GetSecurityDescriptorGroup() work for retrieving other elements of the security descriptor. The GetSecurityDescriptorOwner() function accepts a security descriptor as input and returns a SID containing the owner information.

The code actually calls the GetFileSecurity() function twice. The first call determines the size of the buffer needed to hold the security descriptor. The second call retrieves the security descriptor if the buffer is large enough to hold the data. Notice that this code uses the Marshal.AllocHGlobal() function to allocate the buffer for the SecurityDescriptor buffer.

Once the code obtains a security descriptor, it uses the GetSecurityDescriptorOwner() function to retrieve the SID. Notice that this second function accepts the uninitialized OwnerSID as an out value. If you try to initialize OwnerSID and send it as you did for the GetFileSecurity() function, the function will fail with an invalid parameter error. The GetSecurityDescriptorOwner() function points out that you won't always interact with the Win32 API functions in the same way. Be prepared to send an initialized variable in one case and an uninitialized in other cases. At this point, you have a SID and can use the LookupAccountSid() function to retrieve the applicable information. Figure 15.3 shows the output from this example.

FIGURE 15.3:

The example application will tell you who owns a particular file.

Using the *RegGetKeySecurity()* and *RegSetKeySecurity()* Functions

Another area where you need to use the Win32 API to control security is the registry. If you want to determine the current security state of the registry, then you need to use the RegGetKeySecurity() function. Likewise, you'll use the RegSetKeySecurity() function to set the registry security. Listing 15.5 shows the first part of the process—determining the current security state. This listing only shows the essentials and lacks information such as the Win32 API calling syntax. (You can find the complete source code for this example in the \Chapter 15\C#\SecureRegistry and \Chapter 15\VB\SecureRegistry folders of the source code located on the Sybex Web site.)

Listing 15.5   Reading a Registry Entry

```
private void btnRead_Click(object sender, System.EventArgs e)
{
    IntPtr          KeyHandle;   // Registry key handle.
    Int32           Result;      // Result of a call.
```

```
IntPtr          SD;          // The security descriptor.
Int32           SDSize;      // Size of the security descriptor.
Int32           LastError;   // Last Win32 API error.
IntPtr          OwnerSID;    // SID of the owner account.
Boolean         IsDefault;   // Is this a defaulted account?
Int32           NameSize;    // Size of the account name.
Int32           DomainSize;  // Size of the domain name.
StringBuilder   Name;        // Account name.
StringBuilder   Domain;      // Domain name.
SID_NAME_USE    Use;         // Account use.

// Open the registry key entry.
Result = RegOpenKeyEx(HKEY_LOCAL_MACHINE,
                      @"Software\LockedKey",
                      0,
                      REGSAM.KEY_ALL_ACCESS,
                      out KeyHandle);

// Get the security information size.
SDSize = 0;
SD = new IntPtr(0);
Result = RegGetKeySecurity(KeyHandle,
               SECURITY_INFORMATION.OWNER_SECURITY_INFORMATION,
               SD,
               out SDSize);

// Get the security information.
SD = Marshal.AllocHGlobal(SDSize);
Result = RegGetKeySecurity(KeyHandle,
               SECURITY_INFORMATION.OWNER_SECURITY_INFORMATION,
               SD,
               out SDSize);

... Lookup SID and Display Information ...

// Free the memory we allocated.
Marshal.FreeHGlobal(SD);

// Close the registry key.
RegCloseKey(KeyHandle);
}
```

You might find it hard to imagine, but unlike many other objects in the .NET Framework, the RegistryKey object doesn't include any method for obtaining a handle. Unfortunately, many of the Win32 API calls require a handle, so you need to open the registry key using the RegOpenKeyEx() function. Translating this function into code that .NET can understand requires a few additional tricks. For example, you need two versions of the function. The first accepts an IntPtr as an input for use with handles you create using any of the registry functions that return a handle, while the second accepts a UInt32 value that corresponds to the standard registry handles such as HKEY_CLASSES_ROOT.

After the code opens the registry key for this example, it uses the RegGetKeySecurity() function to obtain a security descriptor for the registry key. This security descriptor works precisely the same as the security descriptor used with a file in Listing 15.4. In fact, once the code obtains the security descriptor, it uses the same display code as shown in Listing 15.4 with a few slight modifications. See the source code for additional information. As usual, the code frees the memory used for the security descriptor and closes the registry key handle.

Adding security to a registry entry is like any other Windows object. Listings 15.1 and 15.2 show how to work with the security descriptors that Windows requires. Once you create a security descriptor, you use the RegSetKeySecurity() function to add security to a specific registry key. Here's the function declaration you need for this function.

```
// This function sets registry security.
[DllImport("AdvAPI32.DLL", CharSet=CharSet.Auto, SetLastError=true )]
public static extern Int32 RegSetKeySecurity(
    IntPtr hKey,
    SECURITY_INFORMATION SecurityInformation,
    IntPtr pSecurityDescriptor);
```

Notice that the function accepts three inputs. The first is the registry key handle. Listing 15.5 shows how to open a registry key and obtain a handle for it. The second is the SECURITY_INFORMATION enumerated value that defines the values contained in the security descriptor. Here's a listing of the possible values.

```
// This enumeration tells what type of information we want to retrieve
// or set in the registry.
public enum SECURITY_INFORMATION : uint
{
    OWNER_SECURITY_INFORMATION              = 0x00000001,
    GROUP_SECURITY_INFORMATION              = 0x00000002,
    DACL_SECURITY_INFORMATION               = 0x00000004,
    SACL_SECURITY_INFORMATION               = 0x00000008,
    PROTECTED_DACL_SECURITY_INFORMATION     = 0x80000000,
    PROTECTED_SACL_SECURITY_INFORMATION     = 0x40000000,
    UNPROTECTED_DACL_SECURITY_INFORMATION   = 0x20000000,
    UNPROTECTED_SACL_SECURITY_INFORMATION   = 0x10000000
};
```

Notice that you can set the owner, group, DACL, or SACL information individually or in combination. The final input value, pSecurityDescriptor, accepts the security descriptor. As mentioned earlier, you build the security descriptor using the same techniques as you use for a file or other Windows object.

Working with Remote Unmanaged Components

In general, once you add the proper code to your components, maintaining security becomes a matter of configuration. When working in the Win32 API environment, the tool of choice for component security configuration is the DCOM Configuration Tool, which is available on most NT-based systems by default and downloadable for Windows 9x systems. The DCOM Configuration Tool is a powerful utility that helps you to work with the components registered on a client machine. You can set the component to execute remotely or locally. In addition, this utility lets you modify the security setup for the component.

You can also use this utility to modify general DCOM operation on a client machine. For example, even though UDP/IP is the normal protocol used to create a connection between the client and the server, you can set it to any of the protocols that both client and server support. This means that you could create a secure connection between client and server by using an encrypted protocol instead of a plain text protocol like UDP/IP.

Although there are many tasks you can perform with the DCOM Configuration Tool, such as setting the endpoint communication protocols, the following sections concentrate on the security features of the program. When you need to perform additional component configuration, you might want to look at the other areas of the program as well. For example, you use this utility to redirect component execution from the local machine to a remote location. You'll also see a few general details when security needs require their mention.

Setting Up the General DCOM Environment

Microsoft assumes certain defaults when setting up DCOM on your machine during the Windows installation process. Normally, these defaults work just fine, but you may find that you either need to change the features supported by the DCOM or the protocols used to communicate between client and server.

The first thing you need to do is start the DCOM Configuration Tool. Use the Run command on the Start menu to display the Run dialog, then type **DCOMCnfg** in the Open field can click OK. You'll see the initial Distributed COM Configuration Properties dialog box. The Applications tab of this dialog displays all of the registered out-of-process servers that are installed on the client machine, including managed components that you register using the RegAsm utility. It's important to note that this dialog box only contains registered components—it doesn't matter whether the component is managed or unmanaged.

NOTE   Windows XP replaces the DCOM Configuration Tool with an MMC snap-in that is part of the Component Services console. The MMC snap-in version lets you configure individual components, but doesn't allow you to configure the DCOM settings overall. To gain access to the overall settings, use the older version of the DCOM Configuration Tool. You can obtain this older version as part of the Windows Resource Kit or from another version of Windows such as Windows 2000. Some older versions of Microsoft's programming tools might also include this tool. Don't use the Windows 9x version of the tool because it doesn't include all of the features of the NT-based version.

The Default Properties tab contains the general settings for DCOM on your machine. The Default Authentication Level list box controls how DCOM handles communication security between the client and server. The default setting is Connect, which means that security is handled only once per connection. See the "Setting the Authentication Level" section of the chapter for additional details.

The Default Impersonation Level list box controls what the server can do on the user's behalf when it comes to identification. For example, this setting affects what will happen if the server has to create another component to satisfy a user request. This setting controls identification issues such as creating the component in such a way that it looks like the user has created it directly. The matter of impersonation level affects what kinds of things the server can do for the client and how it does them. The default setting for this field is Impersonate. The following list defines the various levels of impersonation that DCOM supports:

Anonymous   This is the least secure impersonation level. The server performs processing tasks for the client without knowing the identity of the client application. Unfortunately, this setting limits the server to performing tasks that an anonymous user could perform—which means that many resources will be out of reach.

Identity   This level of impersonation lets the server to identify the client application. This means the client will gain full access to the resources and services available on the server as long as the client makes the call directly. The server can't impersonate the client, even for local service and resource requests.

Impersonate   This is the highest level of impersonation that the Windows authentication service supports natively. It lets the server impersonate the client locally, which means that the server will impersonate the client for any services or resources that the server has to request to satisfy a client request. The Impersonate level only allows client impersonation on the local server; a server can't impersonate the client on other servers.

Delegate   This is the most secure impersonation level. The server performs all tasks as if it were the client. This includes requesting services and resources on other servers. Windows authentication service doesn't support this level of impersonation.

The Provide Additional Security for Reference Tracking check box tells the server to track connected client application requests. Checking this option uses additional server resources—both memory and processor cycles. However, it does enhance server security because a client won't be able to artificially set a server process's reference count to 0, which could kill the process prematurely. The effect of killing a process prematurely is that other clients will likely crash when they attempt to free reference pointers to objects that no longer exist.

> **WARNING**   Securing the server and the components that reside on it still don't secure the data that gets transferred between client and server. Make sure that you always use some type of secure communication protocol to transfer data from one point to another—especially when working on a public network. Check the various options in the "Setting the Authentication Level" section of the chapter for details on how you can use built-in DCOM settings to make your data more secure (a good encryption product will only enhance the security you can get by default).

Using the General DCOM Security Options

You'll find the general DCOM security settings on the Default Security tab of the Distributed COM Configuration Properties dialog box. This dialog box includes three main security areas: access, launch, and configuration. The access area determines who can connect to your machine to use DCOM. The launch area determines who can remotely run applications on your machine. Finally, the configuration options determine who has permission to configure the DCOM settings on your machine. The following list tells you about these areas in more detail.

> **NOTE**   None of the settings in this section will override application specific settings. Windows uses the application specific settings first.

Default Access Permissions   This option defaults to the same access level permissions provided by the system as a whole. In other words, if a person has permission to access your hard drive in some way, they usually have permission to access the applications they find there. Of course, access doesn't necessarily mean the ability to execute. The Default Access Permissions option determines who can access applications on the machine.

Default Launch Permissions   DCOM applications normally recognize three groups for launching purposes: Interactive Users, Administrators, and System. You must specifically assign a user to the Interactive Users or Administrators groups before they'll have launch permission. Only system-level services can use the System account. This particular dialog box also lets you to add specific groups that can't launch an application. However, you need to remember the rules for using an ACL when adding deny entries. The ACL always goes from the top of the list to the bottom and acts on the first entry it sees. So, if a user is part of two groups, one that is allowed to launch DCOM applications and another that isn't, you need to put the deny group first. Otherwise, the user can launch DCOM applications based on the group entry that's allowed to launch applications.

Default Configuration Permissions   This list includes anyone who can configure DCOM on a machine. Normally, the System account and the Administrators group have full configuration control. Everyone else can read the configuration, but not change it. You must provide read permission to anyone who will launch or access applications. You can also use the Special Access setting that allows you to customize settings, but this is a difficult entry to set up and normally you won't need to use it.

All three settings work the same way, so I'll discuss them as a single entity, even though each area affects a different area of DCOM communication. Clicking Edit Default on the Default Security tab displays a Registry Value Permissions dialog box for launch permissions. This dialog box lets you add and remove users from the access list.

Click Add and you'll see an Add Users and Groups dialog box. This dialog box presents a list of domain users and groups; you can also choose from a list for the local machine. Using each list has advantages. Using the local machine's list helps you control the security settings on a machine-by-machine basis. On the other hand, using the domain list means that you only need to change the settings on one machine to add a new user to a group that will affect all machines that are running DCOM applications.

Working with Component Level Security

Component level security works much like general security except it affects just one application. To access this level of security, choose a component from the list on the Applications tab of the Distributed COM Configuration Properties dialog box. Click Properties and you'll see a Properties dialog box for that component. Select the Security tab.

You can choose between general security and component level security for all three areas discussed in the "Using the General DCOM Security Options" section of the chapter. If you choose the default security option, then DCOM uses the options set on the Default Security tab of the Distributed COM Configuration Properties dialog box. Otherwise, you'll need to click the individual Edit button to set the security you want for that area of component level security for the selected component. Since the actual process of setting component level security is the same as default security, this section doesn't discuss the various options.

Setting the Authentication Level

There are two ways to set the authentication level for your component: at the DCOM or individual component level. Both authentication level settings determine the minimum authentication requirements for the client and server. In other words, this setting determines how the client and server exchange security information during a session.

You'll find the Default Authentication Level setting on the Default Properties tab of the main Distributed COM Configuration Properties dialog. As previously mentioned, the default general setting is Connect. The component specific setting appears on the General tab of the component's Properties dialog box. The default setting, in this case, is Default. These two settings represent a minimalist approach to DCOM security. You can use other settings to improve security. The following list describes each of the Default Authentication Level settings.

Default   At the individual component level, this setting means that the component uses the general DCOM setting. At the DCOM level, this setting means that DCOM as a whole will use whatever security the authentication method uses in general. For example, Windows 2000 Security Services uses Connect level authentication. The results of using this setting vary according to the authentication method used.

None   The client and server don't authenticate each other. You must use this setting when creating anonymous connections. However, this setting also works in a small workgroup situation where physical security is high and there aren't any connections to the outside world. This setting reduces overall network traffic to the lowest possible level, but also represents the greatest security risk.

Connect   One-time authentication takes place during object creation. The client and server verify each other's identity during this initial request. There's a good chance a third party could break network security when using this mode since the client and server don't have any way to verify either packets or requests. The advantage to this method is that initial authentication places limits on what the user can do and it minimizes network traffic.

Call   Authentication occurs for every call while DCOM maintains a connection. This moderately high security level ensures the client and server verify each other's identity for each method call, which may involve several packets. You'll notice a slight increase in network traffic when using this authentication level and there's no guarantee of complete security from third party intrusion.

Packet   This is the first of three levels of truly secure DCOM communication settings. DCOM encrypts the sender's identity and packages it with the packet. This means that the receiver can verify the authenticity of the sender with every packet, which greatly reduces the probability of third party intrusion. However, this method also bloats the size of the packet and greatly increases DCOM related network traffic. This setting represents the most reasonable level of protection for a network that allows outside access.

Packet Integrity   DCOM encrypts the sender's identity and a packet signature as part of the packet. Using these two forms of authentication ensures the sender authorization and packet integrity. However, this method won't ensure that a third party hasn't read the packet and it does increase network traffic over Packet authentication. Only use this setting when the integrity of the data is essential, but you don't care who reads the packet.

Packet Privacy   This is the paranoid security level. Not only does the packet contain the sender's identity and a packet signature, but DCOM also encrypts the packet to ensure that a third party can't read it. This level of authentication greatly increases network traffic and could actually slow communications to a crawl when used on slower traffic media like a dial-up connection. Use this level of authentication to ensure safe financial transactions and the transmittal of critical confidential information from one site to another.

Summary

This chapter discusses some of the more interesting security features you can access from the Win32 API. The SACL and DACL let you access and manage security information in a way that Win32 applications also understand. You've also discovered techniques for modifying registry security, as well as working with resources such as files. Finally, this chapter has helped you discover techniques for working with unmanaged components and controls, which is an important skill since you're likely to need to access them for the near future.

Having a security plan in place is one of the most important things an organization can do. A plan helps everyone coordinate their efforts and makes it less likely that a hole will develop that a cracker could exploit. This book has provided you with a wealth of security information you can use to create the development portion of a security plan. Unfortunately, development security is one of the areas that many organizations fail to consider. Give your organization an edge in the security arena by planning for the security needs of your next application. This means considering the use of both managed and unmanaged techniques—the very techniques discussed in this chapter.

Congratulations! You've reached the last chapter of the book. If you've read from the beginning to the end of the book, you know that it covers a lot of ground. I encourage you to continue to use the book as a reference. However, security is a very big topic. Make sure you contact me at JMueller@mwt.net if you have any questions about this book. Also, look on my Web site at http://www.mwt.net/~jmueller/ for updates and additional information.

Glossary

This book includes a glossary so that you can find terms and acronyms easily. It has several important features you need to know. First, every major acronym in the book appears here—even if there's a better than even chance you already know what the acronym stands for. (I mentioned some acronyms in passing or as part of amplifying information that don't appear here.) This way, there isn't any doubt that you'll always find everything you need to use the book properly.

Second, these definitions are specific to the book. In other words, when you look through this glossary, you're seeing the words defined in the context in which they're used in this book. This might or might not always coincide with current industry usage since the computer industry changes the meaning of words so often.

Finally, I've used a conversational tone for the definitions here in most cases. This means that the definitions might sacrifice a bit of puritanical accuracy for the sake of better understanding. The purpose of this glossary is to define the terms in such a way that there's less room for misunderstanding the intent of the book as a whole.

A

Abstract Syntax Notation One (ASN.1)   A specialized language that determines the method of transferring data between dissimilar systems. The language defines a common syntax that ensures the data the recipient receives is the same as the data the sender sent. ASN.1 is an ISO/ITU (International Organization for Standardization/International Telecommunication Union) standard that originally appeared as an addition to the Open System Interconnection (OSI) model. The language first appeared in 1984 as part of the Consultative Committee for International Telegraphy and Telephony (CCITT) X.409 standard and eventually became the separate X.208 standard in 1998.

Active Directory Services Interface (ADSI)   A set of APIs used to access Active Directory, the central repository of information in Windows. Active Directory is a hierarchical database used to store many types of information in a somewhat free-form format. ADSI allows access to both Active Directory data and the schema, which means you can use it to create new database elements, as well as remove elements that are no longer in use.

ADSI   See Active Directory Services Interface

Advanced Encryption Standard (AES)   The mathematical basis for performing symmetric encryption and decryption of data. The algorithm originally appeared as the Rijndael algorithm, after it's inventors (Joan Daemen and Vincent Rijmen). This is a block cipher that can accept a number of data block sizes and key lengths. Many

companies now use this algorithm as a replacement for the DES and Triple DES algorithms.

AES   See Advanced Encryption Standard

API   See Application Programming Interface

Application Programming Interface (API)   A method of defining a standard set of function calls and other interface elements. It usually defines the interface between a high-level language and the lower-level elements used by a device driver or operating system. The ultimate goal is to provide some type of service to an application that requires access to the operating system or device feature set.

ASN.1   See Abstract Syntax Notation One

Attribute   An attribute expresses a feature peculiar to an object. When referring to a database, each field has attributes that express what type of information the field contains, the length of the field, the field name, and the number of decimals. When referring to a display, the attribute expresses pixel color, intensity, and position. In programming, an attribute can also specify some type of object functionality, such as the method used to implement security.

Authentication   The act of validating the identity of a caller. This task can include any of a number of validation techniques, such as the use of passwords.

Authorization   The act of providing access to specific services or resources based on the authenticated identity of a caller or other entity. Authorization gives the requesting party permission to use the specific service or resource.

B

Biometrics   A statistical method of scanning an individual's unique characteristics, normally body parts, to ensure that they are who they say they are. Some of the scanned elements include voiceprints, irises, fingerprints, hands, and facial features. The two most popular elements are irises and fingerprints because they're the two that most people are familiar with. The advantages of using biometrics are obvious. It's unlikely the user will lose their identifying information and, with proper scanning techniques, the identifying information can't be compromised either.

Buffer Overrun   A memory condition normally associated with a variable in which the application assigned more data to the variable than the variable is capable of holding. The excess data runs into other memory locations, which corrupts the information in those memory locations. In many cases, the buffer overrun affects other variables. However, when used maliciously, a buffer overrun can also overwrite other areas of memory such as code blocks or the application stack, causing the application to fail or perform tasks that the originator didn't intend.

C

CA   See Certificate Authority

Certificate Authority (CA)   An organization or group that independently verifies the identity of a requestor and issues credentials that reflect that identity. The credentials are in the form of a certificate that the requestor can use for a number of purposes, such as identification of an email source or signing a component. To provide any value, both parties in an information exchange must trust the CA. In some cases, this means using a public CA such as VeriSign. However, in other cases, it means that third parties must trust the private company issuing the certificate. For example, some Windows server versions provide the means to issue private certificates.

CLR   See Common Language Runtime

Common Language Runtime (CLR)   The engine used to interpret managed applications within the .NET Framework. All Visual Studio .NET languages that produce managed applications can use the same runtime engine. The major advantages of this approach include extensibility (you can add other languages) and reduced code size (you don't need a separate runtime for each language).

Common Object Request Broker Architecture (CORBA)   This protocol describes data and application code in the form of an object. This is the Object Management Group's (OMG) alternative to Microsoft's Component Object Model (COM). Although CORBA is incompatible with COM, it uses many of the same techniques as COM to create, manage, and define objects. CORBA was originally designed by IBM for inclusion with OS/2.

CORBA   See Common Object Request Broker Architecture

Cracker   A hacker (computer expert) who uses their skills for misdeeds on computer systems where they have little or no authorized access.

A cracker normally possesses specialty software that allows easier access to the target network. In most cases, crackers require extensive amounts of time to break the security for a system before they can enter it. Some sources call a cracker a black hat hacker.

Cryptographic Service Provider (CSP)   A specialty company that certifies the identity of companies, developers, or individuals on the Internet. This identification check allows the company to issue an electronic certificate, which can then be used to conduct transactions securely. Several levels of certification are normally provided within a specific group. For example, there are three levels of individual certification. The lowest merely verifies the individual's identity through an Internet mail address; the highest requires the individual to provide written proof along with a notarized statement. When you access a certified site or try to download a certified document such as a component, the browser will display the electronic certificate onscreen, allowing you to make a security determination based on fact.

Cryptography   The process of changing text or other data into an unreadable form (cipher text) to protect the information during a transfer, storage, or other transition, and then changing the unreadable form back into the original format. The first part of the process is known as data encryption, while the second part of the process is decryption. Asymmetric cryptography relies on a public and private key pair for encrypting and decrypting the data. Symmetric cryptograph relies on a single private key for both data encryption and decryption.

CSP   See Cryptographic Service Provider

D

Data Encryption Standard (DES)   A method of data encryption that relies on symmetric key encryption. This methodology was originally introduced in 1975 and standardized by ANSI in 1981.

Data Range   The list of acceptable values for any variable including control properties. A data range determines the set of data inputs that will work with a particular variable. For example, if a variable accepts only characters, the data range would include the letter A, but not the number 1.

Data Stream   One of several methods to send or access information that resides either in local or remote storage. A data stream consists of a series of bits taken from any location within a data storage unit (such as a file). The information can flow continuously (as in an Internet transfer for music) or in blocks (as occurs when reading data from a file on the local hard drive). The reading and writing sequence need not use blocks of any given size and the transfer often works with individual bits rather than characters or words.

Database Management System (DBMS)   A method for storing and retrieving data based on tables, forms, queries, reports, fields, and other data elements. Each field represents a specific piece of data, such as an employee's last name. Records are made up of one or more fields. Each record is one complete entry in a table. A table contains one type of data, such as the names and addresses of all the employees in a company. It's composed of records (rows) and fields (columns), just like the tables you see in books. A database may contain one or more related tables. It may include a list of employees in one table, for example, and the pay records for each of those employees in a second table. Sometimes also referred to as a Relational Database Management System (RDBMS) that includes products such as SQL Server and Oracle.

DBMS   See Database Management System

DCOM   See Distributed Component Object Model

DDoS   See Distributed Denial of Service

Declarative Security   A type of .NET Framework security that relies on attributes to declare the security requirements of an assembly, class, property, event, or other major application element. The compiler evaluates the attribute at compile time and places a token for the security requirement in the assembly manifest. This feature makes it easy to determine security requirements before the application runs. However, declarative security can open an application to possible review by crackers. In addition, it's less flexible than using in-code security programming such as imperative security.

DER   See Distinguished Encoding Rules

DES   See Data Encryption Standard

Deserialization   The act of converting a serialized data stream into an object using the class description as a template. The application performing the conversion must have access to the class template and know the method of serialization.

Digital Certificate   A specially encoded key pair used to identify a caller. A Certificate Authority (CA) issues the digital certificate on behalf of

the caller after verifying the caller's identity. The recipient must trust both the caller and the CA before digital certificate can lend credence to the source of the transmitted data. The most common use of digital certificates from a user perspective is as an email attachment that enables the recipient to identify the caller with confidence. However, digital certificates are also used in other forms of data exchange.

Digital Signature Algorithm (DSA)   The mathematical basis for encrypting and decrypting digital signatures used with the Digital Signature Standard (DSS) introduced by the National Institute of Standards and Technology (NIST). DSS also relies on Secure Hashing Algorithm 1 (SHA-1) to provide the hashing functionality.

DISCO   See Discovery of Web Services

Discovery of Web Services (DISCO)   A service associated with the Internet that's designed to make it easier to locate and use SOAP services. This particular service is SOAP specific and a single vendor, Microsoft, currently supports it. The DISCO service relies on a special protocol named SOAP Contract Language (SCL) to allow the discovery of services by remote computers.

Distinguished Encoding Rules (DER)   A technique for exporting a digital certificate from a memory or other data store to disk. The most common way to use this technique is to encode ASN.1 objects into a sequence of octets. DER provides unique encoding for all ASN.1 values.

Distributed Application   An application that resides on more than one machine; normally a client and server, but not necessarily limited to this configuration. The application could include multiple levels of clients and servers, commonly referred to as tiers. The application is composed of multiple interchangeable elements. For example, a server component could service more than one application type. The application elements are loosely coupled (both systems only require access to self-describing messages) and the developer can replace each element with updates as needed as long as the new element provides the same interface to the client.

Distributed Component Object Model (DCOM) A transport protocol that works with the component object model (COM), and is used for distributed application development. This protocol enables data transfers across the Internet or other non-local sources, but is usually limited to a Local Area Network (LAN) or Wide Area Network (WAN) environment. DCOM adds the capability to perform asynchronous, as well as synchronous, data transfers between machines. The use of asynchronous transfers prevents the client application from becoming blocked as it waits for the server to respond.

Distributed Denial of Service (DDoS) A specialized form of DoS attack where the cracker relies on a multitude of zombie machines to perform a denial of service attack on a target network. The cracker may not even know how many machines are involved in the attack since this technique often relies on virus programs to install the required software on an unsuspecting host.

DLL See Dynamic Link Library

Document Type Definition (DTD) A document that defines how an application should interpret markup tags within an HTML, XML, or SGML document. In some cases, such as HTML, the DTD is an actual specification. In other cases, such as XML, the DTD is an external document supplied by the user or the vendor. A DTD can define every characteristic of a document as long as those characteristics are defined using standard tags and attributes.

Domain An area of control in a network. Members of a domain can share resources controlled by one or more member servers. One or two servers normally control the security of the network; these servers are normally called domain controllers.

DSA See Digital Signature Algorithm

DTD See Document Type Definition

Dynamic Link Library (DLL) A specific form of application code loaded into memory by request. It's not executable by itself like an EXE is. A DLL does contain one or more discrete routines that an application may use to provide specific features. For example, a DLL could provide a common set of file dialogs used to access information on the hard drive. More than one application can use the functions provided by a DLL, reducing overall memory requirements when more than one application is running. DLLs have a number of purposes. For example, they can contain device-specific code in the form of a device driver. Some types of COM objects also rely on DLLs.

E

ECMA See European Computer Manufacturer's Association

European Computer Manufacturer's Association (ECMA) A standards committee originally founded in 1961. ECMA is dedicated to standardizing information and communication systems. For example, it created the ECMAScript standard used for many Web page designs today. You can also find ECMA standards for product safety, security, networks, and storage media.

eXtensible Access Control Markup Language (XACML) A technique for creating secure Web service data communication. This standard lets developers add specialized XML tags that define the security policy for data communication needs such as a Web service. Many developers view XACML as the next step beyond Security Assertions Markup Language (SAML). In fact, XACML is a high-level protocol that relies on SAML to perform many of the low-level tasks.

eXtensible Hypertext Markup Language (XHTML) A cross between XML and HTML specifically designed for Internet devices such as Personal Digital Assistants (PDAs) and cellular telephones, but also usable with desktop machine browsers. Since this language relies on XML, most developers classify it as an XML application builder. The language relies on several standardized namespaces to provide common data type and interface definitions. XHTML creates modules that are interpreted based on a specific platform's requirements. This means that a single document can serve the needs of many display devices.

eXtensible Markup Language (XML) 1. A method used to store information in an organized manner. The storage technique relies on hierarchical organization and uses special statements called tags to separate each storage element. Each tag defines the characteristics of a data value and can contain attributes that further define each data entry. 2. A standardized Web page design language used to incorporate data structuring within standard HTML documents. For example, you could use XML to display database information using something other than forms or tables. It's actually a lightweight version of standardized generalized markup language (SGML) and is supported by the SGML community. XML also supports tag extensions that allow various parts of a Web-based application to exchange information. For example, once a user makes a choice within a catalog, that information could be added to an order entry form with a minimum of effort on the part of the developer. Since XML is easy to extend, some developers look at it as more of a base specification for other languages, rather than a complete language.

G

GAC See Global Assembly Cache

Global Assembly Cache (GAC) A central repository used by the .NET Framework for storing public managed components. The GAC contains only components with strong names, ensuring the integrity of the cache. In addition, the GAC can hold multiple versions of the same component, which ensures that applications can access the version of a component that they need, rather than the single version accessible to all applications.

Globally Unique Identifier (GUID) A 128-bit number used to identify a Component Object Model (COM) object within the Windows registry. The GUID is used to find the object definition and allow applications to create instances of that object. GUIDs can include any kind of object, even nonvisual elements. In addition, some types of complex objects are actually aggregates of simple objects. For example, an object that implements a property page will normally have a minimum of two GUIDs: one for the property page and another for the object itself.

GUID   See Globally Unique Identifier

GXA   Global XML Architecture

H

Hacker   An individual who works with computers at a low level, such as directly in hardware design or with software like drivers (hardware or software), especially in the area of security. A hacker normally possesses specialty software or other tools that allow easier access to the target hardware or software application or network. The media defines two types of hackers, which include those that break into systems for ethical purposes and those that do it to damage the system in some way. The proper term for the second group is *crackers* (see *Cracker* for details). Some people have started to call the first group "ethical hackers" or "white hat hackers" to prevent confusion. Ethical hackers normally work for security firms that specialize in finding holes in a company's security. However, hackers work in a wide range of computer arenas. For example, a person who writes low-level code (like that found in a device driver) after reverse engineering an existing driver is technically a hacker. The main emphasis of a hacker is to work for the benefit of others in the computer industry.

Hierarchical   1. A method of arranging data within a database that relies on a tree-like node structure, rather than a relational structure. 2. A method of displaying information on screen that relies on an indeterminate number of nodes connected to a root node. 3. A chart or graph in which the elements are arranged in ranks. The ranks usually follow an order of simple to complex or higher to lower.

HTML   See Hypertext Markup Language

Hypertext Markup Language (HTML)   1. A data presentation and description (markup) language for the Internet that depends on the use of tags (keywords within angle brackets <>) to display formatted information onscreen in a non-platform-specific manner. The non-platform-specific nature of this markup language makes it difficult to perform some basic tasks such as placement of a screen element at a specific location. However, the language does provide for the use of fonts, color, and various other enhancements onscreen. There are also tags for displaying graphic images. Scripting tags for using scripting languages such as VBScript and JavaScript are available, although not all browsers support this addition. The <OBJECT> tag addition allows the use of ActiveX controls. 2.One method of displaying text, graphics, and sound on the Internet. HTML provides an ASCII-formatted page of information read by a special application called a browser. Depending on the browser's capabilities, some key words are translated into graphics elements, sounds, or text with special characteristics, such as color, font, or other attributes. Most browsers discard any keywords they don't understand, allowing browsers of various capabilities to explore the same page without a problem. Obviously, there's a loss of capability if a browser doesn't support a specific keyword.

I

IETF   See Internet Engineering Task Force

IIS   See Internet Information Server

IL   See Intermediate Language

Imperative Security   A type of .NET Framework security that relies on the use of programming statements to perform security tasks. This form of security doesn't appear within the manifest, so CLR must evaluate it at runtime. While imperative security is more flexible and less likely to cause cracker intrusions, it's also more difficult to find in the code and doesn't provide the self-documenting efficiency of declarative security.

Impersonation   Using the name and/or credentials of another object to obtain access to resources or services. For example, when a user makes a request of a server, the server may use impersonation to request services or resources from another server on the user's behalf. Although impersonation is a necessary and useful strategy for managing services and resources, it can also become a security problem when a third party that isn't allowed to impersonate a caller does so without the caller's knowledge.

Infrared Data Association (IrDA)   The standards association responsible for creating infrared data port standards. These ports normally are used

to create a connection between a portable device (such as a laptop or PDA) and a stationary device or network. Devices include printers, PCs, modems, and mice.

Infrastructure   The underlying base of an organization or system. One way to view infrastructure is as a foundation on which all other elements of a system or organization are attached. Many vendors use this term to indicate the compatibility of their product with existing installations.

Initialization Vector (IV)   The seed (numeric) value provided as input to many encryption and hash algorithms.

Intermediate Language (IL)   The common language that all .NET compilers output. The Common Language Runtime (CLR) interprets the tokens that reside in the IL. The use of a tokenized output ensures that all languages can share the functionality provided by the .NET Framework. Because CLR understands this one common language, any compiler that produces it is compatible with .NET.

Internet Engineering Task Force (IETF)   The standards group tasked with finding solutions to pressing technology problems on the Internet. This group can approve standards created both within the organization itself and outside the organization as part of other group efforts. For example, Microsoft has requested the approval of several new Internet technologies through this group. If approved, the technologies would become an Internet-wide standard performing data transfer and other specific kinds of tasks.

Internet Information Server (IIS)   Microsoft's full-fledged Web server that normally runs under the Windows Server operating system. IIS includes all the features that you'd normally expect with a Web server: FTP and HTTP protocols along with both mail and news services. Older versions of IIS also support the Gopher protocol; newer versions don't provide this support because most Web sites no longer need it.

Internet Protocol (IP)   The information exchange portion of the TCP/IP protocol used by the Internet. IP is an actual data transfer protocol that defines how the sender places information into packets and transmits from one place to another. TCP (Transmission Control Protocol) is the protocol that defines how the actual data transfer takes place.

IP   See Internet Protocol

IrDA   See Infrared Data Association

IV   See Initialization Vector

IWAM   Web Application Management Interface

J

JIT Activation   See Just-in-Time Activation

Just-in-Time Activation (JIT Activation)   Server resources are always scarce, so good resource management techniques are essential. The latest component resource management techniques normally include gaining access to resources only when needed, then releasing them immediately. However, older components were designed to gain access to all of the resources required to perform a task early, then hold onto those resources until no longer needed. Using JIT activation means that even if a client holds onto a component reference, Windows can still use physical resources required by that component until they're needed again by the application. Windows monitors all of the components that are marked as JIT enabled. When a certain time period has elapsed without any method calls, the component deactivates, and the resources that it's using are returned to the resource pool. As far as the application is concerned, the component is still active and the reference to it is still valid. The next time the application makes a method call to the deactivated component, Windows reactivates it and allocates the resources that it requires. This entire process occurs in the background without any programmer input. Newer technologies, such as .NET, have extended JIT to include every aspect of the application.

L

LDAP   See Lightweight Directory Access Protocol

Lightweight Directory Access Protocol (LDAP)   A set of protocols used to access directories that's based on a simplified version of the X.500 standard. Unlike X.500, LDAP provides support for TCP/IP, a requirement for Internet communication. LDAP makes it possible for a client to request directory information like email addresses and public keys from any server. In addition, since LDAP is an open protocol, application developers need not worry about the type of server used to host the directory.

M

MD5   See Message Digest 5

Message Digest 5 (MD5)   The mathematical basis for creating a message digest (a value) based on the content of the message. The basis of this technology is that no two messages will produce the same message digest. Consequently, the recipient can validate the content of a message by performing the calculation and comparing it to the message digest value. MD5 is a one-way hash, which means that it isn't used for encrypting and decrypting the data. Professor Ronal Rivest created MD5 in 1991 to verify the authenticity of digital signatures.

Microsoft Management Console (MMC)   A special application that acts as an object container for Windows management objects like Component Services and Computer Management. The management objects are actually special components that provide interfaces that allow the user to access them within MMC to maintain and control the operation of Windows. A developer can create special versions of these objects for application management or other tasks. Using a single application like MMC helps maintain the same user interface across all management applications.

MMC   See Microsoft Management Console

MSADC   Microsoft Advanced Data Connector

N

NTLM   See Windows NT LAN Manager Security

O

Object Identifier (OID)   A number that uniquely identifies an object class or attribute, along with the object's definition. One of the most common uses for the OID is as part of the ASN.1 language. OIDs are issued by a central agency normally called a National Registration Authority (NRA). Each country has its own NRA. The NRA in the United States is the American National Standards Institute (ANSI). Every entity that requests an OID receives a root OID that can be used to create additional OIDs for individual objects. For example, Microsoft has an OID of 1.2.840.113556. Microsoft has added branches to this OID for a variety of purposes within Windows. For example, there's one OID for Active Directory classes and another for Active Directory attributes. A specific OID example is the IPSEC-Data object with an OID of 1.2.840.113556.1.4.623. As you can see, branches are added using a dot syntax.

OID   See Object Identifier

Open Software Foundation (OSF)   A standards group responsible for defining communication standards such as the Distributed Computing

Environment (DCE) and Remote Procedure Call (RPC) used by both DCOM and CORBA. The OSF is now part of The Open Group.

OSF   See Open Software Foundation

P

Passport Unique Identifier (PUID)   The unique identifier assigned to a caller authenticated by Passport. Adding the PUID to the response stream of a Web request lets the caller maintain an authenticated status without going through the authentication procedure for each request.

Patch   When applied to software, a term that normally defines a small piece of code designed to provide an upgrade. (Some vendors are stretching the size of some patches so they're almost as large as the actual application.) In most cases, a patch will repair a programming error. It could also improve security or add application features. The methods of creating a patch include complete executable replacement or executable modification using an external application. Patches can also affect application data and support files.

PDA   See Personal Digital Assistant

Personal Digital Assistant (PDA)   A small hand-held device such as a Palm Pilot or Pocket PC. These devices are normally used for personal tasks such as taking notes and maintaining an itinerary during business trips. Some PDAs rely on special operating systems and lack any standard application support. However, newer PDAs include some level of standard application support because vendors are supplying specialized

compilers for them. In addition, you'll find common applications included, such as browsers and application office suites that include word processing and spreadsheet support.

Proxy   1. When used in the COM sense of the word, a proxy is the data structure that takes the place of the application within the server's address space. Any server responses to application requests are passed to the proxy, marshaled by COM, and then passed to the application. 2. Generally, any intermediary object that acts as an interface between a client and server. The object can perform any of a number of tasks, such as short-term storage of data to reduce data transmission requirements. In addition, the intermediary object normally marshals data between the client and server to ensure the recipient obtains data in a form it can use.

PUID   See Passport Unique Identifier

R

Remote Procedure Call (RPC)   One of several methods for accessing data within another application. RPC is designed to look for the application first on the local workstation and then across the network at the applications stored on other workstations.

Role-Based Security   A method for controlling access to an object based on the requestor's job function within an organization. In other words, if the requestor has a specific job function (or role), then they're allowed to access the object. This method of maintaining security is an extension of groups. However, unlike groups, a requestor must perform a specific job function before access is granted. This security methodology began with COM+ applications. It also appears as part of applications based on the .NET Framework.

RPC   See Remote Procedure Call

S

SAM   See Security Access Manager

SAML   See Security Assertions Markup Language

Secure Hashing Algorithm 1 (SHA-1)   The mathematical basis for encrypting and decrypting data used with the Digital Signature Standard (DSS) introduced by the National Institute of Standards and Technology (NIST). DSS also relies on Digital Signature Algorithm (DSA) to provide the digital signature functionality.

Secure Socket Layer (SSL)   A digital signature technology used for exchanging information between a client and a server. Essentially an SSL-compliant server will request a digital certificate from the client machine. The client can likewise request a digital certificate from the server. Companies or individuals obtain these digital certificates from a third-party vendor like VeriSign or other trusted source who can vouch for the identity of both parties.

Security Access Manager (SAM)   A database containing information about a caller and their security settings. Some texts also call this the Security Accounts Manager. In either case, the information normally appears within a special hive of the registry. Windows secures this hive to make it difficult to access using the Registry

Editor. The SAM can also use alternative input sources such as Active Directory.

Security Assertions Markup Language (SAML)   A technique for securing XML-based data communications that depends on the use of specialized tags. This technology defines mechanisms to exchange authentication, authorization, and non-repudiation information between client and server. It relies on a single sign-on technique to ensure the user doesn't receive constant requests for authentication information. SAML follows a four-step process in which the caller makes a service or resource request, the SAML server requests authentication information, the SAML server uses the authentication information to open a session with the remote server, and, finally, the caller receives an URL to use to access the service or resource.

Security Identifier (SID)   The part of an access token that identifies the object throughout the network; it's like having an account number. The access token that the SID identifies tells what groups the object belongs to and what privileges the object has.

Serialization   The act of converting an object or other complex data into a data stream (normally bytes) in preparation for transmission or offline storage. The method of serialization determines the ability of the application to convert the data stream back into an object later.

SHA-1   See Secure Hashing Algorithm 1

SID   See Security Identifier

Simple Mail Transfer Protocol (SMTP)   One of the most commonly used protocols to transfer text (commonly mail) messages between clients and servers. This is a stream-based protocol designed to allow query, retrieval, posting, and distribution of mail messages. Normally, this protocol is used in conjunction with other mail retrieval protocols like point of presence (POP). However, not all uses of SMTP involve email data transfer. Some Simple Object Acess Protocol (SOAP) applications have also relied on SMTP to transfer application data.

Simple Object Access Protocol (SOAP)   A Microsoft-sponsored protocol that provides the means for exchanging data between COM and foreign component technologies like Common Object Request Broker Architecture (CORBA) using XML as an intermediary. SOAP is often used as the basis for Web services communication. However, a developer could also use SOAP on a LAN or in any other environment where machine-to-machine communication is required and the two target machines provide the required infrastructure.

SMTP   See Simple Mail Transfer Protocol

Sniffer   A device or piece of software designed to examine raw network packets and to present those packets in human-readable format. A sniffer is commonly used to locate and repair network errors. It can also be used by crackers to break into networks by allowing them to view sensitive data like user passwords.

SOAP   See Simple Object Access Protocol

Socket   An object that creates a connection between an application and a network protocol. The socket is a specially written driver, in most cases, that manages the particulars of a communication session. The application sends and

receives data using the socket, rather than communicating directly with the network protocol.

SSL   See Secure Socket Layer

T

TCP/IP   See Transmission Control Protocol/Internet Protocol

Transmission Control Protocol/Internet Protocol (TCP/IP)   A standard communication line protocol (set of rules) developed by the United States Department of Defense. The protocol defines how two devices talk to each other. TCP defines a communication methodology where it guarantees packet delivery and also ensures the packets appear at the recipient in the same order they were sent. IP defines the packet characteristics.

U

UDDI   See Universal Description, Discovery, and Integration

UDP   See User Datagram Protocol

Uniform Resource Identifier (URI)   A generic term for all names and addresses that reference objects on the Internet. A URL is a specific type of URI. See Uniform Resource Locator (URL).

Uniform Resource Locator (URL)   A text representation of a specific location on the Internet. URLs normally include the protocol (http:// for example), the target location (World Wide Web or www), the domain or server name (mycompany), and a domain type (com for commercial). It can also include a hierarchical location within that Web site. The URL usually specifies a particular file on the Web server, although there are some situations when a Web server will use a default filename. For example, asking the browser to find http://www. mycompany.com, would probably display the DEFAULT.HTM or INDEX.HTM file at that location. The actual default filename depends on the Web server used. In some cases, the default filename is configurable and could be any of a number of files. For example, Internet Information Server (IIS) offers this feature, so the developer can use anything from an HTM to an ASP or an XML file as the default.

Universal Description, Discovery, and Integration (UDDI)   A standard method of advertising application and other software-related services online. The vendor offering the service registers at one or more centralized locations. Clients wishing to use the service add pointers to the service to their application.

URI   See Uniform Resource Identifier

URL   See Uniform Resource Locator

User Datagram Protocol (UDP)   Allows applications to exchange individual packets of information over an IP network. UDP uses a combination of protocol ports and IP addresses to get a message from one point of the network to another. More than one client can use the same protocol port as long as all clients using the port have a unique IP address. There are two types of protocol port: well known and dynamically bound. The well-known port assignments use the ports numbered between 1 and 255. When using dynamically bound port assignments, the requesting applications queries the service first to see which port it can use. Unlike TCP/IP, UDP/IP provides very few error recovery services, making it a fast way to deliver broadcast messages and perform other tasks where reliability isn't a concern.

W

W3C   See World Wide Web Consortium

Web Services Description Language (WSDL)   A method for describing a Web-based application that's accessible through an Internet connection, also known as a service. The file associated with this description contains the service description, port type, interface description, individual method names, and parameter types. A WSDL relies on namespace support to provide descriptions of common elements such as data types. Most WSDL files include references to two or more resources maintained by standards organizations to ensure compatibility across implementations.

Web Services Development Kit (WSDK)   An alternative name for Web Service Enhancements (WSE). See the definition for WSE.

Web Services Enhancements (WSE)   A Microsoft product that enables the developer to add enhancements such as WS-Security to Web applications such as Web Services. This product adds special features to the Visual Studio .NET IDE that make it easier to secure Web applications and make them more reliable.

Windows NT LAN Manager Security (NTLM)   A security scheme based on a challenge/response scenario. The server challenges the client, which must then provide an appropriate username and password. If the username and associated password are found in the server's security list for the service that the client has requested, then access to the service is granted. This security scheme is relatively easy to break and has been replaced by more reliable security schemes like Kerberos in later versions of Windows.

World Wide Web Consortium (W3C)   A standards organization essentially devoted to Internet security issues, but also involved in other issues such as the special <OBJECT> tag required by Microsoft to implement ActiveX technology. The W3C also defines a wealth of other HTML and XML standards. The W3C first appeared on the scene in December 1994, when it endorsed SSL (Secure Sockets Layer). In February 1995, it also endorsed application-level security for the Internet. Its current project is the Digital Signatures Initiative— W3C presented it in May 1996 in Paris.

WSDK   See Web Services Development Kit

WSDL   See Web Services Description Language

WSE   See Web Services Enhancements

X

XACML   See eXtensible Access Control Markup Language

XHTML   See eXtensible Hypertext Markup Language

XML   See eXtensible Markup Language

Index

Note to the Reader: Page numbers in **bold** indicate the principle discussion of a topic or the definition of a term. Page numbers in *italic* indicate illustrations.

W

X

Z